Presidents, Governors, and the Politics of Distribution in Federal Democracies

Tensions between central authorities and subnational units over centralization and fiscal autonomy are on top of the political agenda in many developing federal countries.

This book examines historical changes in the balance between the resources that presidents and governors control and the policy responsibilities they have to deliver. It focuses on Argentina and Brazil, the most decentralized federal countries in Latin America, with the most powerful subnational governments in the region. Using formal modeling, statistical tools, and comparative historical analyses, it examines substantive shifts in the allocation of resources and the distribution of administrative functions and explains under which conditions these changes occur. In doing so, it presents theoretical and comparative implications for the study of fiscal federalism and the functioning of developing federal democracies.

This text will be of key interest to scholars and students of federalism, intergovernmental relations, decentralization, and subnational politics and more broadly to those studying comparative politics, democratization, political elites, public policy, and economics.

Lucas I. González is Researcher at the National Council for Scientific and Technical Research (CONICET) and the Universidad Católica Argentina (UCA), and full-time Professor at the Universidad Nacional de San Martín (UNSAM) in Buenos Aires, Argentina.

Routledge Studies in Federalism and Decentralization
Series editors: Paolo Dardanelli
Centre for Federal Studies, University of Kent, UK
and
John Kincaid
Lafayette College, USA

The series publishes outstanding scholarship on federalism and decentralization, defined broadly, and is open to theoretical, empirical, philosophical, and historical works. The series includes two types of work: first, it features research monographs that are substantially based on primary research and make a significant original contribution to their field. Second, it contains works that address key issues of policy-relevant interest or summarize the research literature and provide a broad comparative coverage.

1   **Presidents, Governors, and the Politics of Distribution in Federal Democracies**
    Primus Contra Pares in Argentina and Brazil
    Lucas I. González

Formerly Routledge Series in Federal Studies, *edited by Michael Burgess and Paolo Dardanelli, Centre for Federal Studies, University of Kent, UK*
    This series brought together some of the foremost academics and theorists to examine the timely subject of regional and federal studies, which since the mid-1980s became key questions in political analysis and practice.

Minority Nations in Multinational Federations
A comparative study of Quebec and Wallonia
Edited by Min Reuchamps

Comparative Federalism and Intergovernmental Agreements
Analyzing Australia, Canada, Germany, South Africa, Switzerland and the United States
Jeffrey Parker

Federalism and Ethnic Conflict in Ethiopia
A Comparative Regional Study
Asnake Kefale

Federal Democracies
Edited by Michael Burgess and Alain-G. Gagnon

The Case for Multinational Federalism
Beyond the All-encompassing Nation
Alain-G. Gagnon

Explaining Federalism
State, Society and Congruence in Austria, Belgium, Canada, Germany and Switzerland
Jan Erk

Multinational Federations
Edited by Michael Burgess and John Pinder

Mastering Globalization
New sub-states' governance and strategies
Edited by Guy Lachapelle and Stéphane Paquin

Multinational Federalism and Value Pluralism
The Spanish case
Ferran Requejo

Regional Interests in Europe
Edited by Jörg Mathias

New Borders for a Changing Europe
Cross-border cooperation and governance
Edited by James Anderson, Liam O'Dowd and Thomas M. Wilson

Region, State and Identity in Central and Eastern Europe
Edited by Kataryna Wolczuk and Judy Batt

Local Power, Territory and Institutions in European Metropolitan Regions
In search of Urban Gargantuas
Edited by Bernard Jouve and Christian Lefevre

The Federalization of Spain
Luis Moreno

Paradiplomacy in Action
The foreign relations of subnational governments
Edited by Francisco Aldecoa and Michael Keating

Remaking the Union
Devolution and British politics in the 1990s
Edited by Howard Elcock and Michael Keating

The Regional Dimension of the European Union
Towards a 'Third Level' in Europe?
Edited by Charlie Jeffery

The Political Economy of Regionalism
Edited by Michael Keating and John Loughlin

The Territorial Management of Ethnic Conflict, 2nd edition
Edited by John Coakley

Protecting the Periphery
Environmental policy in peripheral regions of the European Union
Edited by Susan Baker, Kay Milton and Steven Yearly

The End of the French Unitary State?
Edited by John Loughlin and Sonia Mazey

Presidents, Governors, and the Politics of Distribution in Federal Democracies

Primus contra pares in Argentina and Brazil

Lucas I. González

Routledge
Taylor & Francis Group

LONDON AND NEW YORK

First published 2016
by Routledge
2 Park Square, Milton Park, Abingdon, Oxon OX14 4RN

and by Routledge
711 Third Avenue, New York, NY 10017

First issued in paperback 2017

Routledge is an imprint of the Taylor & Francis Group, an informa business

British Library Cataloguing in Publication Data
A catalogue record for this book is available from the British Library

Library of Congress Cataloging in Publication Data
Names: González, Lucas I. (Lucas Isaac), author.
Title: Presidents, governors, and the politics of distribution in
federal democracies : primus contra pares in Argentina and Brazil /
Lucas I. González.
Description: New York, NY : Routledge, 2016. | Series: Routledge
studies in federalism and decentralization | Includes bibliographical
references and index.
Identifiers: LCCN 2015037388| ISBN 9781138943858 (hardback) |
ISBN 9781315672205 (ebook)
Subjects: LCSH: Central-local government relations–Argentina. |
Central-local government relations–Brazil. | Intergovernmental fiscal
relations–Argentina. | Intergovernmental fiscal relations–Brazil. |
Federal government–Argentina. | Federal government–Brazil.
Classification: LCC JL2020.S8 G77 2016 | DDC 320.481/049–dc23
LC record available at http://lccn.loc.gov/2015037388

ISBN 13: 978-1-138-48734-5 (pbk)
ISBN 13: 978-1-138-94385-8 (hbk)

Typeset in Baskerville
by Wearset Ltd, Boldon, Tyne and Wear

To Inés and Beli

Contents

List of figures		xi
List of tables		xii
Preface		xiv

Introduction   1

1   **The federal distributive game**   10
A game-theoretical framework on the distribution of power in federal democracies 10
Actors, preferences, and strategies over the distribution of resources and functions 24
A game-theoretical analysis on fiscal transfers 34

2   **Power, crises, and distribution in Latin America**   54
A statistical analysis 54
Results and discussion 70
The distribution of funds and functions in Argentina and Brazil 74
Final comments 75

3   ***Pares contra primus***   89
Introduction 89
A brief methodological justification of the comparative historical analysis 90
The historical struggles for the distribution of funds and functions 91
The distribution of resources, tax authority, and functions (the dependent variable) 97
Pares contra primus *101*
The Alfonsín presidency (1983–1989) 101
Primus inter pares *(1983–1987) 103*

The federal distributive game (1983–1987) 113
Pares contra primus *(1987–1989) 117*
The Sarney presidency (1985–1990) 129

4   *Primus inter pares*   164
Introduction 164
The Collor (1990–1992) and the Franco (1992–1994)
    administrations 165
The setting of the federal distributive game during the Collor de Mello
    presidency 171
The Itamar Franco government (1992–1994) 178

5   *Primus contra pares*   197
Introduction 197
The Menem presidency (1989–1999) 198
The federal distributive game during the Menem presidency 205
The 1994 constitutional reform and the second Menem
    administration (1994–1999) 225
The Cardoso presidency (1995–2002) 231

6   Conclusions   276
Some projections of the federal distributive game 276
The federal distributive game and its implications for the performance
    of federal democracies 284
Some comparative notes for federal democracies 298

Index   311

Figures

1.1 Normal form game (payoff matrix) 36
1.2 Normal form game including expected costs and probability of conflict 38
3.1 Distribution of cases according to the values of key variables 102
3.2 Synthesis of the main variables during Alfonsín (1983–1989) 110
3.3 Normal form game for Alfonsín (1983–1987) 113
3.4 Normal form game for Alfonsín (1987–1989) 121
3.5 Synthesis of the main variables during Sarney (1985–1990) 137
3.6 Normal form game for Sarney (1987–1990) 141
4.1 Synthesis of the main variables during Collor (1990–1992) 171
4.2 Normal form game for Collor de Mello (1990–1992) 176
4.3 Synthesis of the main variables during the Franco administration (1992–1994) 182
5.1 Synthesis of the main variables during Menem (1989–1999) 205
5.2 Normal form game for Menem (1991–1993) 208
5.3 Synthesis of the main variables during Menem (1993–1999) 228
5.4 Synthesis of the main variables during Cardoso (1995–2002) 241
5.5 Normal form game for Cardoso (1995–1998) 242

Tables

1.1 Preferences of presidents and governors   31
2.1 Regression results for fiscal (FT) and administrative
    transfers (AT)   66
2.2 Regression results   67
2.3 Regression results   68
2.4 Regression results   69
2.5 Regression results   70
2.6 Regression results data for Argentina   76
2.7 Regression results data for Brazil   77
2.8 Variable description and data sources   78
2.9 Variable description and data sources for Argentina and
    Brazil   79
3.1 Distribution of cases according to the values of key
    variables   101
3.2 Values taken by the main variables during Alfonsín
    (1983–1989)   111
3.3 Revenue and expenditure share of subnational units in
    Argentina (1983–1989)   125
3.4 Synthesis of the reforms and impacts on the federal
    balance (1987–1989)   126
3.5 Values taken by the main variables during Sarney
    (1985–1990)   138
3.6 Revenue and expenditure share of subnational units in
    Brazil (1986–1989)   145
3.7 Synthesis of the reforms and impacts on the federal
    balance (1987–1989)   148
4.1 Operational balance in Brazil (1990–1994)   170
4.2 Values taken by the main variables during Collor
    (1990–1992)   172
4.3 Values taken by the main variables during Franco
    (1992–1994)   180
4.4 Revenue and expenditure share of subnational units in
    Brazil (1990–1995)   190

4.5	Synthesis of the reforms and impacts on the federal balance (1993–1994)	191
5.1	Fiscal deficit in Argentina (1987–1999)	203
5.2	Values taken by the main variables during Menem (1989–1999)	206
5.3	Revenue and expenditure share of subnational units in Argentina (1990–1998)	225
5.4	Synthesis of the reforms and impacts on the federal balance (1991–1993)	226
5.5	Provisional decrees issued or re-issued in Brazil (1985–May 2001)	234
5.6	Operational balance of the public sector in Brazil (1993–2001)	237
5.7	Values taken by the main variables during Cardoso (1998–2002)	238
5.8	Revenue and expenditure share of subnational units in Brazil (1994–2000)	260
5.9	Synthesis of the reforms and impacts on the federal balance (1995–1998)	261
6.1	Synthesis of the results by period of reform (1983/1985–2000)	286

Preface

I began studying federalism because I was impressed by the intensity of conflicts between the central government and the governors and the implications of these struggles both in Argentina and Brazil. Several presidents, some ministries of economy, and more than a few scholars have blamed governors for many of these countries' misfortunes. Many of them believe that governors' fiscal profligacy and pressures on the federal budget have been crucial factors that have led to hyperinflation, soaring debts, and macroeconomic turmoil. Argentina had single-digit poverty rates during the 1980s. More than 50 percent of the population was pulled under the poverty line by 2001. Several times, the Minister of Economy who stayed in office for the longest period during the 1990s publicly accused governors for the country's macroeconomic mismanagement. Their Brazilian counterparts did the same several times, claiming that governors made their country "ungovernable."

Several governors, on the contrary, claimed that the central government ransacked their districts' revenue and fiscal autonomy, forcing them into deep fiscal imbalances and making them unmanageable. These changes imposed by central rulers had huge impacts on policy outcomes, among them, disrupted social services such as basic health care and elementary education (which have to be delivered by provinces or states, and municipalities), unpaid salaries, strikes (even by police forces), and hence, protests and turmoil. Several died during violent incidents, including a primary school teacher shot in the head by a provincial policeman in Neuquén. The teacher demanded an increase in his meager salary.

As a reaction to these changes, some governors asked their peers to boycott the central government, and some openly confronted it. The core of these conflicts centered on the distribution of fiscal revenue between the states and the central government. But not only tax revenue, federal transfers, state debt, or the distribution of administrative functions were at stake. In extreme conditions, it was also macroeconomic stability, the delivery of basic social services, and even the integrity of the federation as well as the survival of democracy. This is the core topic of this research.

I do not intend to explain complex historical conflicts and tensions that can be traced back to the very origins of the two federations. I rather try to explore under what conditions these tensions and struggles between units of government have contributed to drastic changes in the distribution of funds and functions among units and to some of the aforementioned outcomes. The limitations of my research are several, and those are my exclusive responsibility. Despite them, I would not have finished this work without a lot of help from a lot of people during the process. This section is a modest expression of my immense gratitude to them.

First of all, to Guillermo O'Donnell. It is impossible for me to list all that I have learned having one of the most renowned scholars in the field reading and discussing my work. I would just like to mention only three of the most important lessons he gave me. First, through his work and advice he has shown that good scholars are much more than research assistants of established theories. Good scholars try to critically understand one of the many relevant and intricate puzzles in politics and society, especially those that dramatically affect citizens' lives. Available theories do not always help us to do that and, in these cases, reformulating and developing new theoretical arguments becomes crucial. Second, O'Donnell has shown how theory and case can be deeply interwoven to understand the aforementioned puzzles more rigorously. Third, he repeatedly insisted that tools are not the ends but the means to answer a substantial question in a research. This helped me particularly when I seemed to be drowning in the specificities of formalization, empirical tests, and historical details. The limited results in this research following these recommendations are a problem of the advisee and not of a lack of good advice or clear guidance.

I would also like to specially thank Fran Hagopian, Michael Coppedge, and Scott Mainwaring as well as my colleagues at Notre Dame, especially Ángel Álvarez, Saibal Basu, Claudia Maldonado, Carlos Mendoza, and Juan Moraes for all the years we shared together, for their generosity, and for all they taught me along the way. Several professors at Notre Dame also supplied crucial help and guidance; among them, special thanks to Ben Radcliff, Peri Arnold, Rodney Hero, and Christina Wolbrecht.

Special thanks also to the Department of Political Science and the Graduate School at the University of Notre Dame, the Kellogg Institute, The Coca Cola Foundation, the Fulbright Commission, and the Institute for International Education for their financial support for conducting research for this project, and to the authorities of the Instituto Universitário de Pesquisas do Rio de Janeiro (IUPERJ), especially to Fabiano Santos, Argelina Figueiredo, and Maria Regina Soares de Lima; the Universidad Nacional de San Martín, especially to Carlos Ruta, María Matilde Ollier, Carlos Acuña, Gabriela Ippólito, and Marcelo Cavarozzi; the Universidad Católica Argentina, especially to Enrique Aguilar and Marcelo Camusso; la Universidad de San Andrés, especially to Marcelo Leiras; the Universidad Católica de Córdoba, especially to Mario Riorda, Martín

Lardone, and Marcelo Nazareno, for their generosity and institutional support.

For their time during discussions and for reading early drafts, many thanks also to Kent Eaton, Maria Escobar-Lemmon, Edward Gibson, Al Montero, Brian Pollins, Tim Power, Richard Snyder, Eliza Willis, Kurt Weyland, and Wendy Hunter. I also had the honor of having some of the best Argentine scholars who specialize on the broad topic of this research helping me, among them Ernesto Calvo, Marcelo Escolar, Tulia Falleti, Catalina Smulovitz, Ana María Mustapic, and Marcelo Leiras. Some colleagues were critical and generous advisors along the way. Special thanks to Alejandro Bonvecchi, Alberto Fohrig, Sebastián Freille, Agustina Giraudy, Carlos Gervasoni, Germán Lodola, Víctor Mazzalay, Marcelo Nazareno, and Julio Saguir. I appreciate the time during interviews and help several Argentine scholars and policy experts gave me along this work: Oscar Cetrángolo, Sergio Berensztein, Julián Bertranou, Luis Tonelli, Juan Carlos Torre, Pedro Pírez, and Miguel Brown.

I interviewed and discussed several sections of my research with some of the very best Brazilian scholars. I would like to express my deep gratitude to George Avelino Filho, Argelina Figueiredo, Fernando Limongi, Marcus Melo, Carlos Pereira, Fabiano Santos, Celina Souza, and Lucio Rennó. Without them, my understanding of the case would have been even more limited. For their time and generosity, many thanks also to Fernando Luiz Abrucio, Octavio Amorim Neto, Marta Arretche, Paulo Arvate, Ernani Carvalho, Paulo Fábio Dantas Neto, Eli Diniz, Antônio Araújo Fernandez, Peter Fischer-Bollin, José Antônio Gomes de Pinho, Eduardo Kugelmas, Jairo Nicolau, Inês Pessanha, Lourdes Sola, Maria Regina Soares de Lima, Gabriela Tarouco, Maria Hermínia Tavares de Almeida, Maria Antonieta Del Tedesco Lins, Kurt Von Mettenheim, and Jorge Zaverucha.

I also want to thank the Routledge Series Editor and the two anonymous reviewers for their comments and suggestions. Any errors are the sole responsibility of the author.

While conducting fieldwork research in Argentina and Brazil during 2006, 2007, and 2009, I received crucial support from over a hundred interviews with bureaucrats, staff, state and federal politicians, and their political advisors in the state executives and state legislatures of Amazonas, Ceará, Bahia, Pernambuco, Rio Grande do Norte, Rio de Janeiro, and São Paulo, Buenos Aires, Córdoba, Chaco, Santa Fe, and Salta. My special gratitude to Antônio Kandir and Lúcio Alcântara for all the time they spent giving me details and contacts for understanding key reforms in Brazil. Oscar Cetrángolo showed the same generosity in helping me understand crucial negotiations between the central government and governors in Argentina.

I received valuable research assistantship from Santiago Alles, Ana Bovino, Facundo Galván, Julieta Lenarduzzi, Ignacio López, and Ignacio Mamone. To all of them, my sincere gratitude.

Lastly but not least, my deepest gratitude to my family. Both Inés and Beli had to deal with a husband and a dad that, during most days, shared more time with the computer, books, and notes than with them. Their love and generosity have been immense and their company and support the necessary strength for conducting this work. Many thanks also to my parents, sister, and grandparents who were always close to me.

This work is the result of wonderful people who helped me and stayed close to me along the way. Many thanks to all of them.

Introduction

Tensions between central authorities and subnational units over how much centralization is desirable and how much subnational fiscal autonomy the different states may enjoy are on top of the political agenda in some developing federal countries (such as Argentina, Brazil, India, Nigeria, and Russia) as well as in some developed democracies (ranging from Belgium, Italy, and Spain to Canada, the United States, and the United Kingdom). The degrees of centralization and subnational autonomy have changed dramatically in some cases, oscillating between federal disintegration and secession when the center is extremely weak (Yugoslavia and more recently the conflict over Crimea in Ukraine may be examples of this) to a very powerful central government capable of destroying federalism by overwhelming lower-level governments (such as in Putin's Russia and to a lesser extent in Venezuela under Chávez). When are these extreme situations more likely to occur?

Among the abovementioned cases, Argentina and Brazil have the most powerful subnational governments and are the most decentralized federal countries in Latin America.[1] Being politically and administratively strong, provincial and state governments looted national coffers several times in recent history. Argentine governors were able to more than double the share of revenue they controlled in three years (it increased more than 2.5 times, from 16.5 percent of the total government revenues in 1985 to 41.6 percent in 1988) without any substantial increase in the functions they had to deliver. Brazil also underwent a similar trend: governors almost doubled their share of revenue in three years (it rose 1.6 times, from 18.6 percent in 1987 to 30 percent in 1989) (IMF, 2001). The 1988 Constitution substantially increased the amount of money transferred to the states (and municipalities) without specifying changes in the functions they were supposed to deliver. As a consequence, the federal government kept most of its functions, losing an estimated $12.6 billion worth of revenues to subnational units (Souza, 1997, 94). These changes represented a positive balance between resources and services to deliver[2] for subnational officials (they got more revenue without new functions to deliver). But they also contributed to a profound fiscal crises for the central government and large macroeconomic crises, which resulted in dramatic events, including hyperinflation, large devaluations in the currency, fiscal and financial debacles, and debt defaults.

The resources and autonomy of subnational units have also been assaulted by the central government. During the 1990s, the Argentine president trimmed provincial revenue (their share decreased from 42 percent in 1993 to 17 percent in 1996), centralized federal funds (15 percent of the total transfers to the provinces to finance the federal pension system), and decentralized former federal education and health care services to the provinces without new funds to finance them. The total cost for the provinces was $1.2 billion per year. The decentralization of health care and education, arguably among the most important reforms in the post-transition to democracy in this country, as well as the deductions to finance the pension system dramatically modified the federal balance, favoring the central government and forcing provinces into deep fiscal imbalances. Something similar happened in Brazil: the president drastically reversed the decentralizing trend initiated during the 1980s by reducing transfers to the states (the subnational share of revenue decreased from 37 percent in 1990 to 29.7 percent in 1999), increasing the policy functions they were responsible for, and tightening central controls on their spending and capacity to issue debt.

Both the Argentine and Brazilian subnational units lost an important share of revenues, got new functions (in some cases, without new resources), lost tax authority and capacity to finance their budget with their own resources, and suffered more controls (particularly tight in Brazil) in their spending and capacity to issue debt. According to recent OECD data (2015, 28), the share of revenue of subnational units decreased to 15 percent of the total revenue in Argentina and 24.3 percent in Brazil in 2012. As a result, provinces are less autonomous in fiscal terms today than they were during the late 1980s and early 1990s. These fiscal re-centralization processes triggered large budget deficits in the provinces and hence shortages in the delivery of basic services, such as health care and education. In many cases, provincial authorities could not pay for salaries or afford basic supplies, having to face protests, demonstrations, strikes (even by police forces), and sometimes turmoil and violence. This oscillating distribution of resources and functions has occurred despite federal rules that should, in principle, institutionalize relations and ease conflicts between the two levels of government. What determines these changes in the distribution of resources among units in these federal democracies? When are these changes in the distribution of resources more likely to occur?

In responding to this question, I address the conditions under which central rulers are more likely to challenge subnational autonomy (and, in extreme situations, suppress it) or those under which provincial leaders are more likely to threaten common federal arrangements (and, in critical conditions, reject them). Recent developments in Russia and Venezuela may illustrate some of these conflicts. Regional pressures dominated Russian politics during the first half of the 1990s. President Boris Yeltsin, a relatively weak president, was unable to resist demands from very strong governors. As a consequence, he had to increase transfers considerably and grant regional and local governments substantial revenue-raising powers. But fiscal demands were only the beginning. Some regions pressed for more institutional autonomy, and some even threatened to secede. The decentralizing trend was drastically reversed after the election of Vladimir Putin in March 2000. Putin began a profound centralization process to contain pressures from the regions and put regional elites under federal control. After centralizing revenue and tax authority, he decreed the elimination of regional elections and replaced elected governors with executives selected "by recommendation of the president." The resulting centralization process, the most extensive of all in the post-Soviet era, has raised concerns about the democratic status of the union.

Venezuela went through a relatively similar process. Despite being historically weak, governors got stronger during the late 1980s and early 1990s. The decentralizing trend was reversed in 1998, when Hugo Chávez got to power with the largest margin of votes in Venezuelan history. Fiscal centralization came first, but the process did not end there: Chávez also reduced the autonomy of sub-national units and trimmed the power of governors by eliminating the Senate, which had the effect of increasing his control over Congress and reducing the influence of opposition governors over the legislature. The boundaries between fiscal centralization and political domination (or hegemony in extreme cases) have been easily crossed by the most powerful presidents who wished to concentrate political resources. Despite being debilitated and challenged by presidential assaults, opposition subnational leaders were one of the few and among the most important checks to president Chávez (and Nicolás Maduro, to some extent).

The rules regulating the distribution of funds and functions among units are not a stable feature of the federal setting. Some federations have moved toward becoming more institutionalized, but in others, these rules are still subject to the praetorian dynamics by which the winners of the distributive game, either presidents or governors, impose costly reforms on the other actors, and both of them tend to see this as a way (and sometimes the only way) to survive politically. In the most extreme situations, the winner can even try to make the other actor (institutionally) disappear. In this work, I explore when are these extreme centralizing and decentralizing changes more likely to occur.

This is a work about power relations in federal democracies.[3] These relations, broadly speaking, can refer to struggles over the monopolization of the means of coercion among regional and central powers, the control of political, administrative, and taxing powers, and the distribution of fiscal resources from the central government to subnational units.[4] I mainly focus on this last crucial dimension because it affects who gets what, how, and when in the federal system.[5] When I refer to the distribution of resources, I analyze those funds that are transferred by the central government as well as those collected by sub-national units. Transfers from the central government include legally mandated (also called automatic) funds, discretionary transfers, and budget allocations made by ministries of the federal executive in the provinces or states (such as infrastructure, housing projects, and social plans) (see Chapter 3 for details).

Despite the relevance of transferred funds in a federation, analyzing them without considering the distribution of functions that each of the units (central and subnational) have to fulfill and how these functions affect their (net) resources would put significant limitations on the study. That is why I also consider how the centralization or decentralization of administrative functions and policy responsibilities has affected relations among units of government. I assess two dimensions on the struggles among units in a federation: resources and responsibilities,[6] calling the difference between the two the *balance* between the resources presidents and governors have and the functions or policy responsibilities they have to deliver.

The distribution of resources and functions has crucial policy implications, as it affects subnational governments' budgets and policy decisions. Federal and subnational authorities in Argentina and Brazil have been claiming that the 1990s decentralization policies have produced imbalances between the amount of revenue they receive and the functions they have to perform. This work will contribute to a better understanding of these imbalances, helping us to elucidate which outcomes would be more likely to occur out of the balance of power at a certain moment in time in these two countries.

Despite their relevance, the causes of changes in the distribution of resources and functions and their implications for the functioning of developing federal democracies remain understudied. The literature on the topic has provided several explanations for decentralization policies in Latin America (implemented mainly during the 1990s), but not many for the shifting distribution of resources between levels of government. Decentralization policies have been explained relying on static institutional factors (Garman *et al.*, 2001; Willis *et al.*, 1999), "thick" historical analyses (Angell *et al.*, 2001; Díaz Cayeros, 2006; Dickovick, 2011; Eaton 2004; Eaton and Dickovick, 2004; Gibson and Falleti, 2004; Souza, 1997), or individual as well as partisan preferences (Falleti, 2005; Grindle, 2000; O'Neill, 2005; Treisman, 1999). However, these explanations have some important shortcomings: (1) most cannot account both for the centralization and decentralization in the distribution of funds across time (most studies seek to explain only the latter process, as they mainly focus on the causes of decentralization policies); (2) those that do a better job at this task tend to rely mainly on historical details for a single case, without major comparative analysis or theory building; and (3) the vast majority of them focus on the national executive, failing to incorporate other crucial political actors (governors and legislators).

This work intends to explain under what conditions substantive shifts in the allocation of resources and functions are more likely to occur.[7] The central argument is that changes in the allocation of fiscal resources and administrative functions are a reflection of changes in the distribution of political power in a tri-partite set of actors: presidents, governors, and congressmen, struggling under different economic and fiscal conditions. More specifically, substantive shifts in the allocation of revenue and the distribution of administrative functions are more likely to occur when either presidents or governors concentrate institutional and partisan resources and the other actor is weak and unable to oppose reforms effectively, when they are pressed by fiscal urgency, and when they have to cope with hard budget constraints. In other words, presidents imposed centralizing reforms on states and provinces when they were able to concentrate political power and divide the governors under large fiscal pressures and hard budget constraints.

On the other hand, governors imposed decentralizing reforms when they were able to coordinate and concentrate political power against a weak president in an adverse fiscal context and under hard budget constraints. The status quo prevailed when one of the crucial conditions was not met, that is, when neither the president nor the governors concentrated political power or when either of them was able to sabotage reforms despite having the fiscal incentives to alter the federal balance and/or when these political actors were powerful but did not have the fiscal incentives to alter the status quo (that is, when they had fiscal alternatives for funding or when they faced soft budget constraints). Under those conditions, negotiations over the federal balance were deadlocked, and no reforms were passed in Congress.

The study shows that static institutional variables are important, but it also underscores the role of more dynamic factors, such as presidents' and governors' electoral, partisan, and public support, budget constraints, and an important structural factor, fiscal crises. This work also presents an argument to explain why federal institutions that regulate the allocation of funds to states have been relatively more stable in some developed federal democracies than in developing ones, where they have been highly contested.

It also clarifies why in some cases, such as Argentina, presidents and governors have been prone to engage in praetorian struggles with profound effects over the stability of federal rules.[8] Argentina has faced recurrent conflicts and instability, with both presidents and governors imposing costly reforms on each other. There were also devastating consequences in terms of policy outcomes. The decentralization of fiscal revenue during

1988 contributed to generate profound imbalances for the federal budget, which in turn affected the stability of Alfonsín's government. The centralization of revenue and the decentralization of education and health care services in the early 1990s, the provincial incapacity to deliver them (both in fiscal and administrative terms) as well as the economic decline followed by the 2001–2002 economic collapse, translated into serious shortages in the delivery of social services in the provinces. This, in turn, led to social turmoil and violent protests to demand better services and increases in salaries for provincial employees. In Brazil, presidents and governors have faced more difficulties to impose reforms unilaterally. This resulted not only in more negotiations on the reforms in the legislative arena than in Argentina, but also in more protracted institutional changes, and, as a consequence, fewer tensions between president and governors. In the end, federal institutions in Brazil have been more likely to protect presidents and governors from each other's potential assaults.

I justify the need to study cases with strong governors, as opposed to those with weak ones, because the dynamics among units are essentially different. In most unitary countries, and especially those with weak governors, the decision to centralize or decentralize funds and functions is usually taken at the national level. But in federal countries with strong governors these decisions depend on struggles among units, which clash for keeping or increasing their power and allocating scarce resources. I selected Argentina and Brazil as the main cases for the comparative study and for the goal of theory building, because they are relatively similar (Lijphart, 1971). They are developing federal democracies because the institutions regulating the distribution of funds and functions (the dependent variables) in these cases tend to be very much contested (i.e., their institutional frameworks are not (or have not been) stable and formalized). They are also presidential systems of government, which tend to make presidents (and governors) salient actors. And they are the federal democracies with the (formally) most powerful subnational governments in the region. But they also have variation on the outcome to be explained, in terms of the amount and share of fiscal decentralization, the central government's controls and level of discretion over subnational units, the administrative functions that are centralized or decentralized, and the stability of federal rules.

Although the theory is developed mainly from these two federations, it is also tested in a larger number of cases in Latin America in Chapter 2. The main aim of this chapter is to empirically assess the capacity of the theoretical argument developed in Chapter 1 for Argentina and Brazil to account for changes in the distribution of funds and functions across cases and time in Latin America. Furthermore, I compare the two main cases with others in the region (Mexico and Venezuela), and with others outside it (Russia and the United States) in the conclusions. The main aim of these comparisons is to have even more variation in the main independent variables and in the outcomes, to further theorize about the implications of the main argument.

The main period of analysis in both cases is between the transitions to democracy until the early 2000s. Though the theoretical argument is not time bound, these were periods of profound reforms, both decentralizing and centralizing, in which we can identify sharp variation in the distribution of funds and functions between units of government. I also make some references to earlier periods in an historical section (in Chapter 3) and some projections of the federal struggle in the conclusions, making some references to Néstor Kirchner's and Cristina Fernández's presidencies in Argentina and Luiz Inácio Lula da Silva's term in office in Brazil.

This study is divided into three main sections; each of them seeks a main goal and uses a specific methodological approach to reach it: the first part (Chapter 1) presents the main argument by means of a simple formal model; the second section (Chapter 2) explores the role of the main variables in the argument and alternative explanations, making use of statistical analysis; and the third section (Chapters 3–5) examines the cases in light of the theoretical framework through a comparative historical study.

In Chapter 1, I develop the theoretical argument to explain shifts in the distribution of resources and functions in federal democracies, highlighting the main assumptions and identifying key political actors and their preferences, strategies, and interactions under different contexts. Here, I make use of some simple formal modeling and game-theoretical tools. I also present the most relevant theoretical approaches and arguments on the topic, stressing some of their limitations.

In Chapter 2, I test my explanation and alternative arguments to account for changes in the distribution of resources and functions in federal democracies in a large-N study. Relying on a statistical analysis, I use a large sample of cases to get the broadest possible range of variation in the key variables. I analyze the relevance of the different arguments in the four Latin American federations—Argentina, Brazil, Mexico, and Venezuela—and in three unitary countries—Chile, Ecuador, and Uruguay. Examining the role the main and alternative variables play in these countries allows me to get more variation and gain statistical control in the analysis.

In Chapter 3, I present a brief historical introduction to the cases, and in Chapters 3–5, I apply the game-theoretical framework presented in Chapter 1 to a comparative historical analysis of Argentina and Brazil since their transitions to democracy (in 1983 and 1985 respectively) until the early 2000s. Here, I study the role played by key political actors involved in the struggles and the strategies they decided to take under different fiscal conditions. In this section, the main goal is to specify the causal links between the variables centering on actors and their interactions, applying the game-theoretical tools presented in Chapter 1.

Finally, I conclude with some of the work's theoretical and comparative implications for the study of fiscal federalism and the functioning of developing federal democracies, identifying the conditions under which we can expect either presidents shattering subnational governments or governors pressing to disintegrate federal arrangements.

Notes

1 The power of governors is defined and measured based on an index of gubernatorial power and the degree of decentralization is measured out of the revenue and expenditure share of subnational units (see Chapter 2 for definitions and measures of these variables).
2 I call the difference between the resources presidents and governors have and the functions or policy responsibilities they have to deliver the federal balance.
3 Federal countries are those characterized by a political arrangement in which, as Dahl puts it,

> some matters are exclusively within the competence of certain local units—cantons, states, provinces—and are constitutionally beyond the scope of the authority of the national government; and where certain other matters are constitutionally outside the scope and authority of the smaller units.
> (Dahl, 1986, 114)

I would add that, in the definition used in this work, in a federation both of these units have democratically elected authorities.
4 This distribution has been called "vertical" distribution (also called "primary," in Argentina) and it concerns how resources are distributed among the different levels of government (federal and provincial or state-level in this work) as opposed to "horizontal" (or "secondary") distribution, which concerns how resources are allocated across subnational units (provinces and states).
5 And also because it can be observed, measured (contrary to many other aspects which are much more difficult to capture, such as public policy coordination among units of government), and has changed over time (and gives us the possibility to have variation on the dependent variable). The level of decentralization includes several other policy domains, such as regulatory policy, that transfers cannot capture. I analyze some of them in the historical analysis.
6 A third dimension, besides the fiscal and administrative ones, which is also crucial for analyzing the distribution of power in a federal democracy, is political. We can refer to it as political autonomy of subnational units or political decentralization, and it basically consists of the establishment or reestablishment of democratically elected autonomous subnational governments (Falleti, 2005; Willis *et al.* 1999, 8). I include it in the comparative historical analysis of the cases, but as political autonomy does not have variation during the years covered by this work, I do not include it in the theoretical section. There, I work with two main dependent variables: the degree of fiscal and administrative decentralization.
7 A shift in the expenditure or revenue share of subnational units is substantive when any decentralizing or centralizing trend represents total changes above the standard deviation for each country (7 percent for Argentina and 4 percent for Brazil). I analyze all shifts in the distribution of functions in the period of analysis, since each reform in this area represents a substantial change in federal relations.

8 I use the term "praetorian," paraphrasing Huntington (1968), to refer to a situation in which political actors confront each other nakedly, without political institutions being able to mediate and ease conflicts among them. There is a fundamental difference though; while Huntington was referring to praetorian politics in authoritarian regimes, I use the term in a democratic setting (even though institutional mediation is weak).

References

Angell, Alan, Pamela Lowden, and Rosemary Thorp, *Decentralizing Development: The Political Economy of Institutional Change in Colombia and Chile* (Oxford: Oxford University Press, 2001).

Dahl, Robert, "Federalism and the Democratic Process"; in: Dahl, Robert, *Democracy, Identity, and Equality* (Oslo: Norwegian University Press, 1986).

Díaz Cayeros, Alberto, *Federalism, Fiscal Authority, and Centralization in Latin America* (Cambridge: Cambridge University Press, 2006).

Dickovick, J. Tyler, *Decentralization and Recentralization in the Developing World: Comparative Studies from Africa and Latin America* (University Park, PA: Penn State University Press, 2011).

Eaton, Kent, *Politics Beyond the Capital: The Design of Subnational Institutions in South America* (Stanford, CA: Stanford University Press, 2004).

Eaton, Kent, and Tyler Dickovick, "The Politics of Re-Centralization in Argentina And Brazil," *Latin American Research Review*, Vol. 39, No. 1, 2004, pp. 90–122.

Falleti, Tulia, "A Sequential Theory of Decentralization: Latin American Cases in Comparative Perspective," *American Political Science Review*, Vol. 99, No. 3, 2005, pp. 327–346

Garman, Christopher, Stephan Haggard, and Eliza Willis, "Fiscal Decentralization, A Political Theory with Latin American Cases," *World Politics*, Vol. 53, No. 2, 2001, pp. 205–236.

Gibson, Edward L. and Tulia Falleti, "Unity by the Stick: Regional Conflict and the Origins of Argentine Federalism"; in: Gibson, Edward L. (ed.), *Federalism and Democracy in Latin America* (Baltimore: Johns Hopkins University Press, 2004).

Grindle, Merilee, *Audacious Reforms: Institutional Invention and Democracy in Latin America* (Baltimore: Johns Hopkins University Press, 2000).

Huntington, Samuel, *Political Order in Changing Societies* (New Haven: Yale University Press, 1968).

IMF (International Monetary Fund), *Government Finance Statistics* (GFS), 2001.

Lijphart, Arend, "Comparative Politics and the Comparative Method," *The American Political Science Review*, Vol. 65, No. 3, 1971, pp. 682–693.

O'Neill, Kathleen, *Decentralizing the State: Elections, Parties, and Local Power in the Andes* (Cambridge: Cambridge University Press, 2005).

OECD, *Revenue Statistics in Latin America and the Caribbean* (Paris: OECD Publishing, 2015).

Souza, Celina, *Constitutional Engineering in Brazil: The Politics of Federalism and Decentralisation* (London: Macmillan, 1997).

Treisman, Daniel, "Political Decentralization and Economic Reform: A Game Theoretical Analysis," *American Journal of Political Science*, Vol. 43, No. 2, April 1999.

Willis, Eliza, Christopher da C.B. Garman, and Stephan Haggard, "The Politics of Decentralization in Latin America," *Latin American Research Review*, Vol. 34, No. 1, 1999, pp. 7–56.

1   The federal distributive game

A game-theoretical framework on the distribution of power in federal democracies

Research question and justification

Argentina and Brazil have very "decentralized federalisms" (in Lijphart's, 1999, terms) and very long federalist traditions, with subnational governments in charge of several functions (including education, health care, or social programs) and accounting for almost half of the total public expenditures during the 1990s (Dillinger and Webb, 1999, 1; IMF, 2001). Having considerable political power, governors have exerted pressure over Congress, which passed laws decentralizing national resources on several occasions, at times causing fiscal and financial instability at the national level. However, subnational governments are far from invulnerable to central governments; presidents have recently undermined their power by centralizing fiscal resources, decentralizing functions without new resources, and imposing central controls on spending and debt issuing. This has limited subnational units' autonomy and, in many cases, challenged their capacity to cope with the functions for which they are responsible (especially those recently decentralized to them). How can we account for this changing distribution of resources and functions (from sub-national predation to central dominance) if, out of relatively unvarying federal institutions, we should expect a more or less stable distribution of power between levels of government? Scholars have not yet provided compelling explanations for these (often sharp) changes in the distribution of funds and administrative or policy responsibilities between levels of government and their implications for the functioning of democratic federations.

In addition, if we pay attention to the recent fiscal (re-)centralization processes in Argentina and Brazil, some facts have not been sufficiently addressed by the literature. Subnational governments are less autonomous in fiscal terms today than they were during the late 1980s and early 1990s. Argentine subnational governments lost more than 130 percent of their share of revenues in three years (from 41.6 percent in 1993 to 16.5

percent in 1996). Brazil underwent a similar (although not as dramatic) centralizing trend, reducing its share of subnational governments' revenue from 37 percent in 1990 to 29.7 percent in 1999, almost a 25 percent cut during the period (IMF, 2001 and IPEA Data). In addition, subnational governments got new functions (in the case of Argentina, without new resources), lost tax authority and capacity to finance their budget with their own resources, and suffered more controls (particularly tight in Brazil) in their spending and capacity to issue debt. Why have these two countries experienced this erosion of their subnational fiscal autonomy if they have the strongest subnational governments in Latin America? This is even more puzzling if we take into consideration recent trends toward more political, fiscal, and administrative decentralization across the region (Falleti, 2003, 2010; Garman *et al.*, 2001b; IADB, 1997; Willis *et al.*, 1999). How can we account for this weakening of Argentine and Brazilian governors if, inferring solely from the federal institutions and recent decentralization policies across the region, we should expect them to be stronger, and not weaker? More administrative and political power should mean more fiscal resources, not fewer. As subnational leaders are more powerful, they should have greater capacity to get more funds from the center, not fewer. In addition, supporters of decentralization policies have claimed that more administrative decentralization means more power for subnational governments (World Bank, 1997), and not more dependency on central governments. Some administrative, political, and fiscal features cannot be explained by purely institutional or policy-analysis frameworks.

The effects of institutional configurations and the relevance of the issue

The literature is divided over the effects of federal institutions in developing democracies. Some scholars claim that they profoundly affect the dynamics among levels of government and the governance of the country by generating centrifugal forces and veto points that constrain centralized policy decisions (Abrucio, 1994, 1998; Abrucio and Samuels, 1997; Ames, 1995, 2001; Mainwaring, 1995, 1997, 1999; Samuels, 2000a, 2000b, 2003a, 2003b; Samuels and Mainwaring, 2004; Stepan, 1999, 2001). Others stress that we should be paying attention to the influence of other institutional resources available to the presidents in their negotiations with Congress (such as agenda control and decree power) that affect how government functions instead of broad institutional configurations, such as the presidential and federal frameworks (Cheibub *et al.*, 2002; Cheibub and Limongi, 2002; Figueiredo and Limongi, 1995, 1997, 2000). In the topic of this research, I claim that we need to re-focus the discussion.

In the aforementioned debate, one of the core questions is who exerts more influence over federal legislators and ultimately has more political resources to control Congress. Several scholars have argued that in order to determine that, we have to look at the institutional configurations that influence the capacity of federal executives to craft coalitions in Congress. In the case of Brazil, some researchers stress that the presidential system, the federal structure, and the electoral laws, particularly the open-lists proportional representation system, augment the level of fragmentation and regionalization of the party system, ultimately affecting governance—or the capacity of the president to form majorities in Congress (Ames, 2001; Mainwaring, 1999; Samuels, 2000a). These institutions configure a centrifugal political system in which regional governments, particularly the governors, are clearly favored at the expense of the central government's capacity to govern. This is mainly the case because governors control resources and influence career prospects for federal legislators; while presidents do not have that degree of control over either of them. In a similar vein, Stepan (1999, 2001) argues that Brazil is one of the most "demos constraining" federations in the world. Brazilian federalism introduces so many veto points that it challenges the capacity of the federal government to produce many reforms (even when a majority of the population favors them), certainly contributing to the continuation of a structurally induced status quo (Stepan, 2001, 339).

In an opposed position, Cheibub and Limongi (2002) emphasize that, despite the centrifugal characteristics of Brazilian institutional configurations, presidents have governed and have been able to pass reforms relying on relatively disciplined federal legislators and broad coalitions in Congress (see also Figueiredo and Limongi, 1995, 1997, 2000). For these authors, the characteristics of the decision-making process—more specifically, the legislative powers of the president and the centralized legislative organization in Congress—are more important determinants of what the government actually does than the federal configuration, the characteristics of the party system, or the electoral laws (Cheibub and Limongi, 2002, 167).[1]

In the case of Argentina, several scholars have also argued that institutional configurations, more specifically electoral rules such as the closed-lists proportional representation electoral system and nomination procedures in which the president can veto a provincial candidate on the list, favor party discipline emanating from the national executive (particularly if he or she is the leader of the party).[2] As a consequence, the executive has been able to pass several reforms relying on relatively broad legislative support (Jones, 2002; Mustapic, 2000, 2002; Mustapic and Goretti, 1992; Willis et al., 1999). Others have shown that, despite these institutional configurations, support for the executive has changed across time and across issues (Llanos, 2001), and sometimes, on some issues, there can be tensions between national party lines and provincial interests (Eaton, 2001c, 2002b).

Figueiredo and Limongi (1995, 1997, 2000) (as well as Diniz, 1997; Santos, 1999a, 1999b) find empirical evidence to support the claim that presidents in Brazil have received much support for most of their initiatives;[3] Jones (2002), Mustapic (2000, 2002), and Mustapic and Goretti

(1992) do the same for the Argentine case. Yet, I do not want to look at all presidential initiatives, but only to those related to fiscal transfers. Support for the president has changed dramatically across different policies (Desposato, 2002, 11; Eaton, 2001c, 2002b)[4] and across time (Llanos, 2001). In those areas in which the interests of subnational governments are critically at stake, governors may have strong incentives to intervene (their resources can be affected) and legislators' provincial interests may conflict with the national party line (Eaton, 2001c, 114; 2003). In those cases, negotiation dynamics may be different from what is actually recorded in congressional roll calls, and several bills are probably not sent to Congress or do not reach the floor when presidents sense that there is large opposition among subnational leaders (as the historical case analyses show in the following chapters). In sum, although I agree with the claim that presidents get much support for their bills in Congress, I also argue that under certain conditions, and on some specific issues, legislators can face tensions between interests and pressures from presidents and governors.

Hence, I argue that we have to differentiate between the effects of relatively static institutional rules (some of which tend to show some change over time, although less frequently than the sharp and recurrent changes in the dependent variable) and their overall consequences across issues and time, on the one hand, and more dynamic and contextual factors on the other, which can have specific effects on certain issues during key periods of time. As I claim in the section on legislators' preferences, the power of the president, the distribution of power inside Congress in federal countries, and the allocation of selective incentives are other crucial factors that affect legislators' behavior in relation to fiscal reforms.

Furthermore, I argue that in those areas in which the distribution of resources to subnational governments has to be decided, the negotiation process involves not only dynamics inside Congress (whether and how governors affect voting in the chambers), but also negotiations between governors and the president outside the legislative arena. As we will see in the following pages, in negotiations involving this particular issue, there is variation in how relevant Congress can be, ranging from being *the* main arena for negotiations to a reactive institution (as Morgenstern and Nacif, 2002 have argued about Congresses in Latin America) for previous negotiations established among presidents and governors. In some circumstances dealing with the federal distribution of resources, the crucial negotiations have been carried out between the president and the governors (individually or collectively). The actor advancing the reforms was the one in charge of leading negotiations in Congress once she (or they) crafted enough support inside and outside the legislature. This was the case for several substantive reforms to the system of federal distribution of funds and functions in Argentina—specifically, the changes to the revenue-sharing regime in 1988, and the 1992–1993 and 2000 fiscal pacts. Similar negotiations, although with variation in the relevance of Congress, occurred in Brazil during the struggles over the Social Emergency Fund as well as the Kandir, Camata, and Fiscal Responsibility Laws. All these reforms profoundly changed the mechanisms for the distribution of funds and functions in both federations. Hence, in the topic under study, it is critical to explore struggles and negotiations between presidents and governors outside the legislative arena to get a more accurate picture of how those previous arrangements influenced (if they did) decisions taken by legislators and Congress. If we pay attention to the dynamics in Congress and the results of voting on the floor (as measured by roll calls) exclusively, we may lose a crucial component of the negotiation process over fiscal reforms in federal democracies.

The role of political actors

We can claim that strong presidents who had political support (in Congress and in public opinion) to centralize resources weakened subnational governments in Argentina and Brazil, despite federal institutions that should protect their autonomy. However, both powerful and weak presidents (in relation to Congress, public opinion, and governors) have centralized and decentralized resources and responsibilities in different periods of time. The literature on federalism and on decentralization, in particular, has not provided convincing theoretical accounts about the conditions under which presidents centralize or decentralize resources and functions (Eaton, 2004). We only have more or less detailed descriptions of the processes, but no theoretical arguments to explain why they followed one path or the other.

In addition, most of the studies on the topic have almost exclusively focused on the role of presidents, spelling out their preferences, strategies, and the conditions under which they decide to give power away. But most of these studies have systematically neglected other crucial actors, such as governors and legislators (e.g., O'Neill's 2003 work). In federations with strong governors, presidents sometimes have to interact with other powerful actors besides Congress and party leaders. In these countries, presidents usually negotiate changes and reforms in Congress (for instance, when presidents need to pass reforms on "national" issues, such as reforms to liberalize the economy or privatization); other times, they negotiate directly with governors *and* at the same time or after that in Congress (as in the aforementioned examples of the fiscal pacts in Argentina or the Kandir and Camata laws in Brazil). When does Congress (or when do legislators) intervene and when should we expect direct negotiations between governors and the president? The literature has not yet provided answers to these questions.

State of research

Most of the works that have addressed the factors conditioning the distribution of power in federal democracies can be clustered (only for analytical reasons) into two main bodies of research: the literature on federalism and the literature on decentralization. The former explores, in simplified terms, the origins and effects of an institutional framework, the federal system, while the second group of studies does basically the same for a policy outcome, decentralization. Studies on federalism have been predominantly conducted from an historical,[5] a legal (juridical),[6] and an economic perspective.[7] The first has explored the origins of this institutional framework, but generally without dealing with what has caused changes in it over time. The last two areas have focused primarily on the consequences of this institutional framework.

Another area of research that has recently blossomed, especially since the 1990s, is decentralization. Scholars in this area have extensively studied the causes and consequences[8] of this policy. Although exploring some of the consequences is a very important task in itself, I contend that we cannot have a clear picture of them without identifying the factors that led governments to decentralize (and also centralize) resources and functions in the first place. As indicated by O'Neill (2005, 4) "[d]etermining what motivates decentralization seems a necessary and prior question to determining what its consequences may be; it is a missed step that can throw the best analysis of consequences awry."

The arguments on the factors that have shaped the decentralization of funds and functions have been focused on several possible causes. Even though different works combine arguments, for analytic reasons they can be grouped into three main approaches: decentralization "by economic collapse," "from democratization and social mobilization," and "from outside." Studies on the topic can also be classified into three main theoretical and methodological perspectives: institutionalism, historical analysis, and rational choice.

In the decentralization "by economic collapse" perspective, recent decentralization processes in Latin America are seen as a consequence of the economic and fiscal collapse of the import substitution industrialization strategy and central planning during the late 1970s and early 1980s. The post-crisis period was characterized by economic adjustment in many countries of the region (and transition to democracy in most of those having authoritarian regimes). The general explanation is that, under fiscal crisis and financial constraints, central governments tended to implement adjustment policies and to decentralize functions (or "delegate" the crisis) to subnational governments (Bird *et al.*, 1995; García Delgado, 1997; Rondinelli *et al.*, 1983). Hence, more fiscal centralization (or more administrative decentralization) is to be expected in contexts of economic and fiscal crisis and adjustment reforms because presidents are pressed to stabilize national accounts, and they can do so by centralizing resources or decentralizing functions (without decentralizing funds to deliver them).

This approach offers relevant insights for some federal cases (for instance, Argentina or Brazil during the 1990s). However, decentralization policies have not been exclusive of the neoliberal reforms during the late 1980s and 1990s. Montero and Samuels (2004, 14) and Eaton (2001a, 22; 2004, 69–71) show that both developmentalist and neoliberal governments have historically decentralized and re-centralized. Furthermore, centered in the period under consideration in this work, some governments decentralized under conditions of fiscal instability (Argentina and Brazil in the late 1980s) while others re-centralized under similar situations (Argentina in the early 1990s and Brazil in the mid and late 1990s) (Montero and Samuels, 2004, 15). Despite these facts, I recognize that economic and fiscal crises played a role in some federations (and probably in some unitary cases) during critical periods and explore if this explanation can be extended to other countries in the region and periods of time.

For scholars in the second approach, which I call decentralization "from democratization and social mobilization," these policies are linked to transitions to democracy in Latin American countries (federal and unitary alike) and considered a consequence of sociopolitical pressures released after transitions from authoritarian rule. Democratic transitions and consolidation processes, political reforms to "renew" the political system, as well as increased political competition and participation created pressures to decentralize (Angell *et al.*, 2001; Beer, 2004; Bird *et al.*, 1995; Gómez Calcaño and López Maya, 1990; Manor, 1999; Souza, 1996, 1997; Tendler, 1997). The broad implication in this explanation is that decentralization policies are linked to a democratic transition from an authoritarian past. But this is not necessarily true for many cases.[9] As stated by Montero and Samuels (2004, 18), correlation is insufficient to establish causation, and in many cases there is little evidence that democratization caused decentralization. For Eaton (2001a, 3), "decentralizing governments have been both democratic and authoritarian and ... centralizing governments have also been both democratic and authoritarian."[10] In addition, there is a logical link between democratic transition and democratization with increased political competition and more subnational demands, which in some countries translated into decentralization processes. But in many others they have not necessarily been immediately articulated into decentralization policies from the central government. Other scholars in this approach, without explicitly considering the role of democratic transitions, have argued that more pressures from civil society to increase democratic participation and social accountability should be linked to more decentralization (Angell *et al.*, 2001; Beer, 2004; Gómez Calcaño and López Maya, 1990). I empirically assess these claims in the statistical chapter.

The third approach, named decentralization "from outside" pressures, incorporates international financial institutions (IFIs) and contends they have played an important role in promoting decentralization in Latin American countries, especially during the 1990s (Lardone, 2008; Stallings, 1992, 1995; Teichman, 2001). For Willis *et al.* (1999, 7, 16), IFIs have advocated decentralization as an antidote to the costs of over-centralization and have used lending programs to attain this objective. For this approach, decentralization policies are implemented due to "recommendations" (influences or impositions, depending on different interpretations) given by IFIs. Escobar-Lemmon (2001, 41) argues that the more adjustment recommended by IFIs, the higher the chances that a country will fiscally decentralize. However, Manor (1999), while recognizing the role played by international organizations (especially the World Bank and the IMF) in supporting decentralization, considers that the decisions to decentralize were seldom donor-driven and in many cases these organizations tended to lag behind governments in less developed countries, especially in federations with long histories of decentralization (and re-centralization). Moreover, these organizations have not played a role in many cases, a fact that severely weakens the possibility of generalizing the argument. These claims are also supported by evidence presented by Falleti (1999; quoted in Montero and Samuels, 2004, 16) and O'Neill (2005, 79–84). I consider that there is empirical evidence in the three aforementioned works to sustain that IFIs have not played a significant role across the region, especially in federal countries. But still, in Chapter 2, I explore whether there is a link between adjustment (in which IFIs' advice has played a role in some countries) and more decentralization in fiscal (as claimed by Escobar-Lemmon) and administrative terms.

More generally, Willis *et al.* (1999, 17) consider that "[i]nternational financial institutions, fiscal crises, political liberalization, and democratization, are factors common to virtually all Latin American countries, albeit in different degrees." The authors highlight that "decentralization does not appear to follow a common pattern" and in this sense, they call to "look at the ways in which these pressures are managed by the politicians who initiate and vote on decentralizing reforms" because, for them, "decentralization results from a bargaining process among politicians at different levels of government" (Willis *et al.*, 1999, 17). I agree with the last part of this argument and, based on it, I present a model to be tested empirically. However, I slightly diverge from its first part and argue that even though the aforementioned factors could be relevant for some particular countries, they cannot be generalized across the region.

Most studies focus on the factors that explain the causes for the implementation of decentralization policies. These works, conducted from a public policy perspective, fail to account both for the centralization and decentralization in the distribution of resources and functions across time (Díaz Cayeros, 2006 and Dickovick, 2011 are exceptions to this). I present a theoretical framework to account for changes in the distribution of funds and functions rather than to explain a policy outcome only.

Studies on federalism and decentralization can also be grouped according to the theoretical and methodological approaches they use. From an institutional approach, electoral systems such as closed- or open-list proportional representation (PR) rules, and party nomination procedures, are crucial to understanding why these policies were implemented (Calvo and Abal Medina, 2001; Escobar-Lemmon, 2001; Garman *et al.*, 2001b; Haggard and Webb, 2004; Montero, 2001a, 2001b; Montero and Samuels, 2004; Penfold-Becerra, 2004a, 2004b; Samuels, 2000a, 2000b, 2003a, 2003b; Willis *et al.*, 1999). PR with closed-lists electoral system and national as well as provincial-level nominations controlled by the president would give the national executive more political control over subnational governments and, hence, more leverage to centralize funds (Garman *et al.*, 2001b, 212). In contrast, an open-list PR electoral system and federal and state-level nominations controlled by subnational leaders would tend to buttress subnational politicians and their capacity to influence national decisions. I call this approach "static institutionalism," as these variables do not tend to change much over time.

One important critique to this perspective is its over-emphasis on static outcomes and the vagueness regarding change. Political institutions, such as parties, electoral systems, and nomination rules shape incentives, strategic decisions, and bargaining processes.[11] They can also help to explain some general characteristics of the distribution of power in federal democracies (Garman *et al.*, 2001b; Willis *et al.*, 1999). Institutional configurations also account for some variation across countries. However, these variables are better at explaining "comparative statics" than processes of change within countries. The distribution of resources and functions has oscillated (sometimes drastically) between more or less centralization and decentralization, while institutional variables, such as the federal system, electoral rules, or nomination procedures inside parties, have remained relatively unaltered or changed marginally across time. Hence, these relatively stable variables do not account for changes in the dependent one.

Some scholars have constructed more "dynamic" institutional indexes that address changes in party systems, such as the effective number of parties that measures the level of party system fragmentation (Laakso and Taagepera, 1979) and the index of party system nationalization (Jones and Mainwaring, 2003). These researchers have argued that the more parties in the party system and the less nationalized these parties are, the more difficult it is for the president to build up governing coalitions and the easier it is for regional politicians to press the national government for favorable reforms (Coppedge, 2001, 5–6; Jones and Mainwaring, 2003, 6). Changes in these indexes may account for changes in transfers or in policy outcomes, such as decentralization. I include them in the statistical analysis (Chapter 2) to examine their empirical relevance.

A second weakness in the literature on federalism and decentralization, characteristic of some studies based on the historical comparative analysis, is its disproportionate reliance on historical details. Historical analyses take into consideration longer-term path-dependent historical dynamics and processes that influence these policies (Abrucio, 1998; Carmagnani, 1993; Díaz Cayeros, 2006; Dickovick, 2011; Eaton 2001a, 2002a, 2004; Eaton and Dickovick, 2004; Falleti, 2000, 2010; Gibson and Falleti, 2004; Souza, 1996, 1997). Historical institutionalists (such as Eaton, 2001a, 2001b, 2001c, 2004) claim that under the same institutional constraints presidents have decentralized or centralized power in accordance with their political goals at a certain moment in time. Therefore, they focus on detailed explanations about the bargaining processes that led to the decentralizion of functions and resources (see also Abrucio, 1998; and Souza, 1996, 1997). This approach is valuable for accounting for the origins and evolution of the process we want to understand, but it has to be complemented by other methodological tools to avoid narrow interpretations and unnecessary specificity in the arguments (or what Coppedge (2012, 101, 120, 214) calls "myopia"). This work addresses this issue by incorporating a quantitative study that attempts to find general patterns in (or systematic factors to account for) the distribution of power across Latin American federations, and a game-theoretical framework, which presents a simplified theoretical argument about the role of political actors, their strategic interactions, and context.

Finally, the vast majority of the works on the topic focus on the national executive, failing to incorporate governors and legislators, and tend to ignore changes in the structure of payoffs these actors face under different fiscal contexts. These last shortcomings, distinctive of some scholars using a rational choice approach, refer to the lack of attention to variations in the structure of payoffs and strategies that political actors pursue due to changes in the economic and fiscal contexts. Rational choice scholars have explored the individual motivations, mainly of the president, and how institutional rules shape politicians' strategic competition (Falleti, 2005, 2010; Grindle, 2000; O'Neill, 2003, 2005; Treisman, 1999). However, most of these arguments present a stable structure of payoffs without examining whether they change under different economic and fiscal contexts, leading to changes in the strategies political actors pursue. We can argue that presidents and governors prefer to have more funds and functions; however, within the context of fiscal strain, presidents got rid of some key social functions as if they had different incentives under those conditions. We need more complex and sophisticated theoretical frameworks to deal with puzzles like this.

In addition, as O'Neill (2003, 2005) stresses, presidential-legislative relations matter little in most of these rational choice arguments (with the exception of very few scholars). The role of Congress and bargaining processes among presidents, legislators, and governors are basically absent. Hence, power relations among these political actors and different levels of government (central and sub-national) remain under-studied. For the sake of simplicity and parsimony, the preferences and strategies of the president have been considered crucial, and those of other key actors have been regarded as less important or simply omitted in the analysis. Ignoring Congress and governors may be a more or less valid analytical strategy in presidential systems with a very strong national executive and very weak legislative and subnational leaders (perhaps one could claim that this is the case of some unitary or highly centralized federal countries in Latin America, although I tend to doubt this argument would be very convincing). But this is certainly not the case of federal countries with relatively strong governors and Congresses that may block initiatives from the executive.

Several works on federalism have analyzed the origins of this institutional structure (Burgess, 2006; Díaz Cayeros, 2006; Gibson and Falleti, 2004; Riker, 1964; Stepan, 1999, 2001; Wibbels, 2005b). However, this work argues that the literature has tended to overlook the tensions that continued to shape these polities after the founding moment (see the historical introduction in Chapter 3). Struggles over the distribution of power and resources continue over time and recurrently modify relations between central and subnational governments. These tensions are the core interest of this work.

A power distributional approach

In order to surmount some of the aforementioned shortcomings in the literature, this study contends that the distribution of functions and resources in federal countries is the result of political bargaining processes (Haggard and Webb, 2004, 235; Montero and Samuels, 2004, 8; Willis *et al.*, 1999, 17) as well as tensions and power struggles among key political actors representing different levels of government (federal and subnational). Therefore, it puts emphasis on political power and strategic interactions among presidents and governors, stressing that changes in the allocation of functions and resources are the consequence of changes in the distribution of political power among political actors under different fiscal contexts. Institutional configurations and the socioeconomic context play a role, but it has to be understood in light of power relations among actors. The balance of power affects who has the political resources to (potentially) change the status quo while the economic and fiscal context affects the urgency of political actors to do that.

This approach, following Thelen (2003, 215) and Knight (1999, 20; quoted in Thelen 2003, 215), can be labeled *power distributional*, because "institutional development is [considered as] a contest among actors to establish rules which structure outcomes to those equilibria most favorable for them." In other words, the institutional configurations that distribute funds and functions in these federations are a reflection of power asymmetries, "for it is such asymmetries that allow more powerful actors [in this

study, either presidents or governors] to impose their institutional preferences on the less powerful actors" (Thelen, 2003, 216). The institutional
configurations that concern us here, then, are forged out of changes in
the balance of power among key political actors and/or out of changes in
the strategies these actors prefer. In the next section, I define what I mean
by the power of the president and governors and in the following develop
the strategies the actors can take using a game-theoretical framework.

The power of the president

Political power can be a very diffuse concept but, according to the objectives of this work, the power of the president depends on the institutional
capabilities given by the constitution and the legal framework (Negretto,
2009; Shugart and Carey, 1992), her partisan power (Coppedge and Mejía,
2001; Mainwaring and Shugart, 1997; Shugart and Carey, 1992), and her
popularity or public support (Neustadt, 1989). The institutional powers of
presidents are established by the constitution, which determines whether
they have authority to introduce legislation (and exclusive authority to
introduce certain types of legislative proposals, such as in budgetary
matters), decree power (either to legislate in some policy areas, where the
decree is law unless it is overturned by Congress; or to legislate by delegation of Congress), veto power (partial or pocket veto), and emergency
powers, which allow the president to suspend civil liberties and take direct
command of government agencies in times of unrest (Shugart and Carey,
1992, 134–143).

Besides this institutional dimension, partisan power is also crucial to
determine the capacity of the federal executive to take action. The president is powerful if she has support from her party and from a majority of
legislators.[12] The popularity of the president or the support the federal
executive receives from public opinion is another important factor, which
may affect the executive capacity to deal with governors and Congress.[13]
We can also include another dimension of presidential power, which consists of the influence presidents have over lower tiers of government, that
is, over state (and local) officials. A distinctive element of presidential
power in federal regimes, especially in less institutionalized and developing countries, is that the power of the president also depends on the
support the president has from governors (especially those from key states
and even mayors from some crucial urban areas) and her capacity to influence them. This support from governors is critical during the electoral
campaign and the election, as well as during the exercise of power in
office.

In sum, presidential power is directly related to greater institutional
and partisan power and to wider public support.[14] If presidents are
powerful in partisan terms but face an adverse (majority of) public
opinion, my assumption is that this will end up negatively affecting their

partisan support (unless presidents do something to revert this trend). Hence, a president having strong partisan powers but weak public support is less powerful than one having strong support in terms of both partisan power and public opinion. As argued, when the president systematically loses public support, we should expect support in partisan terms to decline as well.

The power of governors

Governors are relevant actors in most democratic federations and even in some unitarian states. Politically, they are elected officials who have varying degrees of power over regional branches of national parties (or regional parties), politicians, bureaucracies, and public funds. Administratively, and despite variations across cases, a growing percentage of governors deliver essential functions such as basic health and primary education. In the US, governors have historically been powerful actors in the federal political arena and the most visible figures in state politics (King and Cohen, 2005, 226; Kousser and Philips, 2012, 2). They have also increased their policymaking responsibilities across time, especially in education, welfare, and health programs. King and Cohen claim that as a consequence of enhanced policymaking authority and the high visibility of governors, "people today hold [them] responsible for the quality of government, public policy, and life in their state" (King and Cohen, 2005, 226). Governors have also been historically powerful in other developing federations. Several authors document a clear trend in Latin America out of which governors (and subnational politicians in general) have been increasing their administrative and fiscal relevance as well as their political power (Escobar-Lemmon, 2001; Falleti, 2010; Gibson, 2004; González, 2008; Montero and Samuels, 2004).

Even though several scholars recognize governors' influence in national politics, and despite the fact that many of them consider that we need to understand regional politics in order to grasp political dynamics in the federal arena, we have little conceptual understanding and measurements on the actual power of governors. Following the definition of presidential power, I claim that the power of governors consists of three main dimensions: their institutional powers, their partisan powers or the political control they have over their provinces or states, and the influence they can exert over federal (national level) politics.[15]

I consider that governors are more powerful when they have greater institutional and political control over their provinces or states, and when they exert greater influence over national/federal politics (i.e., they can better coordinate against the central government). The first and second components—the institutional and partisan dimensions—define the power of governors in their provinces; the third component represents the influence they can exert over federal politics.[16]

Out of the three components that define the power of governors, the institutional one has been the most stable over time, granting governors a floor of power and relevance in the federation. Argentine and Brazilian governors have, in general, been substantially powerful within this dimension historically. The partisan dimension has been subject to more variation across states and (in many cases) within states (I present an empirical analysis of this claim). The last dimension, the governors' capacity to coordinate and influence national politics, has changed the most over time. This dimension has been crucial to altering the balance of power in favor of subnational governments.

Hence, as will be analyzed in the cases, the main factors affecting who prevails in the struggles over the distribution of resources and functions, either presidents or governors, have been how powerful the president and governors are in partisan terms and the degree to which governors can coordinate.

On coordination

In relation to the third component of the power of governors, I argue that governors' individualistic behavior tends to predominate over coordination. The main reasons are three-fold: first, because in most cases state leaders see each other as potential political competitors; second, because there is arduous competition among governors to get limited resources for their states; and third, because there are few institutional arenas for cooperation, particularly in Argentina and Brazil; formalized schemes for coordination are usually scarce and typically very ineffectual in terms of political cooperation and policy results.

However, under certain circumstances governors may coordinate against the central government. First, they may do so organized according to partisan lines or coalitions, which serve the purpose of solving their collective action and coordination problems; this is a form of coordination that I call partisan. Partisan coordination against the president is more likely to occur under conditions of divided government between levels in the federation; that is, when the president is from one party (or coalition) and a majority or most governors are from a different party or coalition. Under these conditions, opposition governors may have more incentives to coordinate against the president. On the contrary, if both the president and governors (or a majority of them) are from the same party or coalition, the president may have either more partisan support to increase her power (in case subnational leaders are loyal to the federal executive and partisan coordination is accomplished to support the president), or more partisan tools to deter coordination against the federal executive (in case they are not loyal), whereas governors may have fewer incentives or face larger costs if they coordinate against the federal executive.[17]

Second, governors coordinate around specific regional demands to the central government; this is what I call regional coordination. Regional coordination tends to increase when the expected benefit for governors from a region is more identifiable and concrete and the economic structure of the states is less diversified. In other words, governors tend to coordinate regionally when there is a defined and achievable common objective to attain or an economic activity (or activities) to defend for a more or less homogeneous group of states. Regional coordination is more feasible when the common goal is easily identifiable and the group of states in the region is homogenous, a factor that makes divisions among them less likely. Also, the less diversified state or regional economic structures are, the more dependent these states and regions tend to be on (federal resources and) a single or few sources of growth and fiscal revenue. Under these conditions, governors may have more incentives to defend these economic interests. This is the case, for instance, when governors (and federal legislators) coordinate to defend a fiscal exemption scheme (such as tax-free zones or special regimes for certain economic activities or regions).

In general, then, governors solve their collective action problems and coordinate when the costs of individualistic behavior are too high, when the threat from the central government is elevated, and when the expected gains from cooperation are significant. Most of the time, expected gains from individualistic behavior prevail over those from cooperation among states, even in the case of regional cooperation.

Actors, preferences, and strategies over the distribution of resources and functions

Arguing that the distribution of resources and functions in federal democracies is the result of power struggles among key political actors requires introducing these actors, specifying their preferences and strategies, and exploring the role context plays in determining the payoffs, who moves first, and how they move. The main goal of this section is to develop a theoretical argument regarding the distribution of power in a federation that will guide the analysis of the cases in comparative perspective.

Actors and goals

This study posits that there are three main actors that interact in the negotiations over the distribution of national resources: the president, governors, and federal legislators.[18] Presidents want to stay in power and increase the power they already have; they want to get reelected (if that is possible, or to appoint their preferred presidential candidates to take their place in office) and gain prestige as well as public support. In relation to fiscal resources, presidents try to make the most of the relationship between federal resources and the functions over which they are responsible. In other words, presidents want to improve the balance between the resources they have and the functions they have to deliver (see the federal equation below). In addition, they want to get more control and more discretion over fiscal resources to have more leverage to achieve their goals and consolidate their power. They also want to have control over taxing authority and, by these means, have influence over tax collection and the distribution of revenues. More resources and more control and discretion over them can help presidents to achieve their goals and strengthen their power, avoiding competition and possible challenges from other actors, including governors.

In relation to administrative functions, presidents prefer more functions if they can get political benefits out of them: for instance, if they can control key political interest groups linked to them (such as unions) or distribute positions and resources to achieve political goals. If these functions could mean significant political conflicts, few benefits, and more spending (especially in contexts of fiscal crises), presidents prefer to get rid of them. In this case, there are several options presidents can take, such as the transfer to the private sector (i.e., privatization), to civil society (i.e., cooperativization), or to lower tiers of government (i.e., decentralization of administrative functions). In the latter case (the topic of this research), they would be getting rid of responsibilities for public policies (as in the first two cases), although they may still retain some control over the resources required for delivering them. This would give them, in principle, more leverage to fulfill the functions they are responsible for and have more control over subnational governments.[19]

In relation to subnational governments, presidents want to have governors' (and mayors') political support. This support contributes to increasing and consolidating presidential power. A key assumption made in this work is that fiscal resources are a crucial means to getting political support, including from subnational leaders. Governors, and politicians in general, can also be mobilized by means of collective incentives (Panebianco, 1988). I recognize the relevance of ideology or partisan identity and ideas to mobilize political support. But in this work I focus on the distribution of fiscal resources as selective incentives to mobilize supporters. Hence, presidents try to maximize the control of federal resources and their distribution in order to forge loyal political coalitions among subnational leaders.

In sum, presidents prefer fiscal and administrative centralization as well as control over subnational resources first. If they have to give power away to sub-national governments and decentralize funds or functions they would rather decentralize administrative functions with no additional resources second; and if they have to decentralize funds, they prefer fiscal decentralization with the corresponding decentralization of functions to lower levels of government third. They would decentralize funds and no functions last. In relation to fiscal decentralization, they favor earmarked or conditional transfers over automatic ones.

Governors want to fulfill the functions they are responsible for, be reelected (if that is constitutionally possible), and further their political careers, preferring fiscal autonomy and discretion to federal control of their resources. They compete with presidents over the access to public funds and try to make the most of the relationship between their own resources, those decentralized from the national coffers, and the functions for which they are responsible. They want to have more control over taxes to increase their fiscal autonomy[20] and prefer non-earmarked resources to those specifically allocated from the national government. They want more resources to be decentralized, especially when the national government does not have control over resources' allocation. That would help them fulfill their functions and further their political careers. In relation to administrative functions, they want them if they think they will get political benefits out of them, if they are decentralized with the resources necessary for their implementation, and if they have some leverage in deciding how those resources are to be allocated. If new administrative functions could attract more political conflicts, few benefits, more control from the central government, and more fiscal costs for governors, they prefer them to be centralized at the national level.[21]

In sum, governors prefer more funds first[22] (that is, if they are forced to choose, they have a preference for fiscal transfers over administrative functions); more funds and new functions with the corresponding funding second (in other words, if they are going to receive new functions, they prefer to get them together with the corresponding funds for their provision); and more functions with no funding lastly. In relation to fiscal transfers, they would rather receive automatic or unconditional over earmarked funds.[23]

These general preferences (which I simplify even further in the game below) have a sequential ordering: I argue that both presidents and governors will try to, first, get more resources (and more discretion over them) to fulfill their functions and build up political support. More funds (and more discretion) can be immediately translated into fiscal and political benefits. If they cannot get them, especially in contexts of fiscal crises, they will try to get rid of functions, passing them on to another level.[24]

In relation to federal legislators, I make a strong and simple assumption: they try to maximize their political careers and, for that, they require resources. As claimed by Jones (2002, 180):

> A deputy wishing to further his/her political career, and/or be an effective legislator, requires resources. Independent on whether the deputy wishes to be reelected, move on to higher office, return to

their previous status as an important local leader, or have a successful tenure as a legislator prior to returning to private activity, resources are required.

The vast literature on legislators' behavior has fundamentally stressed the role of institutional variables, such as electoral rules, candidate nomination and selection procedures, roll call rules, committee regulations, individual and collective amendments, and presidential decrees and vetoes, in affecting Congressmen support for presidential initiatives (Ames, 1995; Figueiredo and Limongi, 1995, 1997, 2000; Jones, 2002; Jones *et al.*, 2002; Mainwaring, 1995, 1997, 1999; Mainwaring and Pérez Liñán, 1997; Morgenstern, 2004; Morgenstern and Nacif, 2002; Negretto, 2004; Shugart and Carey, 1992). Although I recognize the relevance of institutional configurations (and, thus, the substantial contributions from this literature), it is also crucial to differentiate their role, which can favor either national or state leaderships and lines of discipline but tends to be relatively static over time, from other more dynamic and contextual factors. Among the latter, I posit that the distribution of power inside the federal legislative body and the distribution of selective incentives are crucial to influencing legislators' behavior.

Calvo (2007, 263) argues that there is little comparative research integrating different institutional and contextual factors to explain legislators' behavior (and, hence, the sources of presidential legislative strength or weakness). Among the latter factors, Calvo includes the role of public opinion (or the positive image of the president), the number of seats the president's party or coalition has in Congress, and the president's capacity to distribute pork. In relation to the first factor, public opinion is relevant because legislators might fear the electoral consequences of supporting executive initiatives opposed by the public. The number of seats strictly relates to what I refer to as presidential partisan powers: the number of seats and the discipline that can be expected from Congressmen occupying them. For Calvo, seats are relevant due to the majorities required to approve laws and avoid vetoes from minority partners in a coalition. Finally, pork is crucial because legislators' support for presidential initiatives "depends critically on the capacity to trade pork for landmark legislation and on the fiscal capacity of the federal government to finance their electoral districts" (Calvo, 2007, 266–268; for the Brazilian case in particular, see also Pereira and Mueller, 2004, 812).[25]

Summing up, when presidents are powerful in partisan terms (that is, as a result of elections), have support from public opinion (they have power to influence), and can deliver selective incentives (or credibly promise to deliver them in the future) legislators in the president's party or coalition have strong incentives to support reforms endorsed by the federal government, especially those related to fiscal issues. The main reason is that presidents can help legislators further their political careers and offer them selective incentives as well as compensations to achieve their political goals. Federal Congressmen, on the other hand, can get access to more funds and further their careers in exchange for partisan support in Congress.

On the contrary, when presidents are weak, lack public support, and cannot deliver selective incentives (or cannot credibly promise to deliver them in the future), legislators, including those who are not partisan allies as well as members of the presidential coalition, have stronger incentives to oppose the federal executive. As the president is weak, the majority of legislators would be from parties that do not support the president or are in the opposition. In cases where presidents are very weak and unpopular, even legislators from their own parties can vote against them. Under the aforementioned conditions, and in relation to fiscal reforms, politicians in Congress would have strong incentives to support decentralizing reforms endorsed by the governors (if they are brought to the vote), especially those related to changes in the distribution of transfers.[26] Having more resources (especially those automatically distributed by the central government), governors can distribute more selective incentives to legislators. More federal transfers, especially automatic ones, mean that the president has fewer resources to influence legislators, while governors may have more. Legislators, as they want to further their careers and need resources for that, would support those partisan leaders who can deliver to them. This is a more dynamic process than many institutional accounts have claimed. In sum, institutional rules matter. But it is also crucial to take into consideration the distribution of power in Congress and the issue that it is being negotiated, especially if this issue refers to the distribution of resources in the federation. In the analysis of the cases I get into the details on how these factors interact and the results we get out of the different possible values they take.

Two premises (on political power and fiscal urgency)

On the power of political actors (or their capacity to take action)

The first premise in this work is that political actors who want to change the status quo (regulating the distribution of resources and functions in the federation) need political power. More specifically, if presidents and/ or governors want to make any change in the distribution of resources and functions, they need political power. If they are politically weak, their capacity to do so diminishes substantially. How strong must presidents and governors be to pass reforms in the status quo? Presidents need a simple majority in Congress and disciplined legislators. This is the threshold for presidential power to be relevant and significant in producing changes in the status quo (unless super-majorities are required). For gubernatorial power, the cut point is when a majority of governors are powerful in their provinces and they can coordinate against a weak president. After these thresholds, changes in the status quo will be more likely when presidents control more seats and get more discipline (or when more powerful governors can coordinate). The power these actors have determines their capacity to take action and reduces the probability of conflict with the other actor. In Przeworski's (1991, 180) words:

> Reforms can progress under two polar conditions of the organization of political forces: The latter have to be very strong and support the reform program, or they have to be weak and unable to oppose it effectively. Reforms are least likely to advance when political forces— in particular opposition parties ... are strong enough to be able to sabotage them and not large enough to internalize the entire cost of arresting them.

Although Przeworski refers to reforms in general and by political forces he especially means political parties and unions, the main idea applies to fiscal reforms in federal countries in which the main political actors are the president and the governors. In order to change the distribution of fiscal resources or the functions each of these levels have to fulfill, especially if they want to modify the legal framework regulating fiscal relations among them, both presidents and governors need political power. One of these actors needs to be powerful enough to pass the reforms while the other has to be weak enough and unable to oppose it effectively. Hence, when weakened governors face a powerful president, their incentives to negotiate and avoid conflict increase because they are not able to oppose the reforms the federal executive is advancing, reducing the probability of conflict. The same logic applies to weak presidents facing strong and coordinated governors. However, because political power is a crucial factor for influencing the capacity of these political actors to take action, it does not necessarily determine their *need* and *urgency* to do so.

On the fiscal context (or the need to take action)

Besides the abovementioned premise on political power, there are four others related to the role of fiscal resources that are also central for this work:

1   Fiscal resources are crucial for presidents and governors; they need them to fulfill their functions in office, build political support, and retain power (or further their political careers).
2   The fewer resources these actors have, the less capable they will be to retain power and further their political careers. When fiscal conditions are more critical, actors will have fewer resources to build up political support, making it more probable that they will have to curtail funds

for the functions they are responsible for. Under such conditions, it will be more likely that they will face challenges to their leadership from a stronger opposition and lose public support (and legitimacy).

3   The availability of funds for these actors to perform their duties and retain power (or further their political careers) diminishes as fiscal crises are larger. Fiscal crisis is simply a proxy for the lack of resources in the hands of presidents and governors (resources that are available to them to fulfill their duties in office and for political purposes), which is the key variable that concerns us here. In the context of scarcity, the availability of these resources to be used for political purposes diminishes. As actors have fewer resources, their incentives to change the status quo ante increase. This is the case because the expected costs of not taking action tend to rise as well as the benefits out of a change. On the contrary, in conditions of economic expansion, these actors have more funds available for political purposes (many of them to be allocated by Congress; others by the executive) and fewer incentives to alter the status quo.

4   Therefore, in contexts of fiscal crisis and resource scarcity, presidents and governors have more incentives to change the status quo regulating the distribution of resources in their favor.[27]

Some authors have claimed that the fiscal context can make presidents either more powerful (under economic affluence) or less (under economic crisis). Benton (2008, 673), for instance, argues that economic factors can shift "the balance of power toward presidents or provinces during times of economic largesse or distress, respectively." My argument is that the fiscal context is not a determinant for either presidential power or for changes in the federal institutions regulating fiscal relations and (or) the centralization/decentralization to sub-national governments. The fiscal context interacts with the political power of presidents and governors; it affects the *incentives* political actors have, but does not determine their *capacity* to change the status quo. In this sense, presidents with weak partisan power under contexts of fiscal crisis are less likely to pass fiscal reforms favorable to them (i.e., Alfonsín and Sarney), but presidents with strong partisan powers under fiscal crisis are more likely to do so (i.e., Menem and Cardoso). Presidents that are able to pass reforms and tilt the federal balance in their favor can maintain or increase the power they have and weaken that of the governors. Hence, I argue that presidents can gain leverage and build up political power under contexts of economic and fiscal hardship and be strong under contexts of fiscal strain (the examples of Menem and Cardoso apply here too); they can also be powerful under more advantageous fiscal conditions (such as Néstor Kirchner and Lula da Silva).[28]

How severe must the economic crisis be before the actors lead to reforms in the status quo? For fiscal crisis, the threshold is when presidents and governors face an imbalanced budget, a fiscal deficit. Changes in the status quo will be more likely when the fiscal deficit the actors face is larger.

In light of these premises, we can give more precision to the general preferences of presidents and governors in relation to the decentralization (or centralization) of fiscal resources and administrative functions. Simplifying the argument:

1   In contexts of fiscal surplus, presidents prefer more fiscal decentralization (they can use them to build up political support) and less administrative decentralization.

2   In contexts of fiscal surplus, governors prefer more fiscal decentralization and more administrative decentralization.[29]

3   In contexts of fiscal crises, presidents prefer fewer fiscal decentralization and more administrative decentralization.

4   In contexts of fiscal crises, governors prefer more fiscal decentralization and less administrative decentralization (see Table 1.1).

In light of these preferences, we should expect that:

In contexts of fiscal crises:

*   If the president is powerful and the majority of governors are weak and uncoordinated, then fiscal decentralization should decline and administrative decentralization should increase.

*   If the majority of governors are powerful and coordinated and the president is weak, then fiscal decentralization should increase and administrative decentralization should decline.

*   If neither of them is more powerful than the other, the status quo will prevail.

In contexts of fiscal surplus:

*   If the president is powerful and the majority of governors are weak and uncoordinated, then fiscal decentralization should increase and administrative decentralization should decline.

Table 1.1 Preferences of presidents and governors

	Fiscal crisis	*Fiscal surplus*
Preferences of the president		
Fiscal decentralization	Less	More
Administrative decentr.	More	Less
Preferences of the governors		
Fiscal decentralization	More	More
Administrative decentr.	Less	More

- If the majority of governors are powerful and coordinated and the president is weak, then fiscal decentralization and administrative decentralization should increase.
- If neither of them is more powerful than the other, the status quo will prevail.

Four assumptions

In this section, I present a simple game played by two main actors: president and governors. Legislators and Congress intervene once this game between presidents and governors has been played, and when the latter decide to take negotiations inside the legislative arena. In order to keep the game-theoretical framework as simple and parsimonious as possible, I make some assumptions that I later relax in the analysis of the cases. The first assumption is that I consider the president and the governors as representatives of the central and sub-national governments, respectively. In the game, I analyze struggles and negotiations among levels in a federal democracy. These levels are the central and subnational governments, which are represented by these two actors. The second assumption follows from the first: both central and subnational governments are considered to behave as unitary actors under certain specific circumstances. These are not completely unrealistic assumptions: the president is the key political actor at the federal level in a presidential system; governors are crucial at the subnational level. In the games, I analyze situations in which one of these actors is powerful. When presidents concentrate power, they tend to get support from other actors in the executive office, and are more likely to act as unitary actors. Considering governors in a federation as unitary actors deserves additional clarifications. As argued, governors' individualistic behavior predominates over coordination, and they are usually divided along partisan, ideological, and even structural lines (González, 2012). However, governors may coordinate against the central government under certain circumstances. In the games, I consider situations in which governors (or more specifically a majority of them) are powerful and coordinated against the central government. Under those circumstances, and for reasons of simplicity in this theoretical section, I consider them to behave as unitary actors. Having said that, in the analysis of the cases I take into consideration divisions, cleavages, and collective action problems governors face, as well as internal conflicts at the executive level: dynamics that account for possible struggles inside these levels of government.

The third assumption is that, in contexts of fiscal restraint and hard budget constraints, the distribution of resources among levels of government may be a zero-sum game. Under scarcity of resources, either presidents or governors will seek to get more funds to survive politically. There are different strategies they can follow, such as cutting spending, issuing debt (nationally or internationally), printing money, or getting resources that belong to other units. All of them are possible strategies; however, I argue that under fiscal crisis the availability of funds through cutting spending, downsizing, printing money, and debt issuing is limited. Eventually, budget constraints may harden,[30] and presidents and governors may turn the distribution of resources into a zero-sum game; in a context of resource scarcity, what one of the actors gets is what the other one loses. In Iversen's (2006, 6) words, limited resources or "fiscal constraints on the state, make every tax or spending proposal [or any change in the distribution of funds and resources] a zero-sum conflict."

Here, as in the previous section on fiscal context, I argue that both presidents and governors need resources to fulfill their functions in office, build up political support, and retain power. I have doubts about arguments stating that the president cares about fiscal stability and governors about spending.[31] I think this is rather a narrow assumption for two main reasons. First, presidents and governors are political actors who want to stay in power and increase the power they have; to do that, they need resources. Macroeconomic stability has been a relevant goal for several presidents, but for many of them it has been crucial after the experiences with hyperinflation during the late 1970s and the 1980s, and that was not clearly the case before that (Allende in Chile, Alfonsín in Argentina, Sarney in Brazil, and García in Peru are only some cases for whom macroeconomic stability was not the most important concern). Second, in a study coordinated by Souza (2006), she shows that in Brazil during the 1990s, different governors embraced fiscal adjustment (a policy sponsored by the central government), and several of them were reelected despite these restrictive policies. Souza also rejects assumptions made by some scholars who consider state politics as "clientelistic, oriented to the status quo (traditional politics), and [based on the] use of public resources to sustain it" (2006, 94).

The fourth assumption refers to the institutional context in which these struggles take place. In industrialized and consolidated federations, the rules that distribute resources among levels of government tend to be relatively stable and can be considered, for analytical reasons, as "given" (in fact, several works on the topic consider them as independent variables). In developing federal countries, on the contrary, I argue that these institutional configurations are much more contested and subject to (sometimes major) changes. In this context, I assume that political actors consider changes in the framework that regulates the distribution of resources as an available option to reverse unfavorable fiscal situations.

Political power, fiscal urgency, and the federal balance

Summing up, the core argument of this work is that changes in the allocation of fiscal resources and the distribution of administrative functions are to be expected when either presidents or governors prevail in their power relations, when they are pressed by fiscal urgency, and when they have to cope with hard budget constraints (they face limited options to access resources). Under these conditions, federal institutions and preexisting institutional arrangements between levels of government in developing federal democracies cannot do much to attenuate the impact of these "battering rams" (borrowing Skowronek's expression; 1993, 28) struggling for resources.

The status quo will not be changed when neither presidents nor governors prevail in their power relations. Presidents can be powerful and governors weak or vice versa, but they all can be weak or relatively powerful. Under the latter conditions, no changes in the status quo are to be expected. Substantive changes occur only when one of these actors prevails over the other (as in Przeworski's account of reforms). The status quo ante will not be changed either when one of these actors prevails over the other but has no fiscal incentives to alter the rules regulating the distribution of fiscal resources, or when presidents and governors can get access to fiscal resources by other less costly means (such as issuing debt or printing money).

A game-theoretical analysis on fiscal transfers

The federal distributive game

In this simple game, there are two actors, president and governors. As indicated before, legislators intervene once this sequence of the game between presidents and governors has been played and either of them decides to take negotiations inside the legislative arena. The president has a certain amount of fiscal resources to deliver functions and for political purposes, which I refer to as r_{jp}, while the governors have r_{jg} resources $(j = 1, m)$.[32] The president also has a series of functions to deliver, called P_{ip}, and the governors $P_{ig}(i = 1, n)$.

Preferences

I assume that presidents and governors compete over the access to public funds and try to make the most of the relationship between the fiscal resources they have and the functions for which they are responsible.[33] That is, the president wants to maximize U, which is the difference between the resources she gets access to and the functions she has to deliver. I call U the net balance between functions and resources for the president:

President has r_{jp} resources; $j = 1, m$

And has P_{ip} functions to deliver; $i = 1, n$

President Max $U = \Sigma(r_{jp} - P_{ip}) =$ net balance

The larger the positive difference between the two terms in the equation, the more funds the president has to consolidate her power by distributing selective incentives. The larger the negative difference in the equation, the larger the deficit in the central government accounts and the fewer funds the president has to fulfill her functions. The same can be said about the governors, who try to maximize X. I call X the net balance between functions and resources for the governors:

Governors have r_{jg} resources; $j = 1, m$

And have P_{ig} functions to deliver; $i = 1, n$

Governors Max $X = \Sigma(P_{ig} - r_{ig}) = $ net balance

I call B the difference between the net balances of presidential and gubernatorial resources and functions, or the difference between the sums of all resources presidents have and the functions they have to deliver, minus the difference between all the resources and functions of the governors. I refer to this difference as the balance of the federal equation. More formally,

$B = U - X$

Strategies

Presidents and governors can reform by either centralizing or decentralizing resources and functions, or maintain the status quo (SQ). If the president has a positive net balance, she has no fiscal incentives to move and reform. The same can be said about governors: they have no fiscal incentives to move if they have a positive net balance. Under those conditions, the status quo will prevail.

If $U \geq 0$, $X \geq 0$, no fiscal incentive to move for president and governors, then status quo (SQ)

If the presidential net balance is less than 0, the president faces a deficit (I call this deficit γ; 0 represents a balanced budget). If the presidential net balance (U) is less than 0, and the gubernatorial net balance (X) is more than or equal to 0, then the president has incentives to move to get a payoff equal to γ and governors to preserve the status quo (SQ).

If $U < 0$, $X \geq 0$, $\gamma = $ deficit $(0 - U)$

The president moves to get a payoff $= \gamma$

If the gubernatorial net balance is less than 0, governors face a deficit (I call this deficit δ). If the gubernatorial net balance (X) is less than 0, and the presidential net balance (U) is more than or equal to 0, then the governors have fiscal incentives to move to get a payoff equal to δ and the president to preserve the status quo (SQ).

If $U \geq 0$, $X < 0$, $\delta = $ deficit $(0-X)$

Governors move to get a payoff $= \delta$

It is also possible that both the president and the governors face a negative net balance. Under those circumstances, both actors have fiscal incentives to move. Whether the actor having incentives to move is going to be capable of getting the payoff (γ or δ) or not is determined by the distribution of political power in the federal game (see Figure 1.1).

When both president and governors have no political power to reform and get the desired payoff, the status quo will prevail (0,0). Another theoretical possibility is when both have political power and none of them can defeat the other in their power relations. When the president has power, fiscal incentives to move, and governors are weak, she will get a payoff equal to γ, imposing a payoff to governors equal to –γ. The same can be said about governors: when they are powerful, have fiscal incentives to move, and the president is weak, they will get a payoff of δ and impose a payoff of –δ to the president. As indicated in the theoretical section, changes in the status quo occur when one of the actors has fiscal incentives to move and prevails in terms of political power over the other.

Expected costs and benefits and the probability of conflict

Whether the weaker actor will accept the reforms imposed by the stronger one or oppose depends on the payoffs as well as the expected costs imposed by the reforms (C) and the probability of conflict (w) associated

		Governors	
		Power	No power
President	Power	0,0	γ,−γ
	No power	−δ,δ	0,0

Figure 1.1 Normal form game (payoff matrix).

with them. The expected costs of changing the status quo for the president are those associated with the political resources that are needed to pass reforms in Congress, divide coordination efforts among governors, and limit their capacity to react to changes endorsed by the federal executive. The expected costs for the president tend to diminish as she has more political power to pass reforms and as governors are less capable of reacting and coordinating to oppose and prevent the implementation of the president's proposed changes. These costs tend to be higher when the change in the status quo ante is more profound and governors are more powerful and coordinated, that is, when governors perceive possible substantive harm and threaten to hamper the reforms. For governors, these are the costs reforms impose on them and the costs linked to the possibility of being fiscally or politically punished in case they decide to oppose reforms rather than supporting them. This threat is more real when the president is more powerful and she has the resources to divide governors.

The president can also lower the costs and divide governors by imposing sanctions to subnational officials that could discourage and divide their coordination efforts and opposition or by offering selective incentives to governors and by these means induce them to change a hostile stance toward the reforms. These selective incentives usually take the form of compensatory resources for governors (e.g., special funds, debt relief, bailouts), discretionary transfers, and more spending of the central government in the provinces (e.g., social spending or public works).

The payoffs of the game set the benefits and rewards actors expect to get out of changes in the status quo of the game. The expected benefits will be larger as the imbalances generated by the status quo ante at the national level are more profound, that is, when the fiscal deficit is larger and hence the payoffs are larger and budget constraints are harder, as other options are less likely to be available. Expected benefits of centralizing reforms are higher when presidents face contexts of fiscal strain and hard budget constraints. Under those conditions, expected benefits from passing reforms for the president tend to increase relative to maintaining the status quo. Hence, the larger the crisis and the fiscal deficit, the stronger the incentives for the president to pass centralizing reforms and the higher the stakes will be. For governors, centralizing reforms under contexts of fiscal strain and hard budget constraints are likely to be a costly option. On the contrary, in contexts of fiscal surplus and soft budget constraints, the expected benefits from centralizing reforms tend to be lower compared to the costs of changing the status quo ante. Under fiscal bonanza, the actors in the game are not urged to stabilize their budgets by getting extra funds (or, under soft budget constraints they may have access to other sources of funding, such as issuing debt or printing money), and the expected benefits from a centralizing reform for the president will tend to be lower than the expected costs in terms of the probability of conflict.

The probability of conflict depends on how powerful the reforming actor is and how weak the opponent to the reforms is. With a stronger reformist and a weaker opponent, the probability of conflict between the two actors would tend to be lower. In cases of centralization, the probability of conflict is higher with a weaker president and more powerful and coordinated governors. Under those circumstances, subnational leaders will resist centralizing reforms. This probability is also higher when governors have strong incentives to take action, that is, under conditions of fiscal crisis. Not having enough resources to carry out their functions or build up their political careers may diminish the costs governors face if they decide to clash against the president. Costs are higher when governors are weak, uncoordinated, and when the president is strong and has resources to selectively reward and divide them. Clashing with the federal executive under these circumstances can be costly for governors in political and fiscal terms. Summing up, if the expected benefits from centralizing reforms for presidents are higher than the expected costs of changing the status quo and compensating governors to get their support, then the president will be more willing to pass these reforms.

Weak governors facing a powerful president can either accept changes or come into conflict with the federal executive. The decision to accept (and negotiate compensations) or clash depends on the costs they face and the probability of conflict. If the costs governors face are large (as imposed by the reforms), governors are strong and coordinated, the president is weak, and the fiscal context is critical (and budget constraints are rigid), incentives to clash with the president would be larger than those to accept reforms and negotiate compensations. We can modify the normal form game to include these new terms into the payoffs (see Figure 1.2).

C is the expected cost of the reform and w is the probability of conflict associated with it. Out of this payoff matrix, in cases when a powerful president decides to move, the expected costs of the reforms for the governors are not large, and the probability of conflict is low (because the president is strong and governors are weak and uncoordinated and cannot

		Governors	
		Power	No power
President	Power	0,0	$(\gamma-C)w,(-\gamma-C)(1-w)$
	No power	$(-\delta-C)w,(\delta-C)(1-w)$	0,0

Figure 1.2 Normal form game including expected costs and probability of conflict.

retaliate), governors will have stronger incentives to accept the reform instead of clashing. This is the *minmax* or security strategy for governors: they expect the president to play a best-response strategy and they want to guard against consequent adverse outcomes. Hence, they play a strategy whose worst-case payoff (for instance, centralization and some compensation out of accepting and negotiating with the president) is better than the worst-case payoff of any other strategy (for instance, centralization, conflict, no compensation, and retaliation from the president). On the contrary, when the expected costs of the reforms for the governors are substantial and the probability of conflict is high (because the president is not very powerful and governors are strong and coordinated), governors will have more incentives to conflict and clash against the reforms rather than accept them. That is, a clash out of a reform is more likely as the expected costs of changing the status quo are larger, the expected benefits from the reform are fewer (or the stakes are higher), and the probability of conflict is larger.

Federal legislators have more incentives to support the federal executive's reform attempts when the partisan influence of the president is larger (which tends to be larger the more partisan power the president has) and when she has larger control over their career prospects (and how large this control is in relation to that of governors) as well as when the president has more funds to further legislators' goals (either during their electoral campaigns or for building support on their districts). On the contrary, federal legislators have more incentives to support the governors' reform attempts when the partisan influence of the president is weaker, the partisan influence of the governors is larger, and governors have more control over their career prospects as well as more funds to further legislators' goals. I get into further details on the legislators' role in the analysis of the cases.

Changes in the distribution of funds and functions

In this game-theoretical section I focused on the factors that affect changes in the funds the federal government distributes to subnational governments. As indicated earlier, changes in the federal balance can take place through reforms in the distribution of transfers or in the functions each level of government has to deliver. As in the case of funds, the distribution of political power and the fiscal context influences the decision to reform; the expected benefits, costs, and the probability of conflict associated with each of these reforms will influence whether the stronger actor will decide to alter the distribution of funds and/or functions. The key issue here is which of these reforms is more or less costly and which are the expected benefits associated with each of them. Very strong presidents under contexts of deep fiscal strain will be more willing to pass reforms that can help the central government balance federal deficits in the short term, even when these are costly options for them and especially for the governors. Centralizing revenue can help the federal administration to cover up deficits in a relatively short time period, but these reforms are likely to be very much resisted by governors. Under other conditions (for instance less powerful federal executives or less fiscal urgency), presidents may be willing to reduce the probability of conflict with governors and opt for the other option, that is, decentralize functions with no revenue to governors (and even offer some compensations to them to ease tensions). I get into further details of these decisions actors make in the analyses of the cases.

Final comments

Sharp changes in the distribution of resources and functions among levels of government in developing federal democracies have frequently resulted in either profound fiscal imbalances for the central government and hyperinflation or in large budget deficits for the provinces and shortages in the delivery of basic services, which were sometimes accompanied by protests and violence. This is a work about the determinants of these changes in the federal distribution of resources and functions.

In this chapter, I presented the theoretical setting of the federal distributive game and analyzed the conditions under which changes in the federal distribution of funds and functions are more likely to occur. Instead of focusing on relatively static institutional rules (some of which have changed over time but less frequently than the sharp and recurrent changes in the dependent variable) to explain changes in the federal distribution of funds and functions, I rely on more dynamic contextual factors, such as the distribution of political power between the federal and subnational governments and the fiscal incentives generated by fiscal crises, as well as on the strategic interaction among actors. According to the values these variables take, we will have different possible settings of the federal distributive game. Strategic interactions between president and governors will result in different equilibria and, under specific circumstances, in changes in the federal balance and the institutions that regulate the distribution of funds and functions between levels of government.

Having presented the core theoretical argument, in the next chapter, I examine the empirical relevance of the core variables using a database for the four Latin American federations and three unitary countries. Having done this, I apply the game-theoretical framework presented in this chapter to analyze the Argentine and Brazilian cases in comparative historical perspective.

Notes

1 This is so because of the organization of the Brazilian Congress (highly central-ized with legislative rights favoring party leaders) and the president's control of the legislative agenda (monopoly of legislative initiative on crucial areas and her decree powers).

2 Party discipline is the "capacity of political parties to get their members in Con-gress to vote in the same way" (Mustapic, 2000, 581).

3 Presidents introduced 86 percent of the bills enacted between 1989 and 1997, and the overall approval rate of executive bills is high: 78 percent. On the other hand, rejection of executive bills is rare: only 24 bills out of the 1,881 they introduced (Figueiredo and Limongi, 2000, 155). See Palermo (2000) for a good review on the topic.

4 For instance, stabilization policies have more or less received support in Argen-tina, notably during the times of economic urgency at the beginning of Menem's term in office, and in Brazil under Cardoso, but these same presid-ents faced strong reactions in Congress when they tried to pass fiscal reforms to change the system of transfers from the federal government. I get into more details on this in the case analysis.

5 Historical analyses have mainly studied the struggles that led to the formation of federal states (Bethell, 1987, 1989, 1993; Carmagnani, 1993; Carvalho, 1993; Chiaramonte, 1993; Faoro, 1979; Fausto, 2006; Love, 1993; Oszlak, 1997; Sawers, 1996; Torres, 1961; Zorraquín Becú, 1953).

6 A legalistic perspective has dealt with the judicial aspects and consequences of the initial contract (the federal constitution) and the legal obligations among levels of government (see, among others, Bas, 1927; Dromi, 1983; Frías, 1970; Vanossi, 1964).

7 The classic works on federalism (Dahl, 1986; Elazar, 1991; Riker, 1964) and fiscal federalism theory (Musgrave, 1959; Oates, 1977; Tiebout, 1956) have inspired a number of studies that approach the topic from a predominantly economic point of view. These works analyze the effects of federalism in areas such as macroeconomic management (Artana and López Murphy, 1994; López Murphy, 1995; Prud'homme, 1995; Prud'homme and Shah, 2002; Tanzi, 1995; Ter-Minassian, 1996, 1997; Wibbels, 2000, 2005a), fiscal efficiency (Finot, 2001; Oates, 1977, 1998; Rodden, 2002, 2004, 2006), fiscal equilibria (Dillinger and Webb, 1999; Rodden, 2002, 2006), intergovernmental fiscal relations (Garman *et al.*, 2001a; Porto, 2003, 2004), expenditure and revenue assignment, inter-governmental transfers, and subnational borrowing (Litvack *et al.*, 1998; Porto, 2003, 2004; Rezk, 1997, 1998, 2000), public employment (Gimpelson and Tre-isman, 2002), the size of government (Stein, 1998; Treisman, 2007), and eco-nomic performance (Treisman, 2007). More recently, several scholars studied it from the standpoint of economic development and policy analysis, focusing on the effects on local governance (Campbell, 2003; Faguet, 2001; Souza, 1997; Tendler, 1997), development strategies (Angell *et al.*, 2001), inter-regional equity and income disparities (Kraemer, 1997; Smoke, 2003), problems of policy implementation (Rondinelli *et al.*, 1983), stability or territorial dissolu-tion (Filippov *et al.*, 2004) and even corruption or ethnic conflict (Treisman, 2007). Other scholars have focused their attention on the politics of federalism, exploring the political dynamics that led to the formation of certain federa-tions (Stepan, 1999; Wibbels, 2005b), or the political consequences in terms of political competition and representation (Escolar, 2013; Gibson, 2004; Gibson and Calvo, 2000; Samuels and Mainwaring, 2004).

8 In economic or fiscal terms (Artana and López Murphy, 1994; Bird, 1990; Dill-inger and Webb, 1999; Finot, 2001; Kraemer, 1997; Litvack *et al.*, 1998; López

Murphy, 1995; Musgrave, 1959; Oates, 1998; Prud'homme, 1995; Rodden, 2002, 2004, 2006; Tanzi, 1995; Tiebout, 1956; Treisman, 2007; Weingast, 1995); or in relation to the public sector (Acuña and Tommasi, 1999; Gimpelson and Treisman, 2002; Stein, 1998; Treisman, 2007), local governance (Souza, 1997; Tendler, 1997), the nationalization of party systems (Leiras, 2010) or development (Angell *et al.*, 2001; Smoke, 2003).

9 Venezuela and Colombia (the latter being unitary), for instance, have experienced relatively recent decentralization processes without an immediate authoritarian past (not at least since the late 1950s), as in the case of the Southern Cone countries. The Bolivian government (also unitary) decentralized funds and functions in 1994, when the Popular Participation Law was passed, after almost 12 years of democratically held elections. Eaton (2004) finds little evidence to support this hypothesis for the (unitary) Chilean and Uruguayan cases.

10 In Argentina, for instance, the military government of Lanusse decentralized revenues when leaving office in 1973 as a way to constrain the Cámpora and Perón governments. The military government that took power in Brazil in 1964 increased administrative and fiscal decentralization as a way to favor Northern and Northeastern states, where the armed forces found a base of conservative support. The post-transition democratic governments also decentralized (Alfonsín, Sarney) and re-centralized (Menem, Cardoso) fiscal resources.

11 Other authors have stressed the effects that "malapportionment" has on the functioning of federal democracies (Gibson, 2004; Gibson and Calvo, 2000; Gibson *et al.*, 2004; Samuels and Snyder, 2001a, 2001b; Snyder and Samuels, 2004; Souza, 1997).

12 The president will be more powerful if she has support from both of them, less so if one or more of them are absent.

13 For Neustadt (1989, 4, 11) presidential popularity or public support is "the power to persuade" and is also related to the president's "capacity to influence the conduct of men who make up government." By that he is mainly referring to members of the executive cabinet, bureaucrats, and, to some extent, federal legislators, whose support is crucial to make decisions.

14 In Chapter 2, I concentrate on the institutional and partisan dimensions of presidential power, as there are data and indexes available for the time period under consideration. I consider the role of presidents' popularity and public support in influencing reform processes in the analysis of the cases, during periods in which the data are available.

15 The popularity of governors is also an important factor, but there are very few data available on this dimension. I consider it in the analysis of the cases whenever there are data available.

16 I further develop the components of the index of gubernatorial powers in the next chapter.

17 Features of the party system also affect partisan coordination, as it tends to be more difficult to achieve the more fragmented (the larger the effective number of parties) and the less nationalized (or the more regionalized) the party system is.

18 Obviously, there could be other actors (such as state or provincial legislators, mayors, or bureaucrats), who may intervene. For reasons of simplicity and parsimony, I will only consider these three as representative of the central government, Congress, and subnational governments respectively, and analyze the role of others when studying the cases (see the assumptions below).

19 Presidents may also want to decentralize resources due to programmatic commitments. In this case, ideas and ideology may play a key role. I do not consider all possible factors for the sake of simplicity and parsimony.

20 I relax these strong assumptions in González (2012), differentiating states and provinces according to structural differences. There, I distinguish relatively developed and economically diversified states that can generate significant tax revenues and would hence prefer to administer their own wealth, have more tax authority, and less redistribution; and less developed and economically less complex states that would prefer fewer tax powers and a stronger central government capable of redistributing more resources from richer states.

21 Falleti (2003, 29–32; 2010, 44–47) and Willis *et al.* (1999, 17) present very similar expectations.

22 I assume that governors prefer more funds as a first-order strategy since they always can have some type of discretion (sometimes minimal) over their allocation (either in the present or expecting to negotiate it in the future), and more money is, in general, good for political (or clientelistic) purposes. They want more discretion as a second-order strategy. They prefer more funds to more discretion because the latter can have a minimal impact if they have few resources.

23 Governors, in general, would like to have more automatic and unconditional transfers first. I stick to this general claim, although governors from more developed states would favor more fiscal authority second, and more earmarked transfers from the central government third. On the contrary, governors from less developed states would favor more earmarked transfers second and the transfer of taxing authority third (see González, 2012).

24 Some functions, currently centralized at the federal level, have not generated major conflicts over whether they should be centralized or decentralized, such as defense and foreign relations. This work focuses on those over which there have been conflicts over their centralization or decentralization, such as social policy responsibilities (health care, education, housing, and social programs). Furthermore, in the case of provincial/state governments, they can either re-centralize functions to the central government or decentralize further to local governments. For the sake of simplicity, I do not develop these dynamics in the game-theoretical framework, although I refer to them in the analysis of the cases.

25 Pereira and Mueller (2004, 812) claim that the president allows for budget amendments proposed by legislators as a means to obtain their support in Congress and increase the probability of electoral success (especially from the members of the presidential coalition).

26 This argument on federal legislators' behavior is circumscribed to fiscal issues (for which political actors have very specific preferences) and not to legislators' behavior in general (where several other dimensions intervene in configuring their preferences). This work does not deal with this broader discussion.

27 Crises can also open up possibilities for presidential action or increase presidential *leverage* for implementing reforms (Skowronek, 1993, 31–32).

28 In Chapter 2's section on results and discussion, I run a set of correlations that show there is a weak or inverse relationship between economic or fiscal variables and presidential political power or popularity, contrary to the theoretical expectations of the aforementioned arguments. Other authors, in line with the previous reasoning, have argued that the fiscal context affects presidential popularity (see, for instance, the immense literature on economic voting). That is, times of economic scarcity negatively affect presidential popularity, while the opposite is to be expected in times of prosperity. In this work, I take presidential popularity as an explanatory variable (it is a dimension of presidential power), which I consider independent from fiscal decentralization (that is, I do not expect more decentralization to directly augment presidential—or gubernatorial—popularity or power, or less decentralization to diminish it). Hence,

I do not explore what the (innumerable) causes for changes in popularity are, although I deal with some of the most obvious in the analysis of the cases (such as corruption scandals during Collor's administration). Despite the independence among variables, I recognize there could be an *indirect* effect among them: under economic hardship, presidents have more incentives to alter the status quo, they may gain more leverage under urgency, and change the institutional settings regulating the distribution of transfers in their favor; if they pass reforms that tilt the federal balance to their favor, they may gain more power and weaken governors. On the contrary, having substantial constraints in terms of fiscal resources and being unable to change the federal status quo can affect presidents' ability to deliver and their political support.

29 Governors want more administrative functions if they have the revenue necessary for their delivery, especially if they have some leverage over the allocation of these resources. Having more funds, we can expect they would want more functions. If new functions would cause large fiscal costs for the governors, more political conflicts for them, and more fiscal control from the central government, I assume governors would prefer functions to be centralized (see section on Actors and Goals).

30 Under hard-budget constraints, presidents and governors may "have neither the ability to print money nor access to unlimited credit" (Weingast, 1995, 4).

31 Falleti (2003, 33), for instance, argues that presidents care about macroeconomic stability while governors "are more preoccupied with increasing their own revenues—if possible through automatic transfers from the central government … regardless of the macroeconomic consequences of their behavior for the country as a whole."

32 Governors' resources are those collected from their districts and those decentralized from national coffers.

33 I further simplify the preferences and strategies presented in earlier sections to keep the game more parsimonious.

References

Abrucio, Fernando Luis, "Os Barões da Federação," *Lua Nova*, No. 33, 1994, pp. 165–183.

Abrucio, Fernando Luis, *Os Barões da Federação: Os Governadores e a Redemocratização Brasileira* (São Paulo: Coleção Comentário, USP, 1998).

Abrucio, Fernando Luis, and David Samuels, "A Nova Política dos Governadores," *Lua Nova*, No. 40/41, 1997, pp. 137–166.

Acuña, Carlos, and Mariano Tommasi, *Some Reflections on the Institutional Reforms Required for Latin America* (Buenos Aires: CEDI, 1999).

Ames, Barry, "Electoral Rules, Constituency Pressures, and Pork Barrel: Bases of Voting in the Brazilian Congress," *Journal of Politics*, Vol. 57, No. 2, 1995, pp. 324–343.

Ames, Barry, *The Deadlock of Democracy in Brazil: Interests, Identities, and Institutions in Comparative Politics* (Ann Arbor: University of Michigan Press, 2001).

Angell, Alan, Pamela Lowden, and Rosemary Thorp, *Decentralizing Development: The Political Economy of Institutional Change in Colombia and Chile* (Oxford: Oxford University Press, 2001).

Artana, Daniel, and Ricardo López Murphy, "Fiscal Decentralization: Some Lessons for Latin America" (Buenos Aires: FIEL, Documento de Trabajo Nº 42, 1994).

Bas, Arturo, *Derecho Federal Argentino* (Buenos Aires: Valerio Abeledo, 1927).

Beer, Caroline, "Electoral Competition and Fiscal Decentralization in Mexico"; in: Montero, Alfred P. and David J. Samuels (eds.), *Decentralization and Democracy in Latin America* (Notre Dame, IN: University of Notre Dame Press, 2004).

Bethell, Leslie, *Colonial Brazil* (Cambridge History of Latin America) (Cambridge: Cambridge University Press, 1987).

Bethell, Leslie, *Brazil: Empire and Republic. 1822–1930* (Cambridge History of Latin America) (Cambridge: Cambridge University Press, 1989).

Bethell, Leslie, *Argentina since Independence* (Cambridge History of Latin America) (Cambridge: Cambridge University Press, 1993).

Benton, Allyson, "What Makes Strong Federalism Seem Weak? Fiscal Resources and Presidential–Provincial Relations in Argentina," *Publius: The Journal of Federalism*, Vol. 39, No. 4, 2008, pp. 651–676.

Bird, Richard, "Fiscal Decentralization in Colombia"; in: Bennett, Robert (ed.), *Decentralization, Local Governments, and Markets* (Oxford: Clarendon Press, 1990).

Bird, Richard, Caroline Freund, and Christine Wallich, "Decentralizing Fiscal Systems in Transition Economies," *Finance and Development*, Vol. 32, No. 3 (4), 1995.

Burgess, Michael, *Comparative Federalism in Theory and Practice* (Milton Park and New York: Routledge, 2006).

Calvo, Ernesto, "The Responsive Legislature: Public Opinion and Law Making in a Highly Disciplined Legislature," *British Journal of Political Science*, Vol. 37, No. 2, 2007, pp. 263–280.

Calvo, Ernesto, and Juan Manuel Abal Medina, eds., *El Federalismo Electoral Argentino: Sobrerrepresentación, Reforma Política y Gobierno Dividido en la Argentina* (Buenos Aires: EUDEBA, 2001).

Campbell, Timothy, *The Quiet Revolution: Decentralization and the Rise of Political Participation in Latin American Cities* (Pittsburg: University of Pittsburg Press, 2003).

Carmagnani, Marcello, (ed.), *Federalismos Latinoamericanos: México/Brasil/Argentina* (México: Fondo de Cultura Económica, 1993).

Carvalho, José Murilho de, "Federalismo y Centralización en el Imperio Brasileño: Historia y Argumento"; in: Carmagnani, Marcello (ed.), *Federalismos Latinoamericanos: México/Brasil/Argentina* (México: Fondo de Cultura Económica, 1993).

Cheibub, Jose Antonio, and Fernando Limongi, "Democratic Institutions and Regime Survival: Parliamentary and Presidential Democracies Reconsidered," *Annual Review of Political Science*, Vol. 5, No. 1, 2002, pp. 151–179.

Cheibub, Jose Antonio, Argelina Figueiredo, and Fernando Limongi, "The Politics of Federalism in Brazil: The Role of Governors in the Brazilian Congress," presented in a seminar on Taxation Perspectives, University of Sussex, 2002.

Chiaramonte, José Carlos, "El Federalismo Argentino en la Primera Mitad del Siglo XIX"; in: Carmagnani, Marcello (ed.), *Federalismos Latinoamericanos: México/Brasil/Argentina* (México: Fondo de Cultura Económica, 1993).

Coppedge, Michael, "Explaining Democratic Deterioration in Venezuela through Nested Induction," paper presented at the Annual Meeting of the American Political Science Association, San Francisco, September 2–5, 2001.

Coppedge, Michael, *Democratization and Research Methods* (Cambridge: Cambridge University Press, 2012).

Coppedge, Michael, and Andrés Mejía, "Political Determinants of Fiscal Discipline in Latin America, 1979–1998," paper prepared for the LASA Congress, 2001.

Dahl, Robert, "Federalism and the Democratic Process"; in: Dahl, Robert, *Democracy, Identity, and Equality* (Oslo: Norwegian University Press, 1986), pp. 114–126.

Desposato, Scott, "The Impact of Federalism on National Parties in Brazil," Working Paper, 2002.

Díaz Cayeros, Alberto, *Federalism, Fiscal Authority, and Centralization in Latin America* (Cambridge: Cambridge University Press, 2006).

Dickovick, J. Tyler, *Decentralization and Recentralization in the Developing World: Comparative Studies from Africa and Latin America* (University Park, PA: Penn State University Press, 2011).

Dillinger, William, and Steven Webb, "Fiscal Management in Federal Democracies: Argentina and Brazil," Policy Research Working Paper 2121, (Washington, DC: World Bank, 1999).

Diniz, Eli, *Crise, Reforma do Estado e Goverabilidade, Brasil, 1985–95* (Rio de Janeiro: Editora Fundação Getúlio Vargas, 1997).

Dromi, Roberto, *Federalismo y Municipio* (Mendoza: Ciudad Argentina, 1983, 2nd ed.).

Eaton, Kent, "Decentralisation, Democratisation and Liberalisation: The History of Revenue Sharing in Argentina, 1934–1999," *Journal of Latin American Studies*, Vol. 33, No. 1, 2001a, pp. 1–28.

Eaton, Kent, "Political Obstacles to Decentralization: Evidence from Argentina and the Philippines," *Development and Change*, Vol. 32, No. 1, 2001b, pp. 101–127.

Eaton, Kent, "The Logic of Congressional Delegation: Explaining Argentine Economic Reform," *Latin American Research Review*, Vol. 36, No. 2, 2001c, pp. 97–117.

Eaton, Kent, *Politicians and Economic Reform in New Democracies: Argentina and the Philippines in the 1990s* (University Park, PA: Penn State University Press, 2002a).

Eaton, Kent, "Fiscal Policy Making in the Argentine Congress"; in: Morgenstern, Scott and Benito Nacif (eds.), *Legislative Politics in Latin America* (New York: Cambridge University Press, 2002b), pp. 287–314.

Eaton, Kent, "La Lógica de la Delegación de Poderes Legislativos: la Reforma de la Promoción Regional Argentina," *Desarrollo Económico*, Vol. 42, No. 168, 2003, pp. 499–518.

Eaton, Kent, *Politics Beyond the Capital: The Design of Subnational Institutions in South America* (Stanford: Stanford University Press, 2004).

Eaton, Kent, and Tyler Dickovick, "The Politics of Re-Centralization in Argentina and Brazil," *Latin American Research Review*, Vol. 39, No. 1, 2004, pp. 90–122.

Elazar, Daniel, *Exploring Federalism* (Tuscaloosa, AL: University of Alabama Press, 1991).

Escobar-Lemmon, Maria, "Fiscal Decentralization and Federalism in Latin America," *Publius: The Journal of Federalism*, Vol. 31, No. 4, 2001, pp. 23–41.

Escolar, Marcelo, "La Ilusión Unitaria. Política Territorial y Nacionalización Política en Argentina," *Revista de la SAAP*, Vol. 7, No. 2, 2013, pp. 441–451.

Faguet, Jean-Paul, "Does Decentralization Increase Responsiveness to Local Needs? Evidence from Bolivia," World Bank Policy Research Working Paper 2561, 2001.

Falleti, Tulia, "New Fiscal Federalism and the Political Dynamics of Decentralization in Latin America," paper presented at the conference, "International Institutions, Global Processes, Domestic Consequences," Duke University, April 9–11, 1999.

Falleti, Tulia, "Not Just What but When and by Whom: Decentralization Trajectories and Balance of Power in Argentina, Mexico and Colombia, 1982–1999," mimeo, 2000.

Falleti, Tulia, "Governing Governors: Coalitions and Sequences of Decentralization in Argentina, Colombia, and Mexico," Ph.D. Dissertation, Northwestern University, 2003.

Falleti, Tulia, "A Sequential Theory of Decentralization: Latin American Cases in Comparative Perspective," *American Political Science Review*, Vol. 99, No. 3, 2005, pp. 327–346.

Falleti, Tulia, *Decentralization and Subnational Politics in Latin America* (Cambridge: Cambridge University Press, 2010).

Faoro, Raymundo, *Os Donos do Poder. Formação do Patronato Político Brasileiro* (Porto Alegre: Editora Globo, 1979).

Fausto, Boris, *História do Brasil* (São Paulo: EDUSP, 1994; 12th ed., 2006).

Figueiredo, Argelina Cheibub, and Fernando Limongi, "Mudança Constitucional, Desempenho do Legislativo e Consolidação Institucional," *Revista Brasileira de Ciencias Sociais*, Vol. 10, No. 29, pp. 175–200.

Figueiredo, Argelina Cheibub, and Fernando Limongi, "O Congresso e as Medidas Provisórias: Abdicação ou Delegação?," *Novos Estudos*, CEBRAP 47, São Paulo, 1997.

Figueiredo, Argelina Cheibub, and Fernando Limongi, "Presidential Powers, Legislative Organization, and Party Behavior in Brazil," *Comparative Politics*, Vol. 32, No. 2, 2000, pp. 151–170.

Filippov, Mikhail, Peter C. Ordeshook, and Olga Shvetsova, *Designing Federalism: A Theory of Self-Sustainable Federal Institutions* (Cambridge: Cambridge University Press, 2004).

Finot, Iván, "Descentralización en América Latina: Teoría y Práctica," *Series Gestión Pública*, No. 12, CEPAL-ILPES, Santiago, Chile, 2001.

Frías, Pedro José, *El Comportamiento Federal en la Argentina* (Buenos Aires: Editorial Universitaria de Buenos Aires, 1970).

García Delgado, Daniel, ed., *Hacia un Nuevo Modelo de Gestión Local* (Buenos Aires: UBA, Flacso, 1997).

Garman, Christopher, Christiane Kerches da Silva Leite, and Moisés da Silva Marques, "Impactos das Relações Banco Central- Bancos Estaduais no Arranjo Federativo pós-1994: Análise do Casfro Banesp," *Brazilian Journal of Political Economy*, Vol. 1, No. 21, 2001a, pp. 40–61.

Garman, Christopher, Stephan Haggard, and Eliza Willis, "Fiscal Decentralization, a Political Theory with Latin American Cases," *World Politics*, Vol. 53, No. 2, 2001b, pp. 205–236.

Gibson, Edward L., ed., *Federalism and Democracy in Latin America* (Baltimore: Johns Hopkins University Press, 2004).

Gibson, Edward L., and Ernesto Calvo, "Federalism and Low-Maintenance Constituencies: Territorial Dimensions of Economic Reform in Argentina," *Studies in Comparative International Development*, Vol. 35, No. 3, 2000, pp. 32–55.

Gibson, Edward L., and Tulia Falleti, "Unity by the Stick: Regional Conflict and the Origins of Argentine Federalism"; in: Gibson, Edward L. (ed.), *Federalism and Democracy in Latin America* (Baltimore: Johns Hopkins University Press, 2004).

Gibson, Edward L., Ernesto Calvo, and Tulia Falleti, "Reallocative Federalism: Legislative Overrepresentation and Public Spending in the Western Hemisphere";

in: Gibson, Edward L. (ed.), *Federalism and Democracy in Latin America* (Baltimore: Johns Hopkins University Press, 2004).

Gimpelson, Vladimir, and Daniel Treisman, "Fiscal Games and Public Employment: A Theory with Evidence from Russia," *World Politics*, Vol. 54, No. 2, January 2002, pp. 145–183.

Gómez Calcaño, Luis and Margarita López Maya, *El Tejido de Penélope. La Reforma del Estado en Venezuela, 1984–1988* (Caracas: CENDES-APUCV-IPP, 1990).

González, Lucas, "Political Power, Fiscal Crises, and Decentralization in Latin America: Federal Countries in Comparative Perspective (and Some Contrasts with Unitary Cases)," *Publius: The Journal of Federalism*, Vol. 38, No. 2, 2008, pp. 211–247.

González, Lucas, "The Distributive Effects of Centralization and Decentralization across Sub-National Units," *Latin American Research Review*, Vol. 47, No. 3, 2012, pp. 109–133.

Grindle, Merilee, *Audacious Reforms: Institutional Invention and Democracy in Latin America* (Baltimore: Johns Hopkins University Press, 2000).

Haggard, Stephan, and Steven Webb, "Political Incentives and Intergovernmental Fiscal Relations: Argentina, Brazil, and Mexico Compared"; in: Montero, Alfred P. and David J. Samuels (eds.), *Decentralization and Democracy in Latin America* (Notre Dame, IN: University of Notre Dame Press, 2004).

IADB (Inter-American Development Bank), *Fiscal Stability with Democracy and Decentralization* (Washington, DC: IADB, 1997).

IMF (International Monetary Fund), *Government Finance Statistics* (GFS), 2001.

Iversen, Torben, "Class Politics is Dead! Long Live Class Politics! A Political Economy Perspective on the New Partisan Politics," *APSA-CP Newsletter*, Vol. 17, Issue 2, Summer 2006.

Jones, Mark, "Explaining the High Level of Party Discipline in the Argentine Congress"; in: Morgenstern, Scott and Benito Nacif (eds.), *Legislative Politics in Latin America* (New York: Cambridge University Press, 2002).

Jones, Mark, and Scott Mainwaring, "The Nationalization of Parties and Party Systems: An Empirical Measure and an Application for the Americas," Working Paper 304, Kellogg Institute for International Studies, University of Notre Dame, 2003.

Jones, Mark, Sebastián Saiegh, Pablo Spiller, and Mariano Tommasi, "Amateur Legislators—Professional Politicians: The Consequences of Party-Centered Electoral Rules in a Federal System," *American Journal of Political Science*, Vol. 46, No. 3, 2002, pp. 656–660.

King, James, and Jeffrey Cohen, "What Determines a Governor's Popularity?" *State Politics & Policy Quarterly*, Vol. 5, No. 3, 2005, pp. 225–247.

Knight, Jack, "Explaining the Rise of Neo-Liberalism: The Mechanisms of Institutional Change," unpublished manuscript, Washington University in St. Louis, 1999; quoted in Thelen, Kathleen, "How Institutions Evolve: Insights from Historical Institutional Analysis"; in: Mahoney, James and Dietrich Rueschemeyer (eds.), *Comparative Historical Analysis in the Social Sciences* (Cambridge: Cambridge University Press, 2003).

Kousser, Thad, and Justin H. Phillips, *The Power of American Governors: Winning on Budgets and Losing on Policy* (Cambridge: Cambridge University Press, 2012).

Kraemer, Moritz, "Intergovernmental Transfers and Political Representation: Empirical Evidence from Argentina, Brazil and Mexico," Inter-American Development Bank, Working Paper 345, 1997.

Laakso, Markku, and Rein Taagepera, "Effective Number of Parties: A Measure with Application to West Europe," *Comparative Political Studies*, Vol. 12, No. 1, 1979, pp. 3–27.

Lardone, Martín, "Bancos Multilaterales de Desarrollo y Reforma del Estado: Un Análisis Comparado de Casos Provinciales en Argentina," paper presented at the Primer Encuentro de la Red de "Federalismo y Política Subnacional: Argentina en Perspectiva Comparada," Buenos Aires, Universidad Torcuato Di Tella, June 27–28, 2008.

Leiras, Marcelo, "Los Procesos de Descentralización y la Nacionalización de los Sistemas de Partidos en América Latina," *Política y Gobierno*, Vol. 17, No. 2, 2010, pp. 205–241.

Lijphart, Arend, *Patterns of Democracy: Government Forms and Performance in Thirty-Six Countries* (New Haven: Yale University Press, 1999).

Litvack, Jennie, Junaid Ahmad, and Richard Bird, *Rethinking Decentralization in Developing Countries*, Washington, DC: The World Bank, Sector Studies Series, 1998.

Llanos, Mariana, "Understanding Presidential Power in Argentina: A Study of the Policy of Privatisation in the 1990s," *Journal of Latin American Studies*, Vol. 33, No. 1, 2001, pp. 67–99.

López Murphy, Ricardo, *La Descentralización Fiscal en América Latina: Problemas y Perspectivas*, Red de Centros de Investigación Aplicada (Buenos Aires: FIEL-BID, 1995).

Love, Joseph, "Federalismo y Regionalismo en Brazil, 1889–1937"; in: Carmagnani, Marcello (ed.), *Federalismos Latinoamericanos: México/Brasil/Argentina*, (México: Fondo de Cultura Económica, 1993).

Mainwaring, Scott, "Brazil: Weak Parties, Feckless Democracy"; in: Mainwaring, Scott and Timothy Scully, *Building Democratic Institutions: Party Systems in Latin America* (Stanford: Stanford University Press, 1995).

Mainwaring, Scott, "Multipartism, Robust Federalism, and Presidentialism in Brazil"; in: Mainwaring, Scott and Matthew Shugart, *Presidentialism and Democracy in Latin America* (Cambridge: Cambridge University Press, 1997).

Mainwaring, Scott, *Rethinking Party Systems in the Third Wave of Democratization: The Case of Brazil* (Stanford: Stanford University Press, 1999).

Mainwaring, Scott, and Aníbal Pérez Liñán, "Party Discipline in the Brazilian Constitutional Congress," *Legislative Studies Quarterly*, Vol. 22, No. 4, 1997, pp. 453–483.

Mainwaring, Scott, and Matthew Shugart, *Presidentialism and Democracy in Latin America* (Cambridge: Cambridge University Press, 1997).

Manor, James, *The Political Economy of Democratic Decentralization* (Washington, DC: The World Bank, 1999).

Montero, Alfred P., "After Decentralization: Patterns of Intergovernmental Conflict in Argentina, Brazil, Mexico, and Spain," *Publius: The Journal of Federalism*, Vol. 31, No. 4, Fall 2001a, pp. 43–64.

Montero, Alfred P., "Decentralizing Democracy: Spain and Brazil in Comparative Perspective," *Comparative Politics*, Vol. 33, No. 2, 2001b, pp. 149–169.

Montero, Alfred P., and David J. Samuels, eds., *Decentralization and Democracy in Latin America* (Notre Dame, IN: University of Notre Dame Press, 2004).

Morgenstern, Scott, *Patterns of Legislative Politics: Roll Call Voting in the United States and Latin America's Southern Cone* (Cambridge: Cambridge University Press, 2004).

Morgenstern, Scott, and Benito Nacif, eds., *Legislative Politics in Latin America* (New York: Cambridge University Press, 2002).

Musgrave, Richard, *The Theory of Public Finance: A Study of Public Economy* (New York: McGraw-Hill, 1959).

Mustapic, Ana María, "Oficialistas y Diputados: las Relaciones Ejecutivo-Legislativo en la Argentina," *Desarrollo Económico*, Vol. 39, No. 156, 2000, pp. 571–595.

Mustapic, Ana María, "Oscillating Relations: Presidents and Congress in Argentina"; in: Morgenstern, Scott and Benito Nacif (eds.), *Legislative Politics in Latin America* (New York: Cambridge University Press, 2002).

Mustapic, Ana María, and Matteo Goretti, "Gobierno y Oposición en el Congreso: La Práctica de la Cohabitación durante la Presidencia de Alfonsín (1983–1989)," *Desarrollo Económico*, Vol. 32, No. 126, 1992, pp. 251–269.

Negretto, Gabriel, "Government Capacities and Policy Making by Decree in Latin America: The Cases of Brazil and Argentina," *Comparative Political Studies*, Vol. 37, No. 5, 2004, pp. 531–562.

Negretto, Gabriel, "Political Parties and Institutional Design: Explaining Constitutional Choice in Latin America," *British Journal of Political Science*, Vol. 39, No. 1, 2009, pp. 117–139.

Neustadt, Richard, *Presidential Power* (New York: Free Press, 1989).

O'Neill, Kathleen, "Decentralization as an Electoral Strategy," *Comparative Political Studies*, Vol. 36, No. 9, 2003, pp. 1068–1091.

O'Neill, Kathleen, *Decentralizing the State: Elections, Parties, and Local Power in the Andes* (Cambridge: Cambridge University Press, 2005).

Oates, Wallace, ed., *The Political Economy of Fiscal Federalism* (Toronto: Lexington Books, 1977).

Oates, Wallace, *The Economics of Fiscal Federalism and Local Finance*, (Northampton, MA: Edward Elgar, 1998).

Oszlak, Oscar, *La Formación del Estado Argentino: Orden, Progreso y Organización Nacional* (Buenos Aires: Planeta, 1997).

Palermo, Vicente, "¿Cómo se Gobierna Brasil? El Debate Brasileño sobre Instituciones Políticas y Gestión de Gobierno," *Desarrollo Económico*, Vol. 40, No. 159, 2000, pp. 493–518.

Panebianco, Angelo, *Political Parties: Organization and Power* (New York and Cambridge: Cambridge University Press, 1988).

Penfold-Becerra, Michael, "Federalism and Institutional Change in Venezuela"; in: Gibson, Edward L. (ed.), *Federalism and Democracy in Latin America* (Baltimore: Johns Hopkins University Press, 2004a).

Penfold-Becerra, Michael, "Electoral Dynamics and Decentralization in Venezuela"; in: Montero, Alfred P. and David J. Samuels (eds.), *Decentralization and Democracy in Latin America* (Notre Dame, IN: University of Notre Dame Press, 2004b).

Pereira, Carlos, and Bernardo Mueller, "The Cost of Governing: Strategic Behavior of the President and Legislators in Brazil's Budgetary Process," *Comparative Political Studies*, Vol. 37, No. 7, 2004, pp. 781–815.

Porto, Alberto, "Etapas de la Coparticipación Federal de Impuestos," Documento de Federalismo Fiscal No. 2 (La Plata: Universidad Nacional de La Plata, 2003).

Porto, Alberto, "Finanzas Públicas Subnacionales: La Experiencia Argentina," Documento de Federalismo Fiscal No. 12 (La Plata: Universidad Nacional de La Plata, 2004).

Prud'homme, Remy, "The Dangers of Decentralization," *The World Bank Research Observer*, Vol. 10, August 1995.

Prud'homme, Remy, and Anwar Shah, "Centralization v. Decentralization: The Devil is in the Details," mimeo, 2002.

Przeworski, Adam, *Democracy and the Market: Political and Economic Reforms in Eastern Europe and Latin America* (Cambridge: Cambridge University Press, 1991).

Rezk, Ernesto, "Experiences of Decentralization and Inter-Governmental Fiscal Relations in Latin America," *Jornadas de Finanzas Públicas*, Vol. 30, No. 10, 1997, pp. 1–26.

Rezk, Ernesto, "Argentina: Fiscal Federalism and Decentralization"; in: Bird, Richard and Francois Vaillancourt (eds.), *Fiscal Decentralization in Developing Countries* (New York: Cambridge University Press, 1998).

Rezk, Ernesto, *Federalism and Decentralization under Convertibility: Lessons from the Argentine Experience* (Córdoba: Institute of Economics and Finance, UNC, 2000).

Riker, William H., *Federalism: Origin, Operation, Significance* (Boston: Little Brown, 1964).

Rodden, Jonathan, "The Dilemma of Fiscal Federalism: Grants and Fiscal Performance Around the World," *American Journal of Political Science*, Vol. 46, No. 3, 2002, pp. 670–687.

Rodden, Jonathan, "Comparative Federalism and Decentralization: On Meaning and Measurement," *Comparative Politics*, Vol. 36, No. 4, 2004, pp. 481–500.

Rodden, Jonathan, *Hamilton's Paradox: The Promise and Peril of Fiscal Federalism* (Cambridge: Cambridge University Press, 2006).

Rodden, Jonathan, John Nellis, and Shabbir Cheema, "Decentralization in Developing Countries: A Review of Recent Experience," World Bank Staff Working Paper 581, Washington, DC, 1983.

Rondinelli, Dennis, John Nellis, and Shabbir Cheema, "Decentralization in Developing Countries: A Review of Recent Experience," World Bank Staff Working Paper 581, Washington, DC, 1983.

Samuels, David, "Concurrent Elections, Discordant Results: Presidentialism, Federalism, and Governance in Brazil," *Comparative Politics*, Vol. 33, No. 1, 2000a, pp. 1–20.

Samuels, David, "The Gubernatorial Coattails Effect: Federalism and Congressional Elections in Brazil," *Journal of Politics*, Vol. 62, No. 1, 2000b, pp. 240–253.

Samuels, David, "Fiscal Straitjacket: The Politics of Macroeconomic Reform in Brazil, 1995–2002," *Journal of Latin American Studies*, Vol. 35, No. 3, 2003a, pp. 545–569.

Samuels, David, *Ambition, Federalism, and Legislative Politics in Brazil* (Cambridge: Cambridge University Press, 2003b).

Samuels, David, and Richard Snyder, "Devaluing the Vote in Latin America," *Journal of Democracy*, Vol. 12, No. 1, 2001a, pp. 146–159.

Samuels, David, and Richard Snyder, "The Value of a Vote: Malapportionment in Comparative Perspective," *British Journal of Political Science*, Vol. 31, No. 4, 2001b, pp. 651–671.

Samuels, David, and Scott Mainwaring, "Strong Federalism, Constraints on the Central Government, and Economic Reform in Brazil"; in: Gibson, Edward L. (ed.), *Federalism and Democracy in Latin America* (Johns Hopkins University Press, 2004).

Santos, Fabiano, "Democracia e Poder Legislativo no Brasil e na Argentina"; in: Lladós, José María and Samuel Pinheiro Guimaraes (eds.), *Perspectivas Brasil y Argentina* (Brasília: IPRI-CARI, 1999a).

Santos, Fabiano, "lnstituicões Eleitorais e Desempenho do Presidencialismo no Brasil," *Dados*, Vol. 42, No. 1, 1999b, pp. 111–138.

Sawers, Larry, *The Other Argentina: The Interior and National Development* (Boulder, CO: Westview Press, 1996).

Shugart, Matthew, and John Carey, *Presidents and Assemblies: Constitutional Design and Electoral Dynamics* (Cambridge: Cambridge University Press, 1992).

Skowronek, Stephen, *The Politics Presidents Make* (Cambridge, MA: Belknap Press, 1993).

Smoke, Peter, "Decentralisation in Africa: Goals, Dimensions, Myths, and Challenges," *Public Administration and Development*, Vol. 23, No. 1, 2003, pp. 7–16.

Snyder, Richard, and David Samuels, "Legislative Malapportionment in Latin America: Historical and Comparative Perspectives"; in: Gibson, Edward L. (ed.), *Federalism and Democracy in Latin America* (Baltimore: Johns Hopkins University Press, 2004).

Souza, Celina, "Redemocratisation and Decentralisation in Brazil: The Strength of the Member States," *Development and Change*, Vol. 27, No. 3, 1996, pp. 529–555.

Souza, Celina, *Constitutional Engineering in Brazil: The Politics of Federalism and Decentralisation* (London: Macmillan, 1997).

Souza, Celina, "Instituições Políticas Estaduais em um Contexto Federativo: Coalizões Eleitorais e Ajuste Fiscal"; in: Souza, Celina and Paulo F. Dantas Neto (eds.), *Governo, Elites Políticas e Políticas Públicas nos Estados Brasileiros* (Rio de Janeiro: Revan, 2006).

Stallings, Barbara, "International Influence on Economic Policy"; in: Haggard, Stephan and Robert Kaufman (eds.), *The Politics of Economic Adjustment* (Princeton: Princeton University Press, 1992).

Stallings, Barbara, *Global Change, Regional Response: The New International Context of Development* (Cambridge and New York: Cambridge University Press, 1995).

Stein, Ernesto, "Fiscal Decentralization and Government Size in Latin America," Inter-American Development Bank Working Paper 368, 1998.

Stepan, Alfred, "Federalism and Democracy: Beyond the U.S. Model," *Journal of Democracy*, Vol. 10, No. 4, 1999, pp. 19–34.

Stepan, Alfred, "Toward a New Comparative Politics of Federalism, (Multi) Nationalism, and Democracy: Beyond Rikerian Federalism"; in: Stepan, Alfred, *Arguing Comparative Politics* (Oxford: Oxford University Press, 2001).

Tanzi, Vito, "Fiscal Federalism and Decentralization: A Review of Some Efficiency and Macroeconomic Aspects," from the Annual World Bank Conference on Development Economics, Washington, DC, 1995.

Teichman, Judith, A., *The International Context: The Politics of Freeing Markets in Latin America* (Chapel Hill, NC: University of North Carolina Press, 2001).

Tendler, Judith, *Good Government in the Tropics* (Baltimore: Johns Hopkins University Press, 1997).

Ter-Minassian, Teresa, "Decentralization and Macroeconomic Management," International Monetary Fund Working Paper 97/155, 1996.

Ter-Minassian, Teresa, *Fiscal Federalism in Theory and Practice: A Collection of Essays* (Washington, DC: International Monetary Fund, 1997).

Thelen, Kathleen, "How Institutions Evolve: Insights from Historical Institutional Analysis"; in: Mahoney, James and Dietrich Rueschemeyer (eds.), *Comparative Historical Analysis in the Social Sciences* (Cambridge: Cambridge University Press, 2003).

Tiebout, Charles, "A Pure Theory of Local Expenditures," *The Journal of Political Economy*, Vol. 64, No. 5, 1956, pp. 416–424.

Torres, João Camilo de Oliveira, *A Formação do Federalismo no Brasil* (São Paulo: Companhia Editora Nacional, 1961).

Treisman, Daniel, "Political Decentralization and Economic Reform: A Game Theoretical Analysis," *American Journal of Political Science*, Vol. 43, No. 2, April 1999, pp. 488–517.

Treisman, Daniel, *The Architecture of Government: Rethinking Political Decentralization* (Cambridge: Cambridge University Press, 2007).

Vanossi, Jorge R., *Situación Actual del Federalismo* (Buenos Aires: Depalma, 1964).

Weingast, Barry, "The Economic Role of Political Institutions: Market-Preserving Federalism and Economic Growth," *Journal of Law, Economics, and Organization*, Vol. 11, 1995.

Wibbels, Erik, "Federalism and the Politics of Macroeconomic Policy and Performance," *American Journal of Political Science*, Vol. 44, No. 4, 2000, pp. 687–702.

Wibbels, Erik, *Federalism and the Market: Intergovernmental Conflict and Economic Reform in the Developing World* (Cambridge: Cambridge University Press, 2005a).

Wibbels, Erik, "Decentralized Governance, Constitution Formation, and Redistribution," *Constitutional Political Economy*, Vol. 16, No. 2, 2005b, pp. 161–188.

Willis, Eliza, Christopher da C.B. Garman, and Stephan Haggard, "The Politics of Decentralization in Latin America," *Latin American Research Review*, Vol. 34, No. 1, 1999, pp. 7–56.

World Bank, *The Long March: A Reform Agenda for Latin America and the Caribbean in the Next Decade* (Washington, DC: World Bank, 1997).

Zorraquín Becú, Ricardo, *El Federalismo Argentino* (Buenos Aires: La Facultad, 1953, 2nd ed.).

2 Power, crises, and distribution in Latin America

A statistical analysis

Introduction

What factors shape the distribution of funds and functions in Latin American federations? In this chapter, I empirically assess the capacity of the theoretical argument developed in Chapter 1 to account for changes in the distribution of funds and functions across cases and time in Latin America. The main hypothesis is that changes in the distribution of funds and functions in Latin American federations are more likely when either the president or subnational actors hold more political power and when the fiscal context in which they interact is more critical. I present statistical evidence to sustain some of the expectations in the argument and discuss some of its limitations.

The immense majority of countries in Latin America, being federal or unitary, with relatively strong or weak subnational governments, have transferred funds and/or functions (or initiated some kind of decentralization policies[1]) during the last two decades. In political terms, this means that where subnational officials are usually appointed, many Latin American countries are electing intermediate governments, and the vast majority of them (in fact, all South American countries) have now elected local authorities.[2] In fiscal terms, new resources have been transferred to lower levels of government across the region (Falleti, 2000, 1; 2005, 327; Rodden, 2006, 25–26; World Bank, 1998, 2001, 2004a).[3] Likewise, new functions and administrative capabilities have also been transferred to subnational governments in several countries. Lower levels of government in Argentina, Bolivia, Brazil, Chile, Colombia, and Mexico (among other countries; see: Di Gropello and Cominetti, 1998; Falleti, 2000) now handle the administration of education and health care services.

This dramatic convergence in Latin America toward the decentralization of funds and functions to subnational governments has generated a vast body of literature and theoretical frameworks to explain the dynamics and characteristics of these policies. A large share of the scholarly works on the topic have been interested in explaining the policy results rather than exploring the dynamics of the bargaining processes that led to the outcome. In the following sections, I first review some of the main arguments, which stress institutional factors (such as electoral rules or party nomination procedures), economic variables (such as fiscal crisis or the level of economic growth), external pressures (from international financial organizations), or demands from civil society as the main factors that promoted decentralization in the region.

In this chapter, I attempt to, first, empirically assess the main theoretical contributions in these frameworks to explain changes in the distribution of funds and functions in all the federal countries in the region (Argentina, Brazil, Mexico, and Venezuela) and some unitary ones (Chile, Ecuador, and Uruguay), stressing some of their shortcomings and limitations. I selected these cases in order to have the widest possible range of variation in the dependent variables. Second, I examine the empirical strength of the argument developed in Chapter 1, according to which the distribution of funds and functions is the result of power struggles between central and subnational governments in federal democracies in conditions of fiscal crises. This claim is valid for federal democracies with relatively autonomous states or provinces. But I also include evidence for unitary countries with more dependent subnational governments (although in some of these countries subnational governments have recently gained more power). This argument can help us to account for the distribution of funds and functions across cases (federal and unitary), and it can provide dynamic explanations for decentralization and centralization processes alike.

In the following sections, I first define what I mean by distribution of funds and functions. Second, I put forward the central hypothesis and operationalize it. Third, I develop a statistical analysis of the main and the competing arguments. I present the results, analyze them, and conclude in the final section.

The distribution of funds and functions

The distribution of funds and functions between the central government and sub-national units includes two main processes: their transfer (or decentralization) from the central government to subnational governments and the (re-)centralization from regional or local units to the federal government. In this chapter, I focus on debates on the causes that affect transfer processes or decentralization policies, although I introduce a theoretical argument to account for both centralizing and decentralizing changes in the distribution of funds and functions.

Before getting into the debates on the causes of the distribution of funds and functions, it is important to define what I mean by that. The distribution of functions refers to the transfer or centralization of administrative powers to deliver services and to the capabilities to decide the institutional structures to support those services.[4] The distribution of funds consists of the centralization or transfer of fiscal resources and the possibility to count on subnational funds, raised subnationally or transferred from the central government, to manage a budget (which is also called fiscal decentralization) (Montero and Samuels, 2004, 7).[5] A comprehensive transfer process from the central government to sub-national governments may include the direct relocation of responsibilities and executive capacities to democratically elected subnational governments, in addition to the corresponding resources for public services and social programs. But these two centralizing or transferring processes do not necessarily move in the same direction at the same time, in the sense that there can be fiscal transfers without administrative functions or vice versa. I get into further details below.

Distribution of funds and functions as a "result of power struggles"

Initially, I agree with historical institutionalist arguments claiming that the distribution of funds and functions has been the result of specific political dynamics characteristics of each country (Eaton, 2001, 2004). However, I explore whether there are common patterns that can be identified across Latin America. In order to find an answer to this question, I make an initial classification of countries in the region by dividing them into two different analytical categories: federal and unitary. These two categories, following Lijphart (1999), are further divided into two more: decentralized and centralized. Thus, we have four possible combinations: centralized and decentralized unitary, and centralized and decentralized federal. This initial classification will be useful to specify the argument put forward in this section.

From the classic works on the origins of federalism (Gibson and Falleti, 2004; Riker, 1964; Stepan, 1999, 2001; Wibbels, 2005) and without getting into the debates surrounding the bargaining processes through which federations emerged, I argue that the literature has tended to overlook the tensions that continued to shape the distribution of power in these polities after their foundings. In federal countries, as indicated in Chapter 1 and developed further in Chapter 3, there is no complete centralization but rather some form of power sharing among units. Tensions and struggles among units do not cease to exist after the federal system was created, and are usually institutionalized in a federal constitution. Struggles over the distribution of power and resources continue over time and recurrently modify the relations between central and subnational governments.

I distinguish between decentralized federal cases (in which governors are generally strong) and centralized unitary countries (with weak or more dependent governors[6]) because the dynamics for transferring and centralizing resources and functions among units are essentially different. In unitary countries, especially those with weak governors, the central government is usually in charge of taking decisions to centralize or transfer resources and functions (probably based on strategic considerations of the national executive, as in the cases analyzed in O'Neill's (2003, 2005) work). But in federal countries with strong governors these decisions are the result of power struggles among units of government, which clash to increase their resources and functions or maintain the status quo if it is favorable for them (interestingly, these cases are not considered in O'Neill's work).

According to the aforementioned considerations, I selected cases based on data availability (the cases I included in the sample are those for which there is reliable and comparable data), but also based on analytical concerns: I included all the federations in the region and some unitary cases in order to have the widest possible range of variation in the independent variables. In addition, I chose cases in all four possible categories of the dependent variable: decentralized federal countries (Argentina and Brazil), more and less centralized federal cases (Venezuela and Mexico), more or less decentralized unitary governments (Uruguay and Ecuador), and centralized unitary countries (Chile).

Main hypothesis

Following the power distributional approach presented in Chapter 1, the main argument in this chapter is that, ceteris paribus, presidents would prefer centralization. But their preferences interact with fiscal conditions. In contexts of fiscal crises, presidents with ample political powers would try to centralize resources and transfer functions. But under fiscal bonanza, they would seek to transfer resources and centralize functions. Strong subnational governments, on the contrary, would pressure the central government to transfer both resources and functions if they have enough funds to secure their implementation, or to transfer resources and keep functions centralized under fiscal constraints. Thus, the political power of the president and governors as well as the fiscal context produce changes in the distribution of fiscal funds and administrative functions, which may vary in non-simultaneous ways.

The relevance of the power of presidents and governors in shaping the magnitude of transfers in federal countries is an indication that struggles among these actors are critical to shaping the outcome. In centralized unitary cases, the most relevant factors should be the power of the president and the fiscal context.

Dependent variable

The magnitude of transfers can be measured in fiscal terms (share of expenditure or revenues at the subnational level) and administrative terms (functions decentralized, for instance, health care, education, housing, and social plans). Fiscal transfers (*expshare*) are measured by the total share of expenditures at the subnational level in relation to the total expenditures of the government.[7] This is a commonly used indicator to measure fiscal transfers or fiscal decentralization (Escobar-Lemmon, 2001, 32; Rodden, 2006, 27)[8] (for the descriptions of the different variables and data sources, see Tables 2.8 and 2.9).

To measure administrative transfers (*admintr*), I develop an index that reflects whether subnational governments are responsible for some basic functions: health care, education, and social assistance. This is a 0 to 6 index (0 denotes complete centralization and 6 complete transfer of these three functions). A score of 2 in each of the functions transferred means that this function is completely carried out at the subnational level. A score of 0 means that the national level performs 100 percent of it; while a score of 1 would mean that both levels (central and subnational) share the delivery of the same function (this is common in education or health care services, in which lower tiers of government deliver primary health care and education, while the central government may be in charge of higher education and complex health care services).

The measures for fiscal and administrative transfers are correlated at 0.78; although it may be regarded as a marked degree of correlation, I decided to use both measures for the regression analyses because of theoretical reasons associated with changes in the preferences of presidents and governors under fiscal crises or fiscal bonanza (see Table 1.1 in Chapter 1). In addition, the statistical results show that the effects of the selected independent variables over these two dimensions of the amount of transfers vary in magnitude and differ under different fiscal contexts (see the statistical and the results section). Another possible measure of fiscal transfers is the revenue share at the subnational level. In this chapter, I use expenditure share not only because it is more widely used, but also because they seem to be measuring very similar phenomena: expenditure share and revenue share at the subnational level are highly correlated (0.94), while administrative transfers and revenue share are correlated at almost the same level as expenditure share (0.72). Finally, I used the revenue share of subnational governments and re-run the different regressions I ran for expenditure share, and substantive results do not change.[9]

Independent variables: political power of presidents and subnational actors

Political power can be a diffuse concept but, in this work, the power of the president is the capacity of the federal executive to take action and depends on the institutional capabilities given by the constitution and the legal framework (Negretto, 2009; Shugart and Carey, 1992), and her electoral and partisan power (see Chapter 1 for a definition).[10] Mainwaring and Shugart (1997) produce an index of the partisan powers of the president that associates the president's share of seats in Congress with the discipline that can be expected from those members. In general, there is agreement on those two components of partisan powers: the size of the president's party or coalition, on the one hand, and party discipline, on the other. Coppedge and Mejía (2001, 7) combine these two characteristics to define a "reliable majority" or the percentage of Congressional seats that the president can count on to vote in favor of her typical bill. I will empirically test whether presidents have tended to centralize resources and functions or to decentralize them and whether the probability to achieve that depended upon their institutional and partisan power.[11]

Governors and subnational actors are powerful if they have institutional and political control over their districts and if they can exert influence at the national/federal level. The first relevant dimension in the power of governors is their institutional powers. Following Schlesinger (1965) and more contemporary authors such as Pereira (2001) and Santos (2001), I define governors' institutional power as composed of three main dimensions: first, tenure power (or the length of term in office and eligibility to serve successive terms); second, agenda-setting power over the state legislature (or the exclusive authority to introduce bills on certain issues, veto power, and decree power); and third, budget power (or the degree of direct gubernatorial control in preparing the budget). The power of governors also depends on the partisan powers or the partisan control they have over the legislature in terms of control of legislative seats.[12] The control over the legislature is crucial, first, in order to have political support over legislation and reforms promoted by the state executive, and second, in order to neutralize control mechanisms that the state legislature can exert over the governor.

Several scholars have debated (at least since the seminal article by Schlesinger in 1965) the main components and the best indicators to measure the power of governors in the United States. Some of these specialists stress two main dimensions: on the one hand, the relevance of gubernatorial institutional powers and, on the other, gubernatorial enabling resources (Beyle, 1990; Dilger *et al.*, 1995).

Gubernatorial institutional power, as measured by Schlesinger (1965), is composed by tenure power (length of term in office and eligibility to serve successive terms); budget power (degree of direct gubernatorial control in preparing the budget); appointment power (extent of control over appointment ranging from no outside approval needed to independently elected officials); and veto power (combination of item veto privileges and votes needed to override veto) (quoted in Mueller, 1985, 424). Beyle (1990) presents an index on gubernatorial powers based on some of the dimensions stressed by Schlesinger, but includes others. The dimensions are: gubernatorial tenure potential, appointment and removal powers, budget-making authority, legislative budget-changing authority, veto powers, and political party strength in the state legislature.

Gubernatorial enabling resources, according to Dilger *et al.* (1995, 560) includes the number of gubernatorial staff per state government employee, the amount of gubernatorial fiscal support per state government employee (funding for the office of the governor and auxiliary boards and commissions that report to the governor), and the governor's appointment and removal powers over state agency heads.

Others criticize these measures because they are incomplete, as they concentrate on immediately quantifiable dimensions, while largely ignoring the governors' informal powers such as personal resources (for instance, charisma and persuasion) and enabling resources (such as staff support) (Bernick, 1979; Dometrius, 1987; Mueller, 1985 and 1987). Dilger *et al.* (1995) also associate the power of the governor with the professionalism of the state legislature,[13] arguing that in the US, more professionalism in the legislative body increases the power of the governor, measured as gubernatorial effectiveness in office. Although one may expect more effective governors are those that are able to dominate a non-professional legislature, the authors argue that "effective governors work with a professional legislature in a cooperative, positive-sum relationship to accomplish their goals" (Dilger *et al.*, 1995, 562).

I made some changes to the original indexes that measure the power of US governors for two main reasons, the first one being the different institutional (constitutional and legal) configurations of state governments in the United States, Argentina, and Brazil, and second, the lack of data available for the latter two cases. Hence, in measuring governors' power in Argentina and Brazil, I include the following dimensions:

1   *Governors' institutional powers:* (a) governor's tenure potential; (b) governor's agenda-setting powers; (c) governor's legislative power (decree power, exclusive initiative, emergency powers, and veto power) or gubernatorial power over the budget (or the authority of the legislature to alter the budget request); (d) governor's control over the provincial/state public administration and capacity to distribute public employment.

2   *Governors' partisan powers:* (a) percentage of votes received by the governor in the state election; (b) governor's partisan control over the state legislature, measured as the number of seats controlled by the governor; (c) whether the governor and the president are from the same party or coalition.

3   *Governors' influence over federal politics:* (a) existence of coordination mechanisms among governors (what I refer to as regional, partisan, defensive, issue, or predatory coordination; see below); (b) existence of more or less formal institutions representing states and provinces (such as the federal councils, or *consejos federales*).

Having the data, I constructed an index of gubernatorial power for Argentina and Brazil. This index is composed of two main dimensions: a) the power of governors in their districts (which includes the electoral support—share of votes—for the governor; whether the main party in the legislature is the party of the governor, coded as 1 in the case that they are the same, 0 otherwise; and the governor's party share of seats in the state legislature); and b) governors' influence over the federal government or how politically linked governors are to it (here, I include a dummy variable for cases in which presidents and governors are in the same governing coalition; coded as 1 in the case that they are politically allied, 0 otherwise). The index is a composed measure of all the aforementioned shares and dummies (which contribute 0.5 points to the index in the case that they are coded as 1, to balance the effect of each measure). The maximum possible theoretical value is 4 but since the dummies are coded 0.5 instead of 1, the maximum possible value is 3; the minimum is 0. I calculated the average value for each year and for all governors and classified the average power of the governors. The gubernatorial partisan power index is "very high" when values range between 3 and 2; "high," for values between 2 and 1.6; "medium," for values between 1.6 and 1.4; "low," for values between 1.4 and 1; and "very low," for values less than 1 (see Chapters 3–5 for more descriptive details on the index).

A key problem to measure gubernatorial power is that there are not enough data available on all the previously presented dimensions for all the countries and years covered by this chapter to get a useful and reliable index across cases. Therefore, I present a much simpler way to measure it. As a rough proxy of the power of subnational governments, using available data, I created an index of political power of subnational actors in federal and unitary countries, which consists of a 0–2 scale. I considered whether subnational politicians are elected and whether they have institutional resources in relation to agenda-setting powers and budget authority (control in preparing and executing at least part of the budget with relative autonomy from the central government). A country receives 2 points in the index if governors are elected and if they have substantive institutional resources in relation to agenda setting and budgeting, and 1 point if only one level is elected and has some institutional resources in relation to agenda setting and/or budgeting.[14] If subnational actors are appointed and hold no significant institutional resources, they receive a score of 0.[15] I assume that appointed subnational leaders are more dependent on the national government and less powerful, while elected ones who control institutional resources (i.e., agenda-setting and budgeting powers; with important gradations across cases) will tend to have more power and autonomy in relation to the central government.[16]

The equations are:

$$\text{fiscal transfers (expshare)} = \alpha + \beta_1(\text{ppowerspres}) + \beta_2(\text{ppowersgov}) + \varepsilon$$

$$\text{administrative transfers (admintr)} = \alpha + \beta_1(\text{ppowerspres}) + \beta_2(\text{ppowersgov}) + \varepsilon$$

where the dependent variable, fiscal transfers (*expshare*), is measured by the total share of expenditures at the subnational level in relation to the total expenditures of the government. Administrative transfers (*admintr*) are measured by an index that reflects whether national or subnational governments are responsible for selected functions.

The partisan powers of the president (*ppowerspres*) are measured by the Coppedge and Mejía (2001)[17] index of partisan powers, and I construct an index of partisan powers of the governors (*ppowersgov*) (see above). I lag its effect to control for the current amounts of transfers (in time t) that are influenced by previous levels of partisan powers (in time t−1). This is so because it is assumed that it takes time for presidents to decide to make changes in transfers, attain Congressional approval for them, and execute them. I also test the effect of the institutional dimension of presidential power (*instpower*) using Shugart and Carey's index (1992, 148–149) and the legislative powers of the president (*legislpowers*), using Negretto's (2009, 137–138) index of legislative powers of the president.

According to this first model (called Partisan Power Model), and ceteris paribus, I expect fiscal and administrative transfers to decrease when the partisan powers of the president are larger and the partisan powers of the governors are lower. On the contrary, and holding all other variables constant, I expect fiscal and administrative transfers to increase when the partisan powers of the president are lower and the partisan powers of the governors are larger, as the preferences of these actors are diametrically opposed. In contexts of crises, I expect fiscal centralization and administrative transfers to increase when the president is more powerful and governors are weaker. Under these fiscal conditions, governors will try to increase transfers and keep functions at the central level, preventing them from being decentralized.

Alternative explanations

I estimate the main and alternative models in separate regressions. But I run a full model (that includes the main variables and the most important from alternative arguments) to get a more rigorous test. In the second model (Institutional Model), I account for the role of three sets of institutional variables on decentralization. First, I include "static" (relatively time invariant) institutional variables, such as proportional representation rules (pr) and closed lists (cl).[18] The equations are:

$$\text{fiscal transfers (expshare)} = \alpha + \beta_1(\text{pr}) + \beta_2(\text{cl}) + \varepsilon$$

$$\text{administrative transfers (expshare)} = \alpha + \beta_1(\text{pr}) + \beta_2(\text{cl}) + \varepsilon$$

Second, I include variables related to the party system, or as I refer to them, more "dynamic" institutional variables (as they tend to change more often over time). Filippov *et al.* (2004) emphasize the relevance of a federally integrated political party system for the stability of the federal arrangement. But besides stability, attributes of the party system, such as the level of nationalization and fragmentation may also influence transfers. For Jones and Mainwaring (2003, 1, 7) a party system is nationalized when the major parties' respective vote shares do not differ much from one province to the next. The authors claim that in highly nationalized party systems, executives might have greater ability to forge legislative coalitions on the basis of national issues (Jones and Mainwaring, 2003, 6). In weakly nationalized party systems, presidents may face more pressures from regional leaders who try to force subnational issues onto the agenda. The fragmentation of the party system also affects the chances of political actors at the central or regional level to build coalitions for decentralizing or centralizing reforms. For Coppedge (2001, 5–6), conventional wisdom argues that when there is a lower number of parties and a larger government majority in Congress, the president's transaction costs of redistributing and allocating resources will be lower. In relation to decentralization outcomes, when a party system is more nationalized and less fragmented, it would be easier, in principle, for central governments to get the majorities in Congress necessary to centralize resources and administrative functions (or it would be more difficult for subnational governments to press the central government to transfer resources and functions). Low nationalization (or more regionalization) and more fragmentation would favor subnational governments to increase their transfers. Intermediate situations, such as relatively fragmented and low nationalized party systems (or vice versa), should mean stability of the status quo ante, because neither presidents nor governors can change the direction of the transfers.

fiscal transfers (expshare) $= \alpha + \beta_1(\text{enp}) + \beta_2(\text{nps}) + \varepsilon$

administrative transfers (expshare) $= \alpha + \beta_1(\text{enp}) + \beta_2(\text{nps}) + \varepsilon$

where the variables related to the party system are: enp, which is the level of fragmentation of the party system, measured by Laakso and Taagepera's (1979) index of effective number of parties; and nps, which is the Jones and Mainwaring (2003) index of nationalization of the party system.

Federal or unitary countries may have experienced different processes of transfer, since federal countries have autonomous political and administrative structures for subnational governments.[19] Therefore, it is highly relevant to incorporate the effect of the federal system in analyzing transfer processes. I also run separate regressions for unitary and federal cases to reveal whether there are specific factors or changes in the magnitudes of the variables affecting the outcome in each set of countries.

fiscal transfers (expshare) $=\alpha+\beta_1(\text{feder})+\varepsilon$

administrative transfers (expshare) $=\alpha+\beta_1(\text{feder})+\varepsilon$

In addition, countries with elected state and local authorities might have also experienced larger transfer processes, as they have political autonomy and incentives to acquire more resources.

fiscal transfers (expshare) $=\alpha+\beta_1(\text{state})+\varepsilon$

administrative transfers (expshare) $=\alpha+\beta_1(\text{state})+\varepsilon$

fiscal transfers (expshare) $=\alpha+\beta_1(\text{muni})+\varepsilon$

administrative transfers (expshare) $=\alpha+\beta_1(\text{muni})+\varepsilon$

In these equations, and in the third place, I include variables to account for whether the country is formally federal or unitary (feder),[20] and whether it elects local (muni) and state authorities (state).[21]

For a third set of arguments based on economic crises, fiscal centraliza-tion and administrative transfers should increase in contexts of economic crisis (see the State of Research in Chapter 1 for a synthesis of this and other arguments on the topic). The equations are:

fiscal transfers (expshare) $=\alpha+\beta_1(\text{gdp})+\beta_2(\text{deficit})+\varepsilon$

administrative transfers (expshare) $=\alpha+\beta_1(\text{gdp})+\beta_2(\text{deficit})+\varepsilon$

where gdp (GDP Model) is the rate of economic growth measured as changes (growth or fall) in the gross domestic product (GDP) (data from World Bank, 2004b), and deficit (Deficit Model) is the fiscal balance of the national government (total income minus total expenditure, as a per-centage of GDP; data from ECLAC-CEPAL, 1997, 2005).

To test the effects of adjustment policies on transfers, the chapter also includes the IADB structural policy (or adjustment) index (spi) (SPI Model) (Escobar-Lemmon 2001, 30).[22]

fiscal transfers (expshare) $=\alpha+\beta_1(\text{spi})+\varepsilon$

administrative transfers (expshare) $=\alpha+\beta_1(\text{spi})+\varepsilon$

For a fourth set of arguments based on social mobilization and democrat-ization, more pressures from civil society to increase democratic partici-pation and social accountability should be linked to more fiscal and administrative transfers (note that both dimensions should increase simultaneously in this argument). To test the effect of the hypothesis, I use indicators of social and political mobilization (*riots, strikes,* and opposition gatherings, *agdemons,* Banks, 1996, quoted in Przeworski *et al.,* 2000).[23] I also include variables related to the level of democratization (political rights, fhpr, and civil liberties, fhcl; Freedom House, 2005)[24] (I call this model the Demo-Mobil Model). The equations are:

fiscal transfers (expshare) $= \alpha + \beta_1(\text{fhpr}) + \beta_2(\text{fhcl}) + \varepsilon$

administrative transfers (expshare) $= \alpha + \beta_1(\text{fhpr}) + \beta_2(\text{fhcl}) + \varepsilon$

fiscal transfers (expshare) $= \alpha + \beta_1(\text{riots}) + \beta_2(\text{strikes}) + \beta_3(\text{agdemons}) + \varepsilon$

administrative transfers (admintr) $= \alpha + \beta_1(\text{riots}) + \beta_2(\text{strikes}) + \beta_3(\text{agdemons}) + \varepsilon$

I also incorporate dummy variables to control for relatively fixed characteristics of the seven cases under study. Dummies set a separate intercept for each country, thus establishing a way to account for all the unmodeled, country-specific variables that are relatively constant for each case over the relatively short period of time considered in this work and might affect levels of decentralization across cases.

I test the effects of these models (Partisan Power, Institutional, GDP, Deficit, SPI, and Demo-Mobil Models) and the full model, first by using ordinary least squares (OLS) regressions. Second, because the data are cross-sectional and time serial, I also perform a regression taking into consideration random and fixed effects by generalized least squares (GLS) to correct for heteroskedasticity. With time series it is also sensible to execute a first-order autocorrelation correction. This test takes into account the fact that the data are correlated with themselves, and thus the error terms are correlated. In order to control for autocorrelation, I run a Prais–Winsten regression—iterated estimates—to correct for first-order autoregressive errors. Finally, in order to avoid overconfidence in the standard errors using GLS, I perform an OLS regression with panel corrected standard errors (Beck and Katz, 1995).

In this chapter, I attempt to avoid the excessive concentration in particular cases or groups of countries of alternative explanations to decentralization through the cross-sectional and time-series statistical testing of the arguments. Hence, I include all Latin American federations (Argentina, Brazil, Mexico, and Venezuela) and three unitary countries (Chile, Ecuador, and Uruguay), in a series of observations between 1979 and 1998.[25] The total number of observations ranges between 45 and 217, depending on the different regressions performed (as indicated in the different models in Tables 2.1–2.5).

Table 2.1 Regression results for fiscal (FT) and administrative transfers (AT)

Variables partisan power model	President power for FT	President power for AT	Governors' power for FT	Governors' power for AT
Partisan powers of the president (lag.) (ppowerspreslag)	-9.14** (3.65)	-1.27*** (0.33)	–	–
Partisan powers of governors (lag.) (ppowersgovlag)	–	–	5.57*** (0.59)	0.41*** (0.07)
Argentina	26.39*** (4.55)	4.15*** (0.25)	10.87*** (1.95)	2.92*** (0.18)
Brazil	16.51*** (4.33)	2.69*** (0.19)	4.22** (2.12)	1.95*** (0.19)
Chile	-6.06 (4.78)	1.75*** (0.29)	-13.99*** (1.68)	0.72*** (0.14)
Ecuador	–	–	–	–
México	8.11 (4.89)	1.52*** (0.31)	-9.12*** (2.04)	-0.08 (0.19)
Uruguay	-8.11 (4.40)	0.79*** (0.19)	-11.97*** (1.71)	0.27* (0.15)
Venezuela	2.01*** (4.42)	1.41*** (0.24)	-12.71*** (1.84)	0.20 (0.15)
Constant	21.69*** (4.39)	1.31*** (0.15)	18.88*** (1.46)	0.91*** (0.10)
R-squared	0.90	0.85	0.91	0.82
Adj R-squared	0.89	0.84	0.90	0.81
Overall R-squared (GLS regression)	–	–	–	–
N (number of cases)	73	109	131	217

Notes
Standard Errors in parentheses.
*   p<0.10.
**   p<0.05.
*** p<0.01 (two-tailed tests).

Table 2.2 Regression results

Variables institutional model	Institutions for FT	Institutions for AT	State-local elections for FT	State-local elections for AT	PR(1) and CL(2) for FT	PR(1) and CL(2) for AT
Nationalization of party system (nps)	−11.73** (6.43)	−0.36 (1.26)	–	–	–	–
Effective number of parties (enp)	0.94** (0.33)	0.19** (0.07)	–	–	–	–
Federal constitut. (feder)	22.49*** (1.80)	1.43*** (0.37)	–	–	–	–
State elections (state)	–	–	3.35*** (0.86)	0.30*** (0.09)	–	–
Local elections (muni)	–	–	5.29*** (1.19)	0.32*** (0.12)	–	–
Proportional representation (pr)	–	–	–	–	10.44* (5.85)	dropped
Closed lists (cl)	–	–	–	–	−15.91** (5.59)	−2.85*** (0.19)
Argentina	12.09*** (1.44)	1.60*** (0.32)	24.80*** (2.34)	0.76*** (0.17)	22.75*** (5.60)	3.62*** (0.20)
Brazil	−0.8*** (1.96)	dropped	19.50*** (2.67)	dropped	dropped	dropped
Chile	dropped	0.01 (0.25)	dropped	−1.26*** (0.27)	dropped	1.00*** (0.26)
Ecuador						
Mexico	dropped	−0.40 (0.38)	8.96*** (2.09)	−2.25*** (1.19)	2.01 (5.53)	0.30 (0.19)
Uruguay	3.70*** (1.29)	dropped	−1.91 (2.13)	−2.29*** (0.19)	dropped	dropped
Venezuela	−13.09*** (1.41)	−1.39*** (0.29)	2.52 (2.17)	−2.02*** (0.18)	−4.43 (5.57)	0.53** (0.18)
Constant	13.58*** (6.86)	1.34 (1.25)	8.04*** (2.59)	3.26*** (0.22)	23.80*** (6.01)	35.67*** (4.74)
R-squared	0.98	0.85	0.84	0.84	0.81	0.97
Adj R-squared	0.97	0.83	0.83	0.83	0.80	0.96
Overall R-squared (GLS regression)	–	–	–	–	–	–
N (number of cases)	56	77	106	141	79	57

Notes
Standard Errors in parentheses.
* p<0.10. ** p<0.05. *** p<0.01 (two-tailed tests).
1 PR: Proportional Representation Rules.
2 CL: Closed Lists.

Table 2.3 Regression results

Variables deficit model	Deficit (continuous) for FT	Deficit (continuous) for AD	Deficit (dummy) for FT	Deficit (dummy) for AD	Deficit * president power (for FT)	Deficit * president power (a) (for AD)	Deficit * president power (b) (for AD)
Deficit (continuous variable)	0.59*** (0.12)	0.05** (0.02)	–	–	–	–	0.067* (0.043)
Deficit (dummy variable)	–	–	-1.52 (1.21)	0.01 (0.13)	-0.73 (1.15)	-0.055 (0.171)	–
Deficit (lag) * power of the president (lag)	–	–	–	–	-4.86*** (1.79)	-0.279 (0.280)	0.067 (0.042)
Partisan power of the president (lag)	–	–	–	–	-0.34 (4.10)	-0.114 (0.550)	-0.80* (0.43)
Partisan power of governors (lag)	–	–	–	–	–	–	1.13*** (0.18)
Argentina	6.68*** (1.42)	3.74*** (0.18)	35.73*** (1.90)	3.72*** (1.19)	9.47*** (2.23)	3.89*** (0.36)	–
Brazil	dropped	3.30*** (0.19)	28.54*** (1.92)	3.22*** (1.19)	dropped	1.84*** (0.46)	–
Chile	-29.91*** (1.56)	0.88*** (0.19)	dropped	1.00*** (0.20)	-29.37*** (1.79)	dropped	–
Ecuador	–	–	–	–	–	–	–
Mexico	-12.72*** (1.45)	1.21*** (0.18)	15.31*** (1.89)	1.16*** (0.19)	-9.65*** (3.11)	0.79 (0.31)	–
Uruguay	-26.60*** (1.54)	0.82*** (0.19)	2.91 (1.87)	0.82*** (0.19)	-25.63*** (1.67)	-0.12 (0.41)	–
Venezuela	-17.35*** (1.40)	0.97*** (0.19)	10.96*** (1.79)	0.89*** (0.19)	-16.29*** (1.92)	0.14 (0.34)	–
Constant	37.32*** (1.12)	1.08*** (0.13)	8.38*** (1.20)	0.99*** (0.16)	37.64*** (1.69)	2.10*** (0.50)	1.44*** (0.33)
R-squared	0.95	0.85	0.93	0.84	0.94	0.85	0.38
Adj R-squared	0.94	0.84	0.92	0.83	0.93	0.83	0.35
N (number of cases)	64	125	64	125	58	79	73

Notes
Standard Errors in parentheses.
* p<0.10. ** p<0.05. *** p<0.01 (two-tailed tests).

Table 2.4 Regression results

Variables GDP model, SPI model, Demo-Mobil model	Changes in GDP (lag) for FT (GDP model)	Changes in GDP (lag) for AD (GDP model)	Structural adjustment for FT (SPI model)	Structural adjustment for AD (SPI model)	Democratiz. and social mobiliz. for FT (Demo-Mobil model)	Democratiz. and social mobiliz. for AD (Demo-Mobil model)
Changes in GDP (lag) (gdpgrlag)	0.001 (0.09)	0.006 (0.006)	–	–	–	–
Structural Policy Index (spi)	–	–	26.69*** (5.63)	3.26*** (1.50)	–	–
Political rights (Fhpr)			–	–	–1.25** (0.57)	–0.06** (0.03)
Civil liberties (Fhcl)			–	–	0.23 (0.75)	0.05 (0.04)
Nr. of strikes (strikes)			–	–	0.22 (0.53)	0.01 (0.03)
Nr. of riots (riots)			–	–	0.73 (0.50)	0.04* (0.02)
Opposit. gatherings (agdemons)			–	–	–0.23 (0.26)	0.01 (0.01)
Argentina	19.67*** (2.28)	3.50*** (0.17)	22.35*** (1.82)	3.09*** (0.17)	7.31*** (1.82)	2.96*** (0.09)
Brazil	15.37*** (2.33)	2.78*** (0.17)	16.37*** (1.32)	2.14*** (0.17)	dropped	1.95*** (0.08)
Chile	–12.29*** (2.20)	0.80*** (0.17)	–13.21*** (2.14)	0.41* (0.19)	dropped	0.62*** (0.09)
Ecuador	–	–	–	–	–	–
Mexico	2.27 (2.18)	0.56*** (0.15)	1.38 (1.82)	0.09 (0.17)	dropped	–0.02 (0.08)
Uruguay	–9.57*** (2.25)	0.36** (0.16)	–9.90*** (2.09)	0.08 (0.17)	dropped	–0.02 (0.08)
Venezuela	–6.44** (2.25)	0.46*** (0.16)	dropped	0.80*** (0.17)	–20.64*** (3.11)	0.02 (0.09)
Constant	18.87*** (2.00)	0.96*** (0.12)	5.50** (2.66)	–0.33 (0.23)	26.64*** (5.75)	1.03*** (0.09)
R-squared	0.84	0.81	0.93	0.91	0.95	0.96
Adj R-squared	0.83	0.80	0.92	0.90	0.95	0.96
Overall R-squared (GLS regression)	–	–	–	–	–	–
N (number of cases)	133	193	54	77	45	114

Notes
Standard Errors in parentheses.
* p<0.10. ** p<0.05. *** p<0.01 (two-tailed tests).

Table 2.5 Regression results

Variables	Fiscal transfers (expshare)	Administrative tranfers (admindes)
Partisan powers of the president (lagged) (*ppowerslag*)	−3.885** (1.997)	−0.705* (0.379)
Partisan powers of governors (lagged) (*ppowersgovlag*)	1.782*** (0.647)	0.057 (0.116)
National deficit (dummy) (*deficit*)	0.871 (0.640)	0.092 (0.174)
Partisan powers of the president *deficit (*ppowerdeficit*)	−1.731** (0.815)	0.279* (0.212)
Changes in GDP (*gdpgr*)	−0.125** (0.050)	0.031** (0.014)
Nationalization of party system (*nps*)	−12.626*** (4.804)	−0.023 (1.031)
Effective number of parties (*enp*)	0.947** (0.433)	0.138 (0.126)
Constant	37.648*** (5.684)	2.342** (1.176)
R-squared	0.98	0.86
N (number of cases)	52	61

Notes
Standard Errors in parentheses.
* $p<0.10$.
** $p<0.05$.
*** $p<0.01$ (two-tailed tests).
Country dummies are not reported for reasons of space.

Results and discussion

Results of the analysis for the full set of observations and countries are displayed in Tables 2.1–2.5. The findings support some of the model's main expectations. The political power of the president and governors (or subnational actors in general) are variables that affect the magnitude of fiscal and administrative transfers for the selected group of countries. These variables perform according to our theoretical expectations and are significant as well as of relatively robust magnitude (Partisan Power Model, Table 2.1). Out of the data, and controlling for third variables, politically strong presidents have tended to increase fiscal centralization, while strong governors have done the opposite: transferred funds.

The institutional dimension of the power of the president is also negatively related to the expenditure share of subnational governments: ceteris paribus, the larger the institutional power index, the smaller the share of expenditures at the subnational level. The coefficient is statistically significant, although significantly less robust than the partisan powers of the president (−1.76 vs. −9.14).[26] This may be an indication that the partisan powers are more relevant than the institutional powers in explaining changes in the dependent variable. The effect of the legislative powers of the president on the dependent variable is also negative, but not statistically significant.

The results also show that political power affects the level of administrative transfers. More partisan power of the president corresponds with more centralization of functions (an increase in partisan powers of the president corresponds with a decrease in the index of administrative transfers), while more political power of the governors is associated with more transfers of functions, holding third variables constant. These findings show that, in general terms, presidents have supported more centralization and governors more transfers. The institutional dimension of presidential power does not show a clear effect on the level of administrative decentralization. The coefficient has a modest impact on the dependent variable (0.108) and moves in the opposite direction of theoretical expectations. Results on the effect of the institutional dimension of presidential power over administrative transfers are inconclusive and unconvincing.

If I run separate regressions for federal and unitary cases, results change. In unitary cases, the partisan power of the president is a robust and significant factor affecting transfers, while the power of governors is statistically insignificant and of very weak magnitude.[27] Thus, while fiscal and administrative transfers in federal countries have depended on the power of presidents *and* the power of governors[28] (as a measure to reflect power struggles among them), in unitary cases transfers have basically depended on the power of the president, the magnitude of which is higher than in federal cases. The power of the president in unitary cases explains a variance of 0.36 (R-squared) for fiscal and administrative transfers, while it explains 0.06 percent for fiscal and 0.19 percent for administrative transfers in federal cases. In federal cases, the power of governors explains 0.21 and 0.12 of the variation of fiscal and administrative transfers respectively.

The federal structure and the election of state and local authorities increase fiscal and administrative transfers (Institutional Model, Table 2.2). The relevance of the federal structure and the role played by the power of governors in federal cases are valuable reasons to sustain Lijphart's (1999) classification in explaining transfers: centralized and decentralized federal and unitary cases. Yet, as unitary countries have also transferred funds and functions, the federal structure by itself does not seem to be a sufficient cause to explain the process (Escobar-Lemmon, 2001, 40); in fact, that is why I argue that a more complex set of factors, related to the power of political actors and the fiscal context, affects the magnitude of transfers in federal and unitary cases.

Some features of the party system also appear to affect transfers. On the one hand, and controlling for third variables, larger fragmentation of the party system (higher effective number of parties) means more fiscal and administrative transfers, and on the other, an increase in the level of nationalization of the party systems produces a decrease in the magnitude of fiscal transfers, as we expected theoretically (Institutional Model, Table 2.2).[29] More static institutional variables (such as electoral rules) do not seem to play a clear role in relation to transfers: closed lists seem to be linked to fewer fiscal and administrative transfers; although I cannot reach conclusive evidence regarding the effect of proportional representation rules.

Deficits at the national level seem to affect transfers of funds and functions (Deficit Model, Table 2.3). An increase in the value of the variable *deficit* (that is, smaller deficits) corresponds with an increase in fiscal transfers (as we expected theoretically). In relation to administrative transfers, an increase in the value of *deficit* (or smaller deficits) translates into relatively more transferred functions (although the coefficient is very low).[30] With the variable *deficit*, I cannot interpret whether there are different effects because of deficits or surpluses on the outcome, as the variable is continuous, and I only test the effects of one unit increase in the value of the variable (that is one unit decrease in the deficit). In order to test in more detail the effects of the fiscal balance of the national government, I included a dummy variable for periods of surplus (0) or deficit (1). With this dummy variable, I can differentiate periods of fiscal bonanza from those of constraint. According to the results, periods of fiscal deficit are linked to more fiscal centralization and more administrative transfers, as expected theoretically.[31]

I also used an interaction term between political power and deficit. The statistical results show that, ceteris paribus, an increase in the political power of the president, in contexts of fiscal deficit, translates into a decrease in fiscal transfers.[32] These results go in line with our theoretical argument: we expected powerful presidents in contexts of fiscal crisis and resource scarcity to have the capacity as well as the incentives to change the status quo. And the data seem to show that, in general, when presidents had political power and were pressed by an unfavorable fiscal context, they have tended to modify the distribution of resources in their favor.[33]

The fiscal deficit is simply a proxy for the lack of funds in the hands of presidents (money that is available to them for political purposes), and it does not say much about the amount and type of resources they have. We still need better indicators on the fiscal constraints faced by presidents and governors to analyze in more detail how they affect changes in the strategies these actors pursue.

Changes (growth or decline) in gross domestic product do not seem to affect either fiscal or administrative transfers (GDP Model, Table 2.4). This variable does not reach the standard levels of statistical significance in the different regression results performed (even when I use its lagged value).[34] These results may constitute some statistical evidence against the transfers by economic collapse hypothesis as a general argument applicable to the selected countries in the region.

The structural adjustment index appears to have an impact on transfers (SPI Model, Table 2.4). Countries that implemented more structural reforms, as measured by the IADB (1997) structural policy index, have also tended to transfer more funds and functions.[35] The problem with this argument is that it seems to be circular: countries implementing reforms (those adjusting) are those that carried out decentralizing reforms, leaving unexplained the main factors that lead a country to adjust or transfer. Escobar-Lemmon (2001, 41) makes a connection between adjustment and advice from IFIs, which we previously ruled out as a general claim applicable to the federal cases in the region (and some unitary). Also, it is a shortsighted argument: it claims that decentralization is a post-debt crisis or 1990s structural-adjustment policy. But transfer processes, as well as recentralizing reforms, have been carried out several times in the history of many countries in the region, especially in federal ones. To test the full explanatory power of this assertion we would need to expand the series of the index to years previous to 1985.

The variables associated with the level of democracy and social mobilization (Demo-Mobil Model, Table 2.4) do not seem to provide conclusive evidence regarding their role in affecting the transfer of funds and functions to subnational governments. The Freedom House civil liberties index does not reach the standard levels of statistical significance. The index on political rights is statistically significant, and it performs in the expected direction (increases in the score—that is, fewer political rights—seem to be associated with less fiscal and administrative transfers).[36] This means that with more political rights, there are more fiscal and administrative transfers (although the impact of this variable is small). The protest and mobilization variables (riots, strikes, and opposition gatherings) are not statistically significant.[37] Out of the results, I find little evidence regarding the role of the democratization and social mobilization hypothesis to explain changes in transfers for the selected cases and years.

I estimate a model that includes all the main variables and some of the most important from alternative arguments to get a more rigorous test (Table 2.5).[38] Most substantive results hold. Presidential and gubernatorial power and their interactions with fiscal deficits are significant, robust, and move in the theoretically expected direction. Despite this, the coefficient for gubernatorial power in the administrative transfers regression does not reach accepted levels of statistical significance. This may be because more variables increase multicollinearity and produce more noise in the estimators (especially considering that the index of administrative transfers tends to be more stable across time than fiscal transfers).[39]

In order to be more confident, I performed some tests to check robustness in the results.[40] The findings are consistent with the original results and substantive conclusions do not change when using generalized least squares (GLS) to correct for heteroskedasticity and Prais–Winsten regression to correct for first-order autoregressive errors. I also performed an OLS regression with panel corrected standard errors (Beck and Katz, 1995) to avoid overconfidence in the standard errors, and results are consistent with previous tests. The variables in these models explain an important amount of the variance in the dependent variable.[41]

The distribution of funds and functions in Argentina and Brazil

In this section, I explore whether the main hypothesis holds for the Argentine and Brazilian cases for the period between their transitions to democracy and the most recent year for which there are comparable data.[42] Instead of testing the hypothesis in the seven countries of the regions for which there are comparable data, I analyze it in the two main cases of this work. To do that, I constructed two databases, one for the 24 provinces in Argentina for 21 years (1983–2004) and the other for the 27 states in Brazil for 21 years (1985–2006). I perform similar tests to those undertaken before in this chapter. Instead of using dummy variables for each country, I include key controls that account for the distribution of legally mandated transfers: (the natural logarithm of) state population and state income per capita.

The empirical evidence seems to support the main theoretical expectations of Chapter 1 and the previous findings of this chapter (see also González, 2008). The key variables perform as anticipated and are significant as well as of relatively robust magnitude. Ceteris paribus, the partisan power of both presidents and governors affect the distribution of funds between the central government and subnational governments (Tables 2.6 and 2.7, Models 1–3). Results suggest that presidents with large partisan powers, both in Argentina and Brazil, have tended to centralize fiscal resources, while strong governors have increased transfers to subnational governments. This seems to be the case for the two dependent variables used in these models: first, (the log of) total federal transfers, both legally mandated transfers and discretionary; and second, the share of subnational revenues. In the first case, I use a log-log model to normalize the dependent variable and facilitate the interpretation of results. Holding third variables constant, a 1 percent increase in the partisan power of the president decreases total federal transfers 0.76 percent. In the second model, and controlling for third variables, a one-point increase in their partisan power (which is a large change since the average is 0.76), Argentine presidents reduced the expenditure share of subnational governments by about 11.5 percent, while governors increased this share by 17.6 percent.[43] Similarly, for a one-point increase in their partisan power (also a large change since the average is 0.35), Brazilian presidents diminished the states' expenditure share by 12.8 percent. Governors, on the contrary, for a one-point increase in their partisan power, augmented it by 3.8 percent (Tables 2.6 and 2.7, Model 2).

Fiscal crises also seem to be important in accounting for changes in primary distribution. In Argentina, a one-point increase in the variable deficit measured as a continuous variable; that is, smaller deficits or larger surpluses correspond to a 0.08 increase in overall fiscal transfers. These values are very similar to those of Brazil (Tables 2.6 and 2.7, Model 1 for both cases).

Powerful presidents under fiscal crises have tended to centralize resources and reduce federal transfers in general. But powerful presidents under contexts of fiscal bonanza have been more likely to increase federal transfers both in Argentina and Brazil (Tables 2.6 and 2.7, Model 3). The interaction term between presidential political power and federal deficit (measured as a continuous variable) for Argentina is robust, statistically significant, and moves in the expected direction. The interaction term for Brazil also moves in the expected direction but does not reach the standards for statistical significance (Tables 2.6 and 2.7, Model 3).

Final comments

The results presented in this chapter provide some empirical support for the main theoretical claims introduced in Chapter 1. First, the political power the actors have is a critical factor explaining changes in the distribution of funds and functions. The empirical evidence seems to justify the theoretical decision to distinguish the factors that affect changes in the dependent variable in federal and unitary cases: while fiscal and administrative transfers in unitary cases have basically depended on the power of the president, in federal countries changes in the distribution of funds and functions have depended on the power of presidents *and* the power of governors. This finding provides empirical support to the theoretical claim that the federal balance is a reflection of power struggles between president and governors.

Second, political power is a necessary but not sufficient factor to explain changes in the distribution of funds and functions. The statistical results show that there is an interaction between the political power of the president and the fiscal context she faces. As we expected in the theoretical chapter, when presidents had political power and were pressed by an unfavorable fiscal context (that is when they have the capacity as well as the incentives to change the status quo) they have tended to modify the distribution of resources in favor of themselves.

This chapter provides empirical evidence supporting the relevance of the main variables in the model. It is also a broader contribution to the literature as a large-n/quantitative analysis of the causes of decentralization to test the validity of the most important competing theoretical approaches in a larger number of cases. But it intends to be something more than an empirical test of a theoretical argument to account both for centralization and decentralization policies across time and its rival explanations. It also pretends to be a contribution to some limitations in the literature on the topic. It does so by evaluating the capacity of the theoretical claim put forward here to help us to, first, overcome static analyses that can account for differences across cases but are relatively poor to explain changes across time (and within cases), and second, to avoid detailed explanations for a single or very few cases (which limits the scope of the explanation).

Table 2.6 Regression results data for Argentina

Variables	Model 1 Total federal transfers (ln) (ingrorignacln)	Model 2 Revenue share (revshar)	Model 3 Total federal transfers (ln) (ingrorignacln)
Partisan powers of the president (ppowers)	-0.763** (0.264)	-11.462*** (1.793)	-0.627*** (0.247)
National deficit (continuum; lagged) (natdeficitlag)	0.078*** (0.013)	–	0.014 (0.013)
Partisan powers of the president *Deficit (lag) (ppowerdeficitlag)	–	–	0.094*** (0.021)
Population (ln) (populn)	0.427*** (0.020)	–	0.426*** (0.020)
Income per capita (ln) (incomepcln)	-0.299*** (0.037)	–	-0.298*** (0.037)
Partisan powers of governors (avg.) (govpower)	–	17.557*** (4.772)	–
Constant	9.48*** (4.11)	22.179*** (8.631)	9.52*** (4.10)
R-squared	0.78	0.26	0.78
Adj R-squared	0.77	0.25	0.77
N (number of cases)	240	143	240

Notes
Standard Errors in parentheses. Models 1 and 3 are log-log models to normalize the dependent variable and facilitate the interpretation of results. Model 2 replicates the models in Table 2.1, with key control variables instead of dummy variables (as there is only one country analyzed).
*   p<0.10.
**   p<0.05.
*** p<0.01 (two-tailed tests).

Table 2.7 Regression results data for Brazil

Variables	Model 1 Total federal transfers (ln) (ingrorignacln)	Model 2 Revenue share (revshar)	Model 3 Total federal transfers (ln) (ingrorignacln)
Partisan powers of the president (ppowers)	-0.722*** (0.082)	-12.817*** (1.451)	-0.804*** (0.142)
National deficit (continuum; lagged) (natdeficitlag)	0.075*** (0.018)	–	0.042 (0.050)
Partisan powers of the president *Deficit (lag) (ppowerdeficitlag)	–	–	0.139 (0.195)
Population (ln) (populn)	0.299*** (0.027)	–	0.299*** (0.025)
Income per capita (ln) (gdppcln)	0.261*** (0.056)	–	0.261*** (0.056)
Partisan powers of governors (avg.) (govrpower)	–	3.831*** (0.494)	–
Constant	13.91*** (0.366)	29.938*** (0.729)	13.77*** (0.411)
R-squared	0.49	0.21	0.49
Adj R-squared	0.48	0.20	0.48
N (number of cases)	329	324	329

Notes
Standard Errors in parentheses. Models 1 and 3 are log-log models to normalize the dependent variable and facilitate the interpretation of results. Model 2 replicates the models in Table 2.1, with key control variables instead of dummy variables (as there is only one country analyzed).
* p<0.10.
** p<0.05.
*** p<0.01 (two-tailed tests).

Table 2.8 Variable description and data sources

	Indicator	Source	Years of coverage
Dependent variables			
Fiscal decentralization	Expenditure share of subnational governments as a percentage of total expenditures	World Bank and IMF (GFS, 2001).	1972–1998/2001
Administrative decentralization	Index of administrative decentralization	Data collected by the author (available upon request).	1972–2005
Independent variables			
Political power of the president	Partisan powers of the president	Coppedge and Mejía, 2001; Mainwaring and Shugart, 1997; Shugart and Carey, 1992.	1982/1983–1998
Political power of the governors	Index of political power of the governors	Database of Political Institutions (DPI, Version 2.0), and primary sources.	1983/1985–2001
Nationalization and fragmentation of the party system	Index of nationalization of the party system	Jones and Mainwaring (2003).	1983/5–2001
	Effective number of parties (for the level of fragmentation)	Laakso and Taagepera (1979), Coppedge (personal web page).	1986–2001
Control variables			
Federalism	Federal system, election of subnational authorities	DPI, Version 2.0.	1979–2002
Electoral rules	Plurality, proportional representation, closed lists	DPI, Version 2.0.	1979–2002
Socioeconomic context	Changes in GDP; fiscal deficit	ECLAC-CEPAL (1997, 2005); World Bank, World Development Indicators, 2004.	1979–2002; 1987–2004
Structural adjustment	Structural policy index	IADB (1997).	1985–1995
Level of democratization and social mobilization	Political rights, civil liberties, riots, strikes, and opposition gatherings	Banks (1996); Freedom House, 2005; Przeworski *et al.* (2000).	1979–2002

Table 2.9 Variable description and data sources for Argentina and Brazil

	Indicator	Source	Years of coverage
Dependent variables			
Fiscal decentralization	Expenditure share of subnational governments as a percentage of total expenditures	World Bank and IMF (GFS, 2001).	1972–1998/2001
Fiscal transfers and provincial tax revenue	Federal transfers and total provincial revenue (disaggregated in different variables)	Dirección Nacional de Coordinación Fiscal con las Provincias, Ministerio de Economía (Argentina) and Secretaría do Tesouro (Brazil).	1983–2004 (Ar.); 1985–2006 (Br.)
Independent variables			
Political power of the president	Partisan powers of the president	Coppedge and Mejía, 2001; Mainwaring and Shugart, 1997; Shugart and Carey, 1992.	1982/1983–1998
Political power of the governors	Index of political power of the governors	Ministry of Interior (Argentina) and Jairo Nicolau's Electoral Database (Brazil).	1983/1985–2004/2006
Control variables			
Socioeconomic context and fiscal balance of the national government	Changes in GDP; fiscal deficit	ECLAC-CEPAL (1997, 2005); World Bank, World Development Indicators, 2004.	1983–2004/2006
Population	Total population (number of inhabitants)	Official Census Data from Argentina and Brazil (INDEC, MECON; IPEADATA).	1983–2006
Poverty	Percentage of the population under the poverty line	Official Census Data from Argentina and Brazil (INDEC, MECON; IPEADATA).	1983–2006

In sum, and coming back to the main argument tested here, I argue that transfer processes have been strongly influenced by the distribution of political power between key actors whose incentives to alter the status quo are influenced by changes in the fiscal context. According to the results obtained in this chapter, presidents in the region and in the two main federations under analysis have tended to favor processes of centralization of fiscal resources, whereas sub-national politicians have been more prone to influence transfer processes.[44] The crucial elements are who has had the political power to decide the direction of the process, and how much the fiscal context has urged these actors to take action.

Notes

1 I prefer to use the term distribution of funds and functions, which includes the transfer (or decentralization) and centralization of funds and functions, instead of fiscal and administrative decentralization because, first, decentralization policies include only the transfer of funds and functions; and second, and more importantly, because I consider that changes in this distribution are the result of political bargaining process rather than the consequence of a policy design. In some cases, I may use transfer and decentralization interchangeably, but I keep on referring to this policy as a result of political negotiations between levels of government.

2 Only three countries elected their mayors directly in 1980. In 1997, 17 countries used this form of election of local authorities while in the other six, mayors were appointed by elected municipal councils (IADB, 1997, 99).

3 The share of revenues and expenditures of subnational governments in Argentina, Bolivia, Brazil, Chile, Colombia, Mexico, Paraguay, and Peru increased from an average of 14 and 16 percent of the total in 1980, respectively, to 29 percent in 2000 (Falleti, 2005, 327).

4 Part of the literature also referred to the transfer of these powers and capabilities as administrative decentralization. But in this work, it also includes the (re-) centralization of those functions.

5 Other scholars include a third dimension: political decentralization, which refers to the establishment or reestablishment of democratically elected subnational governments (Falleti, 2003, 2005; Willis *et al.*, 1999, 8). I explore the influence elected or appointed subnational authorities have on decentralization outcomes in the statistical analysis.

6 I use the term "governors" to refer to subnational authorities in federal and unitary countries (where they can also be called "intendentes," as in Chile, or "prefectos," as in Bolivia). To avoid confusion, on occasions I also refer to them simply as "subnational actors."

7 Revenue share includes the share of revenues from taxes, social contributions, grants, and other sources (such as interests, dividends, sales of goods and services, and others) (IMF 2001, 47).

8 Escobar-Lemmon presents a compelling justification for using this measure of fiscal transfers or fiscal decentralization and quotes relevant studies that have used it (2001, 32), including Bird and Vaillancourt, 1988; Garman *et al.*, 2001; IADB,1997; López Murphy, 1995; Treisman, 2000; Wallis and Oates, 1988; and World Bank, 2000, 216–217. See Panizza (1999), Rodden (2004 and 2006, 25–31), and Treisman (2002 and 2007) for a discussion on measurement of fiscal decentralization.

9 Expenditure share of subnational governments is measured as the total share of expenditures at the subnational level in relation to the total expenditure of the government. "Expenditures" or "expenses" include wages, salaries, and social contributions for public employees, the provision and use of goods and services, consumption of fixed capital, interests, subsidies, grants, and other miscellaneous expenses (IMF, 2001, 62).

10 Partisan powers of the president represent only part of the picture, that of the political bargain between presidents and legislators to pass laws. This is not a minor issue, since fiscal and administrative transfers are important reform processes that need Congressional approval. But another part would require taking into account the role of subnational politicians who also interact with the president and national legislators to advance their political careers and improve the resources of their districts. Partisan powers of the president, although limited, provide an improved measure from others used previously, such as Escobar-Lemmon's (2001, 35) measure of political power of the president, who considered those presidents that used constitutional or delegated decree authority powerful.

11 Another dimension of presidential (and gubernatorial) power is the support they receive from the public. I could not get comparable data for all the countries in the data set and for the years covered in this chapter. I analyze the relevance of public support in the comparative analysis of the cases (Chapters 3–5).

12 Political control over the judiciary, the state bureaucracy, and state resources, although not taken into consideration in this work, can also be important dimensions for the analysis. This control should give governors more leverage over decisions they can make and actions they can implement without the oversight of other relevant institutions. The political control over other institutional bodies, such as the legislature and the judiciary, has not been considered critical in the literature on the American states, as the institutional separations of powers has, in general, been taken for granted.

13 *Legislative professionalism* is the legislature's capacity to engage in the policymaking process with expertise that is comparable to other actors in that process. Most of the indices that measure this concept include differences in legislative pay, staff, and session length (Dilger *et al.*, 1995, 559).

14 In some unitary cases, only authorities for the local level are elected (i.e., Chile). This is a substantial difference from those unitary countries without local elections and unitary systems with elections at the local and regional level (i.e., Bolivia).

15 The crucial difference is between elected governors and those that are appointed. But I also differentiate between regimes in which there are elections for governors with significant institutional resources (these are federal cases with more or less strong governors, coded as 2) and those in which there are only local elections (unitary cases in which subnational politicians such as *intendentes* or *prefectos* are elected, have some institutional capabilities, and can actually establish negotiations over the distribution of resources and functions with the central government in a somewhat similar way to governors in federal cases) (coded as 1). The last category (coded as 0) includes (centralized unitary) cases in which there are appointed subnational authorities without significant institutional resources. With more data available on the cases, this differentiation could be more precise based on the literature's debate on gubernatorial power.

16 I am aware of the theoretical and empirical limitations this measure imposes, but it is the best I could get so far based on the data we have for all the cases under study.

17 Coppedge and Mejía (2001, 7) calculate partisan powers taking into account the percentage of Congressional seats that the president can count on to vote in favor of her *typical bill*. Ideally, we would need to calculate partisan powers for the particular bills that attempt to reform the distribution of fiscal transfers, but the data needed to construct these indexes are not currently available for the cases and years covered by this work. I consider that this issue generates incentives (especially for subnational actors and legislators loyal to them) that may be different from those of other issues in the Congressional agenda. This may justify the analysis of this issue as different from aggregated measures of partisan powers and roll call votes.

18 Pr is "1" if candidates are elected based on the percentage of votes received by their party and/or if the Database of Political Institutions (DPI) sources specifically call the system "proportional representation." When pr is "1," closed list (cl) gets a "1" if voters cannot express preferences for candidates within a party list, 0 if voters can. There are no available data in the DPI regarding the process of nomination at the national or subnational level for the selected countries.

19 Although some formally unitary countries have also increasingly fiscally and administratively decentralized (e.g., Colombia and Bolivia).

20 According to the National Constitution. The variable is coded 1 for federal countries and 0 for unitary.

21 *Muni* is recorded as 0 if neither the local executive nor the local legislature is locally elected, 1 if the executive is appointed but the legislature elected, and 2 if they are both locally elected. No information, or no evidence, is recorded as blank. *State* refers to state or provincial elections, and it is recorded in the same manner as *muni*. Source: DPI, Version 2.0.

22 The SPI index is a simple average of the policy indices of five areas: (i) trade policy, (ii) tax policy, (iii) finance policy, (iv) privatization, and (v) labor legislation. It measures progress in reforming each of these areas and rates countries between 0 and 1; where 0 represents no adjustment and 1 indicates the maximum degree of adjustment possible in all five areas (IADB, 1997, 95–96).

23 *Riots* is the number of violent demonstrations or clashes of more than 100 citizens involving the use of physical force; *strikes* is the number of strikes of 1,000 or more industrial or service workers that involves more than one employer and that is aimed at national government policies or authority; and *agdemons* is any peaceful public gathering of at least 100 people for the primary purpose of displaying or voicing their opposition to government policies or authority, excluding demonstrations of a distinctly anti-foreign nature (Banks, 1996, quoted in Przeworski *et al.* 2000). This is only an indirect test of this hypothesis and more work should be done regarding alternative ways to operationalize it.

24 Freedom House (FH) assigns a rating for political rights (fhpr) and a rating for civil liberties (fhcl) based on a scale of 1–7, with 1 representing the highest degree of freedom and 7 the lowest level of freedom. Escobar-Lemmon uses similar data (2001, 35).

25 The series diverge depending on the variables included into the model, as there is variation in the data available for each country.

26 These results are not reported due to space constraints.

27 The coefficient for the partisan power of the president in unitary cases for fiscal transfers is –6.51 and significant at the 0.01 level (two-tailed test), while the coefficient for the power of governors is 0.77 and insignificant. For administrative transfers, values are 1.26 and significant (at 0.001) for presidential power and –0.05 and insignificant for that of the governors. The number of cases is relatively small for unitary cases (41 for administrative transfers and 17 for fiscal transfers), so results should be taken with caution.

28 Both variables are robust (−12.19 and 8.86, respectively) and significant (at 0.05 and 0.10 levels respectively; two-tailed) for fiscal and administrative transfers (−1.94 and 0.66; significant at 0.001 and 0.05, respectively).

29 For administrative transfers, the nationalization of the party system performs in the expected direction, but it is not statistically significant when all the institutional variables are run together in the model. If I run nps alone, results are significant and in the expected direction.

30 This important information seems to justify the separation of the fiscal and administrative dimensions in the analysis of transfers and not consider both dimensions as part of the same process.

31 The results are in the correct direction and significant for fiscal transfers and in the correct direction but not statistically significant for administrative transfers.

32 The results for administrative transfers and for interactions between power of governors and deficits do not reach the standard levels of statistical significance in this model (see (a) in Table 2.3). But if I use the variable deficit as a continuous one, substantive results hold: partisan powers of the president and governors and deficit are significant and move in the expected direction. The interaction term is not significant. These results may be indicating that we need to test these results with a more precise and sophisticated index for administrative decentralization and in a larger set of observations to avoid collinearity problems present if I use the index, the deficit dummy, and the country dummies in the same model.

33 I run a series of pairwise correlations between some aggregate economic indicators (such as changes in GDP and national deficit or surplus), presidential partisan power, and the revenue-share of subnational governments. Through them, I want to examine the independence (or not) among the main variables in the model (see section on the theoretical premises related to political power and fiscal pressures in Chapter 1). For all the countries and years in the sample, the correlation between fiscal deficits (continuous variable) and the expenditure share of subnational governments is very low (−0.10) and has a negative sign (meaning that an increase in the value of the deficit variable, that is smaller deficits or larger surpluses, is negatively related to the expenditure share, which is theoretically counterintuitive). The correlation coefficient between fiscal deficits and presidential power is −0.02 (if these values are lagged, substantive results do not change). I also run pairwise correlations for the amount of transfers to the provinces in Argentina and the states in Brazil. For Argentina, correlation coefficients are very low: for national fiscal balance and transfers to subnational governments, the correlation is 0.03 and positive; the coefficient between changes in GDP and transfers is 0.05 (again, very weak and with the same sign). If I lag the transfers (considering we have theoretical reasons for doing that), the correlation coefficient is −0.02 for deficits and −0.03 for changes in GDP (moving in the opposite direction to that expected theoretically and still very weak). In the case of Brazil, correlation coefficients are also quite feeble: for national fiscal balance and transfers to subnational governments the value is −0.03; for changes in GDP and transfers the value is −0.06 (again, very weak and with the opposite sign). If I lag transfers, the correlation coefficient is 0.06 for deficits and −0.002 for changes in GDP. These results may indicate that there is not a clear and direct relation between economic hardship and fiscal reforms altering the fiscal balance. As argued, economic hardship affects the actors' incentives to implement reforms, but do not determine their ability (or their power) of doing so. Getting now into the analysis of the independent variables, and for Argentina, the correlation coefficient between the national fiscal balance and presidential popularity (which is

a dimension of presidential power) is 0.3. Although it moves in the expected direction and it is positive, the coefficient is relatively low. The coefficient between changes in GDP and presidential positive image is 0.1. If I lag positive image of the president, the correlation coefficient is –0.2 for deficits (moving in the opposite direction to that we expected) and 0.2 for changes in GDP (in the expected direction). Both coefficients are very weak. The results for the correlation between fiscal and economic variables and presidential partisan power are equally inconclusive. The deficit variable correlates to 0.47 with presidential partisan power (a larger value than all the rest), but this value diminishes to 0.12 if the latter variable is lagged. In addition, changes in GDP and presidential partisan power correlate at –0.15 (opposite direction), or 0.14 if power is lagged. The data for Brazil contribute to the unsatisfying results found before. The correlation coefficient between the national fiscal balance and presidential popularity is 0.3. Its value for changes in GDP and presidential image is 0.2. And if I lag positive image of the president, the correlation coefficient is –0.3 for deficits and 0.2 for changes in GDP. The deficit variable correlates to –0.34 with presidential partisan power (in the opposite direction to that expected), and this value is 0.01 if the latter variable is lagged. Changes in GDP and presidential partisan power correlate to 0.08, or 0.32, respectively, if power is lagged. Results seem to indicate that the expected theoretical relations between fiscal and economic factors and presidential popularity or power as well as changes in federal fiscal institutions do not have substantial empirical support (contrary to Benton's 2008, 673 claim). In the analysis of the cases, I get into the historical details that further weaken these arguments.

34 GDP per capita does not reach the standard levels of statistical significance for fiscal transfers either.

35 If I include the partisan powers of the president and political power of the governors into the model, controlling for spi, the effect of the main variables of this chapter does not change; a result that supports the main argument put forward in this work.

36 If the FH variables are lagged, neither of them reaches the usual level of statistical significance for fiscal transfers. In relation to administrative transfers, both coefficients are of weak magnitude and significant, but while political rights perform in the expected direction (coef: –0.06; std. error: 0.02), civil liberties performs in the opposite one (coef: 0.07; std. error: 0.04). Therefore, we do not seem to find conclusive evidence regarding their role.

37 Only *riots* seems to be significant to explain changes in administrative transfers. However, this variable performs poorly if regressed alone to both dependent variables.

38 There are limits in the number of variables that can be included into a single model. The more variables I add, the fewer cases I get due to missing data. For this reason, the number of cases in Table 2.5 is small, so conclusions should be taken with caution and compared to other models with a larger N.

39 More dynamic institutional variables (such as nps) are also robust and significant, but more static institutional variables (PR and closed lists) are not. These variables are not reported in the table and cannot be included in the model at the same time as the main variables due to problems of multicollinearity. I run them separately and conclusions remain the same.

40 I have not found important problems for multicollinearity. The main independent variables have low values in the VIF test. Furthermore, the F-test is significant and the individual coefficients are relatively large in magnitude and statistically significant (if not, this would also indicate multicollinearity).

41 The adjusted R-squared for *ppowerspreslag*, *ppowersgovlag*, *nps*, and *feder* is 0.94 (for FT) and 0.64 (for AD) in the PCSE regression. This is a relatively high

value, but not unusual using country dummies. Perhaps a more accurate value of the explained variance is the 0.56 for the overall R-squared for the GLS regression.

42 I have neither enough comparable data for the entire time series nor enough variation in the dependent variable to examine when changes in the distribution of administrative functions are more likely to occur. Despite this limitation, I try to find an answer to this question in the comparative historical analysis of both cases (Chapters 3–5).

43 In order to have a single measure for gubernatorial partisan powers for each year (and to contrast it to the partisan power of presidents in relation to the share of expenditures), I calculated the yearly average of the index for all provinces/states in each year and regress it to expenditure share. Despite this gross simplification, results seem to confirm our theoretical expectations.

44 This latter part is in line with the analysis developed by Eaton (2001).

References

Banks, Arthur, *Cross-National Time-Series Data Archive* (Binghamton, NY: Center for Social Analysis, State University of New York at Binghamton, 1996).

Beck, Nathaniel, and Jonathan Katz, "What to Do and Not to Do with Time-Series Cross-Section Data," *American Political Science Review*, Vol. 89, No. 3, 1995, pp. 634–647.

Benton, Allyson, "What Makes Strong Federalism Seem Weak? Fiscal Resources and Presidential–Provincial Relations in Argentina," *Publius: The Journal of Federalism*, Vol. 39, No. 4, 2008, pp. 651–676.

Bernick, E. Lee, "Gubernatorial Tools: Formal vs. Informal," *The Journal of Politics*, Vol. 41, No. 2, May 1979, pp. 656–664.

Beyle, Thad, "Governors"; in: Gray, Virginia, Herbert Jacob, and Kenneth Vines (eds.), *Politics in the American States* (Boston: Little Brown, 1990, 5th ed.).

Bird, Richard, and Francois Vaillancourt, *Fiscal Decentralization in Developing Countries* (New York: Cambridge University Press, 1998).

Coppedge, Michael, "Explaining Democratic Deterioration in Venezuela through Nested Induction," paper presented at the Annual Meeting of the American Political Science Association, San Francisco, September 2–5, 2001.

Coppedge, Michael, and Andrés Mejía, "Political Determinants of Fiscal Discipline in Latin America, 1979–1998," paper prepared for the LASA Congress, 2001.

Database of Political Institutions, Version 2.0.

Di Gropello, Emanuela, and Rossella Cominetti, (eds.), *La Descentralización de la Educación y la Salud: Un Análisis Comparativo de la Experiencia Latinoamericana* (Santiago de Chile: CEPAL, 1998).

Dilger, Robert Jay, George Krause, and Randolph Moffett, "State Legislative Professionalism and Gubernatorial Effectiveness, 1978–1991," *Legislative Studies Quarterly*, Vol. 20, No. 4, November 1995, pp. 553–571.

Dometrius, Nelson, "Changing Gubernatorial Power: The Measure vs. Reality," *The Western Political Quarterly*, Vol. 40, No. 2, June 1987, pp. 319–328.

Eaton, Kent, "Decentralisation, Democratisation and Liberalisation: The History of Revenue Sharing in Argentina, 1934–1999," *Journal of Latin American Studies*, Vol. 33, No. 1, 2001, pp. 1–28.

Eaton, Kent, *Politics Beyond the Capital: The Design of Subnational Institutions in South America* (Stanford: Stanford University Press, 2004).

ECLAC-CEPAL (Comisión Económica para América Latina y el Caribe), *Economic Survey of Latin America and the Caribbean, 1996–1997* (Santiago de Chile: CEPAL, 1997).

ECLAC-CEPAL (Comisión Económica para América Latina y el Caribe), *Economic Survey of Latin America and the Caribbean, 2004–2005* (Santiago de Chile: CEPAL, 2005).

Escobar-Lemmon, Maria, "Fiscal Decentralization and Federalism in Latin America," *Publius: The Journal of Federalism*, Vol. 31, No. 4, 2001, pp. 23–41.

Falleti, Tulia, "Not Just What but When and by Whom. Decentralization Trajectories and Balance of Power in Argentina, Mexico and Colombia, 1982–1999," mimeo 2000.

Falleti, Tulia, "Governing Governors: Coalitions and Sequences of Decentralization in Argentina, Colombia, and Mexico," Ph.D. Dissertation, Northwestern University, 2003.

Falleti, Tulia, "A Sequential Theory of Decentralization: Latin American Cases in Comparative Perspective," *American Political Science Review*, Vol. 99, No. 3, August 2005, pp. 327–346.

Filippov, Mikhail, Peter C. Ordeshook, and Olga Shvetsova, *Designing Federalism: A Theory of Self-Sustainable Federal Institutions* (Cambridge: Cambridge University Press, 2004).

Freedom House, "Freedom in the World," 2005, at www.freedomhouse.org.

Garman, Christopher, Stephan Haggard, and Eliza Willis, "Fiscal Decentralization, a Political Theory with Latin American Cases," *World Politics*, Vol. 53, No. 2, 2001, pp. 205–236.

Gibson, Edward L. and Tulia Falleti, "Unity by the Stick: Regional Conflict and the Origins of Argentine Federalism"; in: Gibson, Edward L. (ed.), *Federalism and Democracy in Latin America* (Baltimore: Johns Hopkins University Press, 2004).

González, Lucas, "Political Power, Fiscal Crises, and Decentralization in Latin America: Federal Countries in Comparative Perspective (and some Contrasts with Unitary Cases)," *Publius: The Journal of Federalism*, Vol. 38, No. 2, 2008, pp. 211–247.

Government Finance Statistics Manual, IMF, 2001.

IADB (Inter-American Development Bank), *Latin America after a Decade of Reforms* (Washington, DC: IADB, 1997).

Jones, Mark and Scott Mainwaring, "The Nationalization of Parties and Party Systems: An Empirical Measure and an Application for the Americas," Working Paper 304, Kellogg Institute for International Studies, University of Notre Dame, 2003.

Laakso, Markku, and Rein Taagepera, "Effective Number of Parties: A Measure with Application to West Europe," *Comparative Political Studies*, Vol. 12, No. 1, 1979, pp. 3–27.

Lijphart, Arend, *Patterns of Democracy: Government Forms and Performance in Thirty-Six Countries* (New Haven: Yale University Press, 1999).

López Murphy, Ricardo, *La Descentralización Fiscal en América Latina: Problemas y Perspectivas*, Red de Centros de Investigación Aplicada (Buenos Aires: FIEL-BID, 1995).

Mainwaring, Scott and Matthew Shugart, *Presidentialism and Democracy in Latin America* (Cambridge: Cambridge University Press, 1997).

Montero, Alfred P. and David J. Samuels, "The Political Determinants of Decentralization in Latin America: Causes and Consequences"; in: Montero, Alfred P.

and David J. Samuels (eds.), *Decentralization and Democracy in Latin America* (Notre Dame, IN: University of Notre Dame Press, 2004).

Mueller, Keith, "Explaining Variation and Change in Gubernatorial Powers, 1960–1982," *The Western Political Quarterly*, Vol. 38, No. 3, September 1985, pp. 424–431.

Mueller, Keith, "[Changing Gubernatorial Power: The Measure vs. Reality]: A Rejoinder," *The Western Political Quarterly*, Vol. 40, No. 2, June 1987, pp. 329–331.

Negretto, Gabriel, "Political Parties and Institutional Design: Explaining Constitutional Choice in Latin America," *British Journal of Political Science*, Vol. 39, No. 1, 2009, pp. 117–139.

O'Neill, Kathleen, "Decentralization as an Electoral Strategy," *Comparative Political Studies*, Vol. 36, No. 9, 2003, pp. 1068–1091.

O'Neill, Kathleen, *Decentralizing the State: Elections, Parties, and Local Power in the Andes* (Cambridge: Cambridge University Press, 2005).

Panizza, Ugo, "On the Determinants of Fiscal Centralization: Theory and Evidence," *Journal of Public Economics*, Vol. 74, No. 1, 1999, pp. 97–139.

Pereira, André Ricardo, "Sob a Ótica da Delegação, Governadores e Assembléias no Brasil pós-1989"; in: Santos, Fabiano (ed.), *O Poder Legislativo nos Estados: Diversidade e Convergência* (São Paulo: FGV Editora, 2001).

Przeworski, Adam, Michael E. Alvarez, Jose Antonio Cheibub, and Fernando Limongi, *Democracy and Development: Political Institutions and Well-Being in the World, 1950–1990* (Cambridge: Cambridge University Press, 2000).

Riker, William H., *Federalism: Origin, Operation, Significance* (Boston: Little Brown, 1964).

Rodden, Jonathan, "Comparative Federalism and Decentralization. On Meaning and Measurement," *Comparative Politics*, Vol. 36, No. 4, 2004, pp. 481–500.

Rodden, Jonathan, *Hamilton's Paradox: The Promise and Peril of Fiscal Federalism* (Cambridge: Cambridge University Press, 2006).

Santos, Fabiano, (ed.), *O Poder Legislativo nos Estados: Diversidade e Convergência* (São Paulo: FGV Editora, 2001).

Schlesinger, Joseph A., "The Politics of the Executive"; in: Jacob, Henry, and Kenneth N. Vines (eds.), *Politics in the American States* (Boston: Little Brown, 1965).

Shugart, Matthew, and John Carey, *Presidents and Assemblies: Constitutional Design and Electoral Dynamics* (Cambridge: Cambridge University Press, 1992).

Stepan, Alfred, "Federalism and Democracy: Beyond the U.S. Model," *Journal of Democracy*, Vol. 10, No. 4, 1999, pp. 19–34.

Stepan, Alfred, "Toward a New Comparative Politics of Federalism, (Multi)Nationalism, and Democracy: Beyond Rikerian Federalism"; in: Stepan, Alfred, *Arguing Comparative Politics* (Oxford: Oxford University Press, 2001).

Treisman, Daniel, "Decentralization and the Quality of Government," Preliminary Draft, November 2000 (from the author's personal webpage).

Treisman, Daniel, "Defining and Measuring Decentralization: A Global Perspective," Preliminary Draft, 2002 (from the author's personal webpage).

Treisman, Daniel, *The Architecture of Government: Rethinking Political Decentralization* (Cambridge: Cambridge University Press, 2007).

Wallis, John, and Wallace Oates, "Decentralization in the Public Sector: An Empirical Study of State and Local Government"; in: Rosen, Harvey, *Fiscal Federalism* (Chicago: University of Chicago Press, 1988).

Wibbels, Erik, "Decentralized Governance, Constitution Formation, and Redistribution," *Constitutional Political Economy*, Vol. 16, No. 2, 2005, pp. 161–188.

Willis, Eliza, Christopher da C.B. Garman, and Stephan Haggard, "The Politics of Decentralization in Latin America," *Latin American Research Review*, Vol. 34, No. 1, 1999, pp. 7–56.

World Bank, *Fiscal Decentralization Indicators* (Washington, DC: World Bank, 1998). Available from: www1.worldbank.org/publicsector/decentralization/fiscalindicators.htm (last accessed October 25, 2015).

World Bank, *Entering the 21st Century: World Development Report 1999/2000* (New York: Oxford University Press, 2000).

World Bank, *Building Institutions for Markets* (Washington, DC: World Bank, 2001).

World Bank, *World Development Report 2004*, Ch.10: "Budgets, Decentralization, and Public Sector Performance to Underpin Effective Services" (Washington, DC: World Bank, 2004a).

World Bank, *World Development Indicators 2004* (Washington, DC: The World Bank, 2004b).

3 *Pares contra primus*[1]

Introduction

In the two previous chapters, I developed a game-theoretical framework to explain changes in the distribution of funds and functions in federal democracies and presented some statistical evidence on the relevance of the main variables. In this chapter, I put forward the comparative historical analysis of the first presidencies after the transition to democracy in Argentina and Brazil. Its main goal is to explain changes in the federal distribution of power in the two cases under analysis by applying the federal distributive game, and by fleshing out, through historical details, the causal explanation put forward in the game-theoretical part of the study.

The period analyzed here was crucial because the post-transition federal balance influenced dynamics and outcomes of the federal game in successive interactions among actors. The main argument is that after long years of centralized military power (in spite of the fact that governors were elected in Brazil in 1982), provincial and state governments demanded more fiscal and administrative power. The fiscal turmoil and the high inflation during this period also generated strong fiscal incentives for governors to demand more revenue. The erosion of presidential power and the inability of federal executives to control pressures from politically strengthened governors led to fundamental changes in the federal balance both in Argentina and Brazil. Institutional arguments, although relevant, cannot account for these sharp and relatively sudden changes. Abrupt reforms were implemented in the context of marginally changing or relatively stable institutional frameworks. Explanations based on the actors' rational behavior give ground to an important part of the core argument presented here, but are not enough by themselves to account for the timing and depth of the reforms. Both presidents and governors expected to have a better federal balance; their rational expectations, although relevant, did not determine who was capable of getting their goals fulfilled.

In this chapter, I first provide a methodological justification of the comparative historical analysis and introduce the historical background of the struggles among levels of government in the federations to show that the distribution of funds and functions has oscillated sharply across time. I also briefly put forward some details about the system of transfers that these two countries inherited after their transitions to democracy. Overall, this section provides valuable background information for the comparative analysis developed in the following section of the chapter.

In the second part, I organize the distribution of all cases according to the main variables and then analyze the presidencies of Raúl Alfonsín and José Sarney. In each of these two cases, I introduce some background information on the historical context, analyze the values the main variables took in each case, and present the theoretical expectations out of the game-theoretical model introduced in Chapter 1. With this framework, I analyze the historical struggles during each of the two administrations and evaluate changes imposed to the federal balance. I explore some implications of these reforms in the final comments of this chapter. The results of the federal distributive game during this initial stage determined who were the winners and losers in relation to the federal distribution of revenue and functions. The actors who were aggrieved in this round of institutional reforms (president and the central government) struggled to contest the next set of interactions in the game and were an important source for changes in the institutional framework regulating federal relations.

A brief methodological justification of the comparative historical analysis

The statistical section highlighted the relevance of key variables and controlled their role in a large number of cases; the game-theoretical analysis did not intend to describe the complex historical dynamics behind changes in the distribution of revenue and functions but rather to contribute to our knowledge on the strategic motivations and interactions among the key political actors, bringing into light how political actors can affect the outcome according to their preferences and changes in the context. Despite the contributions of both of these approaches, the causal link, or the causal mechanism, between the independent and the dependent variables has not been specified so far. The statistical analysis offers a probabilistic approximation of the general tendencies within which specific histories and particular political processes have happened (Coppedge, 2012; George and Bennett, 2004). We still need a more complex explanation about what determines the different outcomes of the negotiations.

A comparative historical analysis can help to further develop the theory by highlighting the causal processes and links among the variables identified as significant in the statistical section and by presenting the historical details of the causal explanation put forward in the game-theoretical part of the study. It can also help exploring how certain historical processes or events shape the payoff structures the political actors face as well as their preferences. In sum, through the comparative historical analysis, I attempt to develop a more complex, detailed, and refined theoretical argument on the causal process that links key independent variables with the outcome this study is addressing.

Przeworski and Teune (1970, 76) argue that theories are evaluated according to four main criteria: accuracy, generality, parsimony, and causality. They consider that these criteria can be contradictory, so that when the accuracy of a theory is maximized, its generality and parsimony may be low. In a similar vein, Coppedge (2012, 52–53) argues that there are three criteria for evaluating a good theory: generality, integration, and thickness. For him,

> each of the three major approaches in comparative politics achieves one [of these criteria] at the expense of the others. Case studies and small-sample comparisons produce thick propositions, large-sample statistical research produces general propositions, and formal theory integrates propositions. This division of labor has developed because these three criteria are locked in a three-way tradeoff: it is very difficult, in practice, to do a good job of satisfying more than one criterion at a time.

Through the integration of the three parts in this study, I combine the three strategies, following Coppedge's (2012, 220–221) call for each approach to do what it does best: the statistical or large-N analysis to sketch the big picture (the main objective is "extension" and "generalization"); the formal model to integrate and give parsimony and clarity to the explanation; and the comparative historical analysis or small-N research to fill in the details and specify the causal mechanisms between variables. The main goal here is "intension," "causality," and "thickness" (Coppedge, 2012, 52, 58, 74–75) or "depth of insight" (Brady and Collier, 2004, 12) of the processes that led to changes in fiscal and administrative decentralization.

The historical struggles for the distribution of funds and functions

In this section, I introduce a brief historical background to the changes in the systems of transfers in Argentina and Brazil until their transition to democracy in 1983 and 1985 respectively. The intent is not to present an exhaustive historical analysis but rather to explore how the distribution of resources has oscillated (sometimes drastically) from periods of relative centralization to others of more decentralization, taking into account a longer time frame.

Governors have been historically influential political actors in Argentina and Brazil. They have traditionally been the most relevant actors in their provinces, and some of them, especially those from larger states, have significantly influenced national politics. They played crucial roles during independence, in the formation of both federations, and, since then, during key periods of their countries' histories. The federal executive has dramatically augmented its power since the formation of both federations by centralizing core functions and powers. By these means, presidents have been able to relatively control the influence of governors over federal politics. Despite this trend, governors have struggled against presidents during certain periods and under particular conditions, resisting changes imposed by the central government and pressing for conditions more favorable to them. According to O'Donnell (2010, 16), the process of state formation involves violent and protracted struggles, after which [central] rulers made some important achievements. One of them is the expropriation of the control of the means of coercion from other political associations (such as cities or feudal lords [or regional caudillos in many Latin American countries]). Another achievement is the expropriation of the means of administration, which led to the centralization of power and the end, or at least marginalization, of patrimonial (and regionally based) kinds of organization. In federal countries, these central government achievements are characterized by particular arrangements for the distribution of political power and administrative capabilities with subnational governments: there is no complete centralization but rather some form of power sharing among levels of government (Dahl, 1986, 114).[2] In effect, the federal regime emerged as a viable option because of the inability of one powerful region (or regions) to impose its dominion over the others through a unitary regime (Gibson and Falleti, 2004, 229). The fact that is critical for this work is that this "original" arrangement (usually institutionalized in a federal constitution), which shapes the political interests of different actors, reflects tensions and struggles among levels of government that do not cease to exist after the founding moment. The federal institutional arrangements out of which the national state is created effectively centralize certain powers at the national level. But there are other issues that continue to be disputed among levels of government in the federation. Struggles over the distribution of certain capabilities and resources continue over time and recurrently modify the relations between central and subnational governments.

Pendular federal relations in Argentina (1930–1983)

Struggles between presidents and governors have been persistent and, although they have been more or less salient in different periods, they recurrently modified relations among levels of government in Argentina. In the nineteenth century, tensions between Buenos Aires and the interior provinces were mainly focused on the distribution of revenues from the port (the most important source of income for the country), the free navigation of internal rivers (as a key source of revenues from trade that would put an end to the monopoly of the port of Buenos Aires in getting these resources), and the free trade versus protectionist economic policy (representing the interest of political elites linked to the port versus those of the interior, respectively) (Burgin, 1975). These tensions translated into struggles and clashes (several of them fierce and bloody) over the distribution of (sometimes scarce) resources in the federation. In the twentieth century, especially after the 1930s, struggles over the distribution of resources continued, but this time mainly focused (although clearly not exclusively) on the 1935 revenue-sharing system, its rules for the distribution of revenues, and the taxes to be collected by the regime. The results of these tensions have been an oscillating distribution of resources, with periods of (sometimes profound) centralization and others of (often equally sharp) decentralization of funds and functions.

The federal revenue-sharing regime (*Régimen de Coparticipación Federal de Impuestos*), created in 1935, regulates fiscal relations between the central government and the provinces in Argentina. Before 1935, each province mostly depended on its own resources. The central government controlled the largest source of revenue coming from overseas trade, and that put it in a position of preeminence in relation to the provinces (Porto, 2003, 7). This distribution of taxing authority and resources lasted as long as the central government had guaranteed the privileged source of income coming from foreign trade. A large crisis in 1930 (in fact, the largest in the history of the country) made trade shrink. With this, revenues raised through tariffs, the central government's main source of income, suffered a huge collapse. Under those conditions, the president had strong incentives to change the rules distributing revenue and tax authority in the federation. The central government created the revenue-sharing regime to centralize taxes and take over taxing powers over which it had shared authority with the provinces.

The Justo government (1932–1938), who ascended to power relying on systematic fraud and the proscription of the Radical Party (UCR), established the sharing of tax revenues in 1935. The revenue-sharing system was a set of rules and procedures to determine how tax collection and revenue were to be distributed among levels of government in the federation. The agreement consisted of provinces delegating exclusive rights over certain taxes to the national government in exchange for an automatic share in the collected revenues. A powerful authoritarian president was able to impose changes in the system that distributed taxing authority and resources. As a consequence of this centralizing process, provinces received a decreasing share of tax revenue: the central government allocated 30.6 percent when the system was created and 19.6 percent in 1946, the year in which it was modified (Pírez, 1986b, 176). Governors resisted losing an important part of their tax authority, but they faced a powerful (authoritarian) central government, and the options were accepting the reforms or being left outside the revenue-sharing system (which would mean receiving no transfers at all). Being weak and pressed by the fiscal context, governors could not solve collective action problems and coordinate against the president and his centralizing reforms.[3]

The original revenue-sharing regime had an expiration date (in 1954) fixed by law. But it was modified several times before that. The military governments passed a series of centralizing reforms between 1930 and 1945, decreeing the creation of a tax on profits in 1943 but declining to share the proceeds with the provinces, despite their constitutional authority over direct taxes (Eaton, 2004, 69). As a reaction to those centralizing trends, after the transition to democracy and the return to provincial elections in 1946, governors pressed the central government to modify the system of transfers. With large support in both chambers, Perón modified the revenue-sharing system between 1947 and 1954 by concentrating functions and resources at the central level (Pírez, 1986a, 22–24). Out of the reforms, the central government received 79 percent of collected taxes, while provinces received 21 percent. Major changes in the revenue-sharing scheme took place once again during the Radical administrations of Frondizi (1958–1962) and Illia (1963–1966). Both presidents were relatively weak and faced strong and coordinated governors, who pressed them for more resources.

A substantial reversion and a new centralizing trend took place during the military government in 1967, in an attempt to stabilize national accounts. A partial reversion in this centralizing trend took place in 1973, during the Lanusse government (this is an indication that military governments centralized and decentralized revenue at different times). The military dramatically lost power and support after the failed government of Onganía. Due to subnational pressures, it decided to decentralize resources.

The decentralizing trend was abruptly reversed after the 1976 military coup, which brought dramatic effects for the provinces. The military junta of the *Proceso de Reorganización Nacional* (1976–1983) reduced transfers to provincial governments by 44 percent (FIEL, 1993, 147). The 1976–1983 Junta also decentralized health care and education services to the provinces as a way to diminish the responsibilities of the national government (and, hence, cut down spending) and reduce its large fiscal deficit.[4] In a significant political move, the military did not decentralize any revenue or tax authority to finance the new services.

In this section, I briefly described the main reforms in the rules regulating the distribution of funds, functions, and tax authority during the recent history of Argentina without getting into any details on their key causes. I analyze the causes of changes in the federal balance in the post-transition period in the following chapters.

The "systoles" and "diastoles" of the Brazilian federation

Since its independence in 1822, Brazil went through several periods of relative centralization and others of more decentralization. General Golbery do Couto e Silva referred to these changes as the "systoles" and "diastoles" of the federation, as the alternating impulses of the beating heart (Silva, 1981). The monarchy (1822–1889) can be divided into a centralized phase between 1822 and 1831, in which Dom Pedro I exerted tight central control and dissolved the 1823 constituent assembly that sought greater provincial autonomy. Following his abdication, Brazil was taken into a second and more decentralized stage during the Regency (1931–1840), in which provinces got more revenue and autonomy after the approval of a reform act in 1834 (de Oliveira Torres, 1961). The third period was initiated as a consequence of provincial revolts and secessionist attempts, after which Dom Pedro II (1840–1889) passed centralizing reforms to preserve the stability and unity of the Empire (Carvalho, 1993, 65). During this period, there were elections for the federal legislature, but all governors were appointed by the central government. Furthermore, provincial administrations did not have fiscal power independent of the center (Eaton, 2004, 39). With the dissolution of the Empire's tight centralized rule, the power of regional leaders increased dramatically during the First Republic (1889–1930; also called the "Old Republic," *República Velha*; "oligarchic republic" or "republic of colonels"; Nunes Leal, 1997). During this period, governors were so powerful and influential that President Manuel Campos Sales (1898–1902) instituted the so-called *política dos governadores* (governors' politics). Subnational leaders were able to reverse the centralizing trend and demand more transfers and autonomy.

Getúlio Vargas initiated a new centralizing trend. The Great Depression created strong fiscal incentives to centralize revenue (Lopreato, 2002, 21), and Vargas had the political power to do so. He reformed the constitution in 1934, expanding the institutional powers of the federal government and creating new taxes, including the income tax (introduced for the first time in Brazil). This tax was under the control of the central government and was not shared with the states (Carvalho, 1996, 46). Vargas also introduced a revenue-sharing system between the federal government, states, and municipalities, through which he redistributed funds favoring loyal states in the interior. Fiscal centralization had a correlation in terms of administrative centralization, especially of the health care system (Brasileiro, 1974, 15; quoted in Eaton, 2004, 79). The centralizing trend gained even more strength during the *Estado Novo* (1937–1945), when the president suspended state elections, named *interventores*, and centralized more functions and resources (by limiting states' exclusive authority over certain taxes, for instance those on motor fuels).[5]

During the Second Republic (1946–1964), after the fall of Vargas, "the pendulum once again swung back in the opposite [decentralizing] direction" (Carvalho, 1996, 48). Governors got a more prominent role and new funds and functions (although they enjoyed less autonomy than during the First Republic due to Vargas's reforms). The 1946 constitution granted governors access to new funds, especially for less developed regions (a practice started by Vargas).

The economic conditions changed at the beginning of the 1960s, with diminishing growth rates and increasing inflation and fiscal deficit. With this reversion, the pattern of fiscal relations at the time turned dysfunctional, generating strong incentives for the 1964 authoritarian government to pass new centralizing reforms to control inflation (Lopreato, 2002, 39, 44). The 1964 military coup opened up a new centralizing trend, especially during the first decade. In a context of growing economic chaos, the military used their power to cut revenue transfers and reduce subnational taxing authority (Eaton, 2004, 114). These reforms centralized tax authority and resources at the federal level, producing an increase in revenues for the union. Despite the reduction in transfers, states retained substantial taxing authority in Brazil, even after Vargas and the post-1964 centralizing reforms imposed by the military. This contrasts to Argentine provinces, which were compelled to delegate an important part of their taxing authority to the central government during the 1930s. In order to strengthen support in loyal states, and as a way to make subnational governments more dependent on the central government, the military created the States' and Municipalities' Participation Fund (*Fundo de Participação dos Estados e Municipios*, FPEM). Between 1965 and 1980, state governments' share of total revenue declined from 31 to 22 percent.

In Brazil, as in Argentina, a growing opposition to the military regime during 1974 led to the adoption of a series of decentralizing reforms. As the opposition gained more political power, as well as articulation and coordination against the central rulers, the military doubled the revenue shares for states and municipalities in 1975 and granted a greater degree of political authority to sub-national elites by allowing direct gubernatorial elections in 1982 (Abrucio, 1998, 86–89; Eaton, 2004, 132–133). Elected governors, empowered and with renewed legitimacy from elections, further pressed the weakened military for more transfers and resources. The military decreed an additional increase in the amount of transfers to states and municipalities through the *Emenda Passos Porto* (EC 23/83) in 1983 and the *Emenda Airton Sandoval* in 1985.

As in the case of Argentina, deep changes in the distribution of funds and functions in Brazil have recurrently taken place since the very origin of the federation. This section has provided some detail of the several, relatively frequent, and sometimes drastic changes in the rules and mechanisms that distribute funds between the central and subnational governments. If we take into consideration long periods in the history of Argentina and Brazil, it is possible to identify trends and major changes in the rules that regulate revenue-sharing regimes, many of them with radical consequences for these countries.

In Argentina, the fact that governors delegated taxing authority to the central government in exchange for automatic transfers in 1934 opened up distinct forms of negotiations among levels of government. Since then, bargaining between governors and presidents has dealt with several issues, but some of the most important have been the total amount of revenue to be shared (called primary distribution), how these funds are going to be distributed among provinces (secondary distribution), which taxes are going to be included under and excluded from the regime, and which are the functions that each level has to perform. These features are the core of the analysis of this work. Brazil has also followed a similar process. "As in Argentina, the institution of revenue sharing [set] in motion generations of conflict over the rules used to divide up these resources" (Eaton, 2004, 79). As claimed by Giambiagi and Além (1999, 193), "[i]n relation to the decentralization of available resources, [subnational governments had] a clear preference for more transfers [especially if they were] obtained without self tax effort."

The distribution of resources, tax authority, and functions (the dependent variable)

Having provided some detail of the changes in the frameworks that regulate the federal balance, I now get into a brief description of the constitutional rules and legal provisions that regulated the distribution of revenues, functions, and tax authority among different levels of government during each federation's transition to democracy. After providing some of these contextual details in the following section, I study the main changes they were subject to after the transition to democracy in the analysis of the cases. Although in the previous sections I referred to fiscal transfers from the central government in general, without disaggregating them, it is important to stress that there are important differences between funds presidents distribute to governors and the funds they receive from the central government.

Legally Mandated Transfers: Initially, we have to differentiate legally mandated, earmarked resources from other transfers presidents can allocate to the provinces. Specific laws regulate the distribution of mandated transfers and, unless these laws are modified, each year the central government distributes the same proportion (not necessarily the same absolute values) of funds out of the total revenues collected from shared taxes. In the case of Argentina, the core of legally mandated transfers from the central government to the provinces is regulated by the Revenue-Sharing Law (*Ley de Coparticipación* and its modifications).[6] The main transfer from the central government to the states in Brazil is regulated through the States' and Federal District's Participation Fund (*Fundo de*

Participação dos Estados e do Distrito Federal, FPE; and the FPM for municipalities).[7]

Other Legally Mandated Transfers: In addition to transfers allocated through the revenue-sharing regime and the *fundos,* there are other legally mandated transfers provinces and states receive, which are regulated by specific laws both in Argentina[8] and Brazil.[9]

Discretionary Transfers: The president in Argentina can also allocate specific funds using her discretion in deciding the amount and destiny of transfers to the provinces (in principle, out of a total regulated by the 1988 revenue-sharing law[10]). The most important discretionary funds are the Contributions from the National Treasury (the ATNs or *Aportes del Tesoro Nacional*).[11] Discretionary transfers from the central government in Brazil are allocated through the so-called "voluntary transfers" (*transferências voluntárias*).[12]

Together, other legally mandated and discretionary transfers have changed over time (in absolute or relative terms as well as in the percentages distributed to each state) following a very different pattern than those distributed through the revenue-sharing scheme and the *fundos.* Hence, the variables that help explain changes in legally mandated transfers might be weaker to explain changes in the distribution of other funds, especially discretionary ones (this is another limitation in some of the abovementioned analyses using time-invariant variables). All these transfers are critical for governors' capacity to deliver and fundamentally to build up political support for their states. This is one of the main reasons why it is crucial to analyze the politics behind the distribution of the largest (possible) amount of transfers from the central government (not only those legally shared) in general, and discretionary transfers, in particular.

Transfers from Central Government's Ministries to Provinces and States: The central government can also allocate specific funds to subnational governments, such as infrastructure plans or social programs. The budget law regulates total amounts and their distribution, and they can be changed each year according to the distribution of power in Congress. That is, their amount and destiny is not regulated by specific regimes; it depends on Congressional approval every year.

All these transfers—legally mandated, discretionary, and from central government's ministries to the provinces and states—have been at the core of the federal game for the distribution of resources between the central government and subnational governments. That has also been the case for the distribution of functions and tax authority between the central government and the provinces.

Federal and provincial functions and tax authority

The 1853 constitution in Argentina reserved all the functions that were not explicitly transferred to the federal government for the provinces.

In Brazil, as in Argentina, the 1988 federal constitution kept residual powers for the states, that is, they have authority over functions not explicitly granted to the federal and the municipal levels, and may carry out all those functions that are not prohibited by the constitution. In both cases, some functions are the exclusive responsibility of the federal government (such as defense, foreign affairs, immigration, and international trade, currency, and banking regulations). For some others in Brazil (such as social insurance and energy), most expenditures are concentrated at the federal level. The functions delegated by the provinces to the federal government have not historically been subject to many conflicts with states (or municipalities) regarding their distribution. Other functions are shared between the federal, provincial or state, and even municipal governments. In Argentina, the federal carta magna stated that provinces and the federal government had concurrent responsibility over social services, such as health care, education, and social plans. In Brazil, public security is mostly a function of states, while housing and urbanism is mostly a municipal one (Mora and Varsano, 2001, 4). Most of these functions, contrary to those that are delegated, have been subject to historical struggles over their distribution and the sources of revenues to finance them. The struggles over these functions are at the core of the analysis in this work.

In relation to tax authority, the Argentine 1853 constitution established that the federal government had exclusive and permanent authority over import and export taxes and postal services (art. 4, 9, and 67), and that it shared authority over indirect taxes with the provinces (art. 4 and 17).[13] The provinces, in turn, had exclusive and permanent authority over direct taxes (art. 67) and shared authority over indirect taxes.[14] The Brazilian constitution also gives exclusive authority to the federal government[15] and the states.[16] One major difference between Brazilian states and Argentine provinces is that the former has retained substantial taxing authority across time.

In sum, provinces in Argentina and states in Brazil have three main sources of revenues: their own tax revenues, transfers from the central government (regulated through the revenue-sharing scheme and the FPE, and other transfers, legally mandated or discretionary, distributed by the federal government), and the revenue they can access through debt. These three sources of revenue have been at the heart of the struggles between the central government and subnational governments, and they represent the core of the analysis in this work. Their distribution determines who gets what, how, and when in the federation.

The previous sections presented the historical background for the struggles over the federal balance that continued after the transition to democracy. These historical antecedents, together with the description of the legal frameworks regulating the distribution of funds, functions, and tax authority among levels of government, are relevant background information for the analysis of the federal distributive game in the following section and chapters.

The settings of federal distributive game in Argentina and Brazil

In the next section, I analyze the dynamics of federal distributive game during the Alfonsín and the Sarney presidencies. Before getting into the details of the struggles during this period, I present a brief synthesis of the distribution of all the cases according to the main variables in the model. This should help us to organize the analysis and the distribution of cases to be studied in this and the following two chapters. The recent (post-transition to democracy) setting of the federal distributive game in Argentina followed different stages: a first one of fiscal crisis and weak presidential and gubernatorial partisan powers, which meant that there was no concentration of power at any level of government (1983–1987), and a second of fiscal crisis, weak partisan powers of the president, and strong governors (1987–1989). Both of them took place under the presidency of Raúl Alfonsín. In a third period, there was a large fiscal crisis combined with strong partisan powers of the president (1989–1993); and in a fourth, a more benign fiscal context interacted with fewer partisan powers of the president (1994–1999). The last two periods were under the Carlos Menem presidency. Later periods were characterized by a weaker president, who had to deal with an increasingly chaotic fiscal context (1999–2001); political turmoil and fragmentation, weak partisan powers at both national and subnational levels (2001–2003); and finally, fiscal surplus and increasingly strong partisan powers of the president (2003–2005). The main changes in fiscal decentralization occurred during the period of fiscal crisis and strong governors (after 1987), which were then modified during the phase of a strong president and fiscal crisis (1989–1994).

Brazil, on the other hand, followed a relatively different pattern: first, a period without any clear concentration of power in any level of government and fiscal crisis (1985–1986), followed by a second in which a weak president and increasingly strong and coordinated subnational leaders had to confront a context of fiscal restraint (1987–1988). These two periods occurred under the Sarney administration. In a third moment, two relatively weak presidents, Fernando Collor de Mello and Itamar Franco during the first part of his administration, and relatively weakened subnational actors, struggled under fiscal crises (1990–1992); in a fourth, during the last months of Itamar Franco and the first part of Fernando Henrique Cardoso's term in office, a stronger president faced a context of fiscal crisis (1993–1998); in a fifth period, a still relatively strong president, although weakened, struggled against governors under a better (but still far from sound) fiscal situation (1998–2002). In a sixth stage, a relatively strong president faced uncoordinated governors in a relatively stable fiscal context (2003–2006, under Lula da Silva's government). The main changes in fiscal decentralization in Brazil occurred during the period of fiscal crisis and strong and coordinated governors (during 1987–1988), which were then partially changed during the phase of a strong president and fiscal crisis (between 1993 and 1994 and later during 1995 and 1998) (see Table 3.1 and Figure 3.1).

Pares contra primus

In this chapter, I develop the main dynamics of the federal distributive game during the Raúl Alfonsín (1983–1989) and the José Sarney (1985–1990) administrations in Argentina and Brazil. During these presidencies, an initial phase of fiscal crises and no clear concentration of power in any level of government was followed by a second period of deeper fiscal crises, weaker partisan powers of the president, and stronger governors. During this period, the *pares* (the governors) struggled against the *primus* (the president) to alter the federal balance. These tensions translated into important political, fiscal, and institutional changes in both federations.

The Alfonsín presidency (1983–1989)

The first presidency after the transition to democracy in Argentina can be divided into two main periods: a first one between the 1983 transition and the 1987 mid-term elections in which neither the president nor governors concentrated substantial political power, and a second between the 1987 mid-term elections and the (anticipated) conclusion of Alfonsín's term in office. The first substantive change in the legal framework regulating

Table 3.1 Distribution of cases according to the values of key variables

	Concentration of power at the presidential level	Without concentration	Concentration of power at the gubernatorial level and coordination
Adverse fiscal context	Menem 1991–1993; Franco 1993–1994; Cardoso 1995–1998. CHANGES IN THE STATUS QUO	Alfonsín 1983–1986; Menem 1989–1990; De la Rúa 1999–2001; Sarney 1985–1986; Collor and Franco 1990–1992; Cardoso 1999. STATUS QUO	Alfonsín 1987–1989; Sarney 1987–1990. CHANGES IN THE STATUS QUO
Fiscal context relatively stable (or not adverse)	Menem 1993–1994; Kirchner 2004–2005; Lula 2003–2006. STATUS QUO	Menem 1995–1999; Cardoso 2000–2002. STATUS QUO	No cases [STATUS QUO]*

Note
* Theoretically expected.

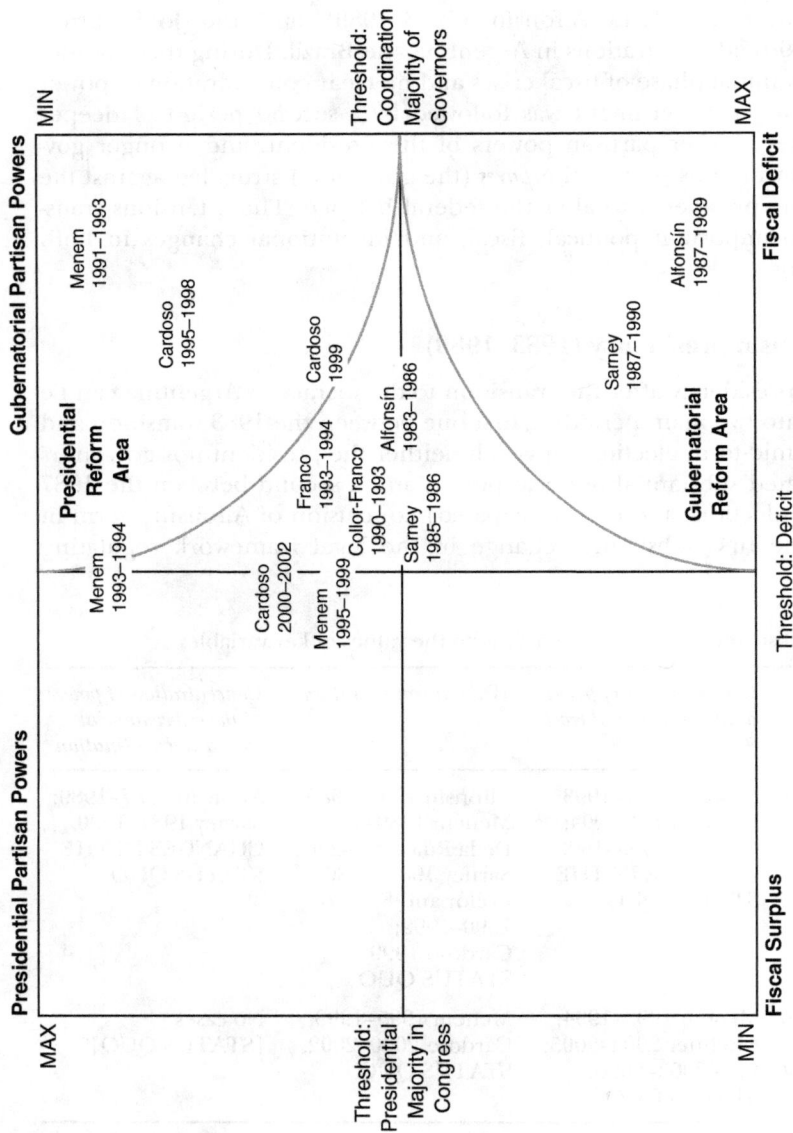

Figure 3.1 Distribution of cases according to the values of key variables.

Note

The area inside both arches is where the probability of changes in the status quo ante is larger, that is, where the partisan power of the president is high and the governors' low (or vice versa) and the fiscal incentives of both actors to alter the status quo are large (because of the fiscal deficit).

revenue transfers after the 1983 transition to democracy was implemented during this second period. In the following sections, I analyze the main causes of deadlock and those that explain reform later on, presenting the main theoretical expectations out of the federal distributive game and examining historical events and processes in light of it.

Primus inter pares (1983–1987)

The historical context

The Argentine transition to democracy was characterized by the absence of both a civil-military pact to settle basic conditions during the transition (a situation which allowed the newly installed democratic government to push ahead with trials against the heads of the *Junta*) and a pact between the two main parties (the *Unión Cívica Radical*, UCR, and the *Partido Justicialista*, PJ) to establish basic agreements for electoral competition (as in Spain, in which the main parties agreed on some fundamental rules for competing in elections). The UCR and the PJ openly confronted one another in electoral contests without those compromises and mutual guarantees (Mustapic and Goretti, 1992, 251).

The collapse of the military regime (after the Malvinas disaster between April 2 and June 14, 1982) and the transition to democracy by rupture (O'Donnell and Schmitter, 1986) contributed to a process of relative political uncertainty (different from the gradual and negotiated transition in Brazil). The military participated in several upheavals during the Alfonsín administration (and later during Menem's), indicating the tensions in civil-military relations and the potential instability of the regime. Another of the factors that contributed to political tensions was that the two main parties had very different public policy priorities, for instance in relation to the role of labor in the economy and regarding their wage demands. After the Peronist setback, Alfonsín and key members of the Radical Party thought the PJ was in the process of disintegration. Therefore, they planned to build a new political movement (the so-called "third historic movement"), centralized around Alfonsín's leadership (Torre and de Riz, 1993, 343). In a crucial move, these UCR leaders tried to neutralize labor opposition, mostly controlled by Peronism, by reforming union organizations to weaken their capacity to defy the government. The president and his allies failed to reorganize the unions, generating a stronger reaction from labor organizations. Challenged by the electoral defeat and internal divisions, crucial PJ leaders accentuated their adversarial stance. They promoted this strategy as a way to strengthen the PJ identity, but at the same time hindered cooperation with the Radical government (Torre and de Riz, 1993, 343). This reaction from the PJ, in addition to the poor macroeconomic results, provoked much opposition to the government policies, weakening the president's capacity to carry out his reform agenda (Acuña,

1994, 32). The macroeconomic situation inherited by the democratic government was chaotic, and it gradually worsened, contributing to further complicated politics during the transition.

This section is organized in two main parts: in the first one, I analyze the values taken by the main independent variables, that is, how powerful Alfonsín and the governors were, as well as the overall features of the fiscal context during the period. In the second part, having information regarding the distribution of political power in the federation and the fiscal incentives the actors had in this particular context, I present the theoretical expectations according to the model developed in Chapter 1. With them, I examine the historical dynamics of the federal game during the presidency of Alfonsín and their outcomes in terms of the federal balance.

Presidential partisan power

Two crucial independent variables in this work are the political power of both the president and the governors. These actors' power influenced their capacity to alter the status quo ante and, together with the fiscal incentives they faced, had an effect on the outcomes of the federal distributive game.

During the 1983 transition to democracy in Argentina, the president was granted substantial political support and legitimacy from the public (contrary to what happened with Sarney in Brazil) vis-à-vis other political actors, including governors (who were key political players during the Brazilian transition), but limited partisan powers in Congress. The president was a charismatic leader, who sent an effective message of tolerance, dialogue, and reconciliation to a country in profound need of it. As a result, Alfonsín's public approval ratings were over 70 percent, according to polls from 1984 (the first year for which there are data available from Nueva Mayoría). Although support from public opinion is an important component of presidential power, it is surely not the only one. Partisan support in Congress is another crucial dimension. And in this one, the UCR did not fare as well as it did in the former. Raúl Alfonsín won the 1983 election with 51.75 percent of the vote, compared to 40.16 percent for his opponent from the PJ, Italo A. Luder. After the electoral results, the UCR had a slight majority in the Chamber of Deputies and ended up in a very weak position in the Senate.[17] Despite some internal divisions, Alfonsín got support from his party in Congress, which in general followed his initiatives "although sometimes with little conviction and after manifesting its resistance" (Torre and de Riz, 1993, 349). Jones (2002, 151) reports that only 39 roll-call votes were taken during the entire presidency of Alfonsín. This may suggest a great level of party discipline in the UCR, as the party seemed not to need roll calls to enforce party discipline.[18]

Due to the particular distribution of power in Congress between the two main parties, both the UCR and the PJ needed support from each other to pass crucial bills. This turned each of the parties into mutual veto players (Mustapic and Goretti, 1992, 252). Each bill required cooperation between the two main parties for passage, a requirement that was some-times hindered by the profound policy differences between them. The PJ victories in 12 provinces out of 22 granted it large support in the Senate.[19] There, the PJ opposition obstructed several bills put forward by Alfonsín, especially on issues related to taxes and fiscal reforms, while in many cases, PJ deputies did not grant the government the quorum needed in the Chamber of Deputies to begin debates. Despite this, it is not possible to conclude that there was a generalized institutional paralysis in Congress and that the PJ was a veto player on all issues. Both parties cooperated in some areas, as Congress passed a total of 645 bills during the Alfonsín administration (Mustapic and Goretti, 1992, 257–259).[20] Mustapic and Goretti (1992, 264) recognize that figures on bills passed in Congress and bill approval rates have to be examined by issue to get a clearer picture of the areas in which both parties cooperated and those that generated more conflict between them. Issues related to international relations (such as the ratification of treaties and accords) had the largest share of support (between 96 and 100 percent, depending on different classifications). However, other issues generated profound divisions, especially those related to fiscal reforms and taxes.[21]

Although Peronist governors and PJ legislators were effective veto players, they did not have enough partisan powers to pass reforms by themselves in Congress. Both the president and his party, on the one hand, and the Peronist governors and legislators, on the other, could veto each others' decisions, but did not have enough political resources to reach quorum without the support of the other party.

Presidential institutional power

The literature on institutional presidential power in Argentina is divided between those who argue that this is an *hyper-presidentialist* system (Nino, 1996), in which the president has clear constitutional superiority in rela-tion to the other branches of government, and those who claim this is a case of *limited centralism* (Mustapic, 2000). According to these scholars, although the Argentine president is undoubtedly powerful, the federal executive still faces difficulties posed by the separation of powers. The role of Congress in the legislative process should not be underestimated, espe-cially in relation to its prerogatives to approve, delay, amend, or reject the executive's initiatives (Llanos, 2001, 69; Mustapic, 2000). Presidents in Argentina have institutional resources they can use, especially decree authority and executive veto power, but this does not mean they always use them or that they use them with the same frequency.

In Shugart and Carey's (1992, 153) index of presidential institutional powers, Argentine presidents are relatively weak in legislative terms but very powerful in relation to government formation.[22] According to Main-waring and Shugart (1997, 49), presidents in Argentina are "potentially dominant," as they have strong veto powers, decree authority, and exclusive introduction.[23] As Mustapic claims, the fact that these authors use this expression ("potentially") to classify the dominant executive reveals that legislative resources are not decisive by themselves but rather that they interact with several other factors that are critical in particular types of executive-legislative relations. Among these factors, one that is critical is the partisan power of the president (Mustapic, 2000, 573).

Alfonsín had several institutional resources to lead negotiations in Congress, but he made limited use of them. Despite not being regulated by the 1853 constitution, Alfonsín issued only ten decrees between 1983 and 1989, mostly related to urgent economic matters (such as a currency change during the Plan Austral),[24] avoiding their use on issues that required deliberation in Congress, such as tax and most fiscal matters. In sum, the president had large institutional resources (although he did not make vast use of them) and much public support, but limited partisan powers in Congress (due to the PJ-controlled Senate).

The power of governors

The governors, who are the other crucial actors in the federal distributive game, were relatively powerful in institutional and partisan terms in their provinces during this period. Although they achieved some coordination in partisan and regional terms, most of them remained divided into two main camps: one favoring the president, linked to him by relatively strong partisan ties, and another very much opposed to him due to opposing partisan incentives. The federal executive weakened both camps through the distribution of selective incentives. This division notably limited governors' influence as a collective actor in the federal distributive game.

Although there is substantive variation across provinces and across time, most governors in Argentina have been historically powerful actors. In this section, I analyze the power of governors in partisan terms, and in the following one I get into some general features of their institutional power. In relation to their partisan power, between 1983 and 1987, a large number of governors got important electoral backing that translated into sizeable shares in the provincial legislatures. During this period, the average governor got elected with 47.8 percent of the vote and controlled 56.3 percent of the seats of the state assembly.[25] Hence, most governors had an important degree of control over their state assemblies and, in all cases, the governors' parties had the largest shares of the seats in the provincial legislative bodies (that is, none of them faced a divided government). The average value of the gubernatorial partisan powers index[26] was relatively high: 1.67 (the highest average value was 1.88 in 1988 and the lowest average value was 1.56 in 1989).

Despite these figures, the capacity of these governors to influence national politics individually was limited in most cases; this influence depended mainly on their ability to coordinate and oppose the president. Governors' influence over federal politics depends, as I argued in the theoretical framework, on coordination mechanisms between them. During the Alfonsín presidency, the most important form of coordination among governors was partisan. Governors from the incumbent party and the opposition achieved different degrees of coordination to support the president and check his power, respectively. Provincial executives in the incumbent party supported the president because they had different incentives, both collective (the UCR party brand and their ideological stances) and selective (they could get material benefits, including more transfers, out of their partisan influences with a Radical president rather than with a Peronist one). Opposition governors also had incentives to coordinate: first, for electoral reasons, the more they weakened Alfonsín, the more they were capable of blocking his reform agenda, thus worsening his presidential performance in office, and making it more probable for them to gain power in the next election; and second, for fiscal reasons: the more they coordinated, the more probable it was for them to extract fiscal revenue from the president. Governors also coordinated regionally, but were influenced by partisan incentives.[27]

Most governors in Argentina are powerful in institutional terms. Corbacho (1998, 608–609) classified provincial constitutions on a continuum from majoritarian to consensual, following Lijphart's (1999) classification. With a maximum of 14 points on the scale representing the most majoritarian constitution and 0 the most consensual, the average value of the 19 constitutions that made a reform after the transition to democracy was 5.84 points in 1984 and 7.55 in 1994, after the reforms (Corbacho, 1998, 607). The main changes occurred in the rules to elect the provincial executive and in the gubernatorial legislative powers.[28] These institutional resources have helped governors to increase their institutional power in relation to other branches of government, especially the legislative. In relation to the executive election, most changes implemented allowed the governors to run for reelection.[29] The possibility of reelection is a crucial factor that enhances gubernatorial control over their provinces in Argentina.[30] Furthermore, a series of recent institutional changes allowed more than half of Argentine governors to re-allocate budget items without asking for authorization from provincial legislatures. In 18 out of the 24 constituents units, governors have these extraordinary powers. Most of the provinces institute these gubernatorial budget powers through the budget law, compelling governors to negotiate them year after year (*La Nación*, November 20, 2007).

Some features of the provincial legislative bodies also contribute to increasing the power of the governor. For instance, most state legislatures (with the exception of few states) lack professional or technical staff, a factor that favors the governor's influence and, sometimes, discretion over the legislative process. A great majority of governors not only have important institutional resources to influence the budget approval process, but they also have large leverage over policymaking, the distribution of resources, and the provincial agenda.

Governors are at the top of the provincial public administration and have the authority to appoint most public employees. Jobs in the provincial public sector tend to be mostly distributed on party-based criteria, going to party activists (or their relatives) and rank-and-file party members (De Luca et al., 2002, 422). Finally, several governors have been able to restrain oversight from the legislative and other institutions, such as the provincial judiciary (e.g., Catamarca during the Saadi's rule and Santiago del Estero under Carlos Juárez). It is important to stress that there is substantive variation across provinces and across time. In some of them, as in the case of Brazil, the governor is the most important political figure and has tight control over other institutions in the state.[31] In some other provinces, and despite the institutional power the governor has, provincial executives rule following more or less consolidated institutional checks and balances, and the control and oversight of the main opposition parties.[32] Despite these differences, in most cases, the capacity of other control institutions to oversee the provincial executive is, to say the least, limited in institutional and operational terms. As indicated by De Luca et al. (2002, 424), "[t]he combination of the governor's control over jobs in the provincial public sector and over the provincial budget (along with control of the party) makes him an extremely powerful force in provincial politics."

In sum, most governors were very powerful in their provinces, both in institutional and partisan terms, but divided in their coordination efforts against the president. Having analyzed the power of the main actors in the federal distributive game, I now get into exploring the fiscal incentives they faced during the period. With these variables, we can get the setting of the game and, according to it, we would be able to apply the theoretical framework to the Alfonsín presidency.

The fiscal context

After the transition to democracy and the heavy legacies left by the military, the skyrocketing inflation and increasing debt burden put the entire public sector in critical condition. The fiscal context generated strong pressures and incentives on both the federal and subnational governments to alter the federal balance.

Alfonsín inherited a chaotic economic situation from the military: a steep recession (that began under Viola in 1981) was combined with a sharp increase in foreign debt, a growing fiscal deficit, rising inflation, and rising unemployment (that reached 10 percent in 1982) (Rock, 1987, 391).[33] Partially because of this heavy legacy and also because of the failed economic programs implemented during his term in office, the Alfonsín administration did not contribute much to economic growth. On average, the economy fell by around 1 percent during the 1980s (the so-call "lost decade"). The fiscal deficit was high, 5 percent of GDP on average, for the period 1987–1989 (4.6 of GDP deficit in 1987, 6.2 deficit in 1988, 3.2 deficit in 1989, and 3.8 deficit in 1990; ECLAC-CEPAL, 1997; comparable data only for these years).

An unfavorable international context partially contributed to the economic recession, augmenting the debt burden, which in turn became another serious restriction to growth: only debt interest payments grew from 2.2 to 9.4 percent of GDP between 1980 and 1983 (Gerchunoff and Llach, 1998, 386, 391). In the context of recession, a mounting debt burden, and a fall in commodity prices, national accounts entered into a rising deficit. The national government first tried to finance the deficit by accessing the local credit market, but it rapidly dried up. The resource most widely used during the 1980s was monetary emission, which led to further economic turmoil (among other reasons, due to lack of investment and erosion in confidence) and fiscal decay (mainly due to the Olivera–Tanzi effect). Under those circumstances, economic actors increased their demand for US dollars, which also augmented the cost of foreign debt, and contributed to a soaring deficit (Gerchunoff and Llach, 1998, 389).

The Alfonsín administration tried to control inflation and the fiscal deficit through several stabilization plans, the most important of them being the Economic Reform Program, also known as the *Plan Austral* (announced in June 1985), and the *Plan Primavera* (August 1988). The 1985 stabilization effort proved to be successful in the short term, contributing to putting inflation under relative control, reducing the fiscal deficit, and helping resume economic growth. The initial achievements of the plan coincided with the beginning of the public proceedings against leaders of the former military juntas, charged for systematic human rights violations (Acuña, 1994, 34). These achievements were echoed at the ballot boxes, allowing the UCR to maintain its Congressional support in the Chamber of Deputies after the 1985 legislative elections.

Despite short-term anti-inflationary stabilization efforts, the main causes of fiscal imbalances were intact: on the spending side, adjustment efforts on salaries and pensions could not be maintained, and the structure of subsidies was enormous. The fiscal adjustment efforts were truncated by divisions inside the ruling party over its desirability and effects, by tensions inside Congress, and, crucially, because most of the provinces were ruled by the opposition, and both Peronists and provincial parties showed strong resistance to the reforms (Torre and de Riz, 1993, 353). Inflation escalated once again during the winter of 1986, and with this, the need to finance fiscal deficits with monetary emission reappeared.

By the end of 1986, as a consequence of the failed stabilization programs and the poor performance of the economy, the government's political resources (such as public support) were more limited than upon entering office, a fact that restrained the president's capacity to pass further reforms (Acuña, 1994, 34). To the serious structural disequilibrium in national accounts we must add provincial pressures for more funds (Gerchunoff and Llach, 1998, 406). Provincial deficits have been the norm rather than the exception. Between 1983 and 2004, only two provinces achieved average surpluses. Between 1983 and 1989, provinces spent, on average, over 10 percent more than their total revenues.[34] Provincial debts also dramatically increased between 1983 and 1988. They rose from almost AR$600 million in 1983 to AR$4.3 billion in only one year (1984), reaching the staggering amount of AR$7 billion in 1988.[35] During the years in which Alfonsín was in office, provincial debt, on average, exceeded 13 percent of total provincial revenues (data from *Dirección Nacional de Coordinación Fiscal con las Provincias*, Ministry of Economy). In this adverse economic and fiscal context, governors had strong incentives to get more resources. As budget constraints became gradually stronger and options to get more funds disappeared (including the capacity of provincial governments to incur debt), the possibility to get resources from the central government became more acceptable. Presidents and governors faced deficits and strong fiscal pressures. Incentives to alter the federal balance became stronger, the larger the deficits and the more they remained over time (see Figure 3.2 and Table 3.2).

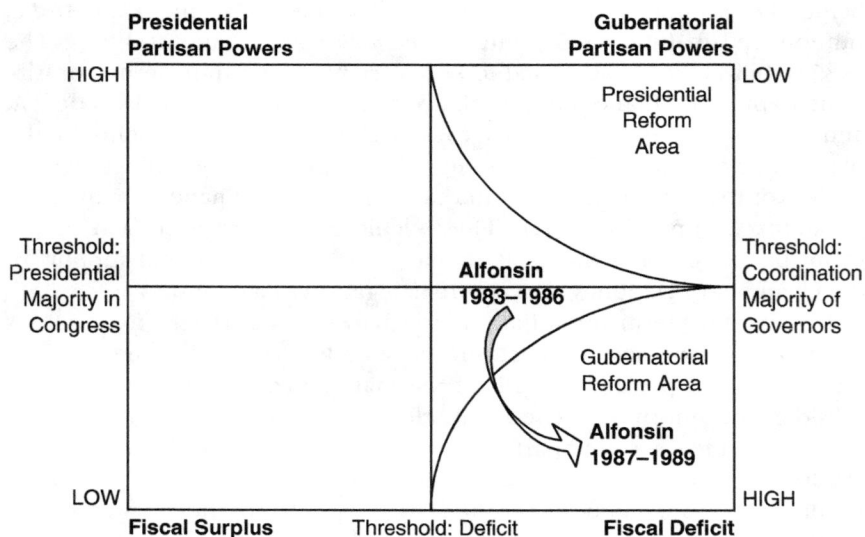

Figure 3.2 Synthesis of the main variables during Alfonsín (1983–1989).

Note
The area inside both arches is where the probability of changes in the status quo ante is larger.

Table 3.2 Values taken by the main variables during Alfonsín (1983–1989)

	Variable	Value	Range high-low[1]	Overall value
Presidential electoral power	Electoral support president	51.75% (1983).	Relatively high	From relatively high to medium range presidential power
	Electoral support opposition	40.1% (1983).	Medium	
	Percentage of seats (Lower Chamber)	50.8% (1983–1985); 50.8% (1985–1987); 44.9% (1987–1989).	Relatively high to medium	
	Percentage of seats (Senate)	39.1% (1983–1985; 1986–1989).	Relatively low	
	Role of opposition	Obstructive/veto.	–	
Presidential legislative power	Use of decree power	Low: ten decrees in six years.	Low	Low legislative power
	Use of veto power	48 bills (7.59% of the total); only one Congressional override of presidential veto.	Low	
Presidential approval rating	Positive image in public opinion	From 72% in October 1984 to 9% in April 1989.	From high to very low	From high to very low approval
Gubernatorial power	Average gubernatorial electoral support	47.8% of the vote.	Medium	Relatively high gubernatorial power
	Average legislative support (% of seats)	56.3% of the seats.	Relatively high	
	Gubernatorial partisan powers index[2]	High: 1.7 (out of a maximum of 3).	High	
	Proportion of allied governors	From 7/22 in 1983 to 2/22 in 1987.	From low to very low	
	Gubernatorial coordination	Relatively low (1983–1987) to high (1988–1989) (opposition).	Relatively low to high	

continued

Table 3.2 Continued

	Variable	Value	Range high-low[1]	Overall value
Economic context	Economic growth	Economy fell by around 1% on average during the 1980s.	Low	Critical economic context
	Inflation	From 101 to 343% between 1980 and 1983. 174% in 1987; 387% in 1988; 4,923.6% in 1989.	High to very high	
	Debt	Increased 700% in 1978–1982. From $46 billion to $65 billion between 1983 and 1989. High debt burden.	High	
	Provincial debt	Provinces issued debt for 17% of total revenues (1983–1999).	High	
	Budget constraints	From soft to harder.	–	
Fiscal indicators	Federal fiscal deficit	14% of GDP in 1982; average 5% of GDP deficit (1987–1989).	Very high	Strong fiscal pressures
	Provincial fiscal deficit	High: between 1983 and 1989, provinces spent, on average, over 10% more than their total revenues.	Very high	

Notes

1 Shares (in percentages) below 30 percent are "low," between 30 and 40 percent are "relatively low," between 40 and 49 are "medium," between 50 and 60 are "relatively high," and over 60 percent are "high."

2 The gubernatorial partisan power index is "very high" when values range between 3 and 2; "high," for values between 2 and 1.6; "medium," values between 1.6 and 1.4; "low" (1.4 to 1); and "very low" (less than 1) (see Chapters 3–5 for more descriptive details on the index).

The federal distributive game (1983–1987)

The settings and the theoretical expectations of the federal distributive game

The initial conditions (or the settings of the game) in terms of the distribution of political power in Congress favored neither the president nor the governors. None of them could prevail over the other in terms of their political power. Although the fiscal context generated strong incentives for them to change the status quo, we would expect no substantial changes in the federal balance as neither of them had enough political power to alter the distribution of fiscal resources in the federation (see Figure 3.3).

The status quo will prevail (0*,0* is the Nash equilibrium) when both the president and governors have fiscal incentives to improve their net balances (U; X) but they have no political power to reform and get their desired payoff (γ or δ).

Expected benefits and costs in the federal distributive game

Both the president and governors expected gains from a change in the status quo, as it was a sub-optimal scenario for them. President Alfonsín sought to reduce pressures and imbalances on the federal budget that contributed to a situation of high deficits and inflation. Governors wanted more funds to run their budgets and fulfill their goals.[36] As the main macroeconomic variables deteriorated and fiscal imbalances skyrocketed, governors had more incentives to solve their collective action problems and coordinate to change the status quo.

At the beginning of the Alfonsín administration, federal legislators had strong incentives to support their party leaders. In the case of the UCR, the president was very popular according to public opinion polls (especially at the beginning of his term in office and shortly after the Austral plan was launched) and had more partisan influence (over career

		Governors	
		Power	No power
President	Power	0,0	$\gamma,-\gamma$
	No power	$-\delta,\delta$	0*,0*

Figure 3.3 Normal form game for Alfonsín (1983–1987).

prospects and access to positions in the federal administration), as well as more fiscal resources to distribute than the governors. But Alfonsín could not count on a majority of the seats in Congress to pass key reforms. After the defeat of their presidential candidate, Peronism was divided into several factions led by powerful leaders of key districts and interior provinces. Partisan coordination among them, at least during the first part of Alfonsín's administration, was very difficult (in fact, conflicts for controlling the presidency of the party were bitter). Even though they had strong fiscal incentives to coordinate, partisan divisions prevented them from doing so.

Both Radical and opposition governors faced elevated costs for reforming the regime-regulating transfers. As there was no revenue-sharing regime between 1984 and 1987, and the president controlled the mechanisms for the distribution of transfers and had large discretion over it (after 1984), the federal executive had fiscal resources to divide governors and compensate them for supporting the president (or not opposing him). This elevated the costs for governors of conflicting with the president. Naturally, the president did not have large incentives to substantially change the mechanisms for the distribution of funds among provinces (he had much discretion in this regard) and limited himself to proposing reductions in the amount of transfers for the provinces to stabilize the large fiscal deficit and, above all, to prevent increasing demands from them.[37] The president also faced large expected costs, as he could not count on a majority in the PJ-dominated Senate. Governors, especially those from PJ, resisted any change in the distribution of transfers endorsed by the president, considerably elevating the costs of the reformist option.

Governors also faced relatively soft budget constraints: first, they had strong incentives to over-spend, as it was likely that the federal government would finance and eventually bail them out (World Bank, 1990). Second, they could also issue debt to finance their spending obligations, a situation that contributed to a growing debt burden and higher inflation. Having to cope with lukewarm budget constraints, governors had more incentives to incur debt and eventually risk being bailed out, rather than confronting the president over changes in the distribution of transfers. This situation changed when the resources of the central government diminished and budget constraints hardened.

The probability of a clash in case either the president or the governors decided to propose reforms was relatively high, as neither of them was powerful enough to pass reforms and both of them could resist and veto eventual changes attempted by the other actor. Neither the president nor governors could put forward their preferred reform option between 1984 and 1987.

The outcomes of the federal distributive game

Once the 1973 revenue-sharing law expired in 1984, both the president and governors pressed members of Congress to pass a new law. However, there was a lack of agreement between the federal executive and governors (especially Peronists and those from provincial parties) on the revenue-sharing law that was to regulate transfers to subnational governments. Thus, no revenue-sharing system regulated transfers from the central government to subnational governments after 1984. In the absence of a revenue-sharing law to distribute transfers between 1984 and 1987, the federal government distributed tax revenues to the provinces according to three different criteria: first, ad hoc political negotiations that did not reflect automatic procedures or transparent criteria; second, contingent factors such as budget deficits and financial needs of the provinces; and third, previous transfers made by the revenue-sharing law 20,221 (Eaton, 2004, 146; Pírez, 1986a, 64–65).

During 1984, governors met to articulate strategies against the central government along partisan and regional lines. Peronist governors and provincial Ministers of Economy and Secretaries of Finance met with representatives of the national government several times during this year. Out of a series of meetings, governors from all parties submitted two proposals requesting the incorporation of new taxes into the revenue-sharing scheme (taxes on liquid fuels) and the increase of redistribution to less developed regions. In June 1984, based on those proposals, provincial ministers demanded a revenue-sharing share of 56.66 percent.[38] The federal Secretary of Finance rejected those demands, arguing they were unrealistic (Eaton, 2004, 146; Pírez, 1986a, 66–67).

The year 1985 commenced without a revenue-sharing law or agreements on how to distribute funds between the central government and the provinces. The federal Secretary of Finance sought to maintain the previous regime for one more year and showed its willingness to support those provinces that accepted to extend the revenue-sharing system with emergency funds (*El Bimestre* no. 19; in Pírez, 1986a, 67). In line with the preferences enunciated in Chapter 1, the federal government sought to maintain the status quo ante, as it was not extremely unfavorable for it and because the reformist option was too costly. Governors, on the other hand, reacted to this initiative and sought to modify the rules for the distribution of funds.

After long and several bitter negotiations, UCR governors and the president reached an arrangement: the president guaranteed AR$510 billion (out of the requested AR$582 billion), distributed according to the shares established by the law that expired in 1984 (*El Bimestre*, no. 19; quoted in Pírez, 1986a, 68). Peronist governors vehemently opposed the agreement, denouncing the Secretary of Finance for allocating only 50 percent of the funds promised by the president to the provinces (a total of AR$255 billion), and claiming they would not be able to pay for salaries.[39] This cut in the amount of transfers agreed to between the president and the governors reflected not only the incapacity of the federal government to pay for them, but also the political clout Alfonsín still had to face such a result.

In April, the Minister of Economy met with the governors from the Radical party first and made the distribution of the agreed amount of federal transfers conditional on their approval of the annual budget in Congress and some emergency measures. He then met the Peronist governors and those from provincial parties. In order to secure the terms of the delicate agreement and force the federal government to comply with it, Peronist governors instructed federal legislators to send a bill to Congress.[40]

Debates on the bill took place on June 26 and 27, 1985.[41] Only two PJ senators spoke addressing the issue. The PJ delegation in the Senate approved the bill with the support of provincial parties against the vote of UCR senators. The bill was then sent to the Chamber of Deputies (*Diario de Sesiones de la Cámara de Senadores de la Nación* [*DS-CSN* from now on], June 26–27, 1985, 744). In the Chamber of Deputies, the bill was sent to the Budget and Finance Commission where the Radicals were able to postpone discussions (*Diario de Sesiones de la Cámara de Diputados de la Nación* [*DS-CDN* from now on], July 3, 1985, 1871). Tensions between the president and the governors and between the UCR and the PJ translated into deadlocked negotiations in Congress. In a clear indication of the lack of a deal on the distribution scheme, the PJ and some provincial parties passed the bill in the Senate but the Radicals vetoed it in the Chamber of Deputies. For the first time in 50 years, Argentina did not have a revenue-sharing system to regulate fiscal relations between the central government and subnational units.

The status quo did not change during 1986 either. Tensions between the central government and the provinces continued, and none of them was able to gather enough political support to pass a reform in Congress, where the debate on the bill was delayed indefinitely. Despite divisions and disagreements, governors and national authorities reached what initially was regarded as a provisional agreement. On March 11, the president and all the governors signed a document, based on a proposal presented by Peronist governors and supported by those from provincial parties, in which the central government would distribute to the provinces a similar amount of funds, in real terms, to that of the second semester of 1985.[42] Governors, especially from the opposition, were able to achieve this because they could solve their coordination problems. They did that because of the fiscal incentives they had (the president wanted to curtail their already insufficient transfers) and because of the high costs the status quo imposed on them. The more they were able to coordinate, the larger the benefits they expected to reach. Radical governors, on the contrary, still backed the president's reform attempts and had few, if any, incentives to support the coalition of parties opposed to the executive.

Peronist governors and those from provincial parties demanded the government to comply with the aforementioned agreement in exchange for supporting the 1986 budget law proposed by the president and his party (*Clarín*, "Hecho político," March 11, 1986). A month after the provisional agreement was reached, the central government sent a bill to Congress to reform the revenue-sharing regime. Instead of complying with the terms of the agreement reached with the governors, the president turned back to the original proposal of 48.5 percent revenue shares for both the federal government and the provinces and 3 percent for the Regional Development Fund (Pírez, 1986a, 72). By doing this, the president was not only reneging on the agreement reached with the governors but also forcing a return to the 1985 status quo ante, which was based on a lack of revenue-sharing rules to regulate the distribution of resources among levels of government.

In sum, during the first half of the Alfonsín government (1983–1987), there were no substantial legal changes in the distribution of fiscal transfers mainly due to political deadlock. Neither the president nor the governors were able to impose their preferences, even though the context of fiscal crisis urged them to do so. The president and his economic team recognized the relevance of getting inflation under control and generating a more tenable fiscal situation. Furthermore, Alfonsín and his party wanted to have some control over opposition governors, and fiscal resources were a means to make them more dependent on the central government. With respect to the revenue-sharing regime, the president wanted to reduce transfers to the provinces (and he made several attempts to do that), although he had fewer incentives than the governors to alter the allocation mechanisms because he had discretion over the transfers to be distributed among provinces. Governors, on the other hand, wanted more funds to perform their functions in office and build up political support. The expected benefits from reforms for the president and governors were high, but the expected costs and the probability of conflict out of changing the status quo ante were even larger for both of them. As predicted by the game-theoretical section, under fragmented power, and despite the strong fiscal incentives, the status quo prevailed.

Pares contra primus (1987–1989)

The power of the president

The political gridlock since 1983 came to an end after the legislative and gubernatorial elections in 1987. The president and his party lost the majority in the Chamber of Deputies in this election, keeping 114 deputies, or 44.9 percent of the seats (from 51 percent in 1983 and 1985). Peronism, on the other hand, got 106 deputies or 41.7 percent of the seats, but it was capable of reaching a majority in the Chamber with the help of center-right and provincial parties. The Senate continued under Peronist dominance.

One of the key elements to explain Alfonsín's electoral defeat in 1987 was a growing inflation that could not be controlled despite the government's efforts (at that time the Austral Plan had already failed). As the main macroeconomic variables could not be put under control, Alfonsín's public opinion approval rates diminished significantly. The military insurrections during the Easter of 1987 also contributed to diminishing the president's popularity in the face of elections. Public opinion data reflect a profound collapse in public support for Alfonsín and his government, which has to be added to the loss of support in Congress after the 1987 elections.[43] As argued in Chapter 1, when the president loses large support in public opinion, we could expect partisan backing to decline as well. After 1987, Alfonsín lost support in public opinion (a trend started before the election), seats in Congress, and discipline inside the party.

The power of governors

While the president diminished his power, the PJ gained more representatives in the Chamber of Deputies as well as additional provincial governments. Out of seven governorships in hands of the UCR in 1983, five of them were lost to the PJ in 1987. The PJ controlled 17 governorships, while the UCR won only in two (provincial parties controlled the other three). Hence, after 1987, Peronism had control over the majority of provincial governorships and a large proportion of the Senate and the Chamber of Deputies.

Most PJ governors were very powerful: eight of them (out of 17) were elected by more than 50 percent of votes; 13 (or more than 80 percent of them) controlled more than the absolute majority of the seats in the legislature from their provinces; and none of them faced a divided government. The average gubernatorial power index during the Alfonsín presidency was 1.63, a high value on the scale introduced in Chapter 1. If these governors were able to coordinate (as in fact they did), there was not much the two UCR governors could have done to support the president and compensate for those pressures.[44] This majority of governors only needed to coordinate in order to cross the threshold after which gubernatorial power can be an active force in bringing about changes in the federal balance.

Between 1983 and 1987, neither the president nor governors prevailed in their power relations. As a consequence, no significant change in the fiscal balance could be passed in Congress. Substantive changes occur only when one of these actors prevails over the other (Przeworski, 1991, 180) and have the fiscal incentives to initiate reforms. And that changed in 1987.

The fiscal context

In early 1987, as the economy further deteriorated, Alfonsín tried to control inflation by relying on price controls. But these measures proved to be ephemeral. At the end of this year, price controls were abandoned, and inflation escalated without restrictions, rising to 174 percent in 1987 and 387 percent in 1988. Gradually, the federal government ran out of resources to finance the fiscal disequilibrium.[45] Under those circumstances, the federal government announced a debt moratorium in April 1988. Tax collection diminished substantially, and revenues from external trade plummeted (as international prices for export products collapsed, leading to a 40 percent deterioration in the terms of trade for Argentina during 1983–1987). Monetary emission as a resource to finance the fiscal deficit also showed its limits, as inflation reached dangerous levels and gradually spiraled out of control. This chaotic fiscal scenario severely affected provincial finances. Subnational deficits skyrocketed, as well as total provincial debt. The total provincial budget deficit went from a AR$1 billion surplus in 1983 to a deficit of more than AR$6 billion in 1988. Total provincial debts also rose from almost AR$600 million in 1983 to AR$7 billion in 1988. As budget constraints became progressively harder, opposition governors sought additional sources of revenue by charging against the central government.

Theoretical expectations under strong governors and fiscal crisis

During this period, the settings of the game clearly favored the governors, especially those from the Peronist opposition (which controlled almost 80 percent of the provinces). Governors were politically powerful in their provinces and faced hard budget constraints, and the fiscal context generated incentives for them to coordinate and change the status quo ante regulating the distribution of resources and functions. Despite having similar incentives to the earlier period, the president was politically weak after the 1987 elections and the failed attempts to control inflation. In the chaotic economic scenario after 1987, Alfonsín had very few fiscal resources to distribute selective incentives among governors and, hence, limited ability to build up political support or to divide provincial executives.

When governors are politically powerful and the president weak, and when they can solve collective action problems and coordinate against the federal government, they face two main strategies: to keep the status quo ante regulating the distribution of federal funds and functions or to change it. Under critical fiscal conditions and hard budget constraints, governors are urged to produce changes to improve their fiscal situation. The optimal strategy for powerful governors would be to extract resources from the central government and force the president to pass decentralizing reforms by bringing negotiations into Congress.

A weak president facing powerful governors who reform the federal distribution of funds or functions in a context of fiscal crisis can either accept
the changes passed by Congress and face the fiscal costs, or veto them and
conflict with the provincial executives. The decision to negotiate or clash
depends on the costs the president faces and the probability of conflict.
The costs are larger when governors take more funds from the central government.[46] When governors seek to reform, they are more powerful and
coordinated, the president is weak, and the fiscal context is critical, the
president's incentives to negotiate with the governors are larger and the
probability of conflict is smaller. Under those conditions, a presidential
veto can mean more conflict against coordinated and powerful governors.
When the president is stronger, governors are less coordinated, and the
fiscal context is more critical (with harder budget constraints), the president has larger incentives to veto and clash against provincial executives.

Federal legislators would have few incentives to support the president
when the president is weak, her public support is diluted, she is less likely
to help federal legislators further their own careers, and the selective
incentives she could offer them to achieve their political goals are fewer
(or she cannot credibly promise to deliver them in the future, especially
under conditions of fiscal strain). Federal legislators will be more likely to
offer support to fiscal reforms favorable for the governors, when governors
are stronger, the president is weaker, governors are more likely to help
legislators further their careers, and governors have more resources (or
when legislators expect governors to have more funds) to distribute
selective incentives (some governors can even run as candidates in the
next presidential race, a situation that may favor even further realign-
ments among legislators).

If the president decides to clash, governors get a payoff equal to $(\delta - C)$
$(1-w)$ and the president gets a payoff equal to $(-\delta - C)w$, where C is the
cost of changing the status quo and w is the probability of conflict linked
to the decentralizing reform. A clash would be more likely when the costs
of changing the status quo for the governors are larger, they have fewer
political resources to pass reforms, and a president is more capable of
reacting to these changes. Under the aforementioned conditions, the
minmax strategy for the president would be to pass the reforms and avoid
conflict by not vetoing them. The Nash equilibrium would be more transfers to the provinces and not clashes against the president. The pay-offs
matrix, or the normal form game, is presented in Figure 3.4.

Expected benefits and costs in the federal distributive game

After the 1987 elections, the expected costs of reforming the regime-
regulating fiscal transfers diminished substantially for opposition governors. First, fiscal resources that were used discretionally by the president
dropped in the context of growing inflation and economic recession. This

		Governors	
		Power	No power
President	Power	0,0	$(\gamma-C)w,(-\gamma-C)(1-w)$
	No power	$(-\delta-C)w^{*},(\delta-C)(1-w)^{*}$	0,0

Figure 3.4 Normal form game for Alfonsín (1987–1989).

limited the president's ability to use selective incentives and divide coordination efforts among subnational leaders. Second, after the 1987 electoral defeat, the president was less capable of blocking reform attempts from the opposition, and had very limited powers to impose sanctions on defiant provinces. Third, the PJ opposition saw in the weak president the possibility to return to power. As the economy deteriorated and the government was unable to control inflation, public support for the government decreased, and the possibilities for the opposition of coming to power increased. Altering the mechanisms for the distribution of federal resources represented benefits for the opposition: it provided access to more funds that could be used for building up political support in the face of the coming presidential elections (scheduled for May 14, 1989) and weakened the possibilities of the president of doing so.

Legislators faced similar incentives: "[b]y increasing the fiscal independence of Peronist governors vis-à-vis the Radical president, automatic transfers made it harder for Alfonsín to influence the behavior of Peronist legislators in Congress" (Eaton, 2002, 224). PJ legislators had incentives to support governors' reform attempts and increase transfers to the provinces, as that would help them receive more funds and further their own political careers.

In the previous period, governors faced relatively soft budget constraints and relatively large collective actions problems. These two components of the federal equation changed after 1987, and that had profound implications for the stability of the status quo ante. On the one hand, as the inflationary crisis continued, governors faced harder budget constraints: first, as public revenues plummeted, the capacity of the federal government to finance and eventually bail out provinces decreased. Second, as public accounts deteriorated and international credit markets practically dried up, governors' capacity to issue debt to finance their spending obligations diminished profoundly. In this context of increasingly hard budget constraints, issuing more debt and risk being bailed out by the federal government was a quite uncertain strategy for governors. In sum, governors faced smaller costs (associated with a weaker president with fewer resources to divide them) and had more incentives for coordinating (linked to larger expected benefits and a lower probability of conflict) against the president to change the distribution of transfers in their favor.

The outcomes of the federal distributive game

As we will see in the case of Brazil during the Sarney administration, the remarkable political weakness of the president after 1987 was combined with a severe fiscal crisis. Under those conditions, governors organized along partisan lines and coordinated against the central government to get more resources. This is a rare form of coordination, which I call predatory, that has tremendous consequences in terms of distribution of resources and the balance of the federal equation.

PJ governors coordinated and contributed to form a majority in the legislature with the support of provincial parties. Urged by an unfavorable economic and fiscal situation, they pressed Congress to approve a new revenue-sharing law.[47] The original revenue-sharing bill was passed in the Senate in June 1985 with the vote of the PJ and provincial parties, but its debate in the Chamber of Deputies was effectively postponed for more than two years, as none of these parties could overcome the UCR veto. After the 1987 elections (that took place during September 6), the federal balance of power changed substantially, and this translated into a new distribution of political forces in Congress. Now, the PJ could reach quorum (to begin deliberations) and pass the bill in the Chamber of Deputies with the support of provincial and other parties (the PJ had 106 seats; provincial and minor parties had 34). But they could also face a presidential veto (partial or total) and a tough negotiation with the Radicals and provincial parties (to get the swing votes) in the Chamber of Deputies after it.[48] Hence, despite having a larger delegation in the Chamber after 1987, the PJ still needed the support from the Radicals to eventually pass the bill and avoid a presidential veto.

Alfonsín faced strong pressures from the PJ deputies and those linked to provincial parties to pass the revenue-sharing bill. He expected tough and costly negotiations in Congress, the results of which were quite uncertain (the PJ could eventually pass the bill in the Chamber of Deputies, and there were some probabilities they could override a veto with the support of some swing votes). Instead of simply suffering the (expected) large costs of uncertain negotiations or the changes in the federal balance he anticipated as a consequence of an alliance between Peronism and provincial parties, Alfonsín and key leaders from the UCR decided to negotiate with the PJ governors and legislators (provincial parties were not invited to the negotiations). They offered Radical support for the PJ revenue-sharing bill in exchange for Peronist backing on some key reforms to the tax system the president had been endorsing. Alfonsín expected these changes in the tax structure to give the central administration some fiscal relief (*Clarín*, "Trata hoy el senado el paquete impositivo," January 7, 1988). With the Radical backing, the PJ had the seats needed to reach quorum, pass the bill, and prevent a presidential veto (the president supported the terms of the negotiation).

On December 21, 1987 (three and a half months after the election), the revenue-sharing bill was submitted for consideration in a special session in the Chamber of Deputies, after the report from the Budget and Finance Commission (where the bill had been delayed for more than two years).[49] The bill reached the floor in a session that took place between December 22 and 23. As a reflection of the agreements negotiated earlier between the president and the governors, legislators voted for the bill without even reading it (as was customary) and without much debate. The bill was then sent to the Senate and voted directly on the floor without a report from any committee (*votación sobre tablas*), a further indication of the previous agreements and the urgency of the decision in Congress.[50] With 40 senators present for the vote, the bill was approved in the Senate and ratified by Congress on January 7, 1988 (as law 23,548). Senators Aguirre Lanari and Romero Feris (PAC-Corrientes) were the only ones to vote against the bill. As deputies did before them, PJ and UCR senators honored the agreement between the central government and the governors (despite the pressures governors had to exert over some senators) and passed the bill. Provincial parties (excepting the PAC) also supported the reform, as it augmented transfers to the provinces (*Clarín*, "Esta madrugada votaban el paquete impositivo," January 8, 1988; "¿Para qué este torrente?," January 9, 1988).

Alfonsín, weakened by the 1987 electoral defeat and by his fruitless efforts to control inflation, could not resist the pressures from governors, especially those in the Peronist opposition. Under a divided government with substantial legislative support for the opposition, the final outcome was a revenue-sharing law that greatly benefited the provinces. Alfonsín had entered into the last two years of his term in office, and the law was negotiated as a temporary regime to regulate fiscal relations between provinces and the central government for 1988 and 1989, until the new administration could reach a new deal with governors. However, the president, governors, and legislators were conscious of the difficulties of approving a law and the perils of not having a revenue-sharing scheme. To avoid this, they included an article by which the approved law would be automatically renewed after the initial expiration date. In fact, this clause made the transitional law effective until today (2016).

The balance of the federal distributive game

Governors notably benefited from this law, as they increased the provincial share of federal revenues to an historic high, 56.66 percent, the exact amount the PJ governors demanded in previous negotiations and the highest proportion since the revenue-sharing regime was created in 1935. The federal government received 42.34 percent of the shared taxes and the rest was divided into 2 percent for promoting the relative development of a group of provinces[51] and 1 percent for the ATN Fund (Law 23,548; article 3). Automatic transfers were increased for all provinces, not merely to those ruled by a particular party or group of parties. The main reason was that the PJ controlled the enormous majority of provinces (20 with the support of provincial parties), and distorting the coefficients for secondary distribution in favor of PJ governors exclusively was a costly decision that would have caused opposition from provincial parties and strong reactions from the two Radical governors. In order to avoid that, the new law increased transfers to all provinces.

Peronist governors also included new taxes in the revenue pool (Law 23,548, Article 2).[52] According to the debates in the Senate, provinces were expected to receive almost 30 percent more in revenues shared by the federal government (29.64 percent; as primary distribution was expected to rise by 8 percent and the volume of shared taxes by about 21 percent).

These were not the only achievements of the governors. In an extraordinary move, which reveals how powerful they had become vis-à-vis the central government, they incorporated limitations on the discretionary power of the president, widely used between 1984 and 1987, curtailing the amount of funds from revenue-sharing that the national executive could allocate on a discretionary basis: only 1 percent of the total, distributed through the so-called ATNs Fund.[53]

Finally, governors eliminated the Regional Development Fund (FDR), regulated by law 20,221, by which the federal government was able to decide and finance public works in the provinces. Under the new regime, revenues from this fund had to be distributed among all provinces according to the coefficients established by the new law. In other words, from 1988 on, previous federal public works for the provinces were to be decided by governors and not by the central government. These funds were now distributed without being earmarked, granting governors discretion over the allocation of these former federal resources.

The total revenue share of the subnational governments almost doubled between 1987 and 1988, increasing from 21 percent to 42 percent during this period (this share was 16.5 percent in 1985). Subnational revenues as a percentage of GDP almost doubled after the 1988 reforms, from 3.37 percent in 1986 (3.68 percent in 1987) to 6.60 percent in 1988. Their expenditure share increased from 39 percent in 1987 to 44 percent in 1988, and 46.7 percent in 1989 (IMF, 2001; Ministerio de Economía, 2000; see Table 3.3).

Table 3.3 Revenue and expenditure share of subnational units in Argentina (1983–1989, in percentages)

Year	Revenue share (a)	Expenditure share (b)
1983	27.40	33.78
1984	27.57	38.97
1985	16.55	29.33
1986	18.14	35.34
1987	20.85	39.20
1988	41.61	44.38
1989	40.82	46.75

Source: Data compiled and adapted from (a) IMF, 2001; (b) Ministerio de Economía, 2000.

Before getting into the details of the absolute transfers from the central government to the provinces after the reforms in the revenue-sharing regime, it is important to bear in mind that the economy contracted by 2.6 percent in 1988 and plummeted by 7.5 percent in 1989. This produced a notorious decline in tax collection and, hence, in the net amount of transfers to the provinces.[54] Despite this overall decline, legally mandated transfers (through the revenue-sharing scheme) remained relatively stable or declined in a much smaller proportion: they went from AR$13 billion in 1987 to AR$12 billion in 1988 and 1989 (constant 2004 prices). Some better indicators of the importance of the changes for provincial finances are the total transfers as a share of total provincial expenditure: they increased from 45 percent in 1987 to almost 50 percent in 1989. Revenue-sharing transfers represented almost 32 percent of total provincial expenditure in 1987, increasing to almost 38 percent in 1989. Revenue-sharing transfers became more relevant for provincial revenue after 1988 while other transfers (legally mandated and discretionary) decreased in relation to total provincial expenditure.

In sum, the balance of the federal distributive game after the 1988 reforms notably favored the governors, as they substantially increased their revenues in real and absolute terms (r_{jg}), while keeping the functions they have to deliver (P_{ig}) basically unchanged. This situation was the opposite for the central government (see Table 3.4).

The reactions from the central government

Alfonsín ended up notably disadvantaged by the changes the 1988 law introduced to the federal balance. The president could have vetoed the law, but he could not resist pressures from the PJ and provincial parties, especially after the electoral defeat in 1987 and his decreasing public support. The president signed the reform to the revenue-sharing scheme to avoid further conflict (and perhaps further losses), and exchanged his support for Peronist collaboration in some immediate tax increases

Table 3.4 Synthesis of the reforms and impacts on the federal balance (1987–1989)

Period of reforms	Subnational revenue (in relative terms)	Subnational functions	Subnational tax authority	Federal balance
Alfonsín 1987–1989	Increased (revenue share more than doubled; from 17% in 1985 to 42% in 1988; the Regional Development Fund was shared among provinces)	No substantial changes	Increased (new taxes included into the revenue-sharing scheme: VAT, on profits, excise, on fuels and lubricants, financial operations, lotteries and sporting events)	Favorable for provinces $X = \Sigma(P_{ig} - r_{ig}) > U = \Sigma(r_{jp} - P_{ip})$

needed by the federal government. Some of these changes were debated in the Senate in the same session as the one in which the new revenue-sharing bill was sanctioned (*Clarín,* "Dan quórum al paquete fiscal," January 6, 1988; "Quorum asegurado" and "Trata hoy el senado el paquete impositivo," January 7, 1988; "¿Para qué este torrente?," January 9, 1988).

Among the reforms in the tax system that Alfonsín could get passed were the creation of the "mandatory savings" regime for 1988 and 1989[55] and tax reforms destined to finance the national social security system (*Clarín,* "Esta madrugada votaban el paquete impositivo," January 8, 1988; *DS-CSN,* January 7–8, 1988, 2414–2415).

Alfonsín also made promises to support changes to labor legislation, once the tax reforms were passed in Congress, and could defer the discussion on this issue until February 1988. That allowed him to give UCR support for the revenue-sharing reforms in exchange for tax system reforms that PJ senators gruntingly accepted, without debating the labor reform in this package (*Clarín,* "Trata hoy el senado el paquete impositivo," January 7, 1988). Facing strong and coordinated governors, Alfonsín had no alternative but to buttress changes and negotiate something in exchange (in this case, a tax increase favorable for the federal government). This is, as expected from the game-theoretical framework, the *minmax* strategy for a weak president facing strong and coordinated governors.

Pressures from Peronist governors did not cease after the reformed revenue-sharing law. Two days after the approval of the new law in 1988, they met in Mar del Plata and demanded more functions and authority to be decentralized from the federal government to the provinces and the sharing of profits from the exploitation of natural resources in the provinces (at that time under central control) (*Clarín,* "Los gobernadores peronistas difunden un documento crítico," January 10, 1988; "Reclaman gobernadores un nuevo pacto federal," January 11, 1988). Once governors secured more resources for the provinces, they demanded new functions, the distribution of fiscal benefits enjoyed exclusively by the central government, and the imposition of limits on the power of the federal government in its relations with subnational governments. These pressures further weakened the Radical government.

The internal divisions among Radicals, the opposition from the reorganized PJ—especially after the 1987 elections—and the unions, the macro-economic turmoil and hyperinflation, and the chaos in the streets (Alfonsín declared a state of siege on May 30, 1989 after looting and unrest in several cities), forced Alfonsín to abandon the government five months before the end of his legal mandate. Fiscal transfers and over-spending at the subnational level contributed to a soaring federal deficit and skyrocketing levels of inflation (price increases reached a monthly 78 percent before his resignation). The 1988 revenue-sharing law, favorable to subnational governments, was one of the key factors to understanding this process. This is a case in which abrupt changes in the federal balance had large implications for the federal government's political stability.

Some partial comments

Both president and governors faced strong fiscal incentives to alter the federal balance in the post-transition to democracy. However, in the first phase, neither of them had enough power to impose these changes on the other actor. In other words, the cutting point for fiscal pressures was crossed (both the federal and provincial executives faced large deficits), but neither of them could cross the one for presidential and gubernatorial power. In this chapter, I showed how the federal executive gradually lost power and how governors increased their political strength and coordination. Under those circumstances, and as we expected theoretically, the powerful actor was able to impose sharp changes on the weaker one.

Many of the governors' demands for redistribution and decentralization were based on a federalist discourse against the excesses of the centralized authoritarian regime and the continuation of the same rules for the distribution of funds and functions during democracy (a similar, and perhaps stronger claim, was also heard from governors during the Brazilian transition to democracy). But far from being based on any ideal principle (such as the subsidiarity principle) or redistributive criteria (such as the percentage of the population under the poverty line), these demands from governors responded to a logic of political survival in their relations with the president: governors faced the dilemma of being fiscally and politically dependent on or dominated by the president, or to consolidate themselves in power by weakening the central government and extracting resources from it. They followed this latter course of action because they had enough political resources, they were capable of coordinating against a weakened president (who could not divide them), and they faced fiscal incentives to take action. In Argentina, federalist claims (or provincial predation of federal resources) or discourses of intergovernmental economic efficiency (or central control and domination over subnational spending) tended to be just rhetorical declarations behind power struggles between political actors fighting for resources and political survival.

The *pares* coordinated and clashed against the *primus*, getting a significant load of fiscal revenue, but also received more than just that. Governors also increased their electoral strength in the face of the upcoming elections, deteriorating the fiscal situation of the federal government and the electoral prospects of the incumbent party. Their actions also had longer-term implications. In a typical case of the "tragedy of the commons" (Hardin, 1968; Ostrom, 1999), governors overgrazed collective resources following a short-term strategy, but adversely affecting the fiscal and economic stability of the entire federation in the longer run.

The Sarney presidency (1985–1990)

The first presidency after the transition to democracy in Brazil, similar to Argentina, can be divided into two main periods: a first one between the 1985 transition and the 1986 elections in which there was no concentration of political power at either level of government, and a second between the 1986 mid-term elections and end of Sarney's term in office in which the president lost power and governors increased it substantially. In both periods, the main actors faced deep fiscal crises. The main reforms in the federal balance were passed during the 1987–1988 Constitutional Assembly. In the next sections, I analyze the values the main variables took, examine the theoretical predictions based on the federal distributive game, and finally use this model to account for the changes during the period.

The historical context: Brazil during the transition to democracy

Before getting into the analysis of the institutional and partisan dimensions of presidential and gubernatorial power, I briefly describe some particularities of the historical context of the Brazilian transition to democracy, which affected the distribution of power among political actors. In 1982, three years before the transition to democracy, the Brazilian military decided to hold direct gubernatorial elections in a search for legitimacy and political support, both of which had been eroding rapidly since the late 1970s, especially during the early 1980s. This election was a defining moment because of its immediate electoral results and its broader political consequences. The party linked to the authoritarian regime, the Democratic Social Party (PDS), won 12 governorships out of 22, with large margins over the opposition in the Northeast. Although these electoral results were relatively favorable for the military regime, the opposition was far from weak: they won in ten states (the Brazilian Democratic Movement Party, PMDB, won in nine, and the Democratic Labor Party, PDT, won in one state) and gained the largest share of the votes in some regions, especially in the more developed Southeast. The results between the party allied with the armed forces and the democratic opposition were close, but this election had one major effect: it gave governors, especially those from the opposition to the military regime, an important degree of legitimacy in a context of authoritarian rule at the national level as well as a chance to show they could govern large states effectively. After all, they were the first elected politicians in a context of military rule. Several scholars have argued that the military giving privileges to subnational governments had important consequences for strengthening regional elites and the functioning of democracy in Brazil (Abrucio, 1998; Eaton, 2004; Hagopian, 1996; Kugelmas *et al.*, 1989; Mainwaring, 1997, 1999; Souza, 1996, 1997) (Interviews with Eduardo Kugelmas, September 12, 2006;

Celina Souza, July 26, 2007). As indicated by Kugelmas *et al.* (1989, 96), "once direct elections were re-established, governors were once again political actors of first order relevance."

In April 1984, after there were guarantees from the military that there would be indirect presidential elections in 1985, the opposition PMDB and a dissident faction from the PDS, the Liberal Front Party (*Partido da Frente Liberal*, PFL) formed an alliance (the Democratic Alliance) and nominated Tancredo Neves (PMDB) as presidential candidate and José Sarney (PFL) for vice-president. Sarney, a conservative leader of the PDS from the Northeast, was nominated as the vice-presidential candidate to provide guarantees to the military in case the democratic coalition won the election and as a way to capture the more conservative votes that the PMDB could not attract. Tancredo, besides his personal capabilities, had some conditions that made him a crucial actor during the transition. First, he was a governor from one of the most powerful states (Minas Gerais) and, as such, he was in condition to negotiate with the military. Due to the gradualism of the Brazilian transition, negotiations with the military government were intense, and many saw Neves as capable of conducting them. Second, as a governor, he was also a crucial spokesman for other governors, who saw him as a peer. He had influence over governors who opposed the military regime (especially those from his party, the PMDB), but he needed to persuade governors from the PDS, which controlled a majority of the governorships, to get votes for him in the Electoral College. Conflicts inside the PDS over the presidential candidate, Paulo Maluf, generated strong divisions in the party, favoring Tancredo.

Tancredo Neves, with the support from the PMDB and the majority of the PDS governors, was indirectly elected president and José Sarney vice-president with 70 percent of the vote in the Electoral College (312 votes, 168 of which were from PDS dissidents). This result was not supposed to happen. The military allowed this indirect election and resisted the movement for direct elections (that mobilized millions in city after city on successive Sundays during 1984) because it assumed it could control the outcome. Neves was the archetypal example of a president elected as a *primus inter pares*. Governors played a crucial role in his election and during the transition process to democracy. Their influence did not end there and continued after the transition, at least during the first years of the democratic regime. The former governor of Minas Gerais, elected president by a large margin and backed by a majority of governors, tragically died before he could take office. His place was taken by the elected vice-president, José Sarney, a member of the Liberal Front Party (PFL).

In the sections that follow, I examine the characteristics of presidential and gubernatorial power during the Sarney administration, as well as the characteristics and incentives generated by the fiscal context. After exploring the main features of the distribution of political power in the federation and the fiscal incentives the actors faced, I elaborate on the theoretical expectations from the model developed in Chapter 1. To finish, I examine the dynamics of the federal game over the distribution of resources and functions during the Sarney presidency and the outcomes in terms of the federal balance.

Presidential partisan power

The power of the president, in partisan and institutional terms, is the first key variable I analyze in the setting of the federal distributive game. Sarney was a political leader and former governor of Maranhão (1966–1971), a small state in the Northeast. He lacked the charisma, and many argued the capacity, for the task his position demanded (Souza, 1997, 57). Even more importantly, he lacked legitimacy and had limited partisan support. He lacked legitimacy because of his role during the military regime as president of the military-sponsored PDS, among other positions in office, and due to the particular way he rose to the presidency. He also had limited political support: after the 1982 elections and until 1986, the opposition from the PDS controlled 49.1 percent of the seats in the Chamber of Deputies, 66.7 percent of the seats in the Senate, and 12 governorships; while the PMDB (allied with Sarney's PFL) occupied 41.8 percent of the seats in the Chamber of Deputies, only 36 percent of the seats in the Senate, and 9 governorships.

The distribution of seats notwithstanding, Sarney received relatively little opposition from Congress during his first 18 months in office (Mainwaring, 1999, 298). It was only after the 1986 elections, and especially after 1987, that his popularity as well as his political support in Congress and from the governors began to wane. During this time, Sarney was an unpopular president, with more than half of Brazilians judging him unfavorably.[56]

After the 1986 elections, Sarney's coalition partners from the PMDB scored an important electoral victory. This party won 53.4 percent of the deputies whereas the PFL won only 24.2 percent (corresponding to 47.8 and 17.7 percent of the vote, respectively). The PMDB won an astonishing 77.6 percent of the seats in the Senate and the PFL 14.3 percent. The PMDB–PFL coalition was the result of historical circumstances and the decisions of opportunistic politicians who, opposing the military-sponsored candidate, backed Neves and ended up supporting his running mate who had become president. The relationship between the chief executive and the main coalition party, the PMDB, was not an easy one. In fact, as later events demonstrated, Sarney's opportunistic partners were not willing to support the president when his administration began losing electoral support and not delivering material benefits to them.

Very importantly also, Sarney did not have a significant regional coalition to support him. In the election for deputies, his party won only in three of the less socioeconomically developed states: his home state of Maranhão, Piauí (another Northeastern state), and the Northern state of

Amapá. As a result of the elections for state governors, the PMDB control-led 22 out of 23 states (or 95.7 percent of the governorships); the PFL won only in Sergipe. Never in the period after the transition to democracy did a party have the same degree of control that the PMDB had over state gov-ernments at this time. And during Sarney's term in office, the main party was not the president's party.

During the first two years in office, especially after the initial success of the *Cruzado* plan, Sarney received support from public opinion, his broad coalition in Congress, and most PMDB governors. However, with the cata-strophic failure of the plan in 1987, as the economic and fiscal conditions deteriorated dramatically, public support began to wane, and so did the partisan backing from his partners in the coalition. The most progressive members of the PMDB deserted the presidential base of political support first, and as the fiscal conditions worsened, the president gradually became isolated. As indicated by Lamounier (1990, 17), the economic failure of the *Cruzado* led to a serious confidence crisis in public opinion, which affected not only the president but also political parties, especially the PMDB, the main basis of support for the president. Some trends that would later reappear became manifest during those years in the Sarney administration: when presidents lose political support from citizens, and this is reflected in electoral results, and when the fiscal conditions deteriorate to a point that presidents cannot lubricate relations with gov-ernors by means of public works, social programs, or discretionary trans-fers (not to mention when they cannot even guarantee the legally mandated transfers, as happened during De la Rúa's term in office in Argentina), governors begin to distance themselves from the government, as do federal legislators. If presidential political support diminishes sub-stantially and fiscal conditions deteriorate acutely, the incentives for gov-ernors to coordinate against the central government increase.

Presidential institutional power

The partisan and institutional dimensions are the most important com-ponents defining the power of the president. This variable (presidential power), together with the power of governors, determines the distribution of power in the setting of the federal distributive game. In this section, I analyze the institutional dimension of presidential power.

Brazilian presidents are relatively powerful in institutional terms, espe-cially if we compare them to other presidential regimes in the region (Mainwaring and Shugart, 1997; Shugart and Carey, 1992). According to Shugart and Carey (1992), Brazilian presidents have relatively extensive legislative and non-legislative powers. The first ones include veto and decree powers as well as the authority to introduce legislation. In Shugart and Carey's (1992, 153) index of presidential institutional powers, Brazilian presidents are considered very powerful, as they score 12 on non-legislative powers (out of a maximum of 16) and 9 on legislative powers (out of a maximum of 24). Mainwaring and Shugart (1997, 49) classify presidents in Brazil as "proactive," as they have decree authority, weak veto powers, and exclusive introduction. Despite their institutional resources, and due to conditions we will explore in the chapters that follow, not all presidents after the transition to democracy have made use of them in the same way and with similar intensity.

President Sarney governed under the authoritarian constitution of 1967 for about two-thirds of his term in office, governing the remaining third under the democratically reformed 1988 charter (Power, 1998, 204). Despite the relative stability of the institutional resources available for Brazilian federal executives after 1988, presidents have not made use of them in the same manner across time. For instance, the use of presidential decree power was limited during the Sarney administration, especially when compared to later presidencies (see Table 5.5, Chapter 5).

Even if we do not compute re-issued decrees, between 1988 and 1999, presidents in Brazil issued two times as many decrees as their counterparts in Argentina (Negretto, 2002, 396–397). Presidents made different use of this institutional resource available to them, and the rate at which they were successful in gaining approval for the MPs they issued varied significantly.[57] Hence, although the institutional dimension is relevant for the analysis of presidential power, we need to consider other key dimensions, such as the support federal executives have in partisan and electoral terms and as well as from public opinion. These other dimensions also make presidents more or less powerful, despite the institutional resources they can use.

The power of governors

The analysis of presidential power has to be complemented with information on the power of governors. Both of them will give us an idea on how power is distributed between levels of government in the federation. This distribution, in turn, is one of the crucial components to defining the setting of the federal distributive game. After having explored the weaknesses Sarney faced as president in partisan and institutional terms, in this and the following sections, I explore the institutional and partisan components defining the power of governors during his term in office.

In institutional terms, governors in Brazil have powers that allow them to be agenda setters: decree (called *medidas provisórias*, MPs, and *lei delegada*, LDs) and veto power (total and partial), exclusive initiative (in tax, budgetary, financial, and administrative matters), and emergency powers.

Furthermore, governors can maintain their original bills sent to the legislative, diminishing the changes this body can propose (Pereira, 2001, 258). Despite these important institutional resources, particularly in relation to the legislature, and the fact that state constitutions in Brazil do not show the dramatic differences we find among Argentine provinces, there is ample variation in the control governors exert over the state assembly and, hence, in the production of policies. Santos (2001, 289–291) conducted a valuable study on executive-legislative relations across Brazilian states. He argues that the combinations of gubernatorial institutional power and the internal organization of the legislature reveal a vast diversity of institutional configurations and party system dynamics in the states, confirming significant variation across territorial units and time (Santos, 2001, 291). Santos's claim can be taken as a justification for studying the governor's institutional resources in combination with their partisan power in the state assembly.

Despite the sharp variation Santos (2001) reports across states (see also Pereira, 2001, 260, 268), Abrucio (1998, 111–112) claims that after the transition to democracy, due to its specific characteristics as well as the institutional legacies from previous periods, several governors had large power over their states in institutional terms. For him, a large majority of state executives had enough power to control (and in many cases manipulate at will) the functioning of the state legislature and the judiciary, the state agenda, and the distribution of resources, including public jobs, through the enormous leverage they had over budgetary appropriations and their execution. Many governors were able to neutralize the checks and balances from the legislative and the judiciary, especially from the *Tribunal de Contas* and the *Ministério Público*, co-opting them with loyal partisans. For Abrucio (1998, 116), this predominance of the executive took place in states as diverse as São Paulo, Paraíba, Goiás, Santa Catarina, Paraná, and Bahia, "showing that this phenomenon has not been circumscribed to the less developed regions of the country." It is not the aim of this work to get into the specificities of this debate, but rather show that the institutional power of governors has wide variation and has to be analyzed together with their partisan control of state assemblies.

The analysis on the institutional dimension of gubernatorial power, as with the study of the president's, has to be complemented with information on their partisan power to get a more accurate idea of how powerful governors were in their states at a moment in time. After the 1986 elections, the PMDB controlled 22 out of 23 governorships.[58] The average governor was elected with more than 55 percent of the votes. This support also translated, in most cases, into gubernatorial control of the state legislature. The average governor controlled a bit over 50 percent of the seats in the state legislative assembly.[59] The average gubernatorial power index for the Sarney presidency was 2.2, a very high value according to our scale.

It is important to differentiate the power of governors in their states, a measure that has an institutional and partisan dimension, from the power of governors in relation to the federal government or over national politics. The fact that governors had an important degree of institutional and partisan power in their states does not necessarily mean that they were able to influence federal politics. In order to explore governors' influence over federal politics we need to study the coordination mechanisms they were able to craft and what the impacts (if any) were of those mechanisms.

Summing up, after the transition to democracy, during most of Sarney's administration, governors had significant institutional resources in their states. The institutional dimension of gubernatorial power has been, in general, relatively stable over time in most states. Furthermore, in partisan terms, most, though not all, governors enjoyed enough electoral support that translated into partisan control over the legislature, which also contributed to their influence in federal politics. The dimension that has changed the most over time has been their capacity to coordinate and influence national politics. In general, governors' individualistic behavior prevailed over coordination although there were some instances of interstate cooperation. The broader form of coordination most easily achieved was defensive: coordination among governors was mainly circumscribed to vetoing changes in the federal balance (I get in some details of this below).

The fiscal context

In 1985, Brazil's transition to democracy occurred under relative political stability (especially when compared to Argentina) but in conditions of profound economic volatility (Stepan, 1989). During the final years of the military regime, the Brazilian economy slowed down and entered a period of stagnation. Between 1980 and 1984, per capita income fell approximately 15 percent. Growth resumed during 1985 and 1986, after the transition to democracy, but decelerated again in 1987, and by 1988 the economy was in recession. Inflation was on the rise, increasing from 223.8 percent in 1984 and 235.5 percent in 1985 to 1,782 percent in 1989. To complete the murky picture, foreign debt soared from $6.6 billion in 1971 to $100 billion in 1984, reaching $105 billion the year Sarney was sworn into office. Debt obligations and interest payments generated substantial fiscal pressures on the federal government, especially in the context of decreasing economic growth. Debt service (amortization plus interests) took up about 30 percent of export earnings in 1974 and increased to 83 percent in 1982 (Baer, 1996, 109). The total public sector debt increased from 23.7 percent of GDP in 1981 to 50 percent in 1985 (the year of the transition to democracy); the central government's debt rose from 4 percent to 17 percent during the same period, reaching 18.3 percent of GDP during the last year of Sarney (Giambiagi and Além, 1999, 157).

The debt problem had also an important correlate at the state level: in 1981, over one-third of Brazil's total external debt was held by state governments (Graham, 1990, 87; quoted in Montero, 2000, 63). The total net debt of sub-national governments increased from 4.2 percent of GDP in

1981 to 6.90 percent in 1985 and almost 9 percent in 1990 (Giambiagi and Além, 1999, 157). Most of this subnational debt was owed to the central government (Bevilaqua, 2000, 9). Hence, not only the federal government but also most of the states suffered strong fiscal pressures from debt obligations. The effective budget revenue of Brazilian states, that is, their budget revenues minus their debt obligations, was 24.5 percent in 1980 (the rest went to debt payments) and 18.2 percent in 1988 (Lopreato, 2002, 141–142). As growth rates decelerated, debt increased, inflation sky-rocketed, and most macroeconomic indicators worsened, the fiscal situation of the central government became more precarious and unstable. The operational fiscal deficit of the central government was 4.7 percent of GDP in 1985, reaching 5.7 percent in 1987 (the year in which the constitutional reform began) and almost reaching 7 percent of GDP in 1989 (the year after the constitutional reform). As economic activity shrank, tax collection through the main state tax, the ICM (called ICMS after 1988) and constitutional transfers contracted, with substantially adverse effects on state budgets (Lopreato, 2002, 119). State fiscal deficits expanded at a rapid pace. In 1986, the overall state deficit was 26 billion cruzados, escalating to 37 billion in 1987 and 843 billion in 1988.[60] According to data provided by the Brazilian Central Bank, the operational balance of states and municipalities was negative during the entire period between 1985 and 1991, reaching the largest deficit in 1987.

In a context of persistent debt expansion, growing inflation, feeble economic growth, and deteriorating fiscal indicators, the option of issuing more domestic debt, borrowing funds from international credit markets, or printing money became increasingly constrained. These options were further constrained with the failure of the first stabilization plans (Lopreato, 2002, 91). All this led to stronger budget constraints for the federal government. At the state level, governors faced similar pressures: spending requirements were rising but budget constraints were increasingly harder, and the need to balance the fiscal deficit was seen as a crucial component for stabilization. The adverse economic and fiscal context generated strong incentives for governors to find new resources. As the states' fiscal deficit increased, the availability of funding (domestic and external) decreased, and budget constraints became stronger, the option of getting resources from the central government gradually became more appealing.

Several attempts to stabilize the inflationary process were implemented after the democratic transition. However, until 1994, all of them had failed to stabilize the economy beyond the short term. However, many analysts agree that these were short-term measures to suddenly stop inflation, without attacking some of its main source, the fiscal deficit (which was exacerbated by the decision to increase salaries and, hence, demand) (de Souza, 1999, 50). The failure in the attempts to reduce inflation and resume growth led to declining presidential popularity, and "that made legislators and governors willing to distance themselves from the president, in turn making it more difficult for Sarney to forge the support needed to implement reforms" (Mainwaring, 1999, 298).

During this period, Brazil's economic performance was highly erratic. One of the worst effects of those failed attempts was that they undermined the credibility of the government in the eyes of the electorate to solve the chronic problem of inflation (Moura, 1993, 6). This further contributed to the erosion of Sarney's political power (see Figure 3.5 and Table 3.5).

The federal distributive game during the 1988 constitutional reform

During the presidency of José Sarney, a crucial arena for negotiations over the distribution of resources and functions was the constitutional assembly elected in 1986 (Eaton, 2004, 155).[61] The constitutional reform was part of a larger democratization movement promoted by several political actors during the transition, including the governors. Reforming the constitution was among the demands these actors made to rid Brazil of its legacies of military rule, secure democratization, and shape a new political order (Kinzo, 1990; Power, 1998b, 201; Souza, 1997, 57). In the coalition pressing for the constitutional reform, governors (and mayors), considered by Souza (1997) to be among the most influential pressure groups, saw this mobilization as an opportunity for decentralizing power, an issue strongly linked to the need to democratize the federation after the transition from

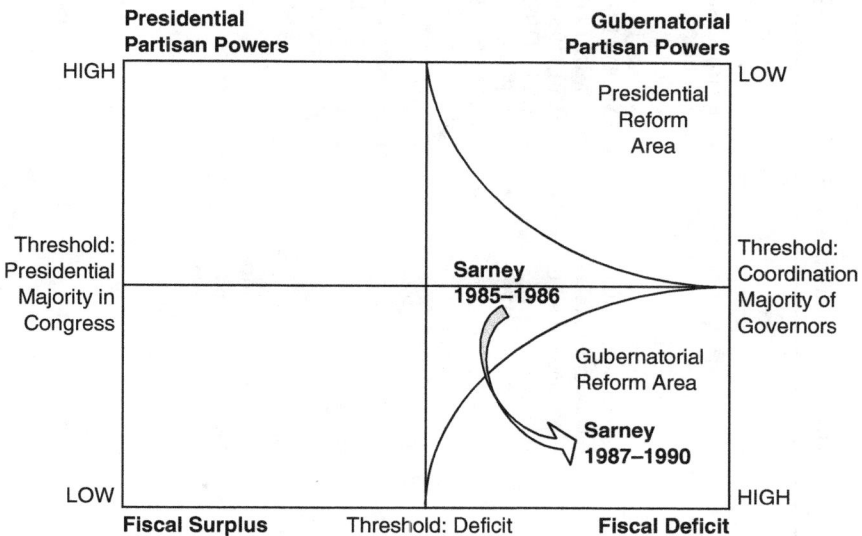

Figure 3.5 Synthesis of the main variables during Sarney (1985–1990).

Note
The area inside both arches is where the probability of changes in the status quo ante is larger.

Table 3.5 Values taken by the main variables during Sarney (1985–1990)

	Variable	Value	Range high-low	Overall value
Presidential electoral power	Electoral support president	Sarney was vice-president elect; turned into president after president Neves died.	Low	Low presidential power
	Electoral support opposition	PDS controlled 49.1% of the chamber, 66.7% of the Senate, 12 governorships.	Relatively high	
	Percentage of seats (Lower Chamber)	41.8% (PMDB) (1982–1986); 24.2% (PFL), 53.4% (PMDB) (1986–1990).	Low (PFL); Medium (coalit.)	
	Percentage of seats (Senate)	36% (PMDB) (1982–1986); 77.6% (PMDB), 14.3% (PFL) (1986–1990).	Low (PFL); relatively high (coalition)	
	Role of opposition	Allied with PMDB.	–	
	Discipline in the coalition/party	76.6% and 76.8% (PFL); 65.7% and 64.7% (PMDB).	Medium (PFL); low (PMDB)	
Presidential legislative power	Use of decree power	200 DLs under the 1967 constitution; 147 MPs under the 1988 constitution.	High	Relatively high legislat. power
Presidential approval rating	Positive image	Average negative 57% (1988–1989, years for which there are data).	Low to very low	From low to very low positive image
Gubernatorial power	Average gubernatorial electoral support	55% of the vote.	Relatively high	High gubernatorial power (opposition)
	Average legislative support (% of seats)	50% of the seats.	Relatively high	
	Gubernatorial partisan powers index	Very high: 2.2 (out of a maximum of 3).	Very high	
	Proportion of allied governors	1/23 governors (PFL), 22/23 in hands of PMDB.	Very low	
	Gubernatorial coordination	From medium (1986–1987) to relatively high (1988–1989).	From medium to relatively high	

Economic context	Economic growth	Nominal growth of 3% for the period. But per capita income fell 15% between 1980 and 1984.	Relatively low	Relatively critical economic context
	Inflation	Average 836% 1985–1990. 1,037% in 1988 and 1,782% in 1989.	From high to very high	
	Debt	From 23.7% of GDP in 1981 to 50% in 1985, average of 45% during the period.	High	
	Provincial debt	Total net debt of subnational governments increased from 4.9% of GDP in 1981 to 6.90% in 1985. Average of 6.3% of GDP during the period.	High	
	Budget constraints	From soft to harder.	–	
Fiscal indicators	Federal fiscal deficit	Average 2.6% of GDP deficit, reaching 4% in 1989.	High	Relatively strong fiscal pressures
	State fiscal deficit	Negative state operational deficit (1985–1991). Avg. 1% of GDP for the period.	Relatively high	

military rule. Besides the expansion of the public sphere for the discussion of political and economic policies, another of the crucial mobilizing issues during the transition to democracy was a critique of authoritarian centralization and the restoration of federalism. These were some of the main programmatic demands the MDB made (Kugelmas *et al.*, 1989, 96). Democratization and decentralization became two strong mobilizing issues or requests that generated "linkages" among governors. Despite ideological, partisan, and regional (or structural) differences, the demands for a constitutional reform served the purpose of horizontally articulating their claims for more democracy and decentralized power. Decentralization and democratization mobilized, linked, and gave governors' claims a substantial degree of legitimacy and public support.

The settings of the federal distributive game

The National Constitutional Assembly (*Assembleia Nacional Constituinte*, ANC) was composed of 559 members: 72 senators and 487 federal deputies. The PMDB, which controlled a majority of the governorships, had the largest share of representatives (54.6 percent of the seats), followed by the party of the president, the PFL (24 percent of the seats). Together, both parties controlled two-thirds of the assembly (Souza, 1997, 58).[62] In the following sections, I analyze each of the different components of the federal equation to explore the expected outcomes (in theoretical terms) of the federal distributive game and assess these theoretical arguments in light of key historical processes and events from the period.

Powerful governors who are able to coordinate in an unfavorable fiscal context can preserve the status quo ante or try to compel the president to pass fiscal decentralizing reforms by bringing negotiations into Congress. These theoretical expectations are similar to those in Argentina after 1987: when governors are powerful, have fiscal incentives to move, and the president is weak, subnational executives will try to get a payoff of δ and impose a payoff of $-\delta$ on the president. In the event that governors decide to take action, a president facing powerful and coordinated governors can either accept the reforms passed by Congress or reject them (by means of a presidential veto) and conflict with provincial executives. This decision depends on the costs the president faces and the probability of conflict. When the costs imposed on the president (and the central government) are larger and she is more powerful (that is, there is a larger probability of conflict), the federal executive would have more incentives to clash. When the president is weaker and the reforms are bearable, the federal executive would have more incentives to negotiate with the governors.

Governors and the president clash when the expected costs of changing the status quo are larger, the political resources the governors have to pass reforms are limited, and the president is more capable of reacting to those reforms (or the larger the probability of conflict). In the case of conflict, governors get a payoff equal to $(\delta-C)(1-w)$ and the president gets a payoff equal to $(-\delta-C)w$, where C is the cost associated with changing the status quo and w is the probability of conflict associated with this reform. The normal form game is the following (see Figure 3.6):

Expected benefits and costs of the federal distributive game

The deterioration in public accounts between 1987 and 1988 prompted state leaders to struggle against the central government to score additional gains in the distribution of revenues (Lopreato, 2002, 107). In fact, state revenues decreased due to the reduction in real terms of transfers to subnational governments. This fueled concerns among the representatives of the states in the Constitutional Assembly and helped galvanize their efforts in defense of more transfers from the central government. The governors faced a relatively weak president who had limited resources to distribute to them to discourage their coordination efforts. Moreover, demands for more democratization and decentralization became issues that linked governors horizontally and gave them substantial support and legitimacy in public opinion. Few political analysts or informed observers, if any, would claim that the president expected substantial gains from changes in the status quo ante; he was hoping not to lose much and to survive politically in a context that was very much unfavorable for him.

Most PMDB legislators had incentives to support governors' reform attempts and increase transfers to the states, as that would help them receive more funds and further their own political careers. They had fewer incentives to support the president's position of retaining the status quo on fiscal transfers, as the federal executive had few resources to distribute among subnational governments and could do little to help them further their careers. Sarney was, moreover, quite unpopular (in fact, he was the most unpopular president in the period after the 1985 transition to democracy), controlled few seats in Congress, and had little leverage to impose discipline among those he did control. Divisions among legislators and

		Governors	
		Power	No power
President	Power	0,0	$(\gamma-C)w,(-\gamma-C)(1-w)$
	No power	$(-\delta-C)w^*,(\delta-C)(1-w)^*$	0,0

Figure 3.6 Normal form game for Sarney (1987–1990).

governors from different regions and parties on several issues before (and during) the constitutional assembly were profound.[63] Despite these tensions, governors and Congress gathered enough political support around the need to democratize the country and decentralize power by calling for the convention.

The president's priorities were mainly short-term issues, like the length of his mandate, the system of government—which, in the case of parliamentarism, directly affected him because he lacked legitimacy, popular support, and partisan power, and the weakening of the federal bureaucracy. Because Sarney's tenure in office was threatened and some decisions adopted during the constitutional reform caused discomfort in the business community, a political coalition called *Centrão* (big center) was created to fight against what they viewed as Leftist features of the constitutional draft. However, the main issues that brought together the *Centrão* were not related to the distribution of fiscal resources and functions in the federation, but rather to those matters that were first-order priorities for the president (such as the defense of the presidential form of government and the length of his mandate) and for some conservative allies, parts of the military, the business community, and large landowners (who were most interested in defeating some of the most "progressive" measures, such as a larger state intervention in the economy, increased powers to expropriate and redistribute land, guarantees of job stability, and prohibitions of private investment and foreign ownership in certain sectors, among others). In addition, decisions about the tax system and the federal organization of the state were already a fait accompli by the time the coalition was formed. Sarney (along with his closest allies) was absent from many negotiations, such as those defining the distribution of resources in the federation, and concentrated his efforts on forming a coalition to defend those issues most related to his immediate political survival.

As the fiscal crisis worsened, governors faced increasingly hard budget constraints. Subnational executives were pressed by their fiscal imbalances, had limited access to federal and international credit, and faced limits on printing money. Although there were limits to the resources governors could extract from the central government, few governors viewed the fiscal and financial situation of the central government as a constraint on their attempts to decentralize more revenues to their states (Souza, 1997, 93). Governors had strong incentives to alter the status quo, solve collective action problems, and coordinate according to regional interests and along partisan lines.[64] For Souza, "the conspiracy against the federal government was facilitated by the existence of a weak president, strong governors, mayors and individual interests of members of the CNA [the constitutional national assembly, ANC]" (Souza, 1997, 84).

The probability of conflict between the president and governors over the reforms imposed on the former was relatively low. Sarney had very strong incentives to prevent these reforms, as they were expected to be very costly for him. However, he had limited political power and little legit-imacy to try to block them. Governors were relatively strong and coord-inated while Sarney was politically weak and fiscally constrained, so he faced limits in his efforts to divide them. As the expected benefits of decentralizing reforms for governors were higher than the expected costs of changing the status quo, changes were more likely to pass in the ANC without the president being capable of vetoing them. This does not mean that Sarney and his coalition could not impose limits on reforms proposed during the ANC, especially on those issues that were first-order priority for the conservative coalition. I get into these bargains in the section below.

The dynamics of the federal distributive game

The constitutional assembly began deliberations on February 1, 1987, and finished a first draft by January 1988, almost a year later. The constitution was finally promulgated on October 5, 1988. The result was an extensive document, consisting of 315 articles and over 200 pages.

The *Centrão* negotiated some changes related to their most important demands (Reich, 1998, 14–15). Presidential lobby efforts, military threats, demonstrations organized by large landowners, and contacts between several political leaders and high-ranking military officers convinced some of the most susceptible representatives in the Assembly.[65] Despite the efforts of the president and his supporters, the constitutional assembly was the political arena in which powerful governors coordinated and exerted pressures against the central government on those issues crucial for them. The *Centrão* proved less capable of limiting those demands. The crucial sub-committee on "Taxation, Sharing and Distribution of Revenues," which recommended increasing federal transfers to subnational govern-ments, was largely dominated by Northeastern, Northern, and Center-West delegates (they represented 54 percent of the sub-committee members). Despite strong regional divisions (especially among the more and the less developed and industrialized states), there was a firm consensus on increasing transfers to states and reducing federal revenues. In previous constitutions, the North and Northeast were entitled to only 2 percent of the federal income tax (IR) and the tax on industrialized products (IPI). The large increase in states' revenues, especially in the transfers to the Northern, Northeastern, and Center-West states, as a percentage of total IR and IPI revenues was a consequence of the power of these subnational interests and their ability to coordinate in the sub-committee. The inclu-sion of the Center-West was a reward for their support in voting for the request sponsored by the other two regions (Souza, 1997, 71).

The constitutional convention was mainly dominated by regional inter-ests, which were quite effective at coordinating a strategy against the central government (Souza, 1997, 70–74).[66] Representatives from the more industrialized and developed states demanded more state taxes and the devolution of taxing authority from the federal to the state (and local) level. In exchange, they endorsed revenue-sharing schemes to benefit the less developed states and regions (such as the North and Northeast). This was a positive-sum game among governors and a zero-sum game between them and the president. Instead of one region vetoing the interests of another or the central government promoting divisions and conflict to prevent cooperation among the regions, most coordination efforts among states and regions ended up benefiting all of them. Increases in one region's revenue were most of the time matched by increases for the others, all at the expenses of the federal government (Rezende, 1990, 163; Souza, 1997, 72). Hence, while representatives from different states and regions disagreed over several issues, such as industrial policy, they coordinated and found a common cause against the federal government in the case of fiscal transfers (Eaton, 2004, 157; Kugelmas, 2001, 36; Montero, 2000, 64; Rezende, 2001, 188). As indicated by Souza (1997, 82),

> [d]espite the intensity of cleavages [among regions and between states], every individual state ... was a winner, not only because their revenues had risen, but also because issues apparently outside the competence of the committee were included in the negotiations, such as the increase in the political representation of the state of São Paulo.

The federal government was stunningly absent during negotiations over fiscal transfers with the states, which contrasted sharply with the intense internal discussions that took place every time a region was penalized by a proposal that benefited another. The president barely had the political capital and resources to survive politically in office and to compensate members of his coalition. He could not offer much to the governors, who knew they were going to get much more at a relatively low cost.

In sum, facing a politically weak president (after 1986) and a deep fiscal crisis, governors coordinated against the central government to get more resources. The president had very limited capacity to divide and deter them from coordinating. This made governors very powerful in relation to the federal government and capable of imposing substantial costs on central authorities. This is the most unfavorable form of coordination against the central government, which I called "predatory": powerful governors solve collective action problems and extract resources from the central government, headed by a weak president unable to obstruct most of these assaults. The outcomes benefited state governors (although to differing degrees) at the expense of the central government.

The outcomes of the federal distributive game

As a consequence of a negotiation process largely dominated by powerful governors and regional interests, the outcomes of the federal distributive game largely benefited subnational governments. They received more constitutionally mandated resources without any clear definition of their responsibilities for providing services, broadened their tax base to include authority over new taxes, and prevented the creation of either constraints on how to spend their money or institutions to enforce fiscal discipline. Governors lobbied in the constitutional assembly to institutionalize their gains and approve a new legal framework regulated by the 1988 constitution. The constitution required three-fifth majorities (in both chambers on two occasions within the life of the same legislature) to be amended and, therefore, these majorities were also needed for any adjustments to the formula for fiscal revenue sharing.

The 1988 constitution raised the shares of federal taxes automatically distributed to the states (through the FPE) and municipalities (through the FPM). The federal government was required to allocate 21.5 percent of the revenues from the income tax (IR) and industrial products tax (IPI) to the FPE (up from 14 percent), representing a 154 percent increase.

Total state tax revenues increased from R$30 billion in 1987 to R$39 billion in 1989. Total federal transfers remained relatively stable between 1986 and 1988 (R$8.85 billion in 1986 and R$8.88 billion in 1988). But in 1989, the year after the reforms, they grew to R$11.5 billion, a rise equivalent to 30 percent for the period.[67] The revenue share of subnational governments was 18.6 percent in 1987, the year before the constitution was reformed. In 1988, the reform year, it increased to 28.5 percent; in 1989, the year in which reforms were implemented and took effect, the revenue share of subnational governments escalated to 30 percent, an increase of more than 1.6 times (IPEA Data; IMF, 2001; see Table 3.6). On the other hand, the expenditure share of subnational governments diminished from 35.4 percent in 1987 to 28.6 in 1989, a 19 percent decrease for the period (IPEA Data; IMF, 2001; see Table 3.6).

The federal government's losses of revenue to subnational levels were estimated at $12.6 billion (Souza, 1997, 94). In relative terms, federal shares of revenue fell from 44.6 percent in 1985 (before the constitutional reform) to 36.5 percent in 1993 (Serra and Afonso, 1999; Souza, 1997, 38). According to Giambiagi (1991, 64), between 1980 and 1990, federal revenues as a share of the total fell 17 percent, while they increased

Table 3.6 Revenue and expenditure share of subnational units in Brazil (1986–1989, in percentages)

Year	Revenue share	Expenditure share
1986	27.49	32.20
1987	18.62	35.45
1988	28.49	29.46
1989	29.95	28.65

Source: Data compiled and adapted from IPEA Data; IMF, 2001.

26 percent for states. States also benefited from other federal transfers vis-à-vis the substantial increases through the revenue-sharing scheme.[68] Significantly, a large part of the revenues decentralized from the central government to subnational governments was not earmarked by the 1988 constitution.

In addition to the increase in resources without new responsibilities (a positive balance in the federal equation), states also expanded their tax base and authority. In 1967, the military decentralized the ICM to subnational governments, but retained control over the establishment of this tax's rate. Members of the 1988 constitutional assembly expanded the base of the ICM, abolishing five former federal taxes, including taxes on transport, energy, fuels, minerals, and communications, which were decentralized to the states to create the ICMS (Mora, 2002, 3; Prado, 2003; Rezende, 2001; Serra and Afonso, 1999; Souza, 1997, 39).[69]

In another move that demonstrated the power of governors in relation to the president, in December 1989 the federal government was forced to convert state debts with foreign creditors into long-term debt with the National Treasury. Out of the 89 state financial institutions in Brazil, 70 were converted into special regimes administered by the Central Bank and federal authorities (Abrucio, 1998, 199). The costs for the central government were enormous. In its attempts to bail out state banks, the federal government spent $2.3 billion between 1984 and 1994, as well as other $31.6 billion in payments to creditors and in judicial procedures (*Folha de São Paulo* [*FSP* from now on], May 29, 1994, 9).

In spite of the substantial increases in fiscal transfers from the central government, states were not made responsible for any new mandated functions. In fact, whereas the 1988 constitution granted municipalities and the central government clear responsibilities, the states did not get a clearly defined set of functions over which they had exclusive authority (Almeida, 1991, 174; quoted in Abrucio, 1998, 196). The constitution established a large amount of common responsibilities between the federal and state governments, especially in the area of social services. But this overlap tended to favor the states, as they were not assigned any specific responsibilities for providing services. In fact, their share of expenditures diminished during the period (see Table 3.6). In the end, the reformed constitution favored subnational governments, but kept the powers to regulate administrative functions in the hands of the central government, limiting the capacity of subnational governments to adopt their own policies. These institutional capacities turned into a critical tool in the hands of the president several years later, when Cardoso used them to exert tighter control over and regulate subnational governments.

The balance of the federal distributive game

In sum, during the constitutional reform, subnational governments increased their taxing power, approved a new mandated revenue-sharing scheme that substantially augmented the amount of funds distributed to them, and removed earmarks that enhanced states' discretion in the use of those funds. The amount of resources available for the central government seriously shrank, due to the increase in spending earmarked by the constitution: mainly larger transfers to states and municipalities and more social spending (Giambiagi and Além, 1999, 112–113). For Melo (2002, 48) the new tax arrangement after the 1988 constitutional reform "represented an effective decentralization of revenue from the union (the central government) to states and municipalities ... without any corresponding decentralization in functions to them. In other words, the union lost revenues, keeping the same functions."

Like the 1988 legal changes to the revenue-sharing scheme during the Alfonsín administration in Argentina, the balance of the federal equation after the 1988 constitutional reforms favored the governors: they got new funds and new taxes (increasing their resources, r_{jg}) without new functions to deliver (P_{ig}), and imposed large costs on the president, as he kept the same functions (P_{ip}) but the amount of funds and tax revenue in his hands decreased (r_{jp}). In other words, the gubernatorial net balance $[X = \Sigma(P_{ig} - r_{ig})]$ improved significantly, while the presidential net balance $[U = \Sigma(r_{jp} - P_{ip})]$ worsened dramatically during the same period. More formally, $X = \Sigma(P_{ig} - r_{ig}) > U = \Sigma(r_{jp} - P_{ip})$. Hence, governors altered the balance of the federal equation $[B = U - X]$ in their favor after the 1988 reforms (see Table 3.7).

The reactions from the central government

Before the 1988 constitutional reform, several analysts raised concerns over the fiscal and administrative weakness of subnational governments and the centralized features of the Brazilian federation in the post-transition to democracy. This situation changed radically after the 1988 reforms. Several economic advisors to the president who valued macroeconomic stabilization more than fiscal decentralization showed their concerns regarding the increase in funds to the states without new functions and controls. The Minister of Finance, Luis Carlos Bresser Pereira (April–December 1987), was among them. Before the constitutional reform, he declared that the proposal to decentralize funds to the states would bankrupt the central government in a short time (OESP 9/20/87, A-1, 5; quoted in Samuels, 2003b, 175). The Minister of Finance who replaced Bresser, Maílson da Nóbrega (1987–1990), coined a famous expression, also used by President Sarney. He argued that the new constitution made the country "ungovernable" (Couto, 1998, 15), claiming that "the 1988

Table 3.7 Synthesis of the reforms and impacts on the federal balance (1987–1989)

Period of reforms	Subnational revenue (in relative terms)	Subnational functions	Subnational tax authority	Federal balance
Sarney 1987–1989	Increased (revenue share increased from 18.6% in 1987 to 30% in 1989).	No substantial changes	Increased (expanded the tax base of the ICM, five federal taxes, on transport, energy, fuels, minerals, and communications, were transferred to the states to create the ICMS)	Favorable for states $X = \Sigma(P_{ig} - r_{ig}) > U = \Sigma(r_{jp} - P_{ip})$

constitution was the greatest fiscal disaster in our nation's history."[70] These reforms resulted, according to them, in a weaker federal government, more powerful subnational governments (which had strong incentives to spend their money), and a troublesome propensity toward severe fiscal deficits (Interview with Lourdes Sola, September 8, 2006).

After the fiscal reforms enacted through the 1988 constitution, states tried to maintain their substantial gains and preserve the status quo. The central government tried to do the opposite. Sarney, in a clear indication of the costs imposed on the central government, expressed his disapproval of the changes enacted during the constitutional assembly in terms of federal relations and worked to reverse some of them. During the negotiations of the 1989 budget (the first one after the promulgation of the constitution), president and governors clashed once again in relation to the way resources should be distributed. Sarney, in an attempt called *Operação Desmonte*, tried to diminish the participation of the central government in several programs and increase the responsibilities of subnational governments in relation to administrative functions. He also diminished discretionary transfers to the states and municipalities and compelled subnational governments to pay back their debts (Abrucio, 1998, 195; Lopreato, 2002, 112; Souza, 1997, 97). The president took a more aggressive stance due to the cost the status quo ante imposed upon the central government after the 1988 constitutional reform. The fiscal imbalances of the federal administration generated more incentives for Sarney to clash against the governors. States once again showed their capacity to coordinate against a relatively weak president. This time, coordination among states was defensive, as governors wanted to preserve the status quo ante against clashes from the president. This form of coordination proved to be quite effective at obstructing the centralizing attempts from the federal executive.

Near the end of his term, instead of trying to reduce fiscal transfers to the states (something that proved to be very difficult), Sarney sought to pass a reform in Congress that would shift functions and policy responsibilities to subnational governments. But Congress blocked these attempts in another indication of the power of governors. In sum, governors got a more favorable federal balance first, and after that, resisted reform attempts from the federal government to reverse some of their gains.

Final comments: the tragedy from the pares

From the accidental beginning of his term in office, President Sarney suffered severe political and fiscal pressures: on the political side, he had to deal with increasing decentralizing pressures from subnational officials, who were strengthened after the transition to democracy by the president's timid political support in Congress and a low level of legitimacy in public opinion. On the fiscal side, he faced a large inflationary crisis and a fiscal deficit of huge proportions, factors that generated strong fiscal pressures on him and the governors to alter the status quo. Despite these unfavorable conditions, Sarney was able to resist subnational pressures from 1985 until the negotiations during the constitutional convention in 1987–1988 (in a very similar situation to the one faced by Alfonsín between 1983 and 1987). In this arena, governors coordinated efficiently and the president was incapable of resisting their pressures. He had neither the political nor the fiscal resources to divide and weaken them.

I claim that when the president is weak and governors are powerful, when governors solve their collective action problems and coordinate, and when these actors are pressed by fiscal urgency and face hard budget constraints, changes in the federal balance favoring subnational governments are expected to occur. This chapter has tried to illuminate through historical details how these factors interacted to produce the expected outcome. Fiscal crises alone are not enough to explain reforms to the federal balance. Both Alfonsín and Sarney faced severe crises beginning the moment they took power. In this sense, the cutting point for fiscal incentives was crossed early on, during the transition. As this chapter has showed, it is the interaction between fiscal incentives and political strength that makes changes more likely.

Institutional rules alone cannot account for those changes either. Under almost the same federal and electoral institutions or party nomination procedures (Calvo and Abal Medina, 2001; Escobar-Lemmon, 2001; Garman et al., 2001; Haggard and Webb, 2004; Montero, 2001a, 2001b; Montero and Samuels, 2004; Penfold-Becerra, 2004a, 2004b; Samuels, 2000a, 2000b, 2003a, 2003b; Willis et al., 1999), presidents were able to resist centrifugal pressures, but they could not do that after a certain moment in time. When presidents lose political support from citizens and votes in elections, and when the fiscal conditions deteriorate to a point that presidents cannot provide selective incentives to governors (from public works, social programs, to discretionary transfers or federal bailouts), subnational officials begin to distance themselves from the president, as do federal legislators (that happened after the 1987 elections in Argentina and the 1986 ANC elections in Brazil). At these moments, governors were able to cross the threshold after which their power can be an influential factor in making changes to the federal balance. The theoretical explanation introduced in this work and the historical analysis presented here are more dynamic accounts of changes in the distribution of revenue under relatively stable or marginally changing institutional frameworks. These institutional variables are better at explaining comparative statics than profound and sharp processes of change within the cases.

This chapter also provides some evidence to answer the question of when presidents are likely to either centralize or decentralize revenue. During the period analyzed here, both presidents resisted the decision to decentralize revenue to the states (under fiscal crises, both of them preferred to centralize revenue). Subnational pressures, rather than presidents' electoral calculations (as claimed by O'Neil, 2003, 2005), were the key factor in explaining changes in the federal balance.

As a result of governors' power and coordination efforts as well as the impossibility of the president to resist them, the *pares* clashed against the *primus*, extracting resources, taxing powers, discretionary authority in the use of funds, and keeping few administrative functions to deliver. The balance of the federal equation ended up being quite favorable for the governors. But only in the short term. The tragedy of the commons analyzed for Alfonsín had its correlate during Sarney's term in office; what began as rational individual behavior (to extract as much revenue and taxing powers as possible from the central government) ended up generating profound aggregated imbalances (the over-grazing of the common pool resources) both for the central government as well as for most states.

Abrupt changes in the Argentine and Brazilian federal balance had implications beyond the distribution of fiscal revenue or administrative functions: they contributed to large fiscal imbalances, hyperinflationary crises, financial turmoil, social mobilization, and political instability (particularly severe in Argentina). The following presidents made use of this situation to negotiate changes in the federal balance with the governors. In the end, it took a profound economic crisis, a powerful president, and long negotiations to reverse the decentralizing reforms enacted during the last years of Sarney's and Alfonsín's terms in office.

Notes

1 *Primus inter pares* is a Latin expression that means "a first among equals." Applied to this work, the *primus* would be the president and the governors would be the equals. The Latin expression has been slightly revised in this chapter to mean "a first against equals" (*primus contra pares*).

2 Out of the federal pact, provinces and states retained some critical powers and delegated others to the central government. This distribution of powers has shaped negotiations among units. In most federations, the central government usually retains crucial prerogatives, such as the power to intervene on subnational governments under certain circumstances or to demand correspondence between subnational legislation and the federal constitution.

3 At the same time, governors found some devices of the revenue-sharing scheme attractive, especially in the short term. They received guaranteed transfers from the central government by law and delegated the costs of collecting resources to national authorities.

4 A very similar move was later on repeated in 1992 during the Menem administration (see Chapter 5).

5 This centralization process did not mean, in fact, that the president eliminated gubernatorial power. As Hagopian (1996, 37) claims, during the Estado Novo "regional oligarchic machines were undermined" but they did not disappear.

6 Since the 1935 law, following the 1947 and 1954 reforms (and the 1956 and 1957 amendments), the main criterion for the distribution among provinces was their population. In 1973, a redistributive factor, income per capita, was incorporated in the division of revenues among provinces. Revenue-sharing

transfers are crucial for most provinces, as they represent an average of 69 percent of all federal transfers (for the period 1983–2004), 42 percent of the total provincial tax revenue, and 35 percent of the total provincial revenues (the partial exception to this is the Federal Capital and to a lesser extent provinces from the more developed central region). The provinces of Formosa, La Rioja, Catamarca, Corrientes, Santiago del Estero, Jujuy, and Chaco received between 80 and 90 percent of their total revenue from federal transfers between 1983 and 2004.

7 The main sources for the fund are the income tax (IR) and the tax on industrial products (IPI), out of which states and municipalities received 20 percent (later modified to 21.5 percent) of the total of those taxes. These funds are distributed according to coefficients determined by the *Tribunal de Contas da União* (TCU), which are calculated according to the state population and the inverse of the state per capita income. In 1989, the National Council for Economic Policy (*Conselho Nacional de Política Fazendária*, or Confaz) established the coefficients for the regional distribution of the FPE: out of the total, 85 percent of the FPE is distributed to states from the North, Northeast, and Center-West regions, and 15 percent to the states of the South and Southeast. The FPE represents an average for the period 1995–2006 of 57 percent of all federal transfers, 27 percent of total states' tax revenue, and 25 of states' total revenue. While Roraima, Acre, and Amapá received more than 88 percent of their total tax revenue from the FPE, São Paulo, Rio de Janeiro, Rio Grande do Sul, and Minas Gerais got between 0.3 and 5 percent of their total tax revenue for the period 1995–2006. The FPE represents 0.5 percent of the total ICMS collected in São Paulo (2.8 percent in Rio de Janeiro).

8 Some of the most important are the revenues collected from gas taxes that are shared with the provinces and other revenues shared from specific taxes that are not included in the revenue-sharing regime (income tax, VAT, and the tax on property). On average, these other legally mandated transfers represent a bit more than a third of the total federal transfers (1983–2004). Bonvecchi and Lodola (2011, 189–191) call them "transfers with medium level of presidential discretionality."

9 In Brazil, other legally mandated transfers include the Compensation Fund for the Export of Industrialized Products (FPEX); the Basic Education Maintenance and Development Fund (FUNDEB); the Unified Health System (SUS); the *Contribuição de Intervenção no Domínio Econômico* (CIDE); the Rural Propriety Tax (ITR); and other minor funds. On average, other legally mandated transfers that are not allocated through the *fundos* represent around a third of the total federal transfers (1995–2006).

10 One percent of total revenue-sharing funds (Law 23,548), although later reforms increased this amount: since 1992, the ATNs fund received 2 percent from the income tax (Cetrángolo and Jiménez, 1997, 16). These are "transfers with high level of presidential discretionality" (for Bonvecchi and Lodola, 2011, 189–191).

11 ATNs represented an average of 11 percent of total revenue-sharing transfers for the period 1985–2004 (or 8 percent of the total fiscal transfers from the central government). After the 1988 revenue-sharing law (and until 2004), discretionary transfers represented an average of 1.28 percent of revenue-sharing transfers and 0.85 percent of the total fiscal transfers from the central government.

12 For the period 1997–2006, voluntary transfers represented an average of almost 2 percent of the FPE or 0.7 percent of all fiscal transfers from the central government.

13 The main federal taxes are the income tax (*impuesto a las ganancias*; representing 18 percent of total tax collection), on personal wealth, the VAT (the most

important tax, representing about one-third of total tax collection), and on foreign trade, fuels, and bank accounts.

14 The main provincial taxes are the gross income tax (*ingresos brutos*), property tax, and automobiles' tax. In addition, through revenue-sharing, provinces receive daily automatic transfers from the central government. Municipalities are in charge of those taxes granted by provincial constitutions and laws.

15 The union has exclusive authority over the income tax (*Imposto de Renda*, IR); on industrial products (IPI; which is a type of value-added tax); import (II) and export (IE); rural property (ITR); large fortunes (IGF); financial transactions (IOF); and social contributions, levied on payroll or turnover of enterprises (Bevilaqua, 2002, 5; Mora, 2002, 8). The IR and the IPI are shared with states through the FPE and municipalities through the FPM. The ITR is only shared with municipalities and the remaining taxes are not shared.

16 Brazilian states have exclusive authority over the value-added, communications, and transportation tax (ICMS). This is their main source of revenues, out of which states receive, on average, 30 percent of the total tax collection. The ICMS's contribution to states' budgets varies significantly across states. Other state taxes are the motor vehicles registration tax (IPVA); the inheritance and gifts tax (ITCMD and the ITBI); and the supplementary capital gain tax. States share part of the ICMS and the IPVA with municipalities.

17 The UCR controlled 129 seats out of 254 in the Lower Chamber (50.8 percent of the Chamber, a percentage that was kept after the 1985 legislative election), and 18 out of 46 in the Senate (39 percent), while Peronism controlled 111 seats and 21, respectively (43 and 46 percent).

18 The UCR was more united than the PJ; it had a single legislative delegation (*bloque legislativo*) in each chamber of Congress during the entire term in office, while the PJ had between four and six legislative blocks (Mustapic and Goretti, 1992, 254), reflecting divisions in the party after the 1983 elections. Among those factions, some were more collaborative and others diametrically opposed the president.

19 The UCR won only in seven provinces and provincial parties in three. Until the 1994 constitutional reform, provincial legislatures elected senators and, by controlling the majority of the governorships, the PJ was able to construct working majorities in the federal Senate.

20 For Mustapic (2005, 268–269), the average bill approval rate during the entire presidency was relatively large: 67.9 percent (404 out of 595 bills). For Calvo (2007, 271), the executive bill approval rate was close to 80 percent during Alfonsín's first year in office, but plummeted to less than 40 percent by 1988.

21 In this area, the PJ granted support only for 6 out of the 39 approved bills for the entire period (1983–1989), manifesting explicit opposition to 20 bills (Mustapic and Goretti, 1992, 266). These data say nothing about the bills for which the PJ did not offer quorum to begin deliberations, those that did not reach the floor, or those that were rejected. The figures only indicate that, among approved laws, those related to fiscal matters and taxes were very few, predominating conflictive relations with Peronism in this issue.

22 They score 2 on legislative powers (out of a maximum of 24), but we have to include decree powers (regulated by the 1994 constitution and specific laws). Since decrees are more restricted than in the Brazilian case (see the Sarney presidency in this chapter), they score as 3, reaching a total of 5. Argentine presidents score 12 on non-legislative powers (out of a maximum of 16).

23 Out of four categories: potentially dominant, proactive, reactive, and potentially marginal executives.

24 Those were very few DNUs compared to Menem's, who issued 336 (Ferreira Rubio and Goretti, 1996, 454–457).

25 In provinces with bicameral state assemblies, this percentage refers to the Chamber of Deputies. Only one-third of the states have a bicameral legislature nowadays (Buenos Aires, Catamarca, Corrientes, Entre Ríos, Mendoza, Salta, San Luis, and Santa Fe). Tucumán had a bicameral legislature until 1991 and Córdoba until 2001 (Almaraz, 2010, 202; Suárez-Cao, 2009, 18). During this period, 9 governors were elected with more than 50 percent of the vote and 18 governors, or more than 80 percent of them, controlled more than 50 percent of the state legislature. In two more cases, the provincial executive had 50 percent of the seats in the assembly, and only in four cases, governors had less than a majoritarian control over the state legislature.

26 See Chapter 2 for details on the index.

27 For instance, during 1984, the year in which the revenue-sharing law expired, Peronist governors from the Northern and river-coastal provinces tried to define a common strategy to demand new resources and administrative powers for the provinces. In February 1984, governors from the Northeastern provinces met with the Minister of Interior to find solutions to the fiscal imbalances in their provinces. In September of that year, governors and Ministers of Economy from the provinces ruled by Peronism voiced their concerns to the central government. Shortly thereafter, governors from the Patagonian provinces met with the Minister of Interior to demand new resources in order to pay for salaries (*Clarín*, January 5, 1984; *La Nación*, January 17 and February 25, 1984; quoted in Pírez, 1986a, 65). These meetings continued during the entire Alfonsín administration (see section on outcomes).

28 Several governors (from Córdoba, Chaco, Chubut, San Juan, San Luis, and Tierra del Fuego) introduced urgency clauses, which compel the legislature to decide on a bill in a certain amount of time (between 30 and 60 days). If the provincial legislature does not decide during this period of time, the bill is considered approved. Other governors (those from Chubut, Río Negro, Salta, and San Juan) have access to DNUs, as the federal executive does.

29 Reelection is banned in three provinces (Corrientes, Entre Ríos, and Mendoza). Catamarca, La Rioja, San Luis, and Santa Cruz allow their governors to run for reelection indefinitely. Sixteen provinces permit a one-term reelection only (Buenos Aires, Chaco, Chubut, Córdoba, Jujuy, La Pampa, Misiones, Neuquén, Río Negro, San Juan, Santa Fe, Santiago del Estero, Tierra del Fuego, and Tucumán) and Salta allows a two-term reelection.

30 De Luca *et al.* (2002, 424) argue that "Of the 33 times since 1983 that an incumbent governor (who had been elected) was eligible to seek immediate reelection, in all but four instances the governor ran. In 25 of these 29 elections, the incumbent was victorious."

31 E.g., San Luis under the Rodriguez Saá brothers, Santiago del Estero under Juárez, Catamarca under Saadi, Corrientes under Romero Feris, Santa Cruz under Kirchner, and Neuquén under Sobisch.

32 That is especially the case of Mendoza, Santa Fe, Buenos Aires, Córdoba, and Capital Federal (see Gervasoni, 2010; and Giraudy, 2015, 40).

33 GDP plummeted by more than 10 percent between 1979 and 1983, the largest decrease since the Great Depression. Net foreign debt jumped from $6.5 billion at the end of 1978 to $43.6 billion after the Southern Atlantic war, an increase of almost 700 percent. In January 1983, the fiscal deficit was 14 percent of the GDP, the deficit in the balance of payments reached $6.7 billion, and the annual inflation rate peaked from 101 to 343 percent between 1980 and 1983 (Gerchunoff and Llach, 1998, 392; Torre and de Riz, 1993, 347, 352–354).

34 The total provincial budget balance went from a AR$1 billion surplus in 1983 to a AR$4 billion deficit in 1984 and more than AR$6 billion deficit in 1988.

35 Provinces issued debt for almost 17 percent of their total revenues during
1983–1999.

36 The 1978 reform process conducted by the military, through which new functions were decentralized to the provinces without any increase in revenues,
generated strong fiscal pressures on provincial budgets and pushed governors
to increase their demands for funds.

37 The option decentralizing more functions without new resources to the provinces was practically not considered by federal authorities because of the high
expected costs this option generated, considering the critical fiscal situation of
subnational units and the fiscal imbalances provincial budgets suffered after
the 1978 decentralization reforms.

38 They reached this figure by taking into account previous revenue-sharing transfers (48.5 percent, according to law 20,221) and the costs of the new services
decentralized by the military in 1978 (8.16 percent).

39 Carlos Menem, at that time the Peronist governor of La Rioja, proposed that
interior provinces should rebel against the central authorities by cutting energy
supplies to the Federal Capital, blocking provincial ports, and retaking the
powers that the provinces delegated to the central government in the national
constitution (*El Bimestre* no. 20; quoted in Pírez, 1986a, 68).

40 Senator Francisco Villada (PJ-Salta), author of the bill he
introduced to the Senate, had its origin in this agreement between the president and governors (*DS-CSN*, June 26–27, 1985, 736–737).

41 Senator Juan Trilla (UCR-Capital Federal), president of the Budget Commission in the Senate, demanded

> this issue to be debated first in the Ministry of Economy—where it should
> be debated because this is a problem related to provincial financing—
> together with the governors. A posteriori, the president of the Republic
> will meet with the governors of each one of the provinces, extending the
> invitation to senators and deputies who deal with budget matters.
>
> (*DS-CSN*, June 26–27, 1985, 733–734)

42 Out of this agreement, governors would have received around 56 percent of
the revenue-sharing funds, equivalent to the annualization of the amount distributed during the second half of 1985 (*Clarín*, "El texto completo," March 11,
1986; *Clarín*, "Alfonsín juzgó histórico el acuerdo firmado con las provincias
por la coparticipación," March 12, 1986), or an increase of about 11 percent in
relation to the previous year.

43 The executive's approval ratings plummeted from a peak of 75 percent in
August 1985 to 36 percent one month before the 1987 election. Alfonsín left
office with an approval rate of 29 percent during April 1988 (data from Nueva
Mayoría).

44 During this period, the struggle between president and governors had a very
strong partisan dynamic (PJ governors opposing the UCR president), although
this had not always been the case. Several times governors coordinated across
partisan lines to oppose as well as support the president. The incentives they
face in the federal distributive game sometimes conflict with their partisan
links.

45 International and local credit markets were practically closed (or they
demanded astronomical interest rates), and debt service was unbearable for
the country (it paid $4 billion in interest during 1987, forcing a reduction of
monetary reserves by $1.1 billion) (Gerchunoff and Llach, 1998, 416).

46 Costs are also larger the more functions the governors seek to re-centralize
without new funds for the central government. This is a theoretical possibility,
which finds no empirical correlates in Argentina (nor in Brazil). One of the

reasons may be found in the history of both countries, as presidents centralized power during the period of consolidation of the central government, retaining several faculties that governors have historically demanded. Another reason can be found in their preferences: governors always want to have more funds and functions, so as to increase their political relevance in the federation. Having more functions is also a first step to claim more funds.

47 The two UCR governors, Eduardo Angeloz (Córdoba) and Horacio Massaccesi (Río Negro), faced the serious dilemma of supporting the bill and getting more transfers, but severely weakening the president from their party. In any case, their influence was not decisive at all in Congress and at that time they were already investing more political resources in getting the presidential bid in the UCR for the 1989 election (Angeloz got the presidential nomination from the party in 1989; Massaccesi got it in 1995).

48 The Argentine Constitution establishes that to override a presidential veto, both chambers need to insist on the original bill with a two-thirds majority of the members present at the moment of the vote.

49 All members in this commission supported the report, except Socialist deputy Estévez Boero (Santa Fe) (*DS-CDN*, December 22–23, 1987, 4838). This result was a clear consequence of a previous agreement between the president and the PJ governors.

50 Senator Romero Feris (PAC, Corrientes) declared that this agreement was crafted between the PJ and UCR without the participation of provincial parties. Senator Brasesco (UCR-Entre Ríos) referred to the agreement as an intra-party consensus, stressing how all the deputies from his province, Radicals and Peronists, supported the bill, despite their partisan differences (*DS-CSN*, January 7–8, 1988, 2385, 2409). Senator Aguirre Lanari (PAC-Corrientes) condemned the agreement between the UCR and the PJ, accusing the Senate of being a rubber stamp ("*un convidado de piedra*") of decisions taken between the president and the governors.

51 Buenos Aires received the largest share (1.5701 percent), while Chubut, Neuquén, and Santa Cruz received 0.1433 percent each.

52 The list of taxes included in the new revenue-sharing scheme between the national government and the provinces was extensive and varied, including the VAT, taxes on profits, excise taxes, taxes on fuels and lubricants, financial operations, and lotteries and sporting events, among many others (*DS-CSN*, January 7–8, 1988, 2378, 2383).

53 The allocation of those funds was left to the Ministry of Interior, who also had to inform the provinces, every three months, the amount that had been disbursed and the criteria used in the distribution.

54 As an indication of that, total provincial revenue diminished from almost AR$37 billion in 1987 to AR$27.9 billion in 1989 and total transfers from the federal government from AR$19 to AR$16 billion, both in this three-year period (constant 2004 prices). Discretionary transfers suffered the sharpest reduction; they went from a peak of almost AR$9 billion in 1987 to AR$1 billion in 1988 and AR$188 million in 1989. This cut was the consequence of the limits imposed by the new law, and, to a lesser extent, of lower tax collection. These changes represented an important limit on the prerogatives of the president to distribute transfers to the provinces.

55 The central government increased the income tax's rates, guaranteeing that this new revenue would be returned to taxpayers after two years. The "mandatory savings" regime ended in 2001, 13 years later (*Clarín*, "Impuesto a las Ganancias: Alpiste, Perdiste," July 26, 2001).

56 Presidential popularity during Sarney's term oscillated between a 57 and a 58 percent negative rating in 1988 (the first year in the data series available).

In 1989, average presidential popularity was negative 58.75 percent and in 1990, negative 52 percent (DataFolha 1988–2001; Lucio Rennó kindly shared these data).

57 Nine of Sarney's MPs were rejected, 11 of Collor's, none of Franco's, and only one of Cardoso's during his first presidency (Negretto, 2002, 388).

58 Amapá and Roraima have been states since 1988; Tocantins since 1989; and the Distrito Federal elected governors beginning in 1991. Seventeen governors, or 74 percent of them, were elected with more than 50 percent of the vote. Of the other six governors, five were elected with more than 47 percent of the vote, and only one with about 40 percent.

59 Ten governors, or more than 45 percent of all the state executives from the PMDB, controlled 50 percent or more of the seats in the state assembly, while six governors were backed by the holders of 45 percent or more of the seats. Only in Piauí and Alagoas do the two PMDB governors (Alberto Silva and Fernando Collor de Mello) have to work with a PFL-dominated assembly.

60 Data from IBGE and COREM are reported in these units.

61 No significant changes in the federal balance were passed between 1985 and 1986 mainly due to the inability of both the president and governors to gather enough political support to pass reforms favorable to them.

62 The remaining 120 seats were distributed among 11 parties, none of which won more than the 37 seats (6.6 percent) the PDS got (Mainwaring and Pérez Liñán, 1997, 457).

63 In particular, the more developed states, especially São Paulo, demanded more tax authority, whereas those from the less developed regions, such as the North and Northeast, pressed for more fiscal transfers from the federal government.

64 The fact that 22 governors were from the same party, the PMDB, and that the president was from another party (although the PMDB and the PFL ran as allies in the presidential election and that discipline inside the PMDB was very low) made partisan coordination an important mechanism for political cooperation among subnational actors. That was especially the case when the president was not able to deliver to governors.

65 On March 22, 1988, the ANC approved the presidential form of government against the parliamentary proposal by 344 votes to 212 (with three abstentions) and the five-year presidential term for Sarney by 304 to 223. Using all of his resources, Sarney was able to marshal enough votes to get these reforms (Lamounier, 1990, 23).

66 No member of the federal administration played an active role in defending the interests of the central government. For Souza, José Serra (a well-known economist from São Paulo's PSDB), rapporteur of the Committee on Tax System, Budget and Finance, was the "most visible but solitary figure in defending the federal government" against subnational pressures for more resources and autonomy. During the debates, Serra claimed that

> it is well known that in the past the federal government enjoyed an excessive concentration of revenues and of tax collection, thus bringing an imbalance in the federation. The constitution will correct this mistake, but it would be another mistake to maintain such an imbalance with changed signs.
>
> (Souza, 1997, 79–80)

67 Total state revenues represented 34 percent of total federal revenues in 1985, and those values were relatively stable until 1988; in 1989, they reached 43 percent. As a percentage of total public sector revenues (including federal, state, and municipal levels), total state revenues increased from 24 percent in 1987 and 1988 to 28 percent in 1989. Legally mandated transfers represented

22 percent of total state tax revenue in 1986, increasing to more than 29 percent in 1989 and 31 percent in 1990. These transfers from the federal government represented 13 percent of total state spending in 1986, increasing to 16 percent in 1989 and 18 percent in 1990.

68 Including two-thirds of the federal fund for education (FUNDEF), the income tax deducted from state and local public servants, and royalties for the exploitation of oil, hydro-electricity, and gas (Souza, 1997, 41, 85).

69 Besides, states were conferred the power (which they did not have before) to set the rates of their ICMS. The ICMS turned into the largest tax in Brazil, representing 26 percent of the revenues collected by all taxes combined in 1990 (Dain, 1992, 43).

70 See Veja, "A ilusão sobre a reforma tributária," August 12, 2009; Revista Bobespa, "Instituições fortes dão base a qualquer governo," January–March, 2006.

References

Abrucio, Fernando Luis, *Os Barões da Federação: Os Governadores e a Redemocratização Brasileira* (São Paulo: Coleção Comentário, USP, 1998).

Acuña, Carlos, "Politics and Economics in the Argentina of the Nineties (Or, Why the Future No Longer is What It Used to Be)"; in: Smith, William C., Carlos H. Acuña, and Eduardo A. Gamarra (eds.), *Democracy, Markets, and Structural Reform in Latin America* (Miami: North–South Center and Boulder, CO: Lynne Rienner, 1994).

Almaraz, María Gabriela, "Ambición Política por la Reelección en las Provincias Argentinas," *Revista SAAP*, Vol. 4, No. 2, 2010, pp. 191–226.

Almeida, Fernanda, *Competências na Constituição de 1988* (São Paulo: Editora Atlas, 1991).

Baer, Werner, *A Economia Brasileira* (São Paulo: Nobel, 1996).

Bevilaqua, Afonso, "State Government Bailouts in Brazil," Texto para Discussão No. 421, Departamento de Economía PUC-Rio, 2000.

Bevilaqua, Afonso, "State Government Bailouts in Brazil," Research Network Working Paper R-441, Inter-American Development Bank, 2002.

Bonvecchi, Alejandro, and Germán Lodola, "The Dual Logic of Intergovernmental Transfers: Presidents, Governors, and the Politics of Coalition-Building in Argentina," *Publius: The Journal of Federalism*, Vol. 41, No. 2, 2011, pp. 179–206.

Brady, Henry, and David Collier, eds., *Rethinking Social Inquiry: Diverse Tools, Shared Standards* (Lanham, MD: Rowman and Littlefield, 2004).

Brasileiro, Ana Maria, "O Federalismo Cooperativo," *Revista Brasileira de Estudos Políticos*, No. 39 (Belo Horizonte: UFMG, 1974), pp. 83–138.

Burgin, Miron, *Aspectos Económicos del Federalismo Argentino* (Buenos Aires: Ediciones Solar, 1975).

Calvo, Ernesto, "The Responsive Legislature: Public Opinion and Law Making in a Highly Disciplined Legislature," *British Journal of Political Science*, Vol. 37, No. 2, 2007, pp. 263–280.

Calvo, Ernesto, and Juan Manuel Abal Medina, eds., *El Federalismo Electoral Argentino: Sobrerrepresentación, Reforma Política y Gobierno Dividido en la Argentina* (Buenos Aires: EUDEBA, 2001).

Carvalho, José Murilho de, "Federalismo y Centralización en el Imperio Brasileño: Historia y Argumento"; in: Carmagnani, Marcello (ed.), *Federalismos Latinoamericanos: México/Brasil/Argentina* (México: Fondo de Cultura Económica, 1993).

Carvalho, José Murilho de, "El Federalismo Brasileño: Perspectiva Histórica"; in: Hernández Chávez, Alicia (ed.), *Hacia un Nuevo Federalismo?* (Mexico: Fondo de Cultura Económica, 1996).

Cetrángolo, Oscar, and Juan Pedro Jiménez, "Aportes del Tesoro Nacional. Discrecionalidad en la Relación Financiera entre la Nación y las Provincias," *Serie de Estudios* No. 21, Centro de Estudios para el Cambio Estructural, 1997.

Coppedge, Michael, *Democratization and Research Methods* (Cambridge: Cambridge University Press, 2012).

Corbacho, Alejandro L., "Reformas constitucionales y modelos de decisión en la democracia argentina, 1984–1994," *Desarrollo Económico*, Vol. 37, No. 148, 1998, pp. 591–616.

Couto, Cláudio Gonçalves, "A Longa Constituinte: Reforma do Estado e Fluidez Institucional no Brasil," *Dados*, Vol. 41, No. 1, 1998.

Dahl, Robert, "Federalism and the Democratic Process"; in: Dahl, Robert, *Democracy, Identity, and Equality* (Oslo: Norwegian University Press, 1986).

Dain, Sulamis, "Impasses de uma Reforma Tributária em Tempos de Crise," in Velosso, João Paulo dos Reis (ed.), *Combate à Inflação e Reforma Fiscal* (Rio de Janeiro: José Olympio, 1992).

De Luca, Miguel, Mark P. Jones, and María Inés Tula, "Back Rooms or Ballot Boxes?: Candidate Nomination in Argentina," *Comparative Political Studies*, Vol. 35, No. 4, 2002, pp. 413–436.

De Oliveira Torres, João Camilo, *A Formação do Federalismo no Brasil*, (São Paulo: Companhia Editora Nacional, 1961).

De Souza, Amaury, "Cardoso and the Struggle for Reform in Brazil," *Journal of Democracy*, Vol. 10, No. 3, 1999, pp. 49–63.

Diario de Sesiones de la Cámara de Diputados de la Nación (DS-CDN), July 3, 1985.

Diario de Sesiones de la Cámara de Diputados de la Nación (DS-CDN), December 22–23, 1987.

Diario de Sesiones de la Cámara de Senadores de la Nación (DS-CSN), June 26–27, 1985.

Diario de Sesiones de la Cámara de Senadores de la Nación (DS-CSN), January 7–8, 1988.

Eaton, Kent, *Politicians and Economic Reform in New Democracies: Argentina and the Philippines in the 1990s* (University Park, PA: Penn State University Press, 2002).

Eaton, Kent, *Politics Beyond the Capital: The Design of Subnational Institutions in South America* (Stanford: Stanford University Press, 2004).

ECLAC-CEPAL (Comisión Económica para América Latina y el Caribe), *Economic Survey of Latin America and the Caribbean, 1996–1997* (Santiago de Chile: CEPAL, 1997).

Escobar-Lemmon, Maria, "Fiscal Decentralization and Federalism in Latin America," *Publius: The Journal of Federalism*, Vol. 31, No. 4, 2001, pp. 23–41.

Ferreira Rubio, Delia, and Matteo Goretti, "Cuando el Presidente Gobierna Solo. Menem y los Decretos de Necesidad y Urgencia hasta la Reforma Constitucional (julio 1989–agosto 1994)," *Desarrollo Económico*, Vol. 36, No. 141, 1996, pp. 443–474.

FIEL (Fundación de Investigaciones Económicas Latinoamericanas), *Hacia una Nueva Organización del Federalismo Fiscal en la Argentina* (Buenos Aires: Ediciones Latinoamericanas, 1993).

160   Pares contra primus

Garman, Christopher, Stephan Haggard, and Eliza Willis, "Fiscal Decentralization, a Political Theory with Latin American Cases," *World Politics*, Vol. 53, No. 2, 2001, pp. 205–236.

George, Alexander, and Andrew Bennett, *Case Studies and Theory Development in the Social Sciences* (Cambridge: BCSIA Studies in International Security-Harvard University, 2004).

Gerchunoff, Pablo, and Lucas Llach, *El Ciclo de la Ilusión y el Desencanto. Un Siglo de Políticas Económicas Argentinas* (Buenos Aires: Ariel, 1998).

Gervasoni, Carlos, "Measuring Variance in Subnational Regimes: Results from an Expert-Based Operationalization of Democracy in the Argentine Provinces," *Journal of Politics in Latin America*, Vol. 2, No. 2, 2010, pp. 13–52.

Giambiagi, Fábio, "Impasse Distributivo e Paralisia Fiscal—Reflexão Acerca da Crise do Setor Público," *Planejamento e Políticas Públicas*, No. 6 (Brasília: IPEA, 1991).

Giambiagi, Fábio, and Ana Claudia Duarte Além, *Finanças Públicas: Teoria e Prática no Brasil* (Rio de Janeiro: Campus, 1999).

Gibson, Edward L., and Tulia Falleti, "Unity by the Stick: Regional Conflict and the Origins of Argentine Federalism"; in: Gibson, Edward L. (ed.), *Federalism and Democracy in Latin America* (Baltimore: Johns Hopkins University Press, 2004).

Giraudy, Agustina, *Democrats and Autocrats: Pathways of Subnational Undemocratic Regime Continuity within Democratic Countries* (Oxford: Oxford University Press, 2015).

Graham, Richard, *Patronage and Politics in Nineteenth-Century Brazil* (Stanford: Stanford University Press, 1990).

Haggard, Stephan, and Steven Webb, "Political Incentives and Intergovernmental Fiscal Relations: Argentina, Brazil, and Mexico Compared"; in: Montero, Alfred P. and David J. Samuels (eds.), *Decentralization and Democracy in Latin America* (Notre Dame, IN: University of Notre Dame Press, 2004).

Hagopian, Frances, *Traditional Politics and Regime Change in Brazil* (Cambridge: Cambridge University Press, 1996).

Hardin, Garrett, "The Tragedy of the Commons," *Science*, Vol. 162, No. 3859, 1968, pp. 1243–1248.

IMF (International Monetary Fund), *Government Finance Statistics* (GFS), 2001.

Jones, Mark, "Explaining the High Level of Party Discipline in the Argentine Congress"; in: Morgenstern, Scott and Benito Nacif (eds.), *Legislative Politics in Latin America* (New York: Cambridge University Press, 2002).

Kinzo, Maria D'Alva, "O Quadro Partidario e a Constituinte"; in: Lamounier, Bolívar (ed.), *De Geisel a Collor: O Balanço da Transição* (São Paulo: Editora Sumaré, 1990).

Kugelmas, Eduardo, "A Evolução Recente do Regime Federativo no Brasil"; in: Hofmeister, Wilhelm and José Mario Brasiliense Carneiro (eds.), *Federalismo na Alemania e no Brasil* (São Paulo: Konrad Adenauer Stiftung, 2001).

Kugelmas, Eduardo, Brasilio Salum Jr., and Eduardo Graeff, "Conflito Federativo e Transição Política," *São Paulo em Perspectiva*, Vol. 3, No. 3, 1989, pp. 95–102.

Lamounier, Bolivar, *De Geisel a Collor: O Balanço da Transição* (São Paulo: Editora Sumaré, 1990).

Lijphart, Arend, *Patterns of Democracy: Government Forms and Performance in Thirty-Six Countries* (New Haven: Yale University Press, 1999).

Llanos, Mariana, "Understanding Presidential Power in Argentina: A Study of the Policy of Privatisation in the 1990s," *Journal of Latin American Studies*, Vol. 33, No. 1, 2001, pp. 67–99.

Lopreato, Francisco Luiz, *O Colapso das Finanças Estaduais e a Crise da Federação* (São Paulo: Editora UNESP-IE Unicamp, 2002).

Mainwaring, Scott, "Multipartism, Robust Federalism, and Presidentialism in Brazil"; in Mainwaring, Scott and Matthew Shugart, *Presidentialism and Democracy in Latin America* (Cambridge: Cambridge University Press, 1997).

Mainwaring, Scott, *Rethinking Party Systems in the Third Wave of Democratization: The Case of Brazil* (Stanford: Stanford University Press, 1999).

Mainwaring, Scott, and Aníbal Pérez Liñán, "Party Discipline in the Brazilian Constitutional Congress," *Legislative Studies Quarterly*, Vol. 22, No. 4, 1997, pp. 453–483.

Mainwaring, Scott, and Matthew Shugart, *Presidentialism and Democracy in Latin America* (Cambridge: Cambridge University Press, 1997).

Melo, Marcus André, *As Reformas Constitucionais no Brasil: Instituições Políticas e Processo Decisório* (Rio de Janeiro: Editora Revan, 2002).

Ministerio de Economía de la Nación, Dirección Nacional de Gastos Sociales, 2000; in Porto, Alberto, "Tamaño y Estructura del Sector Publico Argentino. Visión de Largo Plazo y Comparación," *Documento de Federalismo Fiscal*, No. 1, Universidad Nacional de La Plata, Facultad de Ciencias Económicas, 2003.

Montero, Alfred P., "Devolving Democracy? Political Decentralization and the New Brazilian Federalism"; in: Kingstone, Peter and Timothy Power (eds.), *Democratic Brazil. Actors, Institutions and Processes* (Pittsburgh: University of Pittsburgh Press, 2000).

Montero, Alfred P., "After Decentralization: Patterns of Intergovernmental Conflict in Argentina, Brazil, Mexico, and Spain," *Publius: The Journal of Federalism*, Vol. 31, No. 4, Fall 2001a, pp. 43–64.

Montero, Alfred P., "Decentralizing Democracy: Spain and Brazil in Comparative Perspective," *Comparative Politics*, Vol. 33, No. 2, 2001b, pp. 149–169.

Montero, Alfred P., and David J. Samuels, "The Political Determinants of Decentralization in Latin America: Causes and Consequences"; in: Montero, Alfred P. and David J. Samuels (eds.), *Decentralization and Democracy in Latin America* (Notre Dame, IN: University of Notre Dame Press, 2004).

Mora, Mônica, "Federalismo e Dívida Estadual no Brasil," Texto para Discussão No. 866, IPEA, Rio de Janeiro, 2002.

Mora, Mônica, and Ricardo Varsano, "Fiscal Decentralization and Subnational Fiscal Autonomy in Brazil: Some Facts of the Nineties," *Texto para Discusão*, No. 854, Rio de Janeiro: Instituto de Pesquisa Econômica Aplicada, 2001.

Moura, Alkimar, "Stabilisation Policy as a Game of Mutual Distrust: The Brazilian Experience in Post-1985 Civilian Governments"; in: D'Alva Kinzo, Maria (ed.), *Brazil: The Challenges of the 1990s* (London: The Institute of Latin American Studies, University of London and British Academic Press, 1993).

Mustapic, Ana María, "Oficialistas y Diputados: las Relaciones Ejecutivo-Legislativo en la Argentina," *Desarrollo Económico*, Vol. 39, No. 156, 2000, pp. 571–595.

Mustapic, Ana María, "Inestabilidad sin Colapso. La Renuncia de los Presidentes: Argentina en el Año 2001," *Desarrollo Económico*, Vol. 45, No. 178, 2005, pp. 263–280.

Mustapic, Ana María, and Matteo Goretti, "Gobierno y Oposición en el Congreso: La Práctica de la Cohabitación durante la Presidencia de Alfonsín (1983–1989)," *Desarrollo Económico*, Vol. 32, No. 126, 1992, pp. 251–269.

Negretto, Gabriel, "¿Gobierna solo el Presidente? Poderes de Decreto y Diseño Institucional en Brasil y Argentina," *Desarrollo Económico*, Vol. 42, No. 167, 2002, pp. 377–404.

Nino, Carlos, "Hyperpresidentialism and Constitutional Reform in Argentina"; in: Lijphart, Arendt and Carlos Waisman (eds.), *Institutional Design in New Democracies: Eastern Europe and Latin America* (Boulder, CO: Westview Press, 1996).

Nunes Leal, Victor, *Coronelismo Enxada e Voto: o Município e o Regime Representativo no Brasil* (Rio de Janeiro: Editora Nova Fronteira, 1997, 3rd ed.).

O'Donnell, Guillermo, *Democracy, Agency, and the State: Theory with Comparative Intent* (Oxford: Oxford University Press, 2010).

O'Donnell, Guillermo, and Philippe Schmitter, *Transitions from Authoritarian Rule: Tentative Conclusions on Uncertain Democracies* (Baltimore: Johns Hopkins University Press, 1986).

O'Neill, Kathleen, "Decentralization as an Electoral Strategy," *Comparative Political Studies*, Vol. 36, No. 9, 2003, pp. 1068–1091.

O'Neill, Kathleen, *Decentralizing the State: Elections, Parties, and Local Power in the Andes* (Cambridge: Cambridge University Press, 2005).

Ostrom, Elinor, "Coping with Tragedies of the Commons," *Annual Review of Political Science*, Vol. 2, No. 1, 1999, pp. 493–535.

Penfold-Becerra, Michael, "Federalism and Institutional Change in Venezuela"; in: Gibson, Edward L. (ed.), *Federalism and Democracy in Latin America*, (Baltimore: Johns Hopkins University Press, 2004a), pp. 197–205.

Penfold-Becerra, Michael, "Electoral Dynamics and Decentralization in Venezuela"; in: Montero, Alfred P. and David J. Samuels (eds.), *Decentralization and Democracy in Latin America* (Notre Dame, IN: University of Notre Dame Press, 2004b).

Pereira, André Ricardo, "Sob a Ótica da Delegação, Governadores e Assembléias no Brasil pós-1989"; in: Santos, Fabiano (ed.), *O Poder Legislativo nos Estados: Diversidade e Convergência* (São Paulo: FGV Editora, 2001).

Pírez, Pedro, *Coparticipación Federal y Descentralización del Estado* (Buenos Aires: Centro Editor de América Latina, 1986a).

Pírez, Pedro, *La Coparticipación y Descentralización del Estado Nacional, Revista Mexicana de Sociología*, Vol. 48, No. 4, 1986b, pp. 175–224.

Porto, Alberto, "Etapas de la Coparticipación Federal de Impuestos," *Documento de Federalismo Fiscal* No. 2 (La Plata: Universidad Nacional de La Plata, 2003).

Power, Timothy, "The Pen Is Mightier than the Congress: Presidential Decree Power in Brazil"; in: Carey, John M. and Matthew Soberg Shugart (eds.), *Executive Decree Authority* (Cambridge: Cambridge University Press, 1998), pp. 197–230.

Prado, Sérgio, "Distribução Intergovernamental de Recursos na Federação Brasileira"; in Rezende, Fernando and Augusto de Oliveira (eds.), *Decentralização e Federalismo Fiscal no Brasil* (Rio de Janeiro: Fundação Konrad Adenauer, 2003).

Przeworski, Adam, *Democracy and the Market: Political and Economic Reforms in Eastern Europe and Latin America* (Cambridge: Cambridge University Press, 1991).

Przeworski, Adam, and Henry Teune, *The Logic of Comparative Social Inquiry* (New York: Wiley Interscience, 1970).

Reich, Gary, "The 1988 Constitution a Decade Later: Ugly Compromises Reconsidered," *Journal of Interamerican Studies and World Affairs*, Vol. 40, No. 4, 1998, pp. 5–24.

Rezende, Fernando, "Decentralização e Eficiência: A Tomada de Decisões para o Desenvolvimento sob a Constituição de 1988"; in: Programa das Nações Unidas para o Desenvolvimento (ed.), *Políticas de Desenvolvimento para a Década de Noventa* (Brasília: PNUD, 1990), pp. 141–167.

Rezende, Fernando, "Compensações Financeiras e Desequilibrios Fiscais na Federação Brasileira"; in: Hofmeister, Wilhelm and José Mario Brasiliense Carneiro (eds.), *Federalismo na Alemania e no Brasil* (São Paulo: Konrad Adenauer Stiftung, 2001).

Rock, David, *Argentina, 1516–1987: From Spanish Colonization to Alfonsín* (Berkeley and Los Angeles: University of California Press, 1987).

Samuels, David, "Concurrent Elections, Discordant Results: Presidentialism, Federalism, and Governance in Brazil," *Comparative Politics*, Vol. 33, No. 1, 2000a, pp. 1–20.

Samuels, David, "The Gubernatorial Coattails Effect: Federalism and Congressional Elections in Brazil," *Journal of Politics*, Vol. 62, No. 1, 2000b, pp. 240–254.

Samuels, David, "Fiscal Straitjacket: The Politics of Macroeconomic Reform in Brazil, 1995–2002," *Journal of Latin American Studies*, Vol. 35, No. 3, 2003a, pp. 545–569.

Samuels, David, *Ambition, Federalism, and Legislative Politics in Brazil* (Cambridge: Cambridge University Press, 2003b).

Santos, Fabiano, "Democracia e Poder Legislativo no Brasil e na Argentina"; in Lladós, José María and Samuel Pinheiro Guimaraes (eds.), *Perspectivas Brasil y Argentina* (Brasília: IPRI-CARI, 1999).

Santos, Fabiano, ed., *O Poder Legislativo nos Estados: Diversidade e Convergência* (São Paulo: FGV Editora, 2001).

Serra, José, and José Roberto Rodrigues Afonso, "O Federalismo Fiscal a Brasileira: Algumas Reflexões," paper presented at the "Forum of Federations: An International Conference on Federalism," Mont-Tremblant, Canada, October 6–8, 1999.

Shugart, Matthew, and John Carey, *Presidents and Assemblies: Constitutional Design and Electoral Dynamics* (Cambridge: Cambridge University Press, 1992).

Silva, Golbery do Couto e, *Conjuntura Política Nacional. O Poder Executivo e Geopolítica do Brasil* (Brasília: Editora da UnB, 1981).

Souza, Celina, "Redemocratisation and Decentralisation in Brazil: The Strength of the Member States," *Development and Change*, Vol. 27, No. 3, 1996, pp. 529–555.

Souza, Celina, *Constitutional Engineering in Brazil: The Politics of Federalism and Decentralisation* (London: Macmillan, 1997).

Stepan, Alfred, *Democratizing Brazil: Problems of Transition and Consolidation* (Oxford and New York: Oxford University Press, 1989).

Suárez Cao, Julieta, "Las transformaciones del sistema nacional de partidos. Una visión federalista sobre la competencia partidaria en la Argentina," paper delivered at the conference on "Political Federalism and Fiscal Federalism. Argentina's Inter-governmental Relations in Comparative Perspective," Universidad Católica de Córdoba, Córdoba, June 19, 2009.

Torre, Juan Carlos and Liliana de Riz, "Argentina since 1946"; in: Bethell, Leslie (ed.), *Argentina since Independence* (Cambridge: Cambridge University Press, 1993).

Willis, Eliza, Christopher da C.B. Garman, and Stephan Haggard, "The Politics of Decentralization in Latin America," *Latin American Research Review*, Vol. 34, No. 1, 1999, pp. 7–56.

World Bank, *Argentina: Provincial Government Finances*, World Bank Country Study PUB8176 (Washington, DC: World Bank, 1990).

4 *Primus inter pares*

Introduction

I explored the dynamics of the federal distributive game in the presidencies immediately following the transition to democracy in Argentina and Brazil. This chapter applies the game-theoretical model to the presidencies of Fernando Collor de Mello and Itamar Franco in Brazil. These two administrations had to deal with the reforms to the federal balance introduced during the 1987–1988 constitutional assembly. Several scholars, analysts, and politicians have claimed that one of the several causes of the economic turmoil in this period, and the subsequent political instability, was the subnational pressures on the federal budget generated by these reforms. In the following sections, I analyze the distribution of political power in the federation and the fiscal context the actors faced. Having characterized the setting of the federal distributive game, I analyze the tensions between the need to reverse some decentralizing reforms, a crucial goal the president sought, and the need to preserve the status quo, the governors' main strategy.

Most institutional accounts (especially Abrucio, 1994, 1998; Abrucio and Samuels, 1997; Ames, 1995, 2001; Garman *et al.*, 2001; Mainwaring, 1995, 1997, 1999; Samuels, 2000a, 2000b, 2003a, 2003b; Samuels and Mainwaring, 2004; Willis *et al.*, 1999) would have expected governors to be favored in the Brazilian institutional setting during this particular period in time (due to the federal structure, open-list proportional representation rules, subnationally controlled nomination procedures inside parties, regionally based campaigns, governors' influence over the distribution of patronage, and high fragmentation of the party system). A remarkable outcome during this period is that, in spite of these centrifugal institutional configurations, governors could not get a more favorable federal balance. Deadlock prevailed over changes in it. Even more counterintuitive to these arguments is that, after a period of reforms that favored subnational actors (the 1988 constitutional reform), President Franco could halt and slightly reverse a reform process favoring subnational governments. In line with this, another group of scholars would have claimed that presidents have other institutional resources, such as agenda control and decree power, to influence negotiations with Congress (Cheibub and Limongi, 2002; Figueiredo and Limongi, 1995, 1997, 2000). Out of these specific institutional rules, and not because of broad institutional configurations (such as the electoral and federal frameworks), presidents would be favored in their struggles with governors. However, these formal rules cannot explain the diverse outcomes (deadlock and re-centralization) of the federal distributive game after the 1988 constitutional reform (many of these institutional changes were implemented at that time). The argument presented in Chapter 1 is a more dynamic and integrated account of changes in the federal balance. Historical analysts get into detailed arguments to explain why deadlock and, later on, presidents prevailed over governors. This chapter is historically rooted but applies a theoretical argument to give light to the historical details. It also integrates explanations for both centralizing and decentralizing reforms.

The main argument in this chapter is that the distribution of political power did not favor either the president or the governors. Neither side could concentrate enough political capital and use it to pass substantial reforms. Hence, and despite the strong fiscal incentives to reform the status quo the president faced (and less so the governors), deadlock prevailed for most of the time during this period. Despite this outcome, I also analyze why and how President Franco could slightly reverse the reforms favoring subnational governments. Fiscal imbalances, political crisis, and the outcomes of the federal balance during this period notably influenced the setting of the federal distributive game in the next round of interactions, generating conditions and preparing actors for a profound reforms process. Before analyzing these outcomes, we need to understand how the conditions for reform were made available. This is the main goal of this chapter.

The Collor (1990–1992) and the Franco (1992–1994) administrations

The historical context of the 1989 election

The election of Fernando Collor de Mello, the first direct presidential election in 29 years, marked the high point of the party system's political volatility and the low point of the political system's legitimacy (Mainwaring, 1999, 104; Panizza, 2000, 180; Weyland, 1993, 7). Economic deterioration (after Sarney's failed attempts to stabilize the economy), and a deep erosion in public confidence in the political system characterized the 1989 presidential campaign. Collor made use of this situation. He was a young, charismatic politician from a traditional family in the Northeast and former governor of the small state of Alagoas between 1987 and 1990. He had very few connections to the national political elite and ran as an outsider to the old political system, supported by an ephemeral party structure, the PRN (Party of National Reconstruction), created for the 1989 electoral contest. His campaign was "antiparty and antipolitician" (Mainwaring, 1999, 104), blaming the old political elites and traditional parties for the country's misfortunes. He promised a break from the past in order to combat inflation, fight corruption, downsize the state, reduce poverty, and resume growth.

In the following sections, I analyze the characteristics of the key independent variables (presidential and gubernatorial power and the fiscal context) during the Collor presidency. Then, I put forward the theoretical expectations from the model and study the dynamics of the federal game over the distribution of resources and functions as well as the outcomes in terms of the federal balance during the Collor presidency. I repeat the same structure to analyze the interim presidency of Itamar Franco.

The power of the president

Although supported by 35 million votes (out of a total of 82 million), Collor was far from being a powerful president. He lacked support in Congress and in the state governorships, as well as a solid and disciplined party structure. In the first election round, Collor got 28.5 percent of the votes. Luis Inácio "Lula" da Silva, the leader of the Worker's Party (PT), came in second (with 16.1 percent), and Leonel Brizola (PDT) was third with 15.5 percent. The candidates of the two main historical parties, associated with the Sarney government, received only 5.2 percent of the votes. In the second round, Collor won 53 percent of the votes, while Lula received 47. The former governor of Alagoas capitalized on middle-class fear of Lula's leftist discourse and was backed by the mass media, in particular the giant TV Globo network.

Upon taking office, Collor enjoyed much public support. In April 1990, less than one month after acceding to the presidency (he did that on March 5), 67 percent of the population found him to be a popular president (DataFolha, 1988–2001). Winning the election and being a popular president did not mean, however, that he was able to count on a majority in Congress; on the contrary, his party had a small delegation in both the Chamber of Deputies and the Senate. To make matters worse, the October 1990 Congressional and gubernatorial elections took place at a moment in which the Collor administration faced early difficulties in office and struggled to restore economic stability (Mainwaring, 1999, 106). Collor's popularity plummeted from 67 percent in April 1990 to 9.83 in October (the election month; it fell further to 1.5 by December of that year) (DataFolha 1988–2001). During this Congressional election, the PMDB and PFL remained the two largest parties.[1] No other party received more than 10 percent of the seats in the Chamber of Deputies, and a total of 19 parties won seats in it. This high degree of fragmentation was matched in only a few democracies (Mainwaring, 1999, 106).

Collor counted on the support from his own party, the PRN, which controlled less than 10 percent of the seats in the Chamber of Deputies and in the Senate, and other parties that formed part of his coalition in Congress. Collor was supported by a "minority coalition" (*coalizão minoritária*, in Figueiredo's (2006, 7) terms), which averaged 37 percent of the seats in the Chamber of Deputies for his term and never surpassed 43 percent. In addition, this coalition had the lowest discipline rate in the post-transition period: 69.2 percent between February 1991 and April 1992 (Figueiredo, 2006, 13).

According to Weyland (1993, 4), "[n]either during his political rise nor his time in office did Collor create a firm base of support. Even his conservative allies, such as the clientelist *Partido da Frente Liberal* (PFL), distrusted him as unpredictable and dangerous and backed him only with reservations." Besides not having a strong support base, Collor faced very strong opponents. Among them were members of the PMDB and the PT.[2]

As a consequence of the limited partisan power and the opposition he faced in Congress (as well as his own leadership style), Collor tried to rule by decree (through *medidas provisórias*, MPs), circumventing Congress. Sarney issued 147 MPs in the 525 days that he served under the new constitution, a rate of about one every four days. Fernando Collor doubled this rate: he issued a total of 160 MPs, or about one emergency measure every 48 hours (Power, 1991, 80; 1998, 206, 211). Of this total, only 41 percent were approved in Congress. The great majority of the approved MPs underwent substantial changes, about 33 amendments on average per MP (Negretto, 2002, 393; Power, 1998, 216). Besides, Collor had the largest share of MPs rejected of any president since 1985 (11 out of 160; Chagas, 2002, 344). This is a further indication of the strong opposition he faced in the legislature. In issuing this large number of MPs, Collor claimed that he had broad public support, and the 35 million votes he received in the election gave him the mandate to carry out his proposed reforms, while Congress lacked credibility and public support. Yet, as indicated, his popularity declined sharply during his short term in office: from 67 percent when he assumed office to 1.5 percent by the end of the first year of his term (by September 1992, his support rate was a negative 59 percent; Data-Folha 1988–2001).

The power of governors

In another indication of the uphill climb facing Collor, all 27 states were in the hands of political leaders from different parties than that of the president. The 1990 gubernatorial elections weakened the president in partisan terms and fragmented the party system. The PMDB and PFL were the parties with the largest presence in the states, winning in eight and seven states, respectively. In an unparalleled situation after the 1985 transition to democracy, the party of the president did not win a single state governorship.

During Collor's term in office, many governors were powerful actors in their states. Their institutional power did not change much because institutional rules had been relatively stable since the Sarney presidency. But in partisan terms the picture was more diverse than before. After the 1990 gubernatorial elections, 13 governors out of 27 (48 percent) were elected with 50 percent of the vote or more, a lower percentage than that of the 1986 election (74 percent). On average, governors got 47.5 percent of the votes upon assuming office. In a sharp contrast to the previous period, none of the governors' parties had an absolute majority in the state legislative body, and only six of them had majorities when taking into account coalition parties. Eight governors faced a divided government, that is, an opposition party (or parties) controlled a larger share of the seats than the party of the governor in the state legislative assembly; during Sarney's administration, not a single governor had to cope with such a situation. The average governor's party had less than 30 percent of the seats, and governing coalitions had an average of 40 percent of the seats. These figures suggest that the fragmentation of the party system was high not only at the federal but also at the state level. The average gubernatorial power index for the period in which Collor was president was 1.6, compared to 2.2 during Sarney's term in office.

In sum, governors were not as powerful in partisan terms in their states as they were during the period in which Sarney was president. In addition, they were less influential on the federal scene, since partisan links between president and governors were weaker and different forms of coordination were more difficult to achieve due to the large fragmentation of the party system. No party was a clear winner and none had control over a substantial majority of governorships. Three parties won governorships in the 1982 election (PSD, PMDB, and PDT), two in 1986 (PMDB and PFL), and nine in 1990 (PFL, PMDB, PDT, PTB, PTR, PSDB, PDS, PRS, and PSC). Three different parties (PMDB, PRS, and PDT) won in the three most important Southeastern states; something similar happened in the South (with the PDT, PFL, and PMDB).

The increasing party system fragmentation after the 1990 election challenged different forms of partisan and regional coordination among governors.[3] Coordination was costly because of the lack of partisan links among several state executives.[4] Building up support for the president among governors was as complex and costly as it was in Congress. Regional and partisan fragmentation made coalition formation difficult for the president.

The fiscal context

Collor faced three critical economic problems: surging inflation, an increasing fiscal imbalance, and a deepening economic recession. Inflation increased sharply after the transition to democracy in 1985. Average rates jumped from 235 percent in 1985 to 1,476 percent in 1990. The primary federal deficit was 4 percent of the GDP in 1989. Although the government managed a 2.4 percent surplus in 1990 (see Table 4.1), the deficit increased steadily thereafter. The fiscal deficit rose year-after-year between 1991 and 1993, generating strong fiscal pressures on the federal government and contributing to high inflation rates.

The external debt was $120 billion when Collor took office, growing to $122 billion by the end of his first year as president. The domestic debt was close to $90 billion, of which $57 billion was owed by states to the federal government (Pang, 2002, 125). The net debt of the total public sector as a percentage of GDP remained relatively stable between 1990 and 1993. It marginally increased after that year but grew sharply again after 1995 (Bevilaqua, 2000, 9). States' and municipalities' net debt increased from 7.5 percent of GDP in 1991 to 9.8 percent in 1994 (Giambiagi and Além, 1999, 157).

The unfavorable economic situation, in part worsened by the fiscal disequilibria generated by the large increase in fiscal transfers imposed by the 1988 Constitution, forced the president to take abrupt action. Collor made use of his electoral victory to implement shock measures, decreeing his stabilization plan and anti-inflationary package (called *Plano Collor* or *Plano Brasil Novo*) one day after taking office. The plan was the most radical economic package implemented since the country's return to democracy (Panizza, 2000, 184), and included a drastic reduction in the money supply and the freezing of all short-term financial assets for 18 months (effective from March 16, 1990), as well as wages and prices. Collor sought to reduce the budget deficit by eliminating subsidies, cutting personnel and government agencies, and privatizing deficit-ridden state-owned companies. Aware of the limitations he faced in Congress, Collor tried to pass reforms by surprise and through imposition, avoiding dialogue and consensus with key social, economic, and political actors (Weyland, 1998, 77). A fragmented and demoralized opposition initially compensated the president for the lack of support in Congress. Although some of the reforms were passed, Collor earned for himself more enemies than supporters, a costly burden he would carry for the remainder of his term.

Although the president and his economic team initially reduced inflation (to 480 percent in 1991), the positive aspects of the stabilization plan were short-lived and inflation began to rise again by mid-1990. By 1992, inflation had increased again to 1,157 percent, reaching 2,708 in 1993 (IPEADATA-FGV). Additionally, the plan had a strong recessive impact on the economy due to the dramatic decrease in the stock of liquid assets (frozen by the government's decision).

The states' economic and fiscal situation was not much more comfortable than the federal government's, although it was better than the period before 1988. Only in 1988, after a long period of time, did the states make some gains in the shares of the revenues allocated to them, reversing the process of fiscal centralization that had been under way since at least 1964. However, the economic recession and rising inflation during the late 1980s and early 1990s weakened the fiscal position of the entire public sector and had a profound impact on the states (Lopreato, 2002, 106). The states' tax revenue fell by more than R$3 billion between 1991 and 1992 (decreasing from R$34.6 billion in 1991 to 31.9 in 1992); a similar cut took place in their total revenue (from R$52 billion in 1991 to 49 billion in 1992).

The critical economic situation also impacted state debts and fiscal balance. According to data from the *Banco Central do Brasil*, states' net debt reached 17.15 percent of GDP in 1991 and 17.23 in 1992 (IPEDATA-Banco Central do Brasil). The aggregate primary balance for states and municipalities was positive in each year after the 1988 Constitution took effect until 1994, a reflection of the gains reaped by governors and mayors as a result of the constitutional assembly. Their operational balance, on the other hand, was negative in 1990 and slightly positive in 1991, after the initial success of the Collor Plan, but again fell into deficit during the 1992–1994 period (see Table 4.1). If states faced fiscal pressures, mainly due to the increase in their debts, they were smaller than those prior to 1988.

Drawing from these data, it is reasonable to claim that the economic and fiscal situation at the federal and state level generated incentives, particularly for the president and to some extent for governors, to change it. The cutting point (a fiscal deficit) for the federal government was clearly crossed. Debt pressures and budget constraints contributed to larger fiscal pressures. Several states faced these pressures too, although overall they enjoyed a better fiscal situation after 1988, and budget constraints on them were softer. In the context of stabilization reforms and struggles in Congress, Collor tried to change the federal balance in his favor by

Table 4.1 Operational balance in Brazil (1990–1994, as a percentage of GDP)

Period	Total public sector	Operational balance	
		Central government	States and municipalities
1990	1.4	2.4	−0.4
1991	0.2	−0.1	0.7
1992	1.7	−0.6	−0.7
1993	0.7	−0.7	−0.1
1994	−1.1	1.6	−0.8

Source: Data compiled and adapted from Giambiagi and Além, 1999, 99. Data from the Brazilian Central Bank.

Note
(−) = Deficit.

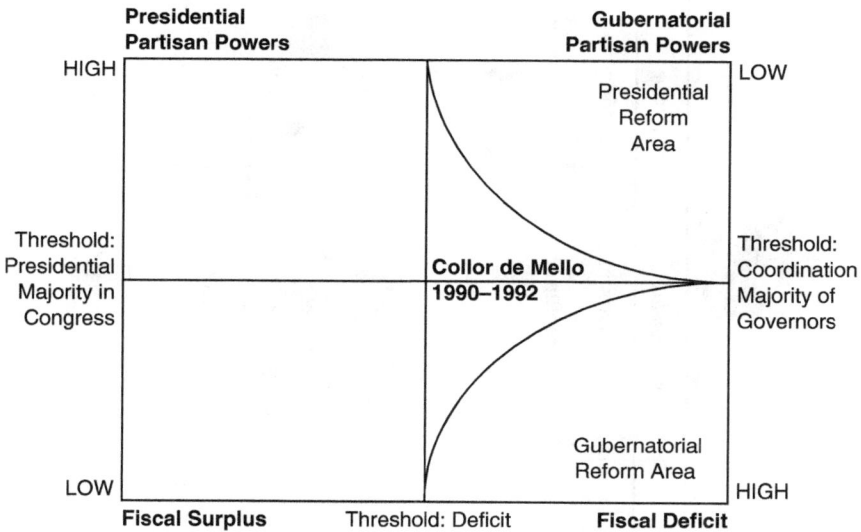

Figure 4.1 Synthesis of the main variables during Collor (1990–1992).

Note
The area inside both arches is where the probability of changes in the status quo ante is larger.

altering the mechanisms for the distribution of funds and functions (see Figure 4.1 and Table 4.2).

The setting of the federal distributive game during the Collor de Mello presidency

The distribution of power did not benefit either the president or the governors. Neither side was able to concentrate enough political capital and use it to pass substantial reforms. The president had only minority control of the Chamber of Deputies and the Senate, and his party did not administer a single governorship. Some governors were relatively powerful in their states, but most of them did not control a substantive share of their seats and faced fragmentation in their state legislative assemblies. In addition, coordination among them was difficult. The large majority of the state executives did not have strong partisan links with the president, and coalitions at the federal level were opportunistic and short term. Coalitions among governors against the president were not easily constructed either. Coordination was undermined by partisan fragmentation as well as the structure of expected costs and benefits faced by subnational officials.

Table 4.2 Values taken by the main variables during Collor (1990–1992)

	Variable	Value	Range high-low	Overall value
Presidential electoral power	Electoral support president	28.5% in the first round; 53% second round.	Low to medium	Low presidential power
	Electoral support opposition	16.1% (PT) first round; 47% (second round).	Low to medium	
	Percentage of seats (Lower Chamber)	7.95% (PRN); 37% average presidential coalition.	Low	
	Percentage of seats (Senate)	PRN won only 2 seats of the 27 being contested (about 7%); less than 10% of total seats. Coalition won between 32.3% and 38.7% of the seats; lowest of 12.9%.	Low	
	Role of opposition	Obstructive (PT and PMDB).	–	
	Discipline in Congress	69.2% between Feb. 1991 and April 1992.	Relatively low	
Presidential legislative power	Use of decree power	Total of 160 MPs (87 originals).	High	High legislative power
Presidential approval rating	Positive image	From 67% upon getting to office to 1.5% by end of 1990. By Sept. 1992, was a –59%.	From high to very low	From high to very low approval

Category	Indicator		Rating	Summary
Gubernatorial power	Average gubernatorial electoral support	47.5% of the vote.	Medium	Relatively low gubernatorial power
	Average legislative support (percentage of seats)	30% of the seats (governors' party); 40% (governors' coalition).	Relatively low	
	Gubernatorial partisan powers index	Medium range: 1.6.	Medium	
	Proportion of allied governors	None.	Very low	
	Gubernatorial coordination	Partisan fragmentation (9 parties got governorships).	Low	
Economic context	Economic growth	-4.35% in 1990; 1% in 1991; and -0.5% in 1992.	Relatively low	Critical economic context
	Inflation	1,038% average 1990–1992.	High	
	Debt	$120 billion in 1990; $122 billion by end of 1990.	High	
	Provincial debt	States net debt reached 17.15% of GDP in 1991 and 17.23% in 1992.	High	
	Budget constraints	From soft to harder.	–	
Fiscal Indicators	Federal fiscal deficit	-4% of the GDP in 1989; surplus in 1990; deficit afterwards.	Relatively High	Strong fiscal pressures for fed. govt./low for states
	Provincial fiscal deficit	Balanced between 1990 and 1994; avg. -0.26% of GDP.	Low	

Expected benefits and costs

The president had strong incentives to modify the status quo. Central government officials calculated that the fiscal pressures the new constitutional reforms imposed on the national budget were a crucial cause of the fiscal imbalances at the federal level. Hence, Collor wanted to reverse some of these reforms. He expected to face relatively large costs in those negotiations, as he did not have enough seats to pass them in Congress. In addition, he did not have substantial support from governors, as none of them were from his party. Opposing them was a costly strategy (Interview with Fernando Limongi, September 12, 2006). Negotiations in Congress were expected to take place on a one-by-one basis and to require costly side-payments in most cases, especially those that pertained to changes in the distribution of funds and functions in the federation. Attempting to pass a reform of the federal distribution of funds and functions by decree (through a *medida provisória*) was expected to be more costly than negotiating a bill in Congress, as the president could anticipate strong reactions from governors and Congressmen.[5]

Governors also faced fiscal pressures in a context of growing inflation and recession, but considering the gains they had reaped from the central government in 1988, they had greater incentives to maintain the status quo regulating the distribution of funds and functions than to change it. Subnational leaders expected few benefits out of reforms to the federal equation.[6]

Finally, most federal legislators had weak incentives to support the president's reform agenda. Most were not linked in partisan terms to Collor, so he had limited capacity to enforce discipline from them or help them further their political careers. Moreover, Collor's popularity had been on the decline since the stabilization plans failed to put inflation under control, and the reforms generated strong opposition from those sectors most affected by them. In contrast, several federal legislators had incentives to support opposition party leaders and state governors who were serious challengers to the president and had realistic chances to run for (and eventually win) the federal executive office in the next election. Several of these governors counted on resources to distribute after the 1988 reforms.

Budget constraints were hard for the president. Although Collor got support from international monetary institutions and the central government was able to finance its fiscal deficit by substantially increasing its debt (by more than 20 percent in a single year), there were also limits to this strategy, and central authorities knew they could not neglect them. Printing money was not the optimal available option, as economic authorities were worried about the growing fiscal deficit and inflation. Reducing the fiscal deficit rather than expanding it was a crucial step to take in the efforts to trim inflation rates. Most of the available options for controlling the federal fiscal deficit and reducing inflation required that the central government impose restrictions on the states. Central authorities wanted to reduce the federal government's transfers to sub-national governments, limit (or even reverse) the decision to finance states' fiscal imbalances, and place limits on the states' spending and capacity to issue debt.

Budget constraints for the states were softer than for the federal government (but gradually hardening as the economic situation deteriorated overall). Most states regularly made use of the inflationary tax, state banks, and debt renegotiations with the central government to reduce the fiscal costs of the status quo ante. Hence, governors had more incentives to keep the status quo than to seek costly changes to it. A difference between this period and the one after 1994 was that governors faced relatively softer budget constraints during Collor's term in office than during Cardoso's (i.e., they could use the inflationary tax and state banks to finance their budget deficits). They also faced similar budget constraints during Sarney's term (relatively soft and gradually hardening), although fiscal pressures on their budgets were larger before 1988 (and that moved them to take action). Despite this, the major difference was not only in relation to the budget constraints faced by the political actors, but also (and fundamentally) the distribution of political power among levels of government in the federation. Cardoso could count on significantly larger support in Congress and in public opinion than Collor, and he had political resources to divide governors, prevent their coordination, and impose reforms and checks to them; differences in this regard were critical.

Theoretical expectations

Given the theoretical expectations of the federal distributive game, the fiscal context the actors faced, as well as the expected costs and benefits, we could argue that the president had incentives to centralize resources and the governors had motivations to defend the status quo ante. Whether the actor that has incentives to move, the president in this case, is capable of getting the payoff (γ) or not depends on the distribution of political power in the federal game. As the president did not have enough partisan power to pass centralizing reforms, and the expected costs and the probability of conflict with the governors were higher than the expected benefits of changing the status quo, the most likely outcome was that no substantial reforms would be passed in Congress during Collor's term in office. As indicated by the equilibrium in the normal form of the game below (see Figure 4.2), deadlock was more likely to prevail over reforms to the status quo ante (0*,0*).

		Governors	
		Power	No power
President	Power	0,0	$\gamma, -\gamma$
	No power	$-\delta, \delta$	$0^*, 0^*$

Figure 4.2 Normal form game for Collor de Mello (1990–1992).

Deadlocked negotiations

The first negotiations with the governors took place in March 1991, a moment in which the recently appointed economic team (with Marcílio Marques Moreira as the head of *Fazenda*) proposed a set of fiscal and tax reforms (called the *Emendão*). According to the government, these reforms needed the support of the governors to be approved in Congress. In August, the president handed the governors a Memorandum of Agreement (*Memorando de Entendimento*), calling upon them to support a series of structural reforms in order to avoid a new "shock" approach to containing inflation. The reform failed mainly due to the intentions of the federal government to roll over state debts using constitutional funds (such as the *Fundos Constitucionais do Nordeste, Norte,* and *Centro-Oeste*) and reduce federal transfers to subnational governments. These funds were crucial for the states controlled by the PFL and the PMDB, the two parties with the largest delegations to Congress, which fiercely opposed any reduction in transfers to them (Abrucio, 1998, 208).

A second attempt to negotiate with the governors failed in late 1991. The central government negotiated a new state debt rollover (and an emergency tax reform) in exchange for fiscal adjustments at the subnational level. Governors, especially from the more indebted states such as São Paulo, Rio de Janeiro, Minas Gerais, and Rio Grande do Sul, actively engaged in the negotiations. After them, federal authorities prepared the rollover deal, giving states 120 days to sign the agreement with the central government. But governors did not meet the terms of the arrangement, since most of them did not want to pay the costs of implementing the adjustment reforms that were to be exchanged with debt rollovers.

In 1992, Collor attempted a third tax reform, which was proposed by the Executive Committee on Fiscal Reform (CERF, also known as *Comissão Ary Oswaldo Matos Filho*). This committee recommended, among other things, to increase federal tax revenue through the creation of a federal

VAT (to be formed by merging the IPI, ICMS, and the ISS) and the creation of a tax on financial transactions (later implemented under the IPMF and CPMF) (Melo, 2002, 87). These reforms would have substantially diminished transfers to states and municipalities by eliminating crucial state taxes (Castro Santos *et al.*, 1992, 41). Accordingly, these attempts generated strong gubernatorial opposition, similar to the opposition displayed during previous reform efforts ("Isenções e Créditos do novo IVA Geram Oposição de Secretários Estaduais," *Gazeta Mercantil,* June 13, 1992; "Dificultades de Aprovação no Congresso," *Gazeta Mercantil,* July 9, 1992; quoted in Melo, 2002, 87, 201). The bill was finally abandoned due to lack of support, and because the impeachment proceedings initiated against the president on September 29 completely dominated debates in Congress.

Between August and September 1992, Collor tried to prevent his impeachment by co-opting governors from the North, Center-West, and especially from the Northeast, making use of the lukewarm links he had with Antônio Carlos Magalhães. The president distributed large amounts of discretionary funds to those regions in his attempt to exchange transfers for their political backing in Congress.[7] The main opposition to Collor came from Southern states, a region in which he lost the presidential election and from which came many competitors for the 1989 presidential bid. Despite this, several analysts claim that some state governors preferred to maintain in office a weak president from whom they could extract fiscal resources (Neumanne, 1992, 177), rather than a strong one who could undo some of the decentralizing reforms implemented in 1988.

By late 1991, Collor's public support had vanished. He also became increasingly isolated in Congress, where he was unable to mobilize political support. Important bills sent to Congress were deadlocked, and the president could not do much to speed up the legislative process (Moraes Valença, 2002, 137). Lacking political support and in the middle of a major corruption scandal, Collor was impeached before he could implement any reform reversing the gains governors had won during Sarney's administration.

If the president was weak and the fiscal context especially pressed the federal executive, but increasingly also the states, to take action, why did the governors not coordinate against the president? The short answer is that they faced weaker fiscal incentives after 1988 and large collective action problems, and any successful attack on the federal government's resources would carry significant costs for them as well. Governors' collective action problems stemmed from their partisan and regional divisions. Collective incentives were very weak and gains from coordination were uncertain. Although governors could not coordinate offensively to secure further privileges from the central government, they did coordinate defensively to retain those they had already gained. They concentrated their efforts on preserving their important achievements in the 1988 Constitution.

Consistent with the predictions of the theoretical model, when neither the president nor the governors are able to concentrate sufficient political power to prevail over the other, and despite having the incentives from an unfavorable fiscal context (especially for the federal government), the status quo would prevail. Under these conditions, the expected costs and the probability of conflict are greater than the expected benefits of the reforms. Although the president actively sought to alter the status quo ante, no substantial modification to the scheme of fiscal relations adopted in 1988 could be passed in Congress.

The Itamar Franco government (1992–1994)

Changes in the setting of the federal distributive game: the president's partisan powers

Itamar Franco's government had limited political support in Congress and, being an interim government, did not have a clear mandate to substantially reverse some of the reforms implemented during the 1988 constitutional assembly. Despite this, the president could put limits on gubernatorial pressures and secure the passage of some bills that both contributed to improving the fiscal balance of the federal government and paved the way for future centralizing reforms.

Even though he faced the same distribution of power in the federal Congress and in state governorships, the Franco administration differed from the Collor government in some important respects. To begin with, Itamar had more congressional experience (he had been a federal senator from the state of Minas Gerais before becoming president) and stronger ties with members of Congress. Sixteen of his 27 ministers were former federal deputies or senators. This helped the president to negotiate with the legislature more effectively than Collor had. His cabinet reflected a broad partisan coalition forged in opposition to the impeached president (Flynn, 1993, 365). In addition to the PFL (which also offered some support to Collor), the new interim president incorporated such major partners into the government coalition as the PMDB and the PSDB, as well as several minor parties, such as the PTB, PSB, and the PP. Among the PSDB's most prominent members, Itamar appointed Fernando Henrique Cardoso as Foreign Minister and, after a short period, as Finance Minister (from May 19, 1993 until March 30, 1994). Itamar's coalition controlled between 60 percent of the seats in the Chamber of Deputies (during the first period) and 55 percent (during the last), a much higher share than that enjoyed by Collor. In the Senate, this share of seats was even larger, as his coalition controlled 74.2 percent between his assumption of power and January 1994, and 61.3 percent from January to December 1994. Moreover, Itamar was able to elicit a higher rate of discipline from the members of his coalition (a low of 72.2 and a high of 77.8 percent for all the parties in the coalition together) than the 69.2 percent Collor achieved between February 1991 and April 1992 (Figueiredo, 2006, 13).

In relation to the institutional resources available to the federal executive, Itamar surpassed both Sarney and Collor in the use of MPs. He issued 505 MPs in his short term in office (Power, 1998, 212), and Congress rejected none (Chagas, 2002, 344).[8] Support in public opinion polls showed ups and downs during Itamar's term in office. He assumed the presidency with a negative 3 percent approval rating (in October 1992) and within one month his support had climbed to 10 percent. His positive image rose again after the stabilization plan began showing some results, and he finished his interim presidency in December 1994 with a 33 percent approval rating (DataFolha 1988–2001).

The distribution of power in Congress granted Itamar slightly more resources than his predecessor, and he enjoyed periods of some public support, while Collor simply saw his support vanish throughout his term in office. The partisan power of the governors in their states and the collective action hurdles they faced, on the other hand, remained basically unchanged after Collor's impeachment.

The fiscal context

Despite some marginal improvements, Collor could neither reduce the deficit nor control inflation. Strong fiscal pressures generated large incentives for the president to change the status quo ante. Governors, who had had stronger incentives to maintain it, faced larger costs and growing pressures to alter it.

Despite some temporary reduction in inflation rates, prices were still on the rise. When Cardoso became Minister of Finance in May 1993, Brazil's consumer price index reached about 2,490 percent. Additionally, the fiscal deficit was soaring. According to data from the Brazilian Central Bank, the primary balance was 0.81 percent, while the operational balance represented a deficit of 0.7 percent of GDP. For Edmar Bacha (2001), a key economic advisor in the Cardoso team, although the nominal balance of the central government (which includes the nominal interest payments on the public debt) indicated a surplus of 0.25 percent of GDP in 1993, the operational deficit (which includes the real, i.e., inflation corrected, interest payments) reached 58.4 percent of GDP (Bacha, 2001, 3). Despite the sharp differences in the data, it was clear that the central government was running larger deficits every year after 1991 and that the economic team considered it was crucial to address the fiscal imbalance in order to control inflation. The cutting point for fiscal deficits was crossed, and that generated incentives for the president to alter the status quo ante (see Table 4.3 and Figure 4.3).

Although revenue allocated to states and municipalities rose from 8 to 12 percent of GDP between the Sarney and Franco administrations,

Table 4.3 Values taken by the main variables during Franco (1992–1994)

	Variable	Value	Range high–low	Overall value
Presidential electoral power	Electoral support president	Interim government.	Low	Medium presidential power
	Electoral support opposition	16.1% (PT) first round; 47% (second round).	Low to medium	
	Percentage of seats (Chamber of Deputies)	Between 55% and 60% (presidential coalition).	Relatively high	
	Percentage of seats (Senate)	74.2% (1992–Jan. 1994) and 61.3% (from Jan. to Dec.1994).	High	
	Role of opposition	Broad coalition. Strong opposition.	–	
	Discipline in Congress	The rate of discipline from the members of his coalition ranged from a low of 72.2% and a high of 77.8% for all the parties in the coalition together.	Medium	
Presidential legisl. power	Use of decree power	505 MPs (141 original).	High	High legislative power
Presidential approval rating	Positive image	−3% (Oct. 1992); 10% (Nov. 1992); 28% (March 1993); −29% (Nov. 1993); 33% (Dec. 1994)	From very low to relatively low	From very low to relat. low approval

Gubernatorial power	Average gubernatorial electoral support	47.5% of the vote.	Medium		Relatively low gubernatorial power
	Average legislative support (% of seats)	30% of the seats (governors' party); 40% (governors' coalition).	Relatively low		
	Gubernatorial partisan powers index	Medium range: 1.6 (out of a maximum of 3).	Medium		
	Proportion of allied governors	19/27 in nominal coalition.	Relatively high		
	Gubernatorial coordination	Partisan fragmentation (nine parties got governorships).	Low		
Economic context	Economic growth	Average 3% 1992–1994.	Medium		Critical economic context
	Inflation	Average 1,653% 1992–1994.	Very high		
	Debt	From R$122 million in 1992 to R$166 billion in 1994.	High		
	Provincial debt	States and municipalities net debt increased from 7.5% to 9.3% of GDP, reaching 9.5% in 1994.	High		
	Budget constraints	From hard to harder.	–		
Fiscal indicators	Federal fiscal deficit	Average –.7% of GDP. Operational deficit 0.7% of GDP in 1992; 0.8% in 1994.	Relatively high		Strong fiscal pressures for fed. govt./low for states
	State fiscal deficit	Average –7% of GDP.	Medium		

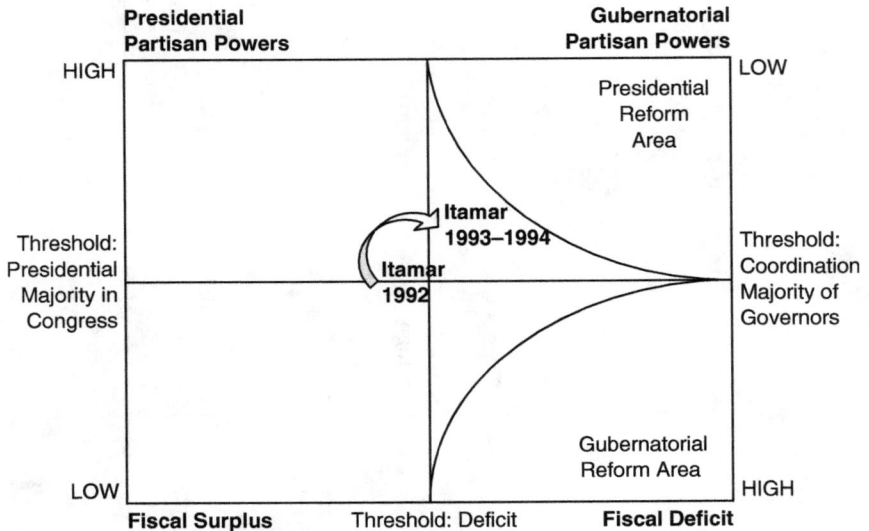

Figure 4.3 Synthesis of the main variables during the Franco administration (1992–1994).

Note
The area inside both arches is where the probability of changes in the status quo ante is larger.

subnational governments were not required to assume any increased responsibilities for tax collection or provision of services. Even more problematic for the central government was that subnational governments' payroll grew by 77 percent between 1985 and 1990. At the time Franco took office, only three states were solvent, and subnational governments owed a total of $49 billion, more than the country's debt to foreign commercial banks (Flynn, 1993, 370).

Despite the positive aggregate primary balance for states and municipalities between 1988 and 1994, the operational deficit of subnational governments climbed marginally: in 1992, it represented 0.7 percent of GDP, and by 1994, it had increased to 0.8 percent (Giambiagi and Além, 1999, 99, 132–133). This is not a substantial change, but reveals that fiscal pressures on the states gradually increased. This is an important difference between Collor's and Franco's administrations, on the one hand, and Cardoso's, on the other. State debts and fiscal deficits eased after 1988; however, as subnational debt and interest rates climbed, states' fiscal solvency, as well as the fiscal benefits they reaped after 1988, gradually (very gradually) deteriorated. Weak presidents were compelled to bail out and roll over state debts. A strong president could force them to reform and accept central controls and restrictions. How? I get into the details on how these changes began during the Itamar government in the following sections.

Expected benefits, costs, and budget constraints

Itamar expected substantial benefits from changes in the status quo. The president faced a deep fiscal crisis that transformed the status quo into a (very) sub-optimal situation, but with the implementation of the reforms he expected to reduce inflation, stabilize the economy, and eventually resume growth, increase tax collection, and, very importantly, augment tax revenue.

Budget constraints remained strong (and grew stronger as time passed without the economic authorities being able to control the main macroeconomic variables). Making more credit available and printing money in a hyperinflationary context were basically fueling the problem rather than controlling its causes. Debt relief could have partially contributed to reducing fiscal pressures on the central government. But economic authorities agreed that getting prices under control required reducing the fiscal deficit and public spending rather than expanding them (Interview with Andre Lara Resende, November 20, 2002). What started to change after the Collor crisis were the expected costs of a reform. As the economic and fiscal crisis imposed high costs on all the key actors in the game, the reformist option gradually became less costly for the president.

Federal authorities (especially economic ones) and some IFIs believed that subnational governments (together with state-owned enterprises and other public institutions, such as state banks) were among the main contributors to the fiscal deficit and the hyperinflationary crisis (whether this was a solid argument or not does not matter much). As actors in the game perceived that the cost of the status quo ante was too high, the costs of reforming it diminished relative to taking no action. As the power and defensive strength of the governors diminished, the power of federal authorities increased.

Federal legislators had stronger incentives to support the president than during the period in which Collor was president. First, the president crafted stronger links with them than Collor had and, thus, had more reliable support in Congress. And second, Itamar enjoyed periods of relative popularity in public opinion. These modest gains in relation to Collor, together with the sense of urgency in the face of significant fiscal and economic crisis (as well as political turmoil), allowed the interim president to gain some timid support from legislators. Despite this, the president did not control a solid majority of seats in either chamber and had limited ability to enforce discipline.

Theoretical expectations

The distribution of power was slightly favorable for the president, who was able to gather more support in Congress than his predecessor. Governors, on the other hand, remained very much uncoordinated and fragmented, although willing to resist centralizing reforms from the federal government. Both sides had clear incentives to get more fiscal revenue as the economic context deteriorated, affecting their net balances. Despite this, as during Collor's administration, governors were in a relatively better fiscal position as they received large transfers without clear responsibilities. Furthermore, they faced softer budget constraints, as they could still finance their deficits using the inflation tax, getting funds from their state banks, and as a last resort being bailed out by the central government when they ran into deep financial disequilibria. In sum, governors were under fewer fiscal pressures after 1988 and before the Real Plan (when the situation was admittedly dire for the country as a whole, but when they enjoyed the inflation tax, state banks, and federal bailouts), rather than after the reform and the control of inflation.

A clash between the president and the governors over the centralizing reforms the president intended to pass was less likely to occur during the Itamar presidency than during Collor's: on the one hand, governors expected lower costs during Franco's term because his reformist agenda was less radical and the expected costs of reforms were lower than during Collor's term (in addition to his less confrontational style). On the other, not changing the status quo ante was increasingly perceived as a costly decision for most actors in the game. All this contributed to reducing the probability of conflict. As the expected costs and the probability of conflict from centralizing reforms diminished, and the expected benefits of changing the status quo increased, some reforms to the federal balance began to appear more plausible. The threshold for having fiscal incentives to reform had been crossed, and Itamar was close to getting a majority in Congress (gubernatorial power, on the contrary, was below the cut point).[9]

The outcomes of the federal distributive game

Macroeconomic stabilization was the government's highest priority, and changes in intergovernmental fiscal transfers were among some of the key measures presented by federal authorities to reduce inflation. In the midst of a hyperinflationary crisis, these proposals for reforming the status quo ante started to gain support from political actors and (more broadly) from public opinion. The first real test of Itamar Franco's relationship with Congress and the governors was the crucially important issue of fiscal reform. This reform, central to any effort to stabilize the economy, included a series of proposals to curtail the extra federal transfers granted to the states and municipalities by the 1988 Constitution.

A first step was taken on January 21, 1993, when the Chamber of Deputies agreed, by 358 to 84 votes, to pass a bill creating a new tax (IPMF, *Imposto Provisório sobre Movimentações Financeiras*) of 0.25 percent on all financial transactions (including checks, ATM transactions, and withdrawals from investments). The bill was also approved in the Senate and turned into *Lei Complementar* 77 on July 13, 1993. The revenues generated by this tax were not to be distributed among states and municipalities, a decision that brought about $712 billion in extra revenue for the federal government, helping it to tackle the large deficit (and finance support for further reforms). In order to get the bill approved, Itamar Franco and Fernando Henrique Cardoso, his Minister of Finance, spent an entire week meeting party leaders of the 19 parties in Congress and negotiating with the governors of the 27 states. Negotiations took almost three months in the Chamber of Deputies and almost a month in the Senate (*Diário do Congresso Nacional* [*DCN* from now on], August 12, 1993, 1948). Instead of imposing a reform package on Congress and the governors, Itamar and Fernando Henrique negotiated an increase in the federal government's revenues, without affecting those of subnational governments. Governors accepted the reform without claiming more revenues for themselves because they recognized the profound crisis in which the central government was immersed. As the economy improved and the president (and his Minister of Finance) gained support in Congress and in public opinion, the main political actors in the federal government gained leverage for negotiating more substantive reforms to the federal equation.

Cardoso and the social emergency fund

After failed attempts to reform state banks and some timid improvements related to state debts, Cardoso's (and his economic advisors from the Department of Economics at the Catholic University of Rio de Janeiro, many of whom were involved in the 1986 Cruzado Plan) first important victory in the efforts to reduce the fiscal deficit of the central government (and thus stabilize the economy) was the creation, through a constitutional amendment, of the Social Emergency Fund (FSE, *Fundo Social de Emergência*). This fund was created for a two-year period to temporarily reverse or at least prevent the worsening of the fiscal crisis and to balance the central government's fiscal deficit. It was expected to provide the central government with $16.1 billion annually, out of which about $12.9 billion would come from a 15 percent cut the federal government imposed on transfers to subnational governments. According to key figures linked to the president (such as Antônio Kandir), the main rationale (and justification) for this fund was that the 1988 Constitution imposed an excessive cost on the central government through large transfers to states and municipalities. The cut this fund imposed on subnational governments was critical in the president's stabilization efforts; without it, the federal

government would have been incapable of balancing its budget, and inflation would have continued (Interview with Antônio Kandir, September 11,
2006; "Democracia e Ajuste Fiscal," *FSP*, February 13, 1994, 2).

Cardoso was able to craft support for these reforms due to two main
factors, which are the key variables analyzed in this work. First, the inflationary and fiscal indicators were spiraling out of control. In this context,
the president, his Finance Minister, and other key political figures in the
country treated these measures as urgent. A sense of urgency, as in Argentina during the late 1980s and early 1990s, played an important role in
reducing the costs of the reforms and the probability of conflict, as well as
in fostering some support and legitimacy for them. Several actors faced
large costs under the status quo ante and had stronger incentives to alter
it. Furthermore, the expected benefits were large: the president sought to
stabilize the economy after the reforms and, as a consequence, stimulate
growth and increase tax revenue (the political gains expected out of these
changes were obviously significant). Second, Itamar and Fernando
Henrique were able to accumulate some political support, which was decisive for passing crucial reforms. Initially, some legislators in Congress
showed resistance to the president's reform attempts, and even some
PSDB members gave only halfhearted support (Bacha, 2001, 5). Governors, mayors, and some members of the president's own legislative coalition opposed the bill creating the FSE, blocking a first vote on the
proposal in January 1994. Cardoso met with the leaders of the main parties
in Congress to discuss the FSE during the first week of February and personally called governors and legislators to craft a basic agreement. Sessions
began on February 1, after an agreement between the government and
the PFL.[10] The stalemate was finally surmounted after the Minister of
Finance threatened to resign if members of Congress did not support the
measure. Leaders of the main parties finally agreed to start the constitutional review that was necessary to pass the reforms and began debate on
February 9 (*DCN*, February 9, 1994, 767). Negotiations were not easy for
the government. The FSE generated strong resistance among the opposition, especially the PT, the PCdoB, PSB, PDT, PV, PPS, and the PSTU, and
even among some members of the governing coalition, such as the PMDB
and the PPR. Legislators from various parties claimed that the FSE
reduced subnational governments' revenues and represented an attack on
the federal system instituted by the 1988 Constitution. Valter Pereira
(PMDB-RS) denounced the reforms, saying:

> The constitutional transfers for states and municipalities, as well as the
> transfers for education, are being challenged. The current tax sharing
> system regulated by the federal constitution was the result of a demo-
> cratic reform that restricted the financial [*sic*] centralization during
> the dictatorial period. With a clear federal inspiration, the decision
> attempted to eliminate the deprivation to which governors and mayors

of the entire country were subjected (during military rule). Cutting the tax shares to these units means reestablishing the centralizing character in the state administration that we so much condemned in the past.

(DCN, February 9, 1994, 769)

Several members of Congress, especially from the PMDB and PPR, criticized the cuts in transfers to states and municipalities as well as those for education and housing that the federal government tried to pass through the FSE. Leftist legislators argued that the bill was part of a large adjustment process, which attempted to reduce funding for health and education as well as public employees' salaries, while it did not cut a cent of interest payments on the foreign and domestic debt (Aldo Rabelo, PCdoB-SP, *DCN*, February 9, 1994, 769). Other members of Congress denounced pressures from the central government, especially from the Minister of Finance, to pass the bill. Members of the PT argued that "Congress cannot be politically responsible for the process of economic decay in the country [and] cannot be made responsible through political blackmail: Either it votes positive, or we have hyperinflation" (Deputy José Genoíno, PT-SP; *DCN*, February 9, 1994, 768).

Supporters of the government in Congress claimed that the bill was crucial to fight inflation, stabilize the economy, bring down the federal fiscal deficit, reduce the size of government, and enhance governability (Luís Eduardo, PFL-BA; Rodríguez Palma, PTB-MT; *DCN*, February 9, 1994, 770). For some of them, the federal government was not imposing its will on the legislative branch of government. On the contrary, they argued that the executive sent the bill to Congress to negotiate it. As evidence of this point, they cited the fact that the original bill had included a 15 percent cut in transfers to states and municipalities, but as a result of negotiations with legislators (especially from the PMDB), governors, and mayors, the federal government finally relented and restored the proposed cuts.

Talks in Congress over this issue were intense. Cardoso finally offered different concessions to overcome the deadlocked negotiations in Congress. PMDB legislators originally made their support for the FSE conditional on eliminating the proposed cuts to transfers to states and municipalities. In negotiations with the federal government and especially with the Minister of Finance, PMDB members of Congress first won the exclusion of local governments from the cuts. Subsequently, they secured a 50 percent reduction in the cut the federal government attempted to impose on the states, and finally they succeeded in eliminating the cuts in the state transfers altogether (Tarcisio Delgado, PMDB-MG, *DCN*, February 9, 1994, 773). These concessions made to governors and mayors as well as the guarantees to keep previous levels or increase financing in real terms for education and housing were crucial to winning support for the

FSE. On February 9, 1994, and despite the divisions it generated, the FSE was passed on the first vote by a margin of 338 to 38 (with four abstentions) (*DCN*, February 9, 1994, 796). Before the second round of the vote, Itamar and Fernando Henrique had to make further concessions to core supporters.[11]

Even though several governors opposed the bill, others such as Antônio Carlos Magalhães (ACM; PFL, Bahia) and Hélio García (PRS, Minas Gerais), who were strong state leaders and crucial supporters during the Cardoso presidential campaign, backed the federal executive in passing the FSE (Abrucio, 1998, 215). Cardoso also received support from South-eastern political elites, where the PSDB was powerful.

Once some of the key governors saw they could not run as possible winning candidates for the 1994 presidential election, they backed Cardoso to prevent Lula from winning power. They supported the FSE, upon which Cardoso's presidential candidacy depended (Abrucio, 1998, 215), because they expected larger benefits from the reforms and for supporting the Minister of Finance (and potential nominee for the presidential ticket). Other key governors, despite not supporting Cardoso's reforms, did not stand in the way of the approval of the FSE.

Besides the fiscal incentives, the political support the president crafted, and the specific concessions he made, Cardoso offered subnational officials a crucial incentive during the negotiations: the possibility for them to be reelected. Most governors wanted to secure their reelection and supported the FSE, or did not actively oppose it, in exchange for that possibility. This concession reduced the costs of the reforms and the probability of conflict. Once this was granted, and after Cardoso was seen as the main political candidate in the governing coalition, most governors focused their political efforts on getting reelected. This result was also a consequence of the growing power Cardoso was able to craft.[12]

The constitutional amendment through which the FSE was enacted contained a sunset provision after which it had to be renegotiated and, if approved, renewed again.[13] This reduced the expected costs of the reform and the probability of conflict, eased negotiations in Congress with subnational officials, and contributed to passing the amendment. Other fiscal reforms and constitutional amendments were sent to Congress to place the federal budget on a more secure footing in the long run, but these long-term reform proposals were vetoed in Congress (Bacha, 2001, 7).

Negotiations over the FSE run parallel to others seeking to restrict state debt emissions through their banks. Both reforms (cutting transfers and restricting state debt issuing) were fundamental in the government's stabilization efforts. Governors historically used state banks to finance their budget needs and, in cases where they ran into financial instability, subnational officials asked the central government for help. There was a perverse dynamic in the relations among states, their banks, and the central government.

Banks would issue debt and lend money to states. When the banks
went bankrupt [because of the large amount lent to the states or
because governors would not pay them back], the Central Bank would
take them over, restructure and clean up their debts, and return them
to the states, for new rounds of debt.

(Nassif, 2002, 48) (see also Guardia, 2004, 114 and Rodden, 2006)

In a context of high inflation and economic recession, state payrolls
expanded to dangerous proportions, reaching over 70 percent of states'
net revenues. Payroll burdens also added to increasing state debts, especially in the amount of bonds state-owned banks issued in the market. As
bond liabilities escalated and the financial situation of subnational governments worsened, several state-owned banks ended up with unmarketable
bonds in their portfolios and faced increasing liquidity problems. Cardoso
took advantage of this situation to press governors to support the FSE in
exchange for bailouts and the temporary swapping of state bank bonds for
Central Bank bonds. State debts were renegotiated in Law 8,727 of November 1993. The main innovation of this law, also known as *Lei do Acordo de
Renegociação das Dívidas*, together with law 7,976/89, was the creation of an
enforcement mechanism to reduce the moral hazard problem in relation
to state debt obligations. Through it, the federal government was authorized to block state tax revenues, especially from the ICMS, in cases of states
violating their debt responsibilities with the central administration
(Rigolon and Giambiagi, 1999; quoted in Leite, 2005, 59). The president's
power and the fiscal incentives governors faced were the key causes of this
outcome. Cardoso could craft support for the reform and governors did
not actively oppose it because they were offered fiscal relief in the short
run in exchange for backing.

The FSE was part of a shock and short-term fiscal adjustment. It took
the government over two months of negotiations to secure its passage. But
the fiscal benefits were substantial: it collected about $15.5 billion in tax
revenue (instead of the original $16.1 billion proposed in the first draft of
the bill) that the central government could use to finance its deficit. States
and municipalities were expected to lose with the original version, but the
central government did not have enough political power to impose large
costs on governors (and mayors), and it needed their support to get the
bill passed. In exchange, subnational officials got some benefits. With the
increase in federal revenue after the FSE and the stabilization plan, transfers also rose from $11.7 billion before the FSE to $13.3 billion after it
(*FSP*, February 25, 1994, 1–4). By negotiating with the governors, the
Franco government, and especially Cardoso, gained some momentum and
legitimacy to pass other crucial fiscal reforms and stabilization measures.
The FSE paved the way for the introduction of the *Plano Real* (the *Real*
Plan), the presidential election of Cardoso, and the reforms he conducted
later to alter the federal balance.

The "Immediate Action Plan" (the Plano Real's formal name) was presented in Congress on December 7, 1993, and in February 1994 Cardoso implemented the first measures in order to stabilize the economy and reduce the chronic inflation rates in Brazil. The plan had two basic components: a fiscal adjustment aimed at reducing government spending, improving tax collection, and solving financial problems with state governments. The plan also implemented a new indexing system to reduce (and eventually eliminate) inertial inflation that would gradually lead to a new currency (Kingstone, 2000, 195).

As a consequence of the new measures, the consumer price index dropped from 46.6 percent in June 1994 to 0.82 percent in September (Bacha, 2001, 24; da Fonseca, 1998, 630; Rocca, 1995, 67, 91). The Plano Real was a success in terms of macroeconomic stabilization. The president was able to craft some political support and legitimacy for the plan and most actors had strong incentives to change the status quo ante. That allowed the federal executive to marginally alter the federal balance against the interests of subnational governments.

The balance of the federal distributive game

After these reforms to stabilize the economy, states' total revenue increased in absolute terms from R$49 billion in 1992 to R$68 billion in 1994 and R$71 billion in 1995, equal to a 45 percent rise in three years. Transfers to states also rose by 65 percent in the same period—in absolute terms, from R$9.7 billion in 1992 to R$14 billion in 1994 and R$16 billion in 1995. In *relative* terms, though, and despite the fact that transfers grew in *absolute* terms, subnational governments lost part of their share of revenues. Their revenue share diminished from 37 percent in 1990 to 31 percent in 1995, while their expenditure share dropped from 53.2 percent in 1992 to 46 percent in 1995 (see Table 4.4).

Despite the absolute increase in federal transfers to subnational governments, the federal government was able to concentrate tax revenue without any change in the federal distribution of functions. The president kept the

Table 4.4 Revenue and expenditure share of subnational units in Brazil (1990–1995, in percentages)

Year	Revenue share	Expenditure share
1990	37.03	50.07
1991	36.27	52.74
1992	34.54	53.23
1993	30.42	49.25
1994	33.18	47.57
1995	31.04	46.09

Source: Data compiled and adapted from IPEA Data.

same functions (P_{ip}) and was able to increase the amount of funds he controlled in absolute and relative terms (r_{jp}). Gubernatorial resources (r_{jg}) increased in absolute terms but diminished in relative terms,[14] without changes in the functions they delivered (P_{ig}). That is, the presidential net balance [$U=\Sigma(r_{jp}-P_{ip})$] improved more than the gubernatorial net balance [$X=\Sigma(P_{ig}-r_{ig})$]. Hence, despite the gains subnational officials made, the president could slightly tilt the balance of the federal equation [$B=U-X$] in his favor after 1994, although changes in absolute terms were not considerable. More formally, $U=\Sigma(r_{jp}-P_{ip})>X=\Sigma(P_{ig}-r_{ig})$ (see Table 4.5).

Final comments

Some of the main factors that played a fundamental role in the implementation of the stabilization reforms and in the initial changes in the distribution of funds among levels of government were the fiscal incentives political actors faced to alter the status quo, the high costs it imposed on them, the hardening of budget constraints, the relatively large expected benefits of the stabilization program, and, fundamentally, the political support Itamar, and especially Cardoso, were able to garner in relation to governors. As claimed in Chapter 1, when political power is concentrated in one level of government (either the central or sub-national), and the crucial actors in the game face strong fiscal incentives to get more revenue in the context of hard budget constraints, changes in the federal balance are likely to occur. This is what happened in Brazil during negotiations for the FSE and after it. When none of these conditions or only some of them take place, the status quo ante is likely to prevail. This is what characterized the setting and the outcomes of the federal game during the Collor and the beginning of Franco's presidency.

Institutional accounts based on aggregate formal norms—such as the federal structure, electoral rules, or party nomination procedures—that

Table 4.5 Synthesis of the reforms and impacts on the federal balance (1993–1994)

Period of reforms	Subnational revenue (in relative terms)	Subnational functions	Subnational tax authority	Federal balance
Itamar 1993–1994	Decrease (revenue share diminished from 37% in 1990 to 31% in 1995). But increased in absolute terms	No substantial changes	No substantial changes	Favorable for the federal government $U=\Sigma(r_{jp}-P_{ip})>X=\Sigma(P_{ig}-r_{ig})$

are thought to generate the centrifugal characteristics of Brazilian institutional configuration cannot adequately explain why deadlock prevailed during this period. Nor can they explain why the reforms implemented during the Itamar Franco government are contrary to the expectation that governors should be the main beneficiaries of this institutional setting. The other side of the debate, represented by scholars who claim that presidents have institutional resources to substantially influence the reform process in Congress, do not seem to have clear arguments to account for why deadlock prevailed during Collor's and the beginning of Franco's term in office. These presidents had to build up political support under a quite similar constitutional framework. This chapter showed how presidential preferences collided with those of governors and how their strategies changed under different fiscal contexts.

The approval in Congress of the FSE represented a watershed moment in the federal distributive game, a gradual but crucial break from the previous period in which the balance of the federal equation clearly favored governors at the expense of the central government. This was also a fundamental reform that paved the way for the implementation of the Plano Real. The entire stabilization program, in turn, was the keystone for Cardoso's ascension to the presidency. This was the beginning of a profound process by which the president was able to curb the power of governors in Brazil, a process by which the *primus* became a *primus* against *pares* and ceased to be one among them. Changes in the distribution of political power, now favoring the president, and in fiscal conditions, shaped the following round of the federal distributive game.

Notes

1 The PMDB got 108 of 503 seats in the Chamber of Deputies, partially reversing the unfortunate results of 1989, but suffered major losses in relation to the 1986 Congressional elections. The PFL went through a similar cycle, winning 83 seats in the Chamber of Deputies, recovering to some extent from the 1989 results, but losing seats in relation to those it had in 1986 (Data provided by Jairo Nicolau).
2 Although Bernardo Cabral (a *pemedebista*) was appointed to the Ministry of Justice, the party never supported Collor.
3 The effective number of parties at the federal level (measured by the Laakso and Taagepera, 1979, index) increased from 2.8 in the period 1987–1989 to 8.7 after the 1990 election (the largest for the period since the transition to democracy).
4 The only region in which there were some partisan connections was the Northeast, where the PFL won six out of nine state elections. There, key party leaders exerted substantial influence among governors and helped them to reduce the costs of coordination, especially through the leadership of Bahia's governor, Antônio Carlos Magalhães (ACM). According to data collected by Roarelli (1994, 164), the states that received the largest shares of discretionary transfers in 1992 were Bahia and Pernambuco, both from the Northeast. Together, these states received around 20 percent of the total of those transfers.

5 Reactions from governors were presumably weaker in cases of reforms related to national issues, such as when the president decided to privatize or lower tariffs by decree, than in attempts to alter the balance of the federal equation (and the distribution of resources) by these same means.

6 There was not much they could extract from the central government without deepening the fiscal crisis and even affecting their own finances, paying a high cost for it. In fact, many analysts feared a tragedy of the commons, as extracting more resources from (or "overgrazing") the central government could lead to higher individual gains in the very short run, but devastating aggregate economic consequences in the medium term.

7 Discretionary transfers to states from those three regions represented 76 percent of the total in 1992 (Roarelli, 1994, 167).

8 Out of this total, 141 MPs were original, 364 were re-issued, and only 5 were derogated.

9 However, this does not necessarily mean that governors were weaker and that the central government could (suddenly) impose costs on them.

10 The PFL agreed to grant a quorum in exchange for the government's support on a bill to eliminate state monopolies in the telecommunication, oil, and electricity sectors (*FSP*, February 2, 1994, 1–4, 1–5).

11 In order to get political backing during the second round of the vote on the FSE, the government granted some ministries to parties in the coalition, the rollover of debt to the agricultural lobby, and the reduction in the time restrictions for government officials to run for office (*FSP*, February 24, 1994, 1–4). Legislative blocks from Center-West and the North also had to campaign to stop a bill introduced by Nelson Jobim (PMDB-RS) that attempted to reduce the number of legislators from those states and increase the number of representatives from other regions, especially São Paulo. They showed willingness to support the FSE when the government agreed to block the proposal.

12 The PT and PCdoB denounced and questioned this informal exchange of support and the intervention of governors to grant the approval of the FSE. José Dirceu (PT-SP) claimed that "this practice of exchanging support for the *Fundo Social de Emergência* for the distribution of television licenses, ministries, and even this agreement with the governors [to grant them the possibility of reelection] is shameful" (*DTR*, March 2, 1994, 1256).

13 In fact, it was renewed four times in 1995, 1997, 1999, and 2003 (see negotiations during Cardoso's presidency).

14 It is important to bear in mind that the crucial goal for presidents and governors is to improve their net balance (between the functions they are responsible for and the revenue they get and collect), in relation to the balance of the other actor. In this sense, the critical factor is how presidential revenues vary relative to the governors' (more than the absolute change in them).

References

Abrucio, Fernando Luis, "Os Barões da Federação," *Lua Nova*, No. 33, 1994, pp. 165–183.

Abrucio, Fernando Luis, *Os Barões da Federação: Os Governadores e a Redemocratização Brasileira* (São Paulo: Coleção Comentário, USP, 1998).

Abrucio, Fernando Luis, and David Samuels, "A Nova Política dos Governadores," *Lua Nova*, No. 40/41, 1997, pp. 137–166.

Ames, Barry, "Electoral Rules, Constituency Pressures, and Pork Barrel: Bases of Voting in the Brazilian Congress," *Journal of Politics*, Vol. 57, No. 2, 1995, pp. 324–343.

Ames, Barry, *The Deadlock of Democracy in Brazil: Interests, Identities, and Institutions in Comparative Politics* (Ann Arbor: University of Michigan Press, 2001).

Bacha, Edmar, "Brazil's Plano Real: A View From the Inside," *Instituto de Estudos de Política Económica*, mimeo, 2001.

Bevilaqua, Afonso, "State Government Bailouts in Brazil," Texto para Discussão No. 421, Departamento de Economía PUC-Rio, 2000.

Castro Santos, Maria Helena de, Maria das Graças Rua, and Carlos Roberto P. da Costa Filho, "A Política Salarial no Governo Collor: Padrões de Negociacão Executivo-Legislativo," Cadernos IUPERJ No. 1, Rio de Janeiro, 1992.

Chagas, Helena, "Relações Executivo-Legislativo"; in: Lamonier, Bolívar and Rubens Figueiredo (eds.), *A Era FHC: Um Balanço* (São Paulo: Cultura Editores Associados, 2002).

Cheibub, Jose Antonio, and Fernando Limongi, "Democratic Institutions and Regime Survival: Parliamentary and Presidential Democracies Reconsidered," *Annual Review of Political Science*, Vol. 5, 2002, pp. 151–179.

Da Fonseca, Manuel A.R., "Brazil's Real Plan," *Journal of Latin American Studies*, Vol. 30, No. 3, 1998, pp. 619–639.

Diário do Congresso Nacional (DCN), August 12, 1993.

Diário do Congresso Nacional (DCN), February 9, 1994.

Figueiredo, Argelina Cheibub, "Formação, Funcionamento e Desempenho das Coalizões de Governo no Brasil," paper prepared for delivery at the 5th Encontro da ABCP, July 26–29, FAFICH/UFMG, Belo Horizonte – MG, 2006.

Figueiredo, Argelina Cheibub, and Fernando Limongi, "Mudança Constitucional, Desempenho do Legislativo e Consolidação Institucional," *Revista Brasileira de Ciencias Sociais*, Vol. 10, No. 29, 1995, pp. 175–200.

Figueiredo, Argelina Cheibub, and Fernando Limongi, "O Congresso e as Medidas Provisórias: Abdicação ou Delegação?," *Novos Estudos*, CEBRAP 47, São Paulo, 1997.

Figueiredo, Argelina Cheibub, and Fernando Limongi, "Presidential Powers, Legislative Organization, and Party Behavior in Brazil," *Comparative Politics*, Vol. 32, No. 2, 2000, pp. 151–170.

Flynn, Peter, "Collor Corruption and Crisis: Time for Reflection," *Journal of Latin American Studies*, Vol. 25, No. 2, 1993, pp. 351–372.

Garman, Christopher, Stephan Haggard, and Eliza Willis, "Fiscal Decentralization, a Political Theory with Latin American Cases," *World Politics*, Vol. 53, No. 2, 2001, pp. 205–236.

Giambiagi, Fábio, and Ana Claudia Duarte Além, *Finanças Públicas: Teoria e Prática no Brasil* (Rio de Janeiro: Campus, 1999).

Guardia, Eduardo, "As Razões do Ajuste Fiscal," in Giambiagi, Fabio, José Guilherme Reis, and André Urani (eds.), *Reformas do Brasil: Balanço e Agenda* (Rio de Janeiro: Editora Nova Fronteira, 2004).

Kingstone, Peter, "Muddling Through Gridlock: Economic Performance, Business Response, and Democratic Sustainability"; in: Kingstone, Peter, and Timothy Power (eds.), *Democratic Brazil. Actors, Institutions and Processes* (Pittsburgh: University of Pittsburgh Press, 2000).

Laakso, Markku, and Rein Taagepera, "Effective Number of Parties: A Measure with Application to West Europe," *Comparative Political Studies*, Vol. 12, No. 1, 1979, pp. 3–27.

Leite, Cristiane Kerches da Silva, "O Processo de Ordenamento Fiscal no Brasil na Década de 1990 e a Lei de Responsabilidade Fiscal," Ph.D. Thesis, Departamento de Ciência Política, Universidade de São Paulo, 2005.

Mainwaring, Scott, "Brazil. Weak Parties, Feckless Democracy," in: Mainwaring, Scott and Timothy Scully (eds.), *Building Democratic Institutions: Party Systems in Latin America* (Stanford: Stanford University Press, 1995).

Mainwaring, Scott, "Multipartism, Robust Federalism, and Presidentialism in Brazil"; in: Mainwaring, Scott and Matthew Shugart (eds.), *Presidentialism and Democracy in Latin America* (Cambridge: Cambridge University Press, 1997).

Mainwaring, Scott, *Rethinking Party Systems in the Third Wave of Democratization: The Case of Brazil* (Stanford: Stanford University Press, 1999).

Melo, Marcus André, *As Reformas Constitucionais no Brasil: Instituições Políticas e Processo Decisório* (Rio de Janeiro: Editora Revan, 2002).

Moraes Valença, Marcio, "The Politics of Giving in Brazil: The Rise and Demise of Collor (1990–1992)," *Latin American Perspectives*, Vol. 29, No. 1, Brazil: The Hegemonic Process in Political and Cultural Formation (Jan., 2002), pp. 115–152.

Nassif, Luís, "Política Macroeconómica e Ajuste Fiscal"; in: Lamonier, Bolívar and Rubens Figueiredo (eds.), *A Era FHC: Um Balanço* (São Paulo: Cultura Editores Associados, 2002).

Negretto, Gabriel, "¿Gobierna solo el Presidente? Poderes de Decreto y Diseño Institucional en Brasil y Argentina," *Desarrollo Económico*, Vol. 42, No. 167, 2002, pp. 377–404.

Neumanne, José, *A República na Lama: Uma Tragédia Brasileira* (Sao Paulo: Geracão, 1992).

Pang, Eul-Soo, *The International Political Economy of Transformation in Argentina, Brazil, and Chile since 1960* (New York: Palgrave, 2002).

Panizza, Francisco, "Is Brazil Becoming a 'Boring Country'?" *Bulletin of Latin American Research*, Vol. 19, No. 4, 2000, pp. 501–525.

Power, Timothy, "Politicized Democracy: Competition, Institutions, and 'Civic Fatigue' in Brazil," *Journal of Interamerican Studies and World Affairs*, Vol. 33, No. 3, 1991, pp. 75–112.

Power, Timothy, "The Pen Is Mightier than the Congress: Presidential Decree Power in Brazil"; in: Carey, John M. and Matthew Soberg Shugart (eds.), *Executive Decree Authority* (Cambridge: Cambridge University Press, 1998), pp. 197–230.

Rigolon, Francisco and Fabio Giambiagi, "A Renegociação das Dívidas e o Regime Fiscal dos Estados," *Textos para Discussão 69*, Banco Nacional de Desenvolvimento Econômico e Social, 1999.

Roarelli, Maria Liz de M., "Análise das Transferências Negociadas por Órgão e Esfera de Governo" (São Paulo: Mimeo, Fundap, 1994).

Rocca, Carlos Antonio, "Brazil's Plano Real: A Chance of Success?" in: D'Alva Kinzo, Maria (ed.), *Growth and Development in Brazil: Cardoso's Real Challenge* (London: Institute of Latin American Studies, University of London, 1995).

Rodden, Jonathan, *Hamilton's Paradox: The Promise and Peril of Fiscal Federalism* (Cambridge: Cambridge University Press, 2006).

Samuels, David, "Concurrent Elections, Discordant Results: Presidentialism, Federalism, and Governance in Brazil," *Comparative Politics*, Vol. 33, No. 1, 2000a, pp. 1–20.

Samuels, David, "The Gubernatorial Coattails Effect: Federalism and Congressional Elections in Brazil," *Journal of Politics*, Vol. 62, No. 1, 2000b, pp. 240–254.

Samuels, David, "Fiscal Straitjacket: The Politics of Macroeconomic Reform in Brazil, 1995–2002," *Journal of Latin American Studies*, Vol. 35, No. 3, 2003a, pp. 545–569.

Samuels, David, *Ambition, Federalism, and Legislative Politics in Brazil* (Cambridge: Cambridge University Press, 2003b).

Samuels, David, and Scott Mainwaring, "Strong Federalism, Constraints on the Central Government, and Economic Reform in Brazil"; in: Gibson, Edward L. (ed.), *Federalism and Democracy in Latin America* (Baltimore: Johns Hopkins University Press, 2004).

Weyland, Kurt, "The Rise and Fall of President Collor and Its Impact on Brazilian Democracy," *Journal of Interamerican Studies and World Affairs*, Vol. 35, No. 1, 1993, pp. 1–37.

Weyland, Kurt, "The Brazilian State in the New Democracy," *Journal of Interamerican Studies and World Affairs*, Vol. 39, Issue 4, 1998, pp. 63–94.

Willis, Eliza, Christopher da C.B. Garman, and Stephan Haggard, "The Politics of Decentralization in Latin America," *Latin American Research Review*, Vol. 34, No. 1, 1999, pp. 7–56.

5   *Primus contra pares*

Introduction

No sequence of the game is played from scratch. Previous stages of the game in time t−1 influenced the dynamics of the game in time t. The erosion of the federal government's fiscal balance, the parallel strengthening of subnational governments', and the sharp macroeconomic disequilibrium generated by gubernatorial predation during the first presidencies post-transition to democracy in Argentina and Brazil contributed to intensifying the presidents' fiscal incentives to alter the status quo ante. Despite these incentives, how can a president pass centralizing reforms against the most powerful governors in the region? How were federal executives capable of doing so after a period in which subnational governments were notably strengthened in relation to the central government? How could presidents erode subnational autonomy in a regional context in which political, fiscal, and administrative decentralization was on the rise? In this chapter, I analyze the process by which the *primus* concentrated political power, clashed against the *pares*, and passed centralizing reforms that notably debilitated them.

Federal institutions, electoral rules, and party regulations can account for comparative statics, but they are inadequate when it comes to explaining this fundamental shift from strong governors, and their pressing demands for funds, to strong presidents and centralizing changes. In the context of basically the same institutional frameworks (with marginal changes), presidents had to deal with strong and coordinated governors, first, and then governors had to face powerful presidents who passed centralizing reforms that favored the federal government. Economic crises, by themselves, cannot explain these reforms either, as Alfonsín, Sarney, and Collor faced them and could not alter the federal balance in their favor as Menem and Cardoso did. Several historical analyses have studied changes during this period, but these accounts are based on ad hoc explanations that cannot account for centralization and decentralization using the same theoretical model.

In the first part of this chapter, I examine the main features of the key independent variables during the Carlos Menem presidency in Argentina.

With some details on the setting, I put forward the theoretical expectations based on the model introduced in Chapter 1. Next, I analyze the dynamics of the federal game over the distribution of resources and functions, and describe the outcomes in terms of the federal balance and the differences from the previous administration. I repeat the same structure of analysis for the presidency of Fernando Henrique Cardoso in Brazil in the second part of the chapter. In the conclusions of this work, I analyze similarities and differences between the Cardoso and the Menem reforms and their implications for the functioning of these two federal democracies.

The main argument in this chapter is that under large fiscal crises, changes to the federal balance were more likely to occur when federal executives were capable of amassing political power and support in Congress. Both Menem and Cardoso had strong fiscal incentives due to the critical situation of the economy after hyperinflation and the reforms endorsed by governors during 1988. They were capable of gaining political support from citizens and votes in elections during the stabilization process. They also distributed selective incentives to governors and federal legislators. As a result, congressmen had more incentives to support presidential reforms than the status quo the governors defended. These resources were crucial for presidents to alter the federal balance. Here I study how they did that.

The Menem presidency (1989–1999)

Carlos Menem, the former governor of an impoverished Northwestern province, ascended to the presidency after winning the first primary in the history of Peronism. Once in office, he built up political support through strenuous struggles inside his divided party by co-opting others in the opposition, allying himself with influential economic and interest groups (and, hence, facing strong resistance from some factions in the PJ and Peronist unions), and winning the support of some sectors of the public that would have never imagined supporting him. He ended up amassing a great deal of political power, but he also faced limits imposed by other influential political actors. Among them, I specifically analyze the role played by governors in the opposition and in the president's own party.

The power of the president

To analyze the setting of the federal distributive game we need to know how power was distributed between the president and governors and the nature of the fiscal incentives these actors faced. I begin by analyzing presidential power. During Menem's first term in office, the president's party had the largest share of seats in both chambers of Congress (the largest delegation, or a plurality, in the Chamber of Deputies and a majority in the Senate), and Peronist governors ruled in most of the provinces. He was able to pass several reforms in Congress, but also faced opposition and had to make substantial concessions to move forward on some of the issues in his agenda.

Menem won the 1989 election with 47.5 percent of the vote against his rival from the UCR, Eduardo César Angeloz (the former governor of Córdoba), who got 31.9 percent. Out of the 1989 electoral results, the PJ won 112 seats or 44.1 percent of the Lower Chamber, versus 90 seats for the UCR (34.4 percent). That guaranteed the president support from the largest delegation, but not control over a majority of the seats. Yet, upon taking office, Menem made an alliance with the Liberals from the Center Democratic Union, UCeDe, and some minor provincial parties (which got a total of 34 seats, or 13.4 percent of the Chamber of Deputies). With the support of these parties, members of an informal governing coalition with the PJ, Menem was granted legislative backing for several of his sponsored reforms. Both in the 1991 and the 1993 legislative elections, the PJ increased its share in the lower house (from 112 to 119 deputies, or 46.3 percent in 1991 (and 124 or 48.2 percent in 1993). The PJ formally won 128 seats but had control over 124 deputies due to a group of dissidents who left the legislative delegation and later formed the *Frente Grande*. The UCR's share fell from 90 to 85 seats or 33.1 percent in 1991 (and 83 seats or 32.3 percent in 1993). Even after those victories, the president did not have control over a majority of the seats in the Chamber of Deputies. It was only after the 1995 election that the PJ won this majority (132 deputies and 51.4 percent), increasing the margin of difference over the UCR to 64 deputies. In the Senate, the PJ had a comfortable majority; it increased its share in this Chamber from 21 seats (or 45.7 percent) for the period 1983–1989 to 26 seats (or 56.5 percent) after the 1989 election.

Menem got considerable support from the PJ, although internal struggles were bitter at the beginning of his term in office. In December 1990, Menem took advantage of a defeat Antonio Cafiero suffered in a plebiscite to reform the constitution of the Buenos Aires province to allow his ree-lection as governor, and finally got a hold of the presidency of the party.[1] Despite the internal struggles at the beginning of his term, Menem's control inside the party ended up being extensive, and early efforts to build non-Menemist factions failed to take hold (Levitsky, 2003, 149), at least during his first years in office (a group of dissidents split from the PJ and formed the *Frente Grande* in 1993 and *Frepaso* in 1994). In the end, the PJ showed a high degree of internal discipline. According to roll-call data collected by Jones (2002), between 1989 and 1991, 97 percent of the PJ legislators who were voting voted with the majority of the party (relative discipline); this figure decreases to 72 percent if we consider the total of those members present at the session (absolute majority). The main opposition party, the UCR, was weakened after the demise of Alfonsín and remained very much divided.

On July 8, 1989, Alfonsín left office with only a 29 percent approval rating; Menem's approval rating was 84 percent just after he assumed office. But it decreased dramatically shortly thereafter as the first efforts to control inflation failed, plummeting to 30.5 percent early in March 1991, before the Convertibility Plan. As the first results of the stabilization plan began to appear, support from public opinion increased substantially again, peaking at over 50 percent by December 1991 (Data from Nueva Mayoría). This backing was reflected in the electoral victories during the 1991 legislative and gubernatorial elections.

In spite of having support from his party and vast sectors of the population, Menem also took advantage of (and some claim that he abused) the institutional resources available to the federal executive. To begin with, he made extensive use of the executive's decree power. According to Ferreira Rubio and Goretti (1996, 454–457), between July 1989 and August 1994, Menem signed 336 necessity and urgency decrees, while between 1853 and July 1989 only 35 decrees had been issued.[2] Furthermore, the approval rate of executive decrees in Argentina had been relatively high, especially due to the rule of "tacit approval" by which Congressional inaction has been interpreted by the Supreme Court as explicit legislative approval without amendments. This substantial participation of the president in the law-making process has been taken as an indication of concentration of power in the hands of the president, leading some scholars to claim that "the president governs alone" (Ferreira Rubio and Goretti, 1996, 473). Others have argued that this was a reflection of an autocratic presidential "style" (Mustapic, 2000, 585, 594). All these institutional resources were available to other presidents before Menem. The key difference between Menem and Alfonsín, for instance, was that the former made vast use of them and, in many cases, pushed them to their constitutional limits (or beyond).

Presidential power and economic (and fiscal) context

The hyperinflationary crisis as well as the chaotic macroeconomic situation after Alfonsín contributed to the expansion of the president's political support. As a consequence of the crisis, the president received considerable backing from the public and many important socio-political groups and institutions (like the leaders of the main parties, the Supreme Court, the Armed Forces, and the Catholic Church). These actors explicitly or implicitly supported the concentration of political power in the executive (Novaro, 1994, 183). Other scholars have also argued that even the Supreme Court and Congress were not significant checks on the powers of the federal executive (Jones et al., 2002). Taking into account this process of concentration of power and the context of economic crisis, O'Donnell (1994) differentiates electoral democracies like the Argentine during the Menem administration (and others in the region sharing similar characteristics) from representative democracies. He calls the former "delegative" democracies and basically characterizes them by executive concentration of power and an overall lack of horizontal accountability.

Despite being a powerful president, bypassing Congress on several occasions to rule by decree, and displaying general features of a delegative democracy during his period in office, Menem met (sometimes strong) resistance and opposition in the legislature as well as in some provincial governments during his ten-year administration. Llanos (2001) shows, for instance, how Menem faced opposition of varying intensity in Congress during several stages of the privatization reforms. For her, there is little evidence "to argue that the weakness of Congress is a permanent feature of the political regime" (2001, 73) and to claim that the president governed alone (Ferreira Rubio and Goretti, 1996, 473). In fact, to the privatization issue we can add the federal distribution of funds and functions, on which, after an initial period of executive dominance, Menem faced increasing resistance from governors and Congress.

Summing up, Menem was a relatively powerful president in partisan terms (especially when compared to Alfonsín) and got support from key political actors and from the public in the midst of hyperinflation, especially after the economy was stabilized in 1991. The fact that the president got support for many of the reforms he tried to pass does not mean, however, that he did not face resistance and opposition to other issues on his reform agenda during different periods of his mandate.

The power of governors

Besides presidential power, the other key variable needed to analyze the distribution of power in the federation is that of the governors. In terms of the institutional dimension of gubernatorial power, there were no substantial changes between the Alfonsín and the Menem administrations. In partisan terms, and on average, governors were slightly more powerful in their districts during Menem's presidency than they were during Alfonsín's. The critical and obvious differences were that the PJ won in most provinces, that most governors (from the PJ and other parties) were politically allied to Menem on most issues, and that the president was able to divide coordination efforts among those opposing him. Partisan links and alliances between presidents and governors are crucial in influencing presidential and gubernatorial power. But it is not the only factor determining it; coordination efforts among governors (which can be partisan, but not exclusively, as there is inter-partisan coordination, even among opposition parties) in favor of or against the president are another critical component of these actors' power.

If we analyze provincial electoral results during the first part of Menem's administration (1989–1991), the average governor got elected with 47.4 percent of the vote and controlled 54.9 percent of the seats in the provincial legislature.[3] As during Alfonsín's term in office, most governors had control over their state assemblies and none of them faced a divided government. With respect to the gubernatorial partisan powers index, the average value was 1.85 (the highest value was 1.95 in 1991; the lowest 1.85, after 1992), higher than the 1.67 average during Alfonsín.

In sum, most governors had an important degree of control over their districts in institutional and partisan terms. The fact that most of them were in the president's party or coalition also made them influential actors at the national level. The president could count on the support from important and powerful political actors. The crucial differences between the Alfonsín and the Menem administrations were not so much how powerful governors were in their districts in institutional terms (variables that were relatively stable over the period), or in partisan terms (although governors were slightly more powerful in partisan terms during Menem's term), but rather how many of them were linked to the president, how much they were able to coordinate in favor or against the federal executive, and how powerful the president was to prevent coordination against him. In this regard, the Menem administration was substantively different from that of Alfonsín; the former governor of La Rioja was able to gather support on most issues from an important group of subnational leaders and divide those opposing him.

During the second half of Alfonsín's term in office (after the 1987 election), opposition governors had strong incentives to coordinate along partisan lines against the central government (see Chapter 3). During Menem's two terms in office, both the president and a majority of governors were from the same party (and from parties allied with the federal executive). Under those conditions, the president had partisan tools to deter coordination against the central government (he controlled resources for campaigns, several nominations, and many positions on the party lists), whereas governors had fewer incentives and faced more costs (politically and fiscally) if they coordinated against the federal executive.[4] Other forms of coordination included some regional dynamics, especially for demanding fiscal exemptions (industrial promotion regimes in La Rioja, Catamarca, San Juan, and San Luis) (Eaton, 2001c) or specific subsidies for certain industries or economic sectors (such as tobacco production for some Northern provinces, and the wool industry for some Southern districts). Through these forms of coordination some governors achieved some fiscal gains for their districts. Despite these gains for the coordinating provinces and others for few districts or regions, these forms of coordination were far from achieving substantial gains for all subnational governments. In fact, the president conceded fiscal compensation and gave rewards to governors in exchange for loyalty, distributing selective incentives to deter major coordination efforts or opposition from the provinces. The stabilization of the economy and the privatization process helped the Menem administration and the Federal Treasury get some fiscal resources to use in the distribution of selective incentives (see below). This contrasts to the Alfonsín administration, for which none of the two sources of income were available.

The fiscal context

The overall economic and fiscal scenario in 1989, when Menem took office, was alarming. Inflation, one of the main concerns for the incoming government, was basically beyond the control of economic authorities: it had escalated to 4,923 percent in 1989 and 20,594 percent between April 1989 and March 1990. Other major worries for the new administration and its economic team were how to reduce the fiscal deficit and the debt as well as resume growth. The federal government deficit was 4.6 percent of GDP in 1987, reaching 6.2 percent in 1988 (ECLAC-CEPAL, 1997, 2005; see Table 5.1).

The debt problem also posed serious challenges for the federal government. During 1989 alone, the external debt jumped from $58 billion to $64 billion. By 1999, the total public sector debt reached $152 billion (*Secretaría de Finanzas*, Ministry of Economy). Under this volatile economic situation, GDP fell 6.9 percent in 1989 and 1.8 percent in 1990. The 1988 revenue-sharing law and its obligation to share more than 56 percent of the total federal revenues with the provinces exerted sharp pressures on the budget of the central government and contributed to fiscal and economic instability (Eaton, 2004, 147). Forced by the critical economic and fiscal situation, the central government had to convert a big part of bank deposits ($1.5 billion) into long-term dollar bonds on January 1, 1990, (Acuña, 1994, 41). The overall economic and fiscal situation in Argentina was much worse than the one in Brazil before the Plano Real.

Table 5.1 Fiscal deficit in Argentina (1987–1999)

Year	Fiscal deficit
1987	−4.6
1988	−6.2
1989	−3.2
1990	−3.8
1991	−1.6
1992	−0.1
1993	1.4
1994	−0.2
1995	−0.6
1996	−3.2
1997	−1.5
1998	−2.4
1999	−4.5

Source: Data compiled and adapted from ECLAC-CEPAL (1997, 2005).

Provincial finances reflected the general macroeconomic turmoil despite the increase in federal transfers after 1988. Total provincial debt increased from AR$3 billion in 1986 to almost AR$6 billion in 1989, and AR$7.5 billion in 1990. Total provincial deficits escalated from AR$3.9 billion in 1989 to AR$6.2 billion in 1990, reaching AR$8.5 billion in 1999.

In a context of growing inflation and the anticipated handing over of the presidency from Alfonsín to Menem, the incoming chief executive negotiated support to pass two laws, the State Reform Law (23,696) and Economic Emergency Law (23,697) (sanctioned by Congress on August 17 and September 15, 1989, respectively). These laws allowed the elected president to declare economic and administrative emergencies and initiate structural reforms, including downsizing the state, selling public-owned companies, privatizing, deregulating, reducing or eliminating subsidies, reforming the Central Bank, and opening up the economy. These initial reforms were the keystone for the stabilization program put forward a year and a half later. After a series of failed attempts to stabilize the economy and control inflation between 1989 and the beginning of year 1991, Menem appointed Domingo Cavallo as the Ministry of Economy on March 1 of that year. On March 27, Cavallo got Congressional approval for the Convertibility Law (23,928), which converted each peso to one dollar, required monetary emission to be backed with Central Bank reserves, and eliminated indexation clauses in contracts.

The macroeconomic context changed substantially after the 1991 plan. The Convertibility Plan proved capable of reducing inflation to 1 percent per month by late 1991. Growth resumed at an annual average of 8.8 percent between 1990 and 1994, the highest rate for a four-year period in a century (Gerchunoff and Llach, 1998, 443). Tax revenues increased substantially, especially the VAT, in a macroeconomic context characterized by lowering inflation, economic growth, and larger consumption. Between 1990 and 1993, federal tax revenues grew from 12.4 percent of GDP to 16.2 percent of GDP; while total revenues expanded from 14.7 to 19.6 percent of GDP. As total tax revenues increased, so did automatic transfers to the provinces. Revenue-sharing transfers rose from 4.7 percent of GDP in 1988 to 7.4 percent of GDP in 1992 (Cetrángolo and Jiménez, 1996).

Despite these signs of improvement in some macroeconomic indicators, especially inflation, growth, and tax collection, others were still a source of concern. Among them were the trade deficit, foreign debt interest payments, and the fiscal deficit, all of which demanded more revenues from the central government. Although macroeconomic stability and growth contributed to easing fiscal imbalances, government spending pushed them up again. After convertibility fiscal deficits eased marginally, but they returned and continued between 1994 and 2002. In 1996 (after the 1995 Mexican crisis), the fiscal deficit rose again to levels equal to those prevailing before 1991, reaching 3.2 percent in that year (see Table 5.1;

ECLAC-CEPAL, 1997, 2005). These deficits generated incentives for the central government to reduce spending and access more funds. Budget constraints increasingly hardened under convertibility mainly because printing money was restricted to the equivalent amount in national reserves (see Table 5.2 and Figure 5.1).

The federal distributive game during the Menem presidency

The settings of the game

During the Menem government, especially between 1991 and 1993, the president had relatively ample partisan powers and made vast use of his institutional powers (especially his decree powers). The settings of the federal distributive game were favorable for the president in relation to the distribution of political power and relatively adverse for the governors. Despite being relatively powerful in their districts, PJ and allied governors were politically subordinated to the president, and those opposing him were uncoordinated and divided along partisan lines and by the selective incentives that the federal executive distributed to them. The adverse fiscal situation and the hyperinflationary crises moved Menem to take action and alter the unfavorable fiscal imbalances and pressures the federal government faced.

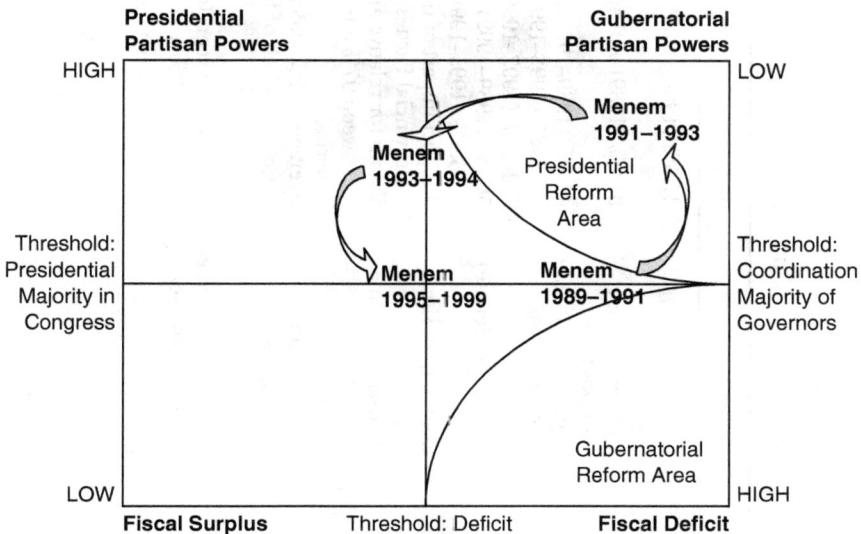

Figure 5.1 Synthesis of the main variables during Menem (1989–1999).

Note
The area inside both arches is where the probability of changes in the status quo ante is larger.

Table 5.2 Values taken by the main variables during Menem (1989–1999)

	Variable	Value	Range high-low	Overall value
Presidential electoral power	Electoral support president	47.5% (1989); 44.9% (1995).	Medium	From relatively low (1989–1991) to high (1991–1994) to relatively low (1995–1999) presidential power
	Electoral support opposition	31.9% (1989) and 45.1% (1995).	Relatively low to medium	
	% of seats (Chamber of Deputies)	44.1% (1989–1991); 46.3% (1991–1993); 48.2% (1993–1995); 51.4% (1995–1997), 46.3% (1997–1999).	Medium to relatively high	
	% of seats (Senate)	56.5% (1989–1992); 58.3% (1992–1995); 55.5% (1995–1998); 50% (1998–1999).	Relatively high	
	Role of opposition	Support in part of the opposition (UCeDe, Provincial Parties, and part of the UCR).	–	
	Partisan discipline	Values for relative and absolute discipline between 97% and 70% for the entire period.	From relatively high to high	
	Approval rate in Congress	Average 58.8% executive bills approval rate. Less than half of bills in 1990; 60% 1993–1994; 30% 1998.	From relatively high to relatively low	
Presidential legislative power	Use of decree power	336 DNU between Jul.1989 and Aug.1994.	Very high	High legislative power
	Use of veto power	109 cases (12%); 11 Congressional overrides.	High	
Presidential approval	Positive image in public opinion	From 84% in 1989; 30.5% early in March 1991; 50% by Dec. 1991; 36.6% 1994–1995; below 20% 1996–1998; 16% 1999.	From high to low	From high to low approval

Gubernatorial power	Average gubernatorial electoral support	47.4% (1989–1991); 50.7% (1991); and 54.7% (1997).	Relatively high to high	Relatively high gubernat. power
	Average legislative support (% of seats)	54.9% (1989–1991); 55% (1991); and 57.1% (1997).	High	
	Gubernatorial partisan powers index	High: 1.85 for the period; (highest value 1.95 in 1991; lowest 1.85 in 1992).	High	
	Proportion of allied governors	From 17/22 in 1989 to 12/23 in 1997.	From very high to high	
	Gubernatorial coordination	Relatively low to medium (1995–1999)	Low to medium	
Economic context	Economic growth	GDP fell 6.9% in 1989; 1.8% in 1990; but economy grew at average of 8.8% in 1990–1994; 2.25% in 1995–1999.	Low to medium	Relatively excruciating (early 1990s) to critical economic context (late 1990s)
	Inflation	4,924% in 1989; 20,594% for April 1989 and March 1990; reduced to one-digit figures after 1992.	Very high to very low	
	External debt	Jumped from $58 billion to $65 billion in 1989. By 1999 it reached $152 billion.	High	
	Provincial debt	$3 billion in 1986 to $7.5 billion in 1990.	High	
	Budget constraints	From hard to harder.	–	
Fiscal indicators	Federal fiscal deficit	4.6% of GDP in 1987, 6.2% in 1988, 3.2% in 1989, and 3.8% in 1990. Average of 2% deficit during the 1990s.	High	Very strong to strong fiscal pressures
	Provincial fiscal deficit	Average provincial deficits as a share of total provincial revenues more than 10% in the 1990s. Provincial deficit increased over 500% and debt over 300% in 1992–1995.	High	

As argued in the theoretical chapter, I expect that a powerful president in a context of fiscal crisis and hard budget constraints would try to get a more favorable federal equation balance (a payoff of γ and impose a payoff of $-\gamma$ to the governors; the Nash equilibrium is indicated with the asterisks in Figure 5.2). If the president centralizes resources or decentralizes functions without resources and the governors accept this reform without clashing, the president gets a total payoff of γ, while governors get $-\gamma$. The president will improve her net balance $\Sigma(r_{jp}-P_{ip})$, as she has to perform the same or fewer functions (P_{ip}) with more resources (r_{jp}). Governors, on the contrary, would get a payoff equal to $-\gamma$, as they have the same or new functions (P_{ig}) to deliver with fewer resources (r_{ig}), suffering a deterioration in their net balance, $\Sigma(P_{ig}-r_{ig})$. If governors decide to clash, the president will get a payoff equal to $(\gamma-C)(1-w)$ and the governors get a payoff equal to $(-\gamma-C)w$. C is the cost of changing the status quo and w is the probability of conflict linked to the centralizing reform endorsed by the president. Figure 5.2 presents the normal form game.

In the case the president expects to pass favorable reforms of the system of transfers, she would also seek to take negotiations inside Congress to institutionalize her gains and change the legal status quo ante in her favor. Weak governors facing a powerful president who takes action in a context of fiscal crisis can either accept the changes passed by Congress at request of the president or conflict with the federal executive. The decision to negotiate or clash depends on the costs they face and the probability of conflict. Costs depend on the characteristics of the reform being implemented. The probability of conflict depends on how powerful and coordinated governors are, how powerful the president is, and how critical the fiscal context is (as well as how strong budget constraints are). The governors have larger incentives to negotiate some form of compensation instead of conflict with the president when they are weaker and less coordinated, the president is more powerful, and the fiscal context is more critical (and budget constraints are harder). A clash is more likely when the expected costs of changing the status quo for the president are larger, her

		Governors	
		Power	No power
President	Power	0,0	$(\gamma-C)w^*,(-\gamma-C)(1-w)^*$
	No power	$(-\delta-C)w,(\delta-C)(1-w)$	0,0

Figure 5.2 Normal form game for Menem (1991–1993).

political resources to pass the reforms are fewer, and the governors are more capable of coordinating and reacting to these reforms.

Having presented the theoretical expectations, I proceed to the analysis of the expected benefits, costs, and the probability of conflict in the next section. With this information, I explore the dynamics of negotiations between president Menem and governors over the distribution of funds and functions between 1989 and 1999.

Expected benefits and costs

The expected benefits for the president of changing the status quo were high: the central government faced strong fiscal pressures over the budget that were reflected in the increasing federal fiscal deficit: the peak was 6.2 percent in 1988, and although it was reduced to 3.2 in 1989, it increased once again in 1990, reaching 3.8 percent. Among the several causes of these pressures, some crucial ones were the high spending level of the central government and the large transfers to the provinces. Menem expected to reduce those pressures and balance the federal government's accounts, and in doing so, get more access to funds for furthering his political goals. Menem faced relatively soft budget constraints, and he got vast support from IFIs, which lent large amounts of money to Argentina to undertake structural reforms during the 1990s. But there were limits to these funds as well as to the adjustment and downsizing of the state to reduce central government spending.

Very importantly too, the president had strong political incentives to change the status quo: as automatic transfers increased substantially after the 1988 revenue-sharing law, they removed an important tool in the hands of the federal executive for building up political support, namely, the ability of the president to make revenue transfers conditional on gubernatorial and legislative backing. Governors received federal automatic transfers which could be used according to their political goals (these funds were not earmarked). In sum, Menem needed to both stabilize national accounts to prevent inflation from reescalating after the 1991 stabilization program and gain more funds to continue building up political support. The president needed both assets: funds and political support.

Governors expected to face relatively large costs in negotiations with the president and, especially, with his Minister of Economy after 1991. They knew the reformist stance was strong and that federal authorities had the political capital to influence them. Expecting relatively large costs in a critical fiscal context but not having sufficient power to coordinate and prevent changes against a powerful president led governors to take a more defensive and less confrontational stance. They wanted to preserve the status quo ante in relation to the revenue-sharing scheme if at all possible; if not, they wanted changes to be the least profound as possible and to negotiate compensation for any of the reforms to come.

PJ legislators had incentives to support the federal executive's reform attempts. The president was popular in public opinion (especially after late 1991), had more partisan influence than any governor (Menem had important control over their career prospects, and he could veto lists proposed by governors; the president also controlled access to positions in the federal administration), and had more funds to further legislators' goals (either in campaigns or for building support on their districts). This contributed to disciplining their behavior in Congress. Contrary to what happened under Alfonsín, federal legislators had few if any incentives to oppose the president. Opposing him meant a larger probability of getting fewer funds for their districts, and they would incur the risk of endangering their political careers inside the PJ, which was under the tight control of the federal executive.[5]

The expected costs of centralizing reforms were relatively high. This has usually been the case: centralizing funds and reducing transfers to the provinces has been such a costly option in terms of reactions from the governors and other subnational officials (such as mayors from large cities) that only authoritarian military rulers could afford doing so. This centralizing option was also costly as a partial consequence of changes in the previous stages of the game. The military government imposed very high costs on subnational governments after the 1978 decentralization of functions without new resources for the provinces. Although governors got substantive benefits from the changes in the revenue-sharing scheme in 1988, these new funds decentralized from the central government were mainly used to cover deficits still mounting after the 1978 decentralization process (and in many cases, though not all, their own fiscal profligacy). These relative gains in the federal balance were slashed by hyperinflation and the collapse of GDP and tax collection during the last months of the Alfonsín administration and the first months of Menem's, forcing provinces into new fiscal deficits and higher debt burdens. The expected costs of reversing those gains in revenue sharing were relatively high for the president, as defensive coordination to sustain them was very likely among governors (including some PJ governors, especially those who had presidential aspirations). That substantially increased the probability of conflict with governors, even those from the president's own party.

Both the president and governors faced increasingly harder budget constraints. In 1991, as part of Cavallo's stabilization attempts, the central government faced a series of restrictions imposed by the convertibility law in terms of money printing and issuing debt. This law also limited the sources of funds and resources the federal executive could use for political purposes. As these funds were limited, central authorities looked for alternative sources of revenues where available. Additionally, the central administration eliminated the rediscounting and monetization of provincial debts. Provincial governments could no longer incur debt and transfer their costs to the federal government (Wibbels, 2004, 217). As a consequence, both governors and the president had greater incentives to alter the federal balance, gain access to revenues, and finance their fiscal imbalances and political goals.

Another important restriction for governors was the collective action problems they faced. Structural divisions among provinces, partisan differences, and the federal government's strategies to divide them contributed to preventing their coordination (see González, 2012). Menem discouraged governors from building up a united front in negotiations with him by two main means. First, he elevated the costs of defection: those who would not negotiate would have to face high costs, including being excluded from the revenue-sharing regime (not only from negotiating the terms of the law but also from receiving funds at all). Second, he increased selective incentives: the president crafted deals with governors individually and delivered particular benefits to each of them, especially to the least developed provinces (González, 2012), to garner support and prevent opposition (see section on compensation and selective incentives below). As the fiscal conditions in some provinces worsened, the president could use bailouts and fiscal rescue packages in exchange for support for the reforms he endorsed. This strategy was very similar to that followed by Cardoso in Brazil.

Negotiations over the decentralization of education and health care services

Menem could not pass a new revenue-sharing law favorable to the central government because the costs of changing it were relatively high. He understood quite well that this was a conflictive strategy; he was himself a governor before being president. In fact, the federal executive did not send a bill to Congress to propose changes to the revenue-sharing scheme between 1989 and 1992.[6]

Instead of centralizing resources by modifying the revenue-sharing law, Menem decided to negotiate a reduction in the costs for the central government by decentralizing functions and the expenses associated with them. This would also result in a positive balance for the central government out of the federal equation (a reduction in P_{ip}, holding relatively constant r_{ip}).

This option also supposed costs, but some contextual reasons played to its favor: first, most governors, especially those from larger provinces, wanted more functions (and criticized the calamities generated by excessive centralization), albeit with more resources, while none of the governors wanted fewer resources. PJ governors had demanded such decentralization, at least since the Mar del Plata meeting in 1988, shortly after the sanction of the new revenue-sharing law. Second, the fiscal situation of the provinces partially improved after the stabilization plan, once growth resumed (although fiscal pressures were still high). Third, the military government had already decentralized functions (without resources) in 1978, so most provinces were already delivering health care and education services.[7] Fourth, a decentralizing trend in the region and abroad favored this option, and funds from IFIs were available for financing this reform (Lardone, 2008). All these factors contributed, at least to some extent, to reducing the costs of carrying out this reform option and the probability of conflict among actors.

Decentralization was a policy (or a "tool") available for the president out of which he could achieve substantial fiscal and political gains. It would be illusory to believe that a president (and less so Menem and his Minister of Economy) wanted to surrender authority over key functions and empower his most serious challengers, the governors (even when the majority of them were loyal to the president). In reality, as the federal distributive game would predict based on the distribution of political power and the fiscal context, he did quite the opposite.

An early bill that attempted to decentralize education to the provinces was sent to Congress by the ministry of Education, Luis Barry, in February 1990, soon after Menem took office. This bill was based on some recommendations made by the National Pedagogic Congress (NPC, *Congreso Pedagógico Nacional*) called during the Alfonsín administration. The main purpose was to improve the education system by decentralizing it, and in the bill the federal government was in charge of guaranteeing the fiscal funds for the decentralized services (see fundaments of the bill introduced February 7, 1990). The bill never reached the floor. One of the main concerns was, as we could expect, who would finance the decentralized services. Provincial authorities distrusted the central government and feared they would end up paying for the costs (Repetto, 2001c, 26). The federal government did not want to pay for them either.

As inflation diminished and the economy recovered after 1991, tax revenues increased (also because of broadened tax bases and higher tax rates), making the total amount of transfers to the provinces grow substantially. In 1990, the total amount of transfers to the provinces was $14.7 billion, reaching AR$20.4 billion in 1991, the year of the negotiations with the central government, and AR$25.1 billion in 1992 (after the decentralization of the new functions); revenue sharing grew from a total of AR$11.6 billion in 1990 to AR$17.6 billion in 1992 (constant 2004 prices; data from *Subsecretaría de Relaciones Fiscales y Económicas con las Provincias*). This increase in provincial revenue resulted in bringing some relief to provincial finances, reducing their demands for more transfers, and easing fiscal relations between the federal government and the governors. More importantly, however, the increase reduced the expected costs of decentralizing functions (provinces had more resources) and lowered the probability of conflict between president and governors.[8]

Taking advantage of these fiscal conditions after the 1991 stabilization plan, the central government decided to initiate negotiations with the governors to decentralize education and health care services. Menem and Cavallo wanted the governors to spend these new funds on social services instead of using them to expand payroll and patronage (Eaton, 2004, 150). Central authorities claimed that this was a real threat to stabilization reforms. But it was also a potential threat to Menem from serious political challengers. Governors could use those funds to build up political support for furthering their careers (and eventually challenge the central government, especially in the case of the most powerful governors).

The federal executive was divided over the way to implement the decentralizing reform. The Minister of Education wanted a gradual decentralization of secondary education with the corresponding financial backing to the provinces, but the Minister of Economy, Domingo Cavallo, wanted decentralization to diminish the national deficit by reducing federal social spending. He even publicly stated that the decentralization of secondary education would save the national government AR$890 million per year (*La Nación*, December 7, 1991, 14; quoted in Falleti, 2003, 143).[9]

In the end, it was clear that the decentralization reform did not have policy goals or intentions to improve education and health care services: Cavallo included the decentralization of secondary schools and the remaining federal hospitals effective from January 1, 1992 in the budget proposal of that year. By doing this, the minister wanted to speed up negotiations and avoid separate discussions on the issue. Governors reacted forcefully and compelled the central government to initiate discussions on the decentralization and how to compensate the provinces for the costs they would incur after schools and hospitals were decentralized to the provinces. Due to the resistance and pressures from some legislators and governors, representatives from the federal executive met with the governors to reach an agreement on the decentralization reform. Governors did not oppose the decentralization of social services per se; their complaint was that the central government coerced them into receiving secondary schools (especially considering that, constitutionally, provinces are exclusively responsible for primary education) and public hospitals, without any compensation. They demanded new funds to finance the decentralized functions (Cetrángolo and Jiménez, 2004, 27; Repetto, 2001c, 27).

Bargaining over the decentralization of education and health care services (secondary schools and national hospitals) with the governors took place between October and December 1991. In those meetings between the president, his ministers, and the governors, the main discussion was not about how to improve the education system but rather about the amount of money the provinces were demanding from the central government to deliver the new services (*Diario de Sesiones de la Cámara de Diputados de la Nación* [*DS-CDN* from now on], December 5–6, 1991, 5306). After bitter discussions and tough negotiations, the central government agreed to compensate governors and give them side payments (see section below). These selective incentives reduced the short-term costs for governors, allowing them to have more funds for political purposes in the present, but put their districts into in a more precarious fiscal footing in the longer run (later demonstrations from teachers and physicians were an indication of that). Governors resisted and negotiated but in the end offered political support for the reforms in exchange for short-term fiscal and financial help and relief distributed by the president, resulting in larger costs for future provincial budgets (necessary to deliver the decentralized services).

Once the president knew he had enough support for the reforms from the governors, he sent the bill to Congress. Debates on the floor took place on November 13, 1991. Debates on how to finance the decentralization of secondary schools were divisive. While some senators in the incumbent party claimed this bill would improve federalism, contribute to a better quality and more efficient education system, and overcome the costs of centralism (*Diario de Sesiones de la Cámara de Senadores de la Nación* [*DS-CSN* from now on], November 13, 1991, 4040–4041), those in the opposition and even some Peronists raised several concerns. To begin with, they questioned why the central government wanted to speed up the approval of the law and demanded more time to conduct debates.[10] Others criticized this decision because it was taken "under pressures of the economic cycle" "to balance [federal] fiscal accounts" (Senator Lafferriere, UCR-Entre Ríos; *DS-CSN*, November 13, 1991, 4048) complaining that "this decentralization means a substantial reduction in revenues for the provinces" (Senator Posleman, Bloquismo-San Juan; *DS-CSN*, November 13, 1991, 4054). Some were also worried about the fiscal imbalances the decentralization policy would produce in the provinces (Senator Malharo de Torres, *DS-CSN*, November 13, 1991, 4043). Some senators were straightforward:

> The central government has been clear. It has to balance its fiscal deficit. Tax collection is not enough even when it has increased it. It needs the revenue from privatizations and from cutting down spending, out of which it unilaterally decides to decentralize all education establishments to the provinces, without considering the different situations in each of them, and without distinctions in their technical and educational capacity.
>
> (Senator Brasesco, UCR-Entre Ríos, *DS-CSN*,
> November 13, 1991, 4056)

Despite the divisions it generated, senators voted for the bill, remaining faithful to the previously bargained agreement between the president and governors (Falleti, 2003, 147; Repetto, 2001c, 28, 37; see also *DS-CSN*, November 13, 1991). The bill was then sent to the Chamber of Deputies. There, the project was debated together with the 1992 national budget proposal.[11] Deputies raised concerns and critiques very similar to those the senators brought up. The decision to decentralize these social services, some deputies claimed, was not based on policies to improve education but rather on a decision to reduce the central government's budget deficit (Deputy Dumón, UCR Buenos Aires and Deputy Marelli, UCR-Misiones; *DS-CDN*, December 5–6, 1991, 5305, 5308, 5343). Others feared this process would repeat the fiscal imbalances and the shortages in the provision of services generated by the decentralization during the military government in 1978 (Deputy Brook, UCR Córdoba; *DS-CDN*, December 5–6, 1991, 5355). Despite the debates and the opposition from several UCR deputies and even some from the PJ (especially those from Buenos Aires province, where the impact of decentralization was largest),[12] both the decentralization bill and the 1992 budget were voted on in the same session. Reflecting that the decision to support the bill was taken before the debates, only 22 deputies were present during the discussion over the contents of the bill. But when the time came to vote, 167 members were present (more than those needed for a quorum). Deputy Matzkin (PJ-La Pampa) asked for a nominal vote, a decision usually taken to enforce discipline during the vote, and the motion was accepted. Congressmen had incentives to pass the bill and get some of the side-payments the president distributed to governors and to some of them. Opposing the president and governors could have meant large costs for legislators in the incumbent party.

Congress merely ratified what was agreed upon between president and governors some days earlier: 156 deputies voted in favor of the bill, eight voted against, and two abstained (*DS-CDN*, December 5–6, 1991, 5356). On December 6, 1991, Congress passed law 24,049 decentralizing all national secondary schools and some few hospitals still in the hands of the federal government to the provinces. Primary, secondary, and tertiary educational services that were still controlled by the national government were decentralized to the provinces in 1992. The remarkable point was that the federal government could finance the payment not from central government revenues but from the provinces' share of the revenue-sharing scheme. This allowed the federal government to exit from a major area of expenditure without any increase in transfers to the provinces (Cetrángolo and Jiménez, 2004, 27; Dillinger and Webb, 1999, 16–17; Gerchunoff and Llach, 1998, 448; Repetto, 2001c, 32–34) and represented a clear change in primary distribution in favor of the central government with losses for all the provinces (Porto, 2003, 53).

The new law, once sanctioned, had to be ratified by each governor in order to sort out procedural aspects of the decentralization (such as the exact date of the decentralization, wages, infrastructure, pensions, and other operational issues). In an indication of the alliances that supported the president's bill and the decentralization, the first governor to sign the agreement with the central government in January 1992 was Bernabé

Arnaudo, the governor of La Rioja (President Menem's native province, one among the districts largely benefited by discretionary transfers). Radical governors, in an attempt to negotiate compensation, did not sign until October and December of 1992.[13] Despite some resistance, all governors signed after negotiating bilaterally with the president, in an indication of the power of the federal executive and the minimax strategy followed by provincial leaders. This is, as predicted by the federal distributive game, the Nash equilibrium point in the contexts of strong presidents, uncoordinated governors, and fiscal crisis. Almost all educational services and national hospitals were decentralized to subnational governments between 1992 and 1994. This new source of expenditure decentralized to the governors represented a favorable balance for the federal government and a large loss in fiscal terms for the provinces.

The fiscal pacts

Although the centralizing strategy was relatively costly, Menem also sought to extract funds from subnational governments to stabilize the central government's accounts. Instead of substantially changing the revenue-sharing law (a decision that would have considerably elevated the costs and the probability of conflict), the president sought to divert provincial funds from the pool of funds before they were distributed to the provinces (the pre-coparticipation, as it is called). This strategy is very similar to that followed by Cardoso during the negotiations for the FSE. The main goal was to finance the central government deficit in the pension system.

The president reduced the relatively high costs of this decision by negotiating on a one-by-one basis with governors, distributing selective incentives, and dividing their coordination efforts. All these strategies, which served the main goal of reducing the costs of the reform and the probability of conflict, were carried out through the so-called "fiscal pacts."

Fiscal Pact I, called "Agreement between the National Government and the Provincial Governments," was signed on August 12, 1992, by the president, members of the national executive cabinet and the governors (except the one from the province of Corrientes, under federal intervention at that moment). In the pact, 15 percent of the revenue-sharing funds were diverted to finance the national social security system, which at that time had a large deficit, "and other operative expenditures in case it is required." This amount represented, according to Deputy Fescina (Partido Federal, Capital Federal) more than 30 percent of the total revenues of the pension system (DS-CDN, August 19–20, 1992, 2081).

Another AR$43.8 million per month were deducted from total provincial revenues and used to finance those districts that were running fiscal deficits. The central government, in exchange, guaranteed a minimum transfer of AR$725 million annually. This guarantee had an expiration date (December 31, 1993), but the deductions from provincial revenues to finance the national social security system were renewed automatically every year (*DS-CDN*, August 19–20, 1992, 2055–2056). The bill with the content of the agreement was sent to Congress during August, 1992. UCR deputies, some from the UCeDe, members of provincial parties (such as the PAC), and some PJ dissidents who formed the *Grupo de los Ocho* voted against the bill, denouncing it as an imposition from the central government to balance its fiscal deficit at the expense of fiscally constrained provinces.[14] Deputy García (UCeDe-Buenos Aires) stressed governors' disadvantageous situation when signing the pact:

> We know that these governors, restrained by a very rigid economic policy that transforms provincial autonomy into utopia, have to do some concessions to deal with the most urgent necessities in their provinces ... governors have sought the way to obtain fresh funds for their provinces to solve some indispensable and immediate matters.
>
> (*DS-CDN*, August 19–20, 1992, 2062, 2068, 2076, 2079)

In the Senate, the opposition (represented mainly by the Radicals and the senators from Corrientes) raised similar concerns to those that the deputies brought up before them.[15] Senators who supported the bill stressed the fact that it would contribute to financing the pension system, which was in a critical situation at that moment. In addition, some stressed that there were no other options available for the central government and that provinces could afford this cut in the transfers because their revenues had increased substantially since 1989 (Senator Britos, PJ-San Luis, *DS-CSN*, August 19–20, 1992, 2316, 2318). In spite of the critics and concerns, and the opposition of the Radicals and the senators from Corrientes, the bill was approved. On the same day, it went back to the Chamber of Deputies, where it was finally sanctioned after being debated directly on the floor (*sesión sobre tablas*). In a process that reveals how much the president or the governors can influence the federal legislature when either of them is powerful, the new law (24,130) was sanctioned in the Senate and the Chamber of Deputies 22 days after the pact was signed.

One year later, the federal government negotiated Fiscal Pact II, called "Federal Pact for Employment, Production and Growth," and signed on August 12, 1993. This fiscal pact eliminated some provincial and local taxes (tax on the transport of fuels, natural gas, and electric energy, *impuesto a los sellos*, and on bank accounts), modified others (such as the tax on net benefits and real estate, increasing exemptions to them), and set limits to provincial tax bases and rates (Articles 1–5, Decree 1807/93). It also imposed severe restrictions on provincial (and municipal) tax authority. The central government compelled provinces to abolish some taxes through the pact (such as those on bank withdrawals), which lapsed for a period but were later on reinstated by the federal administration (Porto, 2003, 53–54, 57).

In exchange for those reforms, and to finance losses in tax collection for the provinces due to the elimination of taxes and the broadening of tax exemptions, the central government increased the guaranteed revenue transfers to a monthly AR$740 million and the fund for financing provincial fiscal disequilibria to AR$45.8 million, but made these increases conditional on provincial implementation of federally designed reform programs.

As part of the agreement, the central government encouraged provinces to transfer provincial pension schemes to the national system, a decision designed to control the deficits they generated (Cetrángolo and Jiménez, 2004, 35; Eaton, 2001a, 13). The central government also promoted the privatization of provincial banks and state-owned companies. By 1998, as a consequence of the pact, 18 out of 26 provincial banks were privatized (Eaton, 2004, 150) in addition to water and electric provincial companies in most of the 24 districts.

The central government was in a favorable position in terms of the distribution of power to negotiate these reforms and the profound restrictions on tax authority and provincial tax collection. Menem broke governors' resistance by taking advantage of the fiscal situation they were in (a factor that reduced the probability of conflict) and by distributing side-payments (to reduce the relative costs of the reforms). He granted financial assistance programs and bailouts, distributed special funds, discretionary transfers, and resources from the central government to build up coalitions and encourage the implementation of the reforms he endorsed. The president exchanged short-term side-payments for structural changes in the relations between levels of government. This appeared to be a rational deal for governors: they faced increasing deficits, soaring debts, and a powerful president who most expected to pass the reforms. Thus, instead of clashing, the core of their strategy was based on extracting side-payments from the federal executive, while differing the costs of the reforms for the future.

The selective incentives distributed by the president took different forms: first, Menem granted compensations to all provinces as a way of reducing overall costs and the probability of conflict with the governors. A crucial one was the financial guarantee clause in the decentralization of social services (article 15 of Law 24,049), which ensured a minimum level of expenditures in each province. If revenues were to fall below a fixed average for the period, the federal government would pay for the difference. But instead of taking into account each year's revenue requirements (updating them according to inflation; or as in Brazil where funds are allocated on a per capita basis), the central government was able to insert a clause by which the average to be computed was a fixed value (not to be yearly updated) calculated on the basis of the period of April–December 1991 (totaling AR$1.2 billion or the difference required to reach this amount). As a consequence of inflation (low during the 1990s, but increasingly high after 2001), this guarantee became useless and the financial requirements incurred by the provinces were mostly financed with their own budgets. As no new specific transfers were created to finance the decentralized functions, all financing was derived from revenue-sharing funds; and as these funds are not earmarked, provincial governments saw the possibility of receiving new funds to finance their overall fiscal situation (by demanding more funds from the central government to administer the decentralized functions). Also, the new decentralized functions represented an important number of public jobs, and governors expected to use them to mobilize political support (Repetto, 2001b, 37).

The federal government also guaranteed a floor of AR$8.7 billion to be allocated annually (or AR$725 million per month) to all provinces in revenue-sharing payments until December 31, 1993. This amount was raised to almost AR$8.9 billion (AR$740 million per month) in the negotiations for the second fiscal pact. Thus, governors were assured a minimum budget to deliver the services. This was not a minor compensation, considering the historical ups and downs of the Argentine economy and the previous collapses in GDP during the 1980s.

Second, as a part of the fiscal agreements between Menem and the governors, the federal government decentralized the administration of new funds to the provinces, but in this case they were earmarked for particular uses.[16] The total amount of money decentralized to each province was not based on the district's social indicators or any other transparent criteria, but rather based on bilateral agreements dependent on the governors' bargaining power and capacity to pressure the president (Repetto, 2001a, 26, 42–48). Governors accepted compensation, even though these funds were earmarked. As indicated in Chapter 1, they preferred new funds, even when they were attached to mandatory expending, over no funds at all or more discretion over the funds they already administered. Governors could use these new funds for credit claiming and building up political support (and in some cases even circumvent some of the legal requirements for spending them).

Finally, Menem also distributed selective incentives to specific districts to negotiate their support. The president bailed out provinces in need of financial help, especially Peronist or those politically allied to Peronism, conditional on support for presidential initiatives or the implementation of structural reforms in provincial public sectors. The national executive also established federal tax exemptions and federal financial assistance for the provinces that agreed to support the reforms.[17] For instance, to foster support for the first fiscal pact, Menem created a special fund (called *Fondo de Compensación de Desequilibrios Regionales*) to deal with financial disequilibria in the provinces and used these resources to negotiate with governors. The amount each province received from this fund was not based on their financial needs or capacity to re-pay, but determined in one-to-one negotiations with the president. The Radical governor of Chubut, Carlos Maestro, supported the reforms sponsored by the president in the first fiscal pact once he had secured his province the largest share from the special fund (AR$3 million per month). Governors who initially criticized the pact but signed it later on (such as Mario Moine of Entre Ríos) received a small share of the fund; but provincial executives who refused to sign the pact (such as Rolando Tauguinas of Chaco) received none of the special funds (*DS-CDN*, August 19–20, 1992, 2105–2106; and *Página 12*, 9 August 1992, quoted in Eaton, 2001b, 110).

Another case in point was the "Fund for Financing Social Programs in Buenos Aires Metropolitan Area" (or *Fondo de Reparación Histórica del Conurbano Bonaerense*), created in 1992. Through this fund, the province of Buenos Aires was granted 10 percent of a federal income tax or about AR$650 million annually (*La Nación*, "En 1998 la lucha será por los recursos," December 14, 1997). The fund was granted in exchange of support from Buenosairean deputies and the province's governor during the first fiscal pact (*La Nación*, "Las provincias exigen una nueva coparticipación," February 1, 1998). Néstor Kirchner, from Santa Cruz, refused to sign the pact in August 1993 but signed it in January 19, 1994, after the president granted him a special fund of AR$1.5 million per month through a reserved decree (usually issued in cases of national security threats, intelligence operations, or defense matters).[18]

Cavallo increased his pressure on provincial governments to sign the second fiscal pact by promising to lift the tax on minimum assets for companies located in provinces that had signed the pact (*Clarín*, August 18, 1993; quoted in Eaton, 2001b, 111). The governors of Chaco and Formosa (Rolando Tauguinas—PACh—and Vicente Joga—PJ) reversed their initial hostile stance after Menem promised federal help with provincial debts and subsidies for cotton producers, the case of Chaco, and the creation of a tax-free zone and public works projects in Formosa. In exchange for the Formosan support, Menem personally rewarded Joga by appointing him as *interventor* of the Peronist party in the neighboring Corrientes province (CGE, 1993, 207; quoted in Eaton, 2001b, 111; Eaton, 2004, 148–149).

Another widely used instrument for crafting political deals by the president were the ATNs (National Treasury Grants). ATNs were used to reward the president's political allies and craft support for the reforms. Menem also used resources from the federal budget selectively, distributed as social plans, investment projects, public works, and infrastructure as a way to build up coalitions or encourage reforms (see González, 2012, for details on the distribution of transfers and ATNs from the central government to the provinces).

In sum, it is possible to claim that governors negotiated and accepted substantial changes in the distribution of resources and functions among levels of government promoted by the federal executive in return for short-term economic relief and compensation. Knowing that coordination was costly and expecting that reforms were going to be implemented because the president was powerful in partisan terms, governors focused their strategy on getting compensation and short-term fiscal relief. This is the governors' minimax strategy, in line with our theoretical expectations.

The outcomes of the federal distributive game

Three major changes resulted from negotiations led by the president over the uncoordinated governors: changes in what the provinces received (modifications in the system of transfers and distribution of revenues), in what they spent their money on (functions performed by each level of government), and in the way provinces could use their money (spending restrictions).

There were two main outcomes of the reforms negotiated between the federal government and the provinces between 1991 and 1994: first, the decentralization of costly new functions to the provinces without the resources necessary to finance them, and second, the reduction in the share of transfers from the central government to the provinces to finance the central government fiscal deficit. It is noticeable that although Menem was politically powerful (he got special powers out of the economic emergency and state reform laws in 1989), he could not pass a new revenue-sharing law that would favor the federal government by centralizing fiscal resources. This was a costly option, and the probability of conflict with the governors was high. Instead, Menem went for a less conflictive option in the short term (during negotiations) and in the longer run: he needed gubernatorial support both to remain in office (he was entering his second year in office) and to implement other reforms (gubernatorial support was crucial for his later reelection plans through a constitutional reform).

The administrative decentralization of health care and education produced dramatic changes in the federal balance. Whereas the central government had administered 1,647 secondary schools in 1987 (or 46.5 percent of the total), by 1997, only 65 remained under its authority (0.8 percent). Some deputies claimed (according to what the budget law indicated) that the total cost of the decentralized services was AR$1.2 billion per year (Deputy Baglini, *DS-CDN*, December 5–6, 1991, 5310; Deputy Clerici, *DS-CDN*, December 5–6, 1991, 5320).[19]

In relation to changes in the revenue-sharing system, the original 57/43 percent formula to divide provincial and national shared taxes contained in the 1988 revenue-sharing law was de facto changed to represent the opposite: in 1994, the central government received 57.7 percent of shared taxes and the provinces 42.3 (Cetrángolo and Jiménez, 1995, 8–9; Porto, 2003, 58). The aforementioned reforms were followed by changes in the value-added tax (VAT) in March 1995 (its bases were broadened and its rates increased from 18 to 21 percent) and corporate income taxes. These changes in the tax system increased the revenue shares of the national government relative to the provinces, which lost about 28 percent of shared revenues in 1994. For Porto (2003, 54), "the already weakened provincial and municipal tax system was further constrained" after these reforms.

The consequences of the fiscal pacts were also shattering for the provinces. Between 1992 and 1995 the provinces lost AR$13 billion as a result of the two fiscal pacts (CECE, 1997, 43). The decentralization of education and health care services demanded a substantial increase in provincial spending and no new legally mandated transfers to the provinces helped them to finance these functions. To the contrary, the central government withdrew funds every month to finance the pension system. This situation is reflected in the amount of money provincial governments spent before and after the decentralization reform. Total provincial spending increased from AR$39.3 billion in 1991, before the decentralization of new functions, to AR$46.9 billion in 1992, AR$53.8 billion in 1993, and AR$57 billion in 1994 after the fiscal pacts, a total increase of almost 70 percent during this four-year period. Provincial deficits also reflect the impact of the newly decentralized services: in 1992, the combined deficit of all provinces was AR$1.2 billion. It jumped to AR$4.1 billion in 1993, AR$4.5 billion in 1994, and AR$6.4 billion in 1995; an increase of over 220 percent during this period. Provincial debt also rose dramatically. It skyrocketed from AR$3.1 billion in 1993 to AR$5.4 billion in 1994 and AR$9.8 billion in 1995, equivalent to a 316 percent increase during the period.

Another important indicator of the critical fiscal situation in the provinces is the decline in the share of total provincial spending financed by revenue-sharing funds in relation to other transfers from the central government. In 1991, provinces could finance 42 percent of their total spending with revenue-sharing transfers; this share dropped to 27 percent in 1995; representing a 15-point drop during the period in which decentralization policies were implemented.[20]

After the decentralization process initiated with the fiscal pacts, provinces ended up being more dependent on federal transfers to match their spending levels and cover fiscal disequilibria and debt increases. The balance of the federal equation favored the president, since the central government had fewer functions and more funds at its disposal, while subnational governments had fewer resources and more administrative functions to deliver. On the side of the central government, decentralization reforms translated into a modest surplus (1.4 percent of GDP) in 1993 (the year after decentralization of health and education). However, the deficit reappeared in 1994 and continued for almost a decade, mainly as a consequence of increasing spending from the federal administration (it was reversed only in 2004).

Another major change linked to the decentralization of functions described above was the shift from unconditional to conditional transfers after 1990. Conditional transfers increased from 12 percent in 1989 and 15.2 percent in 1991, before the fiscal pacts, to 27.6 in 1994, after these negotiations. As Wibbels (2004, 220) indicates, such a percentage change in the type of transfers could be seen as a relatively insignificant change, but these reforms together with the hard budget constraints imposed after 1991 represented a loss of provincial autonomy and more dependency on the central government.

In the federal distributive game, governors followed a minimax strategy: the president was powerful enough and had resources to deliver side-payments to divide them, and coordination was costly. Most of them faced increasing fiscal deficits and soaring debts in their districts. Instead of con-flicting with the central government, they negotiated compensation out of the reforms. Out of the negotiations with the president, governors received a guarantee for a minimum level of transfers, earmarked federal funds, and a AR$44 million fund to finance provincial fiscal disequilibria, which was distributed among governors in a discretionary basis. This was clearly a short-term solution that had long-term consequences for provin-cial autonomy. But, when facing a strong president willing to change the status quo, governors opted for the choice that, out of the unfavorable situation they were in, would give them the largest payoffs (this is the *minimax* strategy). They preferred short-term compensation to defecting and paying the costs of the reforms and of not cooperating with a powerful president.

Once governors faced the common challenge of insufficient funds to deliver the decentralized services after they had spent most of their short-term compensations, they tried to coordinate efforts in more institutional-ized arenas (Falleti, 2001; 2003, 75). These arenas for federal coordination, which were created after the 1978 decentralization of education and health care services, received renewed attention after the 1991–1992 reforms. Despite this new impetus, many of these efforts were fruitless or produced only minor results compared to the costs imposed during the 1992–1994 period (Palanza, 2002, 41, 44). Although there are about 25 federal councils, their relevance, lobby capacity, and degree of institution-alization varied substantially. The CFCE (culture and education), COFESA (health), and CFI (investment) have been among the most active, although their impact and influence on federal decisions has been decisively marginal.

The balance of the federal distributive game

The most substantive reforms in the system that regulates the distribution of funds and functions in the federation were passed by Congress between 1992 and 1994, during the first Menem administration. During these years, Menem had considerable partisan powers (and popularity) and he faced strong fiscal pressures. Despite the fiscal constraints, he also had some resources from a relatively favorable fiscal context after 1991 that allowed him to distribute compensation and selective incentives. The time frame for a setting favoring the central government was relatively short: after the macroeconomic results of the 1991 Convertibility Plan and before the external shock from the 1995 "tequila" crisis and the erosion in his partisan powers. As a consequence, despite increases in revenues in absolute terms, the provincial share of revenues in relation to the central government diminished. In absolute terms, total provincial income increased from AR\$45 billion in 1992 to AR\$52 billion in 1996 (constant 2004 prices). Interestingly, fiscal transfers from the central government remained basically constant during the period, rising from AR\$25.1 billion in 1992 to only AR\$25.8 billion in 1996, while revenue-sharing transfers decreased from AR\$17.6 to AR\$16.1 billion in the same time frame.

In relative terms, the central government concentrated 68.1 percent of the revenues in 1984 while provinces did that with 27.6 percent (and municipalities 4.3 percent). In 2000, after Menem's reforms, the federal government augmented its control over 76 percent of the total revenues, and the provinces decreased it to 18.5 percent (municipalities increased it to 5.5 percent). Provinces lost 49 percent of their total revenue as a consequence of the centralizing reforms implemented during this period. On the expenditure side, the central government was responsible for 64.5 percent of total expenditures in 1984 while provinces controlled 30.9 percent (and municipalities 4.5 percent). In 2000, after the central government got rid of several of its social functions, its share of expenditures decreased to 52.7 percent (or almost a 19 percent rise) while the provincial share augmented to 37.9 percent (a 23 percent increase) and municipalities' to 9.5 percent (an increase of over 110 percent) (Cetrángolo and Jiménez, 2004). This means that the increase of 23 percent in their expenditure has not been matched with new revenue. According to data collected by the Ministry of Economy, in relative terms, the provincial revenue share fell from 37.7 percent in 1991, the year before the reforms, to 16.6 percent in 1996, almost a 21 point decrease during the period (see Table 5.3).[21]

In sum, the presidential net balance $[U=\Sigma(r_{jp}-P_{ip})]$ improved significantly, while the gubernatorial net balance $[X=\Sigma(P_{ig}-r_{ig})]$ worsened dramatically (see Table 5.4).

The main goal driving the reforms in the relations between the central and subnational levels of government was not improving the quality of service delivery and enhancing local accountability (as claimed by IADB, 1997a, 1997b, and World Bank, 1998, or the main supporters of the reforms). Debates on the decentralization in both chambers of Congress took only ten days, despite arguably being among the most substantive reforms during the 1990s. These changes were accomplished at the expense of provincial autonomy and generated important shortages in service delivery at the provincial (and local) level. Provinces (and some

Table 5.3 Revenue and expenditure share of subnational units in Argentina (1990–1998)

Year	Revenue share	Expenditure share
1990	40.70	43.82
1991	37.74	44.16
1992	40.82	46.75
1993	41.61	44.38
1994	20.85	39.21
1995	18.14	35.34
1996	16.55	29.33
1997	27.57	38.97
1998	27.40	33.78

Source: Data compiled and adapted from the Ministry of Economy, *Secretaría de Programación Económica*, various years.

municipalities[22]) could not afford to pay minimum salaries for teachers and physicians or nurses as well as for supplies and basic infrastructure. The decentralized functions were then accompanied by demonstrations, violent protests led by unions, and some popular uprisings (especially during 1995–1996 and 1999–2002). Protests moved from the doorways of national ministries to provincial palaces of government and the governors' residencies. This led some analysts to claim that the fiscal crisis had been decentralized and protests provincialized.

The federal executive achieved two crucial objectives from the reforms: on the one hand, it improved the central government finances; on the other, the president could count on more fiscal resources to craft a position of political preeminence in relation to the governors. By making governors more dependent on the central government he could, on the one hand, appease them and prevent another 1988, and on the other, he could count on provincial support for critical reforms (including his reelection plans through the constitutional reform), especially from less developed provinces (González, 2012). Provincial fiscal dependency and vulnerability is a potential source for economic and social instability in the federation (as the events in 1989–1991 and 2001–2002 revealed) but also a political asset for the president.

Menem got to power as a *par* (peer) among governors, but his strategy for political survival and governability as president led him to become a clear *primus* in his relations with governors. His former *pares* had to pay a high cost for this presidential strategy.

The 1994 constitutional reform and the second Menem administration (1994–1999)

Taking advantage of his partisan power and high public approval rates after the stabilization of the economy and the battles he won in the federal

Table 5.4 Synthesis of the reforms and impacts on the federal balance (1991–1993)

Period of reforms	Subnational revenue (in relative terms)	Subnational functions	Subnational tax authority	Federal balance
Menem 1991–1993	Decreased (revenue share fell from 38% in 1991 to 17% in 1996; the president retained 15% of provincial revenue-sharing funds). Between 1992 and 1995 the provinces lost $13 billion as a result of the two fiscal pacts.	Increased (transferred health, education, housing: more than 1,500 schools, 800,000 students, and 95,000 teachers, total annual cost of $1.2 billion).	Decreased (eliminated provincial and local taxes: tax on the transport of fuels, natural gas, and electric energy, *impuesto a los sellos*, and on bank accounts, replacing them with federal taxes; their revenue is not shared).	Favorable for the federal government $U = \Sigma (r_{jp} - P_{ip}) > X = \Sigma (P_{ig} - r_{ig})$

game against the governors, Menem increased his bet and decided to go for reelection.[23] To do that, he needed to reform the 1853 federal constitution to allow for immediate reelection. In order to pass a law calling for elections to choose representatives for the constitutional convention, Menem needed a two-thirds majority in both chambers of Congress. He could reach that number in the Senate, but lacked sufficient support in the Chamber of Deputies without the votes from the UCR. In order to force negotiations, Menem threatened the opposition, especially the Radicals, by calling a plebiscite. Raúl Alfonsín, the leader of the UCR at that time, argued that he preferred to give support for the constitutional reform, negotiate changes before and during the assembly, and look for compensations rather than leaving the president unchecked in his reformist attempts (Acuña, 1995; Alfonsín, 1996; Carrizo, 1997).

Although the PJ won a plurality of votes and seats in the elections for the 1994 constitutional assembly, none of the parties commanded an absolute majority.[24] This situation limited the power of the president and his capacity to impose his preferred options at the same time that it boosted the ability of the opposition, especially the Frente Grande (which made a remarkable election), to act as a negotiator and potentially veto important decisions. As a result, negotiations were intense and the reforms passed on those issues related to the distribution of funds and functions in the federation did not have a clear winner. Menem wanted reelection and he got it, but at the price of making concessions to several political actors, including the governors.

After his reelection in 1995, Menem clearly did not enjoy the same level of partisan powers that he had during his first term in office. The main reason for this decline in power was rising internal conflict in the PJ after the president reformed the constitution in 1994 to permit his reelection and especially after the 1995 election, which he won with 44.9 percent of the vote. Factionalism and divisions inside the governing party proliferated as several governors began to campaign for a position in the presidential succession race.[25] With low public support, divisions inside the ruling party, and fewer funds to craft legislative coalitions, federal Congressmen had less clear incentives to support the federal executive and more to begin looking for those party leaders with presidential aspirations. Governors, being crucial figures in the main parties and having resources from their districts, tried to get more visibility and some of them (such as Duhalde, Rodríguez Saá, De la Sota, Sobisch, and De la Rúa) began campaigning to get the presidential nomination in the main parties. As presidential power diminished, federal legislators relocated their support to those party leaders they thought would better contribute to their career prospects. As a result of this erosion in presidential power, the PJ lost the 1997 mid-term legislative elections against the Frente Grande and the UCR (now formally allied under the label of Alianza).

The fiscal context during the period 1994–1999 was far from optimal but not as excruciating as it had been during 1989–1991.[26] The fiscal deficit continued to increase at an average rate of 2.8 percent of GDP after a modest surplus in only one year, 1993, the year after the decentralization of social services to the provinces. Fiscal pressures on the central government continued, although Menem did not have the urgency he had at the beginning of his first term in office to alter the federal balance. Provincial budgets entered into structural fiscal imbalances after the decentralization of social services and the fiscal pacts. Fiscal deficits in most provinces were high, and provincial debt increased steadily after the functions were decentralized in 1992. Fiscal pressures on the governors were high, and they had strong incentives to alter the distribution of funds and functions (see Figure 5.3).

Negotiations and struggles for reforms

One of the top priorities of the president in the constitutional assembly was to win the right to run for reelection. In order to guarantee support from the governors and provincial representatives, the president did not bring a strong reformist stance in relation to fiscal decentralization to the assembly. He did not suffer strong fiscal pressures either. Instead, he delayed negotiations, blocked bills favorable to the provinces, and traded some benefits for subnational governments in exchange for the support he needed on critical issues, among them reelection. As a consequence,

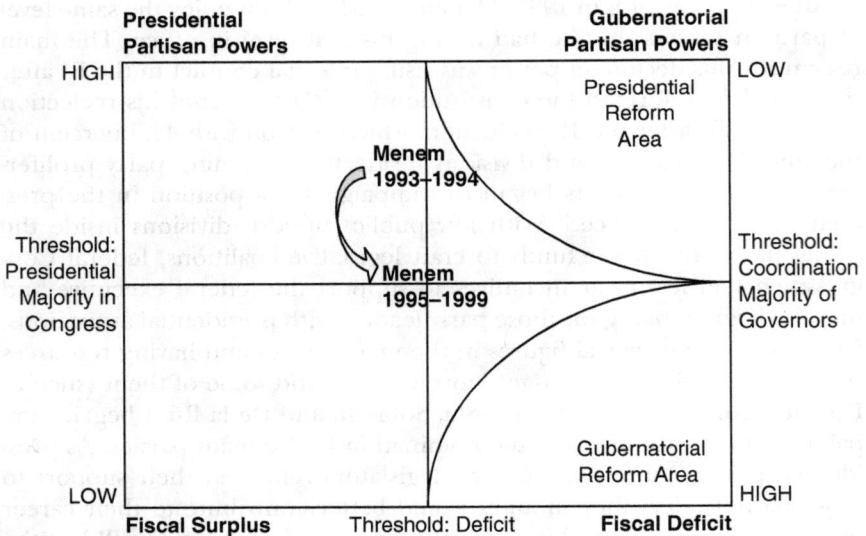

Figure 5.3 Synthesis of the main variables during Menem (1993–1999).

Note
The area inside both arches is where the probability of changes in the status quo ante is larger.

the 1994 constitutional reform had mixed effects on the provincial interests, and no substantive changes to the revenue-sharing scheme were
passed, although clauses on the conditions for reforming it were introduced in the constitutional text.

On the one hand, legislators passed some constitutional changes that
benefited the governors. The new constitution established that changes in
laws governing revenue sharing or in the division of responsibilities among
levels of government had to be approved by an absolute majority of the
members of each chamber (the Senate was the chamber in charge of
introducing the reform bill) and by all the provincial legislatures. Provincial representatives effectively negotiated that further decentralization of
services would only be possible if the provinces accepted them and they
were accompanied by federal funds or new revenue sources to finance
them. These gains for the provinces could also be interpreted as a relative
triumph for the central government: it institutionalized its achievements
after 1992, making it more difficult for the governors to change the
revenue-sharing regime as they had in 1988. Despite these changes, several
legislators from the provinces and eight governors demanded changes in
the distribution of resources and reforms in the revenue-sharing system.
The president effectively put limits to those claims and, in a sagacious
move, bargained to postpone debates. Governors, on the other hand, did
not have enough political power to force discussions and less so to impose
reforms. As a consequence, debates over changes to the revenue-sharing
system were delayed until the president, governors, and legislators called
for a new round of negotiations.[27]

Other reforms encouraged centralization and control by the federal
government. Among those changes were the abolition of the Electoral
College and the direct election of senators. In sum, despite some substantive changes to the constitution, neither the president nor the governors
ended up being clear winners after the reforms. The revenue-sharing
regime as well as the balance of the federal equation remained
unchanged, as we would expect under situations of power stalemate (no
clear predominance by any of the actors in terms of political power) and
relatively weak fiscal urgency.

The federal distributive game during the second Menem administration (1995–1999)

The fiscal context deteriorated in the period after 1995, presidential partisan powers gradually declined (as the primaries for the 1999 presidential
election approached and divisions inside PJ augmented), and public
support rapidly evaporated in the face of corruption scandals (and the
resistance to a new reelection attempt, formally banned by the constitution) and the failure of the government to deal with the social costs of
macroeconomic reforms.[28] In this context, the president was incapable of

further reforming the intergovernmental fiscal system, despite a constitutional mandate to revise the revenue-sharing regime by 1996.

When the president weakened his position after 1995 and lost his influence over how individual legislators could further their careers in the party, dissonances over policy in the party increased (Eaton, 2002, 160). Power over legislators' behavior in the party increasingly swung toward provincial party leaders, who were worried about Menem's adjustment attempts in the provinces.

The central government engaged in long and costly negotiations, out of which it received some benefits, such as the amendment in the rates of some taxes (e.g., on fuels) to finance the deficit of the federal pension system, but did not substantially modify the federal distribution of revenues and funds.[29] Between 1996 and 1999, federal authorities prepared several drafts to reform the revenue-sharing scheme, but none of them reached the floor of Congress for debate. By early 1997, the central government ceded to gubernatorial pressures and paid the revenue-sharing debt it had with the provinces (during 1996, the central government turned into arrears for about AR$200 million in transfers to the provinces), a decision which contributed to a sharp increase in the deficit of the federal government (*La Nación*, "El déficit creció por la deuda con las provincias," February 13, 1997). In 1998, after the mid-term elections, negotiations over the federal distribution of funds were once again on the government's agenda.[30] The draft of the bill never got to Congress, as governors vetoed the presidential proposal. Also in 1998, governors blocked another bill in the Senate that would have instituted direct revenue transfers from the federal government to the municipalities, bypassing the provinces (*La Nación*, "Coparticipación: sin apoyo en el Senado," September 15, 1998; "Los gobernadores del PJ, en pie de Guerra," March 6, 1998). Any attempt to circumvent governors had to deal with their strong reactions. By the end of 1998, when the 1993 Fiscal Pact was due to expire, the federal government asked Congress and governors to extend it. But in order to get this passed in the federal legislature, governors asked for concessions, some of which the federal government granted by increasing the minimum revenue guarantee from AR$740 million per month to AR$850 million per month in 1999 (*Ámbito Financiero*, October 23, 1998; quoted in Eaton, 2004, 152). By that time, as presidential power eroded and gubernatorial pressures escalated, governors won what was probably the last battle of the federal distributive game fought during the Menem administration. Provincial executives got new funds from a special federal tax on cars, airplanes, and yachts (called *Fondo Nacional de Incentivo Docente*) to finance teachers' salaries, a formal responsibility of the provinces since 1992.[31] Provincial pressures increased as governors were more capable of coordinating, even against a president from their own party, pressed by growing fiscal imbalances in their districts. The revenue-sharing scheme remained unchanged, despite the constitutional mandate to reform it before 1996 and the several attempts to alter it from the president. The substantially weakened president could not do much to stop governors' demands. When Menem left office, he passed those legacies to De la Rúa.

Some partial comments

An elected president who, at the time he was a governor claimed the provinces should rebel against the central government because it was not distributing the resources provincial authorities demanded, carried out the most dramatic centralization process in the post-transition period in Argentina. The changes in the federal balance favoring the central government included the centralization of resources, the decentralization of costly functions without revenues to deliver them, the elimination and reduction of provincial tax bases, the imposition of a reform agenda on the provinces, and more control over subnational spending. These reforms had vast consequences and produced large fiscal imbalances in the provinces, including the inability of provincial authorities to pay for salaries of public employees and health care and education personnel, and shortages in the delivery of basic services. This translated into profound social crises in many districts, large demonstrations, and even violent protests.

The main goal the president pursued was to consolidate and remain in power (staying in office even after the term limit by reforming the constitution) and limit the power of governors. Changes in the federal equation were pursued as a means to reach this goal, weakening provincial authorities and shattering the main competitors' intentions to reach power. Despite this, governors worked as a critical check to presidential power. Menem was forced to abandon office after his reelection, although he explicitly campaigned for a second reelection. Governors were one of the most important limits to that attempt.

The political power of the president, his capacity to divide the governors by delivering concessions and side-payments, and the fiscal incentives he faced were the main driving forces behind the reforms. Programmatic ideas or policy goals designed to improve the quality of basic social services and the efficiency or transparency of the public administration were not important factors influencing these changes.

The Cardoso presidency (1995–2002)

Governors in Brazil were notably strong and got substantial legitimacy from public opinion after the transition to democracy. Being strong and fiscally pressured to alter the post-authoritarian status quo ante, they achieved a substantial amount of fiscal benefits during the 1987–1988 constitutional assembly. Abrucio (1998) called them "the barons of the federation" (*os barões da federação*) not only because of the power they amassed in their districts but also because of the influence they had over federal politics. The costs of the changes imposed on the federal government during the Sarney administration were immense, and any effort to solve the chronic federal fiscal deficit (key to stabilizing the economy and controlling inflation) had to deal with altering the federal balance that favored governors.

The first presidency after the transition to democracy appeared to confirm the expectation from those scholars claiming that the "centrifugal" institutional configuration in Brazil not only favored regional interests but also made reforms (and governability) difficult for the president. How did Cardoso pass centralizing reforms against the most powerful governors in the region? In this second section of the chapter, making some parallels to the analysis of the Menem presidency, I respond to this question by analyzing the process by which the *primus* (Cardoso) was able to accumulate political power and negotiate centralizing reforms that notably debilitated the governors. The Brazilian case is even more counterintuitive than the Argentine in terms of the reforms Cardoso passed because its institutional configurations, according to several scholars, did not favor presidential decisions.

I follow the usual structure. First, I explore the values taken by the key independent variables (presidential and gubernatorial power and the fiscal context) to analyze the distribution of power and the actors' fiscal incentives. Next, I introduce the theoretical expectations from the federal distributive game and analyze its dynamics during the presidency of Fernando Henrique Cardoso in Brazil. After that, I describe the outcomes of the federal balance in terms of the distribution of revenue, functions, and tax authority. In the conclusions, I analyze similarities and differences between the Cardoso and the Menem reforms and their implications for the functioning of these two federal democracies.

The historical context

In order to have some details about the power Cardoso was able to accumulate, it is important to get into some of the characteristics of the 1994 presidential campaign. Six months before the 1994 elections, Luís Inácio Lula da Silva, the PT presidential candidate, was supported by about 40 percent of the public, while Fernando Henrique Cardoso, the PSDB (Party of Brazilian Social Democracy) nominee, only by 15 percent.[32] Lula was a popular candidate who ran a very credible presidential race against Collor in 1989 (coming in second with 40 percent of the vote), and he was a strong opponent in 1994. Cardoso was also a serious challenger, but his decision to form an electoral alliance with the PFL and the political right, announced in 1994, cost him much credibility and support among leftist voters (Flynn, 1996, 405). Cardoso was a respected intellectual from São Paulo, who had an important political career, but very few links to the

Brazilian interior, especially the Northeast. This was a region historically dominated by the PFL. PSDB leaders sought an alliance with the PFL as a way to strengthen their party's chances in the election and their electoral backing in the interior of the country (as well as support in Congress in case they won the election).

Within three weeks of the implementation of the Plano Real on July 1, Cardoso surged ahead of Lula in the polls and retained this margin until the electoral contest (Power, 2002, 623), despite his alliance with the PFL. The October 1994 presidential election took place when inflation, gradually brought under control by the Plano Real, was below 2 percent per month. Cardoso campaigned on the results of the plan and voters supported him massively. In addition, an important part of the Brazilian political and economic elites also feared the accession of Lula to power, a leftist union leader. He won the election with 54.3 percent of the votes, one of the highest in Brazilian history (the highest since the election of Eurico Gaspar Dutra in 1945), and took office in January 1995.

The power of the president

Cardoso reached the presidency with substantial public support and was able to build a broad coalition in Congress. Although his party did not control an absolute majority of the seats in parliament, he was able to build a working coalition with other parties. His main electoral partner was the PFL,[33] and other parties, notably the PMDB, PTB, PL, and PPB joined the governing coalition after January 1, 1995. The president's allies changed over time, but they provided substantial support for several issues on his reform agenda. In the Lower Chamber, the PSDB won only 63 seats, an equivalent to 12.3 percent of the total, and it won nine seats (11 percent) of the Upper Chamber. But Cardoso's electoral coalition with the PFL granted him almost 30 percent of the seats in the Lower Chamber and 36 percent of the seats in the Senate (Jairo Nicolau, Dados Eleitorais do Brasil, 1982–2002).

Cardoso had a comprehensive reform agenda in terms of economic and political issues. Several of them needed to be passed through constitutional reforms, which require three-fifths of the members of Congress. Although the president's electoral coalition with the PFL did not reach those numbers, Cardoso was able to achieve a three-fifths majority with the support of other parties that were part of the larger governing coalition formed after January 1, 1995.[34] Cardoso's coalition in Congress reached stunning figures during some periods: 77 percent of the seats in the Chamber of Deputies and more than 90 percent of the Senate, the largest shares since 1985.[35] The flip side of this broad governing coalition was that the president was continually pushed to provide compensations and distribute selective incentives to members of Congress and governors to get their support. Despite the diversity of Cardoso's political allies, the overall discipline rate in the presidential coalition was relatively high during his two terms in office. According to Power, the support rate for Cardoso in ten roll-call votes collected by the newspaper *FSP* on ten important issues was 75 percent (Power, 1998a, 61). Figueiredo (2006, 13), using 562 roll-call votes during both of Cardoso's terms in office, finds a higher rate, ranging from 85.7 percent during the second part of his first term to 90.1 percent in the second half of his second term.

Cardoso got substantial political backing among state governors, another fact that made his term in office exceptional in relation to the previous ones after 1985. To begin with, he had political allies in the five most important states.[36] But Cardoso's support went beyond the largest states and also found loyal leaders in smaller ones, such as Pernambuco during the governorship of Jarbas Vasconcelos (from the PMDB; governor between 1999 and 2006). In total, Cardoso began his term in office with 22 governors that belonged to parties allied to the government coalition in Congress (out of 27) and kept their support during most of his two terms in office (although it fell to 15 during the last year of his presidency).

The president enjoyed broad public support after his success in stabilizing the economy. When he reached office on January 1, 1995, his positive image was 31 percent and one month later, it had climbed to 38.5 percent.[37] Cardoso was himself a very influential figure, a prestigious academic, an experienced politician (he served as senator between 1983 and 1992; Minister of Foreign Affairs, 1992–1993; and Minister of Finance, 1993–1994), and a person with valuable connections to the São Paulo political and business elite and to leaders in Latin America, Europe, and the United States (Flynn, 1993, 406).

Cardoso also made use of the full range of institutional resources available to the federal executive as a result of the 1988 constitutional reform. In pushing forward his reform agenda, he made use of the president's legislative power by relying on decrees (he signed 5,028 MPs; see Table 5.5), the exclusive initiative in areas of public administration, taxation,

Table 5.5 Provisional decrees issued or re-issued in Brazil (1985–May 2001)

	Sarney	Collor	Franco	Cardoso (first term)	Cardoso (second term)	Total
Original	125	87	141	160	76	589
Re-issued	22	73	364	1,750	2,209	5,254
Derogated	2	5	5	11	5	28
Rejected	9	11	–	1	1	22
Negotiated	–	–	–	38	7	45
Total Issued	147	160	505	2,609	2,419	5,840

Source: Based on data from *Presidência da República/ Casa Civil*; Chagas, 2002, 344.

and budget, and the centralization of legislative organization (Figueiredo and Limongi, 2000, 163, 164).

The president issued provisional decrees to pass the Plano Real in 1994 and re-issued the main decrees 65 times during six years, until it was passed by law in 2000. In an indication of the effectiveness the president was able to get out of this legislative tool, only two MPs were rejected during Cardoso's entire term in office (Chagas, 2002, 336; Figueiredo and Limongi, 2000, 156, 164). Figueiredo and Limongi (2000, 164–165) claim that besides the use of decree and veto powers, since Cardoso, presidents have relied on the centralized legislative organization of Congress to marshal support for their bills. Most of these institutional resources were also available to Collor and Franco, but it seems that strong presidents, with substantial support in Congress and in public opinion, can take better advantage and make more extensive and (perhaps) legitimate use of them.

The power of governors

The other crucial variable in this work is the political power of governors. Together with the power of the president, it defines the distribution of power in the federation. Several governors were powerful actors in their states during Cardoso's term in office. However, the majority of them did not coordinate actively to oppose the president. On the contrary, those from the most important states were allies and those in the opposition were divided. Furthermore, for reasons that will be analyzed, most governors ended up in an adverse fiscal condition, a situation that the president exploited to further weaken and divide them. The president's party and coalition controlled most states after the 1994 election.[38] This strong political support from governors continued after the 1998 election, and this really distinguishes Brazil from Argentina, since governors were able to turn against Menem during his second (lame-duck) term. After 1998, Cardoso's governing coalition had nominal support in 21 states. The largest share of governorships was in the hands of the governing party, the PSDB, which got seven, up from six in the previous election. The PMDB followed with six and the PFL also won in six states. During his final year in office, when the PFL and the PTB left the governing coalition, the president had only 15 governors as formal allies.

Several governors were powerful actors in partisan terms in their districts (one of the crucial dimensions of their power), but on the whole they were weaker than they were during the Sarney and Collor administrations. Governors got elected with an average of 48 percent (1995–1998) and 51 percent of the vote (1999–2002).[39] The average index for Cardoso's first period in office was 1.23 (a low value according to the scale introduced in Chapter 2), lower than that during Collor's (1.6) and Sarney's (2.2). These figures indicate that although governors remained powerful actors in their districts in institutional terms,[40] many of them faced stiff competition in state elections and had trouble achieving majorities in their state legislatures.

These values did not change much after the 1998 election. A total of 13 governors out of 27 (48 percent) were elected with 50 percent of the vote or more; a small increase from the 1994 electoral contest (when 41 percent were), equal to the number in 1990, but still lower than that during the 1986 election (74 percent). Twelve governors faced a divided government, one more than in 1994, and four more than during Collor's term in office. None of the governors had to deal with this situation during Sarney's administration. The governors' partisan powers were far greater in 1986 than after 1998, and this is a critical difference between the two periods. The average index for Cardoso's second period in office was 1.37 (a low value in the scale), a bit higher than during 1994. In sum, although several governors were relatively powerful in their districts in partisan terms, the values of their partisan power in aggregate terms were lower than during the previous administrations. Overall, governors faced more electoral competition and had less comfortable majorities in their assemblies than they had during the administration of Collor and Sarney.

The fiscal context after the Real Plan

After getting a picture of the distribution of power in the federation, this section examines the fiscal incentives the president and the governors faced in relation to the distribution of resources in the federation. Although most macroeconomic indicators improved significantly after the introduction of the Plano Real, the central government still faced strong fiscal pressures to stabilize the budget's fiscal deficit and reduce its debt. Among the many factors that contributed to those pressures was the sharp increase in constitutional transfers that governors got in 1988. Despite the gains made after 1988, governors also faced strong fiscal pressures and harder budget constraints after the stabilization of the economy. Their fiscal weakness and the urgency they faced in relation to debt payments were factors that adversely affected them and favored the federal government.

After the Plano Real, most macroeconomic indicators were satisfactory.[41] Despite these optimistic figures, the economy continued to be vulnerable to external shocks, which were especially severe in 1995, 1997, and 1999. In addition to the imbalances generated by external shocks, Brazil's public debt increased substantially during Cardoso's two terms in office, from 30 percent of GDP in 1994 to 56.5 in 2002. The federal government's debt increased from 12.9 to 36 percent, while the states and municipalities' augmented from 10 to 18.8 percent of GDP during the same period. The fiscal pressures from subnational governments after 1988, the increasing demands for state bailouts and state debt rollover, the higher interest rates, and the larger needs to finance the federal fiscal deficit were among the several causes for this sharp increase in debt.

Another source of permanent concern for the federal government was the fiscal deficit, considered by some analysts to be the main difficulty faced by the government (Panizza, 2003, 82). Although the operational balance of the public sector (which includes the impact of real interest payments on debt) improved during the year in which the Plano Real was introduced (there was a 2 percent operational surplus in 1994), it lapsed into an operational deficit by 1995 (1.7 percent of GDP); in 1998 the deficit exceeded 5 percent of GDP (*Banco Central do Brasil, Boletim de Finanças Públicas*, BM NFGFOY). This negative tendency continued for the rest of Cardoso's two terms in office (see Tables 5.6 and 5.7). Between 1995 and 1997, the primary fiscal results systematically worsened at all three levels of government. For Baer (2008, 136–137), this deficit was attributable to a failure to check the rise in expenditures at every level of government, the continuing deficit in the social security system (which rose from 4.9 percent in 1994 to 6 percent in 1998), and "the necessity of the federal government to constantly allocate substantial resources to the states." As Baer puts it, "[t]hese transfers were not wholly constitutional mandated in nature but also resulted from the need to rescue bankrupt state banks" (Baer, 2008, 137).

The latter figures indicate that the fiscal pressures on the federal government were large for the entire period in which Cardoso was president, and especially acute after 1995. As budget constraints became increasingly harder in the context of the stabilization plan (see below) and central authorities faced limits in financing the deficit with debt or monetary emission, changes in the distribution of funds and functions between levels of government became a more attractive option. In addition,

Table 5.6 Operational balance of the public sector in Brazil (1993–2001, as a percentage of GDP)

Years	Operational balance
1993	−0.68
1994	2.00
1995	−1.74
1996	−1.27
1997	−1.76
1998	−5.13
1999	−3.17
2000	−1.31
2001	−1.35

Source: Data compiled and adapted from Banco Central do Brasil.

Note
(−) = Deficit.

Table 5.7 Values taken by the main variables during Cardoso (1998–2002)

	Variable	Value	Range high–low	Overall value
Presidential electoral power	Electoral support president	54.3% (highest since 1945) (1994–1998); 53.1% (1998–2002).	Relatively high	Relatively high presidential power
	Electoral support opposition	27% (Lula's PT) (1994–1998); 31.7% (1998–2002).	Medium	
	Percentage of seats (Chamber of Deputies)	12.3% (PSDB only); 56% coalition (1995–1996); 77% coalition (1996–1998); 74% coalition (1998–2002); 45% coalition (end of 2002).	Low (PSDB); relatively high (coalition; for most of period)	
	Percentage of seats (Senate)	11% (PSDB only); 69% coalition (1995–1996); 90% coalition (1996–1998); 90% coalition (1998–2002); 25% coalition (end of 2002).	Relatively high for most of the period	
	Role of opposition	Coalitional; strong opposition PT, PCdoB.	–	
	Discipline in coalition	From 85.7% during first term to 90.1% in second term.	High	
Presidential legislative power	Use of decree power	5,028 MPs; 2,609 MPs (160 originals) (1995–1998); 2,419 (76 original) (1999–2002).	High	High legislative power
Presidential approval rating	Positive image	From peaks of 27% and low values of around 10% (1995–1998); negative values during the last years (–22% in 2000, –13% in 2001, and –4% in 2002).	From medium to Low	From medium to low approval

Gubernatorial power	Average gubernatorial electoral support	Average of 48% (1995–1998); 51% (1999–2002).	From medium to relat. high	Medium gubernatorial power
	Average legislative support (% of seats)	Governors' party: 28% (1995–1998) and 26% (1999–2002). Coalition: 35% (1995–1998) and 45% (1999–2002).	Relatively Low to Medium	
	Gubernatorial partisan powers index	1.23 (1995–1998); 1.37 (1999–2002).	Low	
	Proportion of allied governors	Six governorships in hands of PSDB. From 22/27 allied during most of the period to 15/27 in late-2002.	High	
	Budget constraints	From hard to harder.	–	
Economic context	Economic growth	Average 2.3% 1995–2002.	Medium	Relatively critical economic context
	Inflation	Average 12.5% 1995–2002.	Low	
	Debt	From R$90 billion in 1994 to R$560 billion in 2002. From 12.9% of GDP in 1994 to 36% of GDP in 2002.	High	
	State debt	Total state debt (debt obligations plus interest rates) from R$3.1 billion in 1995 to R$5.7 billion in 1998, a 184% increase.	Relatively high	
Fiscal indicators	Federal fiscal deficit	Average of –1.6 for the entire period. Peaks of over –5% (1998).	High	Strong fiscal pressures
	State fiscal deficit	Average of –5% (1995–1998); (1999–2002).	High	

economic authorities believed that an important part of the fiscal pressures on the central government after 1988 had a subnational component. Between 1995 and 1998, the deficits of states and municipalities averaged 0.4 percent of GDP. These data contrast sharply to the period from 1988 to 1993, when the average deficit was almost half of this figure (a result of the increased transfers and tax revenue they received after the constitutional reform) (see Table 5.7). In absolute terms, the primary fiscal balance (total revenue excluding financial revenue, credit operations, and disposal of assets) of Brazilian states increased by 470 percent between 1995 and 1998 (from R$ −4.4 billion in 1995 to a whopping −20.8 billion in 1998). The total state debt (debt obligations plus interest rates) grew from R$3.1 billion in 1995 to R$5.7 in 1998, which is equivalent to a 184 percent increase (Data from *Ministério da Fazenda*, STN, COREM). Some authors (Rodden, 2006, 206; Samuels, 2003, 549) have claimed that the soft budget constraints faced by state governments after 1988 and before the Plano Real, especially in relation to debts contracted by their own banks and the successive bailouts from the central government, contributed to the severe fiscal crisis at the state level during the early 1990s.

The fiscal imbalance at the central and subnational levels generated strong incentives for the federal government to stabilize public (national and state) accounts and contain inflation. At the same time, the deepening crisis generated strong incentives for governors to stabilize their budgets and renegotiate their debts with the central government. In a substantial change from previous administrations, governors faced a strong and relatively popular president, who was able to divide them by providing selective incentives (see Table 5.7 and Figure 5.4).

The settings of the game

The distribution of political power favored the president over governors. Cardoso was supported by a relatively large coalition in Congress (the largest since the transition to democracy in 1985), was relatively popular in public opinion (more than any of the previous presidents), and was an influential figure (contrary to the legitimacy problems Sarney faced due to his close ties to the military and the limitations Collor had for being an outsider and having an anti-political establishment stance). Several governors remained relatively powerful in their districts, but overall they had fewer partisan powers than during previous administrations. Moreover, they faced coordination problems as the president increased incentives that divided them. On top of that, an important part of the economic establishment, the mass media, and a portion of public opinion saw governors as one of the key set of actors responsible for the previous hyperinflationary spiral and fiscal profligacy (if not blunt corruption scandals in their states). As Melo (2002, 49) put it, "[t]he issue of subnational finances gradually gained visibility in the public agenda as a cause of fiscal ungovernability."

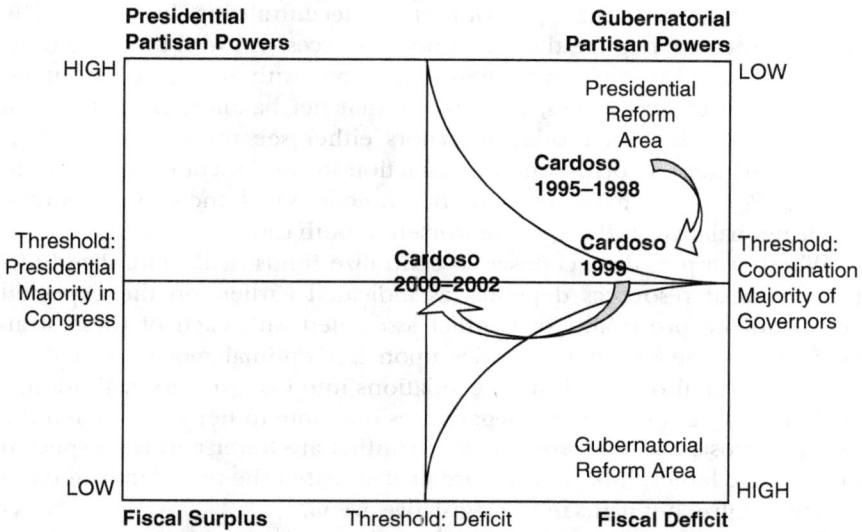

Figure 5.4 Synthesis of the main variables during Cardoso (1995–2002).

Note
The area inside both arches is where the probability of changes in the status quo ante is larger.

Despite the changes initiated during Itamar's presidency, the fiscal context and the hardening budget constraints imposed large costs on both the president and the governors, generating incentives for them to change the status quo. However, the fiscal context interacted with the political power of these actors to produce different outcomes than in the previous stages of the game. On the one hand, governors were politically weaker in relation to the president; fiscal urgency made them more vulnerable, and they depended on debt renegotiation schemes with the central government and bailouts to overcome their fiscal crises. In the previous stages of the federal distributive game, especially between 1987 and 1989, they had more power in their districts and were able to coordinate against a weak president, imposing reforms that translated into more transfers to subnational governments, bailouts, and debt-renegotiation schemes. On the other hand, the president had more partisan power and public support than before, and the critical fiscal scenario generated incentives for him to begin with his reform attempts.

Theoretical expectations

According to the theoretical expectations laid out in Chapter 1, a powerful president facing a context of fiscal crisis, weakened governors, and hard budget constraints should try to improve her balance of the federal equation by either centralizing resources or decentralizing functions. The federal executive might either get more resources (r_{jp}) with the same functions (P_{ip}) or she might have fewer functions with the same resources. Under both circumstances, the presidential net balance, $\Sigma(r_{jp}-P_{ip})$, will improve. On the other side, governors either see their resources (r_{ig}) reduced without a corresponding reduction in the functions they have to deliver (P_{ig}) or they have to take on new functions with the same resources. Their net balance, $\Sigma(P_{ig}-r_{ig})$, will worsen in both cases.

Whether a president chooses to centralize funds or decentralize functions without resources depends, as indicated earlier, on the expected costs and the probability of conflict associated with each of these strategies. Once the president decides upon her optimal move, the federal executive will also try to bring negotiations into Congress to institutionalize her gains and change the legal status quo ante to her favor. When the expected costs and the probability of conflict are lower and the expected benefits are larger, it becomes more probable that the president will try to institutionalize her gains in the legislative arena.

Weak governors facing a powerful president who decides to modify the federal balance in a context of fiscal crisis can either accept the changes passed by Congress at the request of the president or oppose these reforms. If governors decide to clash, the president will get a payoff equal to $(\gamma-C)$ $(1-w)$ and governors get a payoff equal to $(-\gamma-C)w$. The decision to clash or not depends on the costs and the probability of conflict governors expect to face. The larger the expected costs and the probability of conflict, the more probable it is that governors will seek to clash with the president. The normal form game and the Nash equilibrium is the following (see Figure 5.5):

Having analyzed the settings of the game and the theoretical expectations that follow from them, in the next section I explore the costs and benefits the actors expected and how these affected the probability of conflict and the dynamics of negotiations between President Cardoso and the governors over the distribution of funds in Brazil.

		Governors	
		Power	No power
President	Power	0,0	$(\gamma-C)w^*,(-\gamma-C)(1-w)^*$
	No power	$(-\delta-C)w,(\delta-C)(1-w)$	0,0

Figure 5.5 Normal form game for Cardoso (1995–1998).

Expected benefits and costs

The 1988 constitutional changes drove national accounts into deficit and created strong pressures on the federal budget. After the Plano Real, the possibility of financing the central government with the inflationary tax or by printing money were eliminated; rather, interest rates were raised to control inflation. As budget constraints hardened, the expected benefits for the president of a reform to the status quo ante regulating the balance of the federal equation rose. Under the setting of the federal distributive game, governors did not face a weak president as they had in 1988, they were weaker and had stronger partisan links with the president (a fact that prevented strong coordination efforts against him), and they faced larger expected costs to change the status quo ante in their favor. Hence, governors took a more defensive stance (Interview with Antônio Kandir, September 11, 2006). They sought to maintain the balance of the federal equation and keep the benefits they had won in 1988. Coordinating to change the status quo ante once again to gain more benefits was very unlikely. The key problem they faced was that their fiscal situation gradually deteriorated after 1994. During Cardoso's term in office state deficits and debts gradually worsened. Several sub-national executives were trapped with high payrolls, increasing debt payments, and less money for advancing their political objectives. The president used this situation to force negotiations and encourage reforms. Having stronger fiscal pressures and being weaker in relation to the central government meant that governors faced unfavorable conditions for negotiating reforms. They did not expect large benefits from the reforms the president wanted to put forward; they just tried to minimize their losses.

Federal legislators from the PSDB and allied parties had stronger incentives to support the federal executive's reform agenda than to oppose it. The president was relatively popular among citizens and had strong influence inside his party and coalition. Cardoso had control over access to positions in the federal administration, not only for his co-partisans but also for his coalition partners. The federal executive was also able to distribute selective incentives and resources to further legislators' goals (either during their campaigns or for building support on their districts; see negotiations below) (Pereira and Muller, 2004; for Hagopian *et al.*, 2009, a key factor to forge stronger partisan ties and, hence, more presidential backing, was the reduction of state patronage). This contributed to forging some discipline in Congress, despite its historically low levels and high party fragmentation. This fundamental change in federal legislators' behavior has to be understood not only in light of Cardoso's ability to lead negotiations, but also in terms of a change in federal Congressmen's strategies to maximize their preferences. Supporting the president became more attractive in terms of their career prospects and in relation to demands from public opinion. This claim is supported by Hagopian *et al.*

(2009, 362), who argue that during this period strengthening their parties became more attractive for federal Congressmen.

The status quo ante during hyperinflation was costly for most political, economic, and social actors. Most of them did not want to return to the pre-stabilization situation (although some of them had benefited from it). The larger the costs the status quo ante imposed on those actors, the larger the probability that they would support changes to it. The fiscal benefits subnational governments had won in 1988 gradually disappeared in a context of growing fiscal deficits, higher interest rates, and larger debt obligations. Increasing fiscal urgency for the governors translated into a more costly status quo ante.[42] The president used subnational fiscal urgency (especially in relation to debt re-negotiation with the central government) to urge governors to support reforms rather than let them coordinate and begin another round of decentralizing pressures, as in 1988.

In contrast to the state of affairs during the Sarney administration, when the cost of conflict with the executive was low, federal legislators now anticipated significant costs if they decided to conflict with the president. Opposing Cardoso meant fewer funds for their districts and for furthering their political goals, and a greater likelihood of endangering their political careers, especially in terms of access to positions in the federal administration (or the party, in the case of PSDB members) (Interview with Fernando Limongi, September 12, 2006). In relation to more programmatic commitments, opposing the main fiscal reforms endorsed by the president was also perceived as going against the tide of fundamental demands in public opinion, which massively rejected a return to inflation and condemned fiscal irresponsibility (and the corruption associated with it). As debates in Congress indicate (see below), legislators from the incumbent coalition portrayed the opposition as those who wanted a return to inflation and instability.

Budget constraints for the central government hardened substantially in the context of the policies implemented by the economic authorities to curb inflation during and after the Plano Real. Under the new measures to stabilize the economy, the federal government could no longer rely on inflation to reduce the real value of public expenditures. It could not immediately target the rigidities in the expenditure side imposed by the 1988 constitution either. Hence, at the post-1994 inflation rates and the post-1988 fiscal pressures, the primary budget surpluses achieved during the few months before and immediately after the introduction of the Plan Real virtually disappeared. With harder budget constraints and a more critical fiscal situation, the expected benefits for the president to reform the distribution of funds and functions were larger.

Budget constraints also dramatically hardened for subnational governments. On the one hand, the policy of higher interest rates coincided with the end of the five-year grace period for the 1989 debt renegotiation with the states. On the other, the non-renegotiated state debt was contracted at variable rates, all of which combined to generate a sharp increase in the debt and interest rates payments for the lower tiers of government. Before Cardoso, governors paid a low price, or did not have to pay a price at all, for over-spending and for running large deficits because the federal government repeatedly took over and re-financed state debts when governors needed its help. This situation changed under Cardoso. The president took advantage of the gradually unfavorable fiscal context subnational governments faced and their fiscal dependency on the federal government in relation to debt financing to press them to support the reforms endorsed by the central government. As Lopreato claims (2002, 175, 215),

> In the face of their states' financial instability, governors were forced to negotiate individually the rollover of their debts and access to credit or fiscal transfers, and they were pressured to make political concessions and support decisions that were in the interest of the federal government.... States, hostages of the financial crisis, were not able to defend a strong position. The correlation of forces and the critical fiscal situation left the states with few options but to follow the debt re-negotiation conditions (demanded by the central government).

The case of the governor of Minas Gerais, Itamar Franco, is revealing. Itamar declared a moratorium of his state debt to the central government for 90 days as soon as he got into office as governor in January 1999. Besides putting pressure on the federal government to bail out the state, the governor, who had presidential aspirations, took this decision as a political move to weaken the central government. Instead of bailing out the state, the Cardoso administration suspended federal transfers to Minas Gerais and confiscated state bank accounts to pay for the defaulted debt. The governor of Rio Grande do Sul, Olívio Dutra, one of the least favored states out of the 1997 debt renegotiation scheme, also reacted against the central government by initiating a judicial process. The president and economic authorities reacted in the same way they did against Itamar (Rigolon and Giambiagi, 1999, 26). The Itamar and the Dutra incidents were important precedents in the negotiations between the central government and the states. The federal government emerged from these struggles stronger than before, and imposed harder budget constraints on subnational officials.

Why did Collor not do that? Collor faced strong fiscal incentives to alter the federal balance in favor of the central government, and these incentives were similar to Cardoso's. Both of them clearly wanted to revert the decentralizing reforms imposed to the central government during 1988. There were some differences in terms of the restrictions each of these presidents faced. For instance, governors could use the inflationary tax and state banks to finance their budget deficits during the late 1980s, and these options virtually disappeared under hyperinflation and later on during the stabilization period. Despite this, the fundamental difference was not the budget constraints or the fiscal incentives faced by political actors (relatively similar or not deeply different), but essentially the distribution of political power among levels of government in the federation. Cardoso had the political resources to impose limits on governors (as in the case of Itamar) and divide them. Collor did not have the political backing to face governors and impose strong restrictions on them. Moreover, Collor did not have the battery of political resources Cardoso had to prevent coordination among governors (and reduce the probability of conflict). I get into this in the sections below.

The probability of conflict between the president and the governors if the federal executive engaged in substantial reforms of the distribution of funds and functions was lower during the Cardoso administration than during those of Collor and Franco. Facing a relatively strong opponent, governors had more incentives to negotiate than to conflict with the president. Second, governors faced collective action problems and substantial dividing incentives from the president (both selective, e.g., material benefits; and collective, e.g., partisan identity and programmatic commitments), who applied them strategically. Furthermore, the president contributed to diminishing the likelihood of a clash against subnational governments by negotiating with state authorities and granting them concessions. Franco and Cardoso learned from the Collor experience and avoided imposing a broad reform that could raise the probability of conflict by forcing a stronger reaction from governors.

As the expected costs and the probability of conflict from centralizing reforms diminished and the expected benefits of changing the status quo increased, reforms to the status quo ante became a more likely option for Cardoso than for the presidents before him.

The outcomes of the federal distributive game

As predicted by the federal distributive game, Cardoso passed extensive legal and constitutional reforms that substantially altered the federal balance, favoring the central government over subnational governments. A total of 34 constitutional amendments were passed during the Cardoso administration, an average of 4.25 amendments per year. The federal executive proposed most of these reforms. In a detailed analysis of each of these reforms, Couto and Arantes (2003, 119–143) argue that most of them were related to Cardoso's government agenda, particularly on fiscal and budget policies. The constitutional reform agenda was extensive because policy reform attempts in the aforementioned areas could not be implemented without changing preexisting regulations in the 1988 constitution. As part of his reform agenda, Cardoso altered the federal balance by centralizing funds and tax authority, decentralizing new functions to subnational governments, and imposing harder budget constraints (limitations on debt and access to credit) and controls on state spending. Governors reacted to those reforms mainly by seeking to negotiate compensations. This was their minimax strategy. Only in exceptional circumstances did governors decide to conflict with the federal executive (such as Itamar Franco did), and when they did so, they faced large costs. This had an important demonstration effect.

Centralizing funds

The first substantial change in the federal balance was the centralization of revenue by the president through the reduction of federal transfers to subnational governments. The crucial reform in this regard was the extension of the FSE (which was due to expire on December 31, 1995). The FSE authorized the central government to extract 20 percent of the total federal budget allocations from constitutional transfers to states and municipalities and use them on a discretionary basis.

During 1995, Cardoso first demanded of Congress (and the governors) a permanent extension of the FSE, including the clause that reduced transfers to states and municipalities. He justified it as a key reform to continue with his stabilization efforts. The permanent extension of the FSE would have represented a permanent loss for subnational governments. But the president could not get it passed in Congress due to its high costs and the strong reactions from the governors and mayors. Instead, the president had to renegotiate extensions of the law (for as long a term as possible) before each expiration date.

The bill to extend the FSE was sent to Congress on August 15, 1995, almost four months before it was set to expire in December 1995. Governors engaged in intense negotiations with federal authorities during those weeks. State executives were worried about the budgetary impact of revenue losses that followed from reductions in federal transfers due to the FSE. As a consequence of those pressures and as an illustration of the difficulties the federal government had in getting the original bill passed, the FSE deadline lapsed before the bill could be extended in Congress. Between January and February of 1996, state and local governments received their regular transfers (without the cuts imposed by the FSE). Negotiations were arduous, but the federal government finally got the bill passed on March 4, 1996 (almost seven months after its introduction to Congress). The extended fund included a cut in transfers to the states, something Cardoso could not pass in negotiations with subnational governments and Congress in 1994. It took a powerful and popular president, strong fiscal incentives, and long negotiations to achieve these reforms.

The results of this change, despite the concessions, were quite unfavorable to the states, far more so than the version of the bill approved in 1994. Deputies that opposed the extension saw the Social Emergency

Fund as a "fiscal stabilization fund" (as it was later called by the speaker of the committee), which was created to benefit the federal government fiscally and politically. They argued that the main goal of the federal government was to stabilize its fiscal accounts, rather than making any "social" investments from the fund. The strongest complaint from the opposition was the way in which the federal government tried to stabilize its fiscal budget: by taking 20 percent of the total tax collection, about R$20 to 22 billion, from transfers to the states and municipalities (Deputy Inácio Arruda, PCdoB-CE, and Deputy Aldo Arantes, PCdoB-GO, *Diario de Sessões da Câmara dos Deputados* [*DS-CD* from now on], November 2, 1995, 3981, 3983, 3986). As Paulo Bernardo (PT-PR), a member of the Budget Committee, put it, "the federal government wants to solve its fiscal imbalances by imposing costs on the states and municipalities, which are under significant fiscal strain" (*FSP*, "PFL não apóia a prorrogação," April 13, 1997).

Even federal deputies from the main parties in the presidential coalition, PSDB and PFL, recognized that the main goal of the FSE was to stabilize the federal fiscal deficit (*DS-CD*, November 2, 1995, 3985, 3987). The major claim made by the government and the deputies allied to the president was that states would not lose any revenue. In the context of a stabilizing and growing economy as well as raising tax revenues, the extension of the FSE simply meant that they would not get *all* the resources they were expected to get (*DS-CD*, November 2, 1995, 3981–3982).[43] Moreover, they argued that the FSE was necessary to give the federal government some leeway in dealing with a fiscal crisis that was expected to generate a deficit of R$3.18 billion for 1996 and to consolidate the achievements of the stabilization plan (Deputy Arthur Vigilio, PSDB-AM, Deputy Jairo Carneiro, PFL-BA, *DS-CD*, November 2, 1995, 3985, 3987). Menem and Cavallo made similar arguments to Argentine governors and legislators during the 1991 negotiations for the decentralization of health and education.

For most governors, supporting the extension of the FSE was a minimax strategy: they faced large costs if they decided to conflict with the president (as in the case of Itamar, or limitations on their career prospects) and coordination was difficult due to the dividing selective incentives the federal government delivered (at that time, it was renegotiating states' debt and bailouts to state banks). By negotiating with the president, governors expected to extract particular benefits and surmount the fiscal crisis of their states and banks.

Another element to take into account during the negotiations for the extension of the FSE was that Cardoso conducted several reform attempts at the same time, including two crucial ones to the pension system and the federal state bureaucratic administration (*FSP*, March 5, 1996, 1–11). Support for the FSE in Congress was exchanged for concessions in the pension and administrative reforms (which ended up not being approved in Congress). This strategy of conducting several parallel reforms and exchanging support for concessions was characteristic of Cardoso's term in office.[44] This approach also contributed to derailing core negotiations in Congress, to generating attention in the press on the more substantive issues (pension and administrative reform), and to diminishing pressure on the extension of the FSE. Some reforms could probably be seen as having been created only as bargaining chips; they could be abandoned in Congress in exchange for legislative support for crucial reforms (for instance, the reduction in the number of federal legislators for the Center West and the North).

Additionally, as indicated earlier, Cardoso offered the governors the possibility of immediate reelection, a gesture that garnered support for the president's proposals from several governors who did not see him as a challenger and took advantage of the possibility to stay in power for one more term (and perhaps run for the presidency after that). After intense bargaining, delays in the vote, some amendments, and even inconsequential corruption scandals (*FSP*, "Governo usa Verba do FSE para Obter Voto," October 30, 1995), the Chamber of Deputies and the Senate voted for the bill on February 13 and March 4, 1996 (*FSP*, March 5, 1996, 1–11). The fund was expected to collect around R\$20 billion by centralizing 20 percent of the total tax revenue collected by the central government.[45] The president got the expiration date extended only for 18 months (until June 30, 1997), instead of the permanent extension that he wanted initially and the four years he sought later on. Congressmen granted the president this extension because they considered that the bill had to be discussed again before the 1998 election. The fund was renamed Fiscal Stabilization Fund (*Fundo de Estabilização Fiscal*, FEF).[46]

When the new deadline approached (June 30, 1997), Cardoso sought another extension (until December 1999) through a bill sent to Congress in March 1997. As in the previous case, negotiations continued for a longer period than the government wanted, facing more resistance, especially from mayors, that put pressure on deputies. The struggle was also intense this time because the president once again sought to extend the FEF permanently. In reaction, several governors, even some of those allied with Cardoso, opposed the reform. The intense opposition from the governors forced Cardoso to withdraw the proposal for a permanent extension, as he feared that the fund would not be extended under those conditions. The opposition argued that the FEF imposed large costs on the states and municipalities. The fund was created as a temporary measure to reverse a deep fiscal imbalance for the federal government, but now the president wanted to convert this temporary loss for states and municipalities into a permanent one. In a revealing speech, Deputy Giovanni Queiroz (PDT-PA) claimed that

> The Fiscal Stabilization Fund ... was created to stabilize federal accounts ... to take away part of the revenues from the states and

municipalities to stabilize the union.... The institutional imbalance in relation to the federal states is notorious and as legislators who defend their states and municipalities, we cannot allow this bleeding to go on by extending the FEF proposed by the government.

(*DS-CD*, July 11, 1997, 19436)

Deputies from the presidential coalition, on the contrary (and as they did before) stressed the need to have the FEF as a way to control inflation; without it, they argued, the country would return to the disastrous days of the late 1980s and early 1990s. As claimed by Deputy Luiz Carlos Hauly, PSDB-PR, "those who vote against the FEF are voting against our currency, the Plano Real, stability, and the fight against inflation" (*DS-CD*, July 11, 1997, 19429–19430). Cardoso argued that the extension of the FEF did not generate economic losses for states or municipalities, and that this was a temporary measure until the administrative, pension, and tax reforms would stabilize federal and subnational budgets (*FSP*, "Leia trechos da entrevista coletiva concedida pelo presidente da República," September 2, 1997).

Initially, some governors resisted the extension of the FEF, and some deputies supported those criticisms. Governors had a common complaint: they had privatized state companies, fired employees, and opened concessions for public services; in exchange, instead of receiving help from the federal government, they ended up with fewer resources to spend, mainly as a consequence of the FEF (*FSP*, "A nova rebelião," August 15, 1997). Some governors were also mobilized to support the bill.[47] Despite some complaints, most governors had already renegotiated their debt obligations with the central government or were in the process of doing so, and in the end they did not represent an important obstacle for passing the law. Making use of the partisan powers and the majoritarian support in the Chamber of Deputies and the Senate, as well as some concessions to the opposition and other members of Congress, the president got the bill passed.

Some PT deputies condemned the manner in which it was approved and the way the president led negotiations. Deputy Waldomiro Fioravante (PT-RS) argued that,

This fund [the FEF] was approved because ... the president released small quantities [of resources] so that the deputies could take funds to their municipalities to build up a health center, a bridge, or a gym.... But the funds obtained in Brasília through individual amendments do not represent even 10 percent of the funds taken away from municipalities and states through this legislation.

(*DS-CD*, December 8, 1999, 60471)

Jacques Wagner (PT-BA) publicly declared that the intentions of FHC in passing the FEF, which severely affected states and municipalities, were obvious: the FEF for him was the "*Fundo de Eleição do Fernando*" (Fernando's Election Fund) (*FSP*, "Painel," June 26, 1997).

The extension was finally approved by a vote of 342 in favor to 121 against on August 13, 1997, and sent to the Senate, where the bill was passed on November 22, 1997. The extension was granted for two more years, until December 31, 1999.

As this date approached, the president and the governors began a new round of negotiations. The president introduced the bill in the Chamber of Deputies in mid-November 1999. The positions maintained by the government and the opposition were similar to those adopted during previous rounds. The opposition denounced that the president promised he would not renew the fund (now re-named "deviated union's revenue"; *Desvinculação de Receitas da União*, DRU) but he ended up extending constantly this emergency and provisional measure that took funds away from states and municipalities to stabilize the federal deficit (Deputy Nelson Peregrino, PT-BA, *DS-CD*, December 8, 1999, 60464). In addition, the opposition complained that there was not much they could do because the government had the votes necessary to extend the DRU. These votes were secured, they claimed, in exchange for individual amendments the deputies in the governing coalition demanded. Deputy Arnaldo Faria de Sá (PPB-SP) complained that "If you vote for the bill you are going to be giving a blank check [to the president] so that your city and your state will continue being dependent on the federal government, which wants them all subordinated" (*DS-CD*, December 8, 1999, 60469–60470).

Negotiations among party leaders and the executive provided the architecture of agreements for the approval of the bill. As claimed theoretically, when governors are weakened, their influence over legislators is diminished, so the game focused on the dynamics between the president and legislators in Congress. The fragile legislative support had to be constantly secured by Cardoso to avoid defection in the passing of the law. This time, as in the previous negotiations, the government and allied deputies in Congress had to make important concessions to pass the bill. These concessions included the elimination of the Constitutional Fund for the North-Northeast from the DRU (in order to avoid conflict and guarantee support from deputies from those regions), reducing the period of the fund's extension from 2007 to 2003, and finally broadening a series of exemptions for the funds allocated to states and municipalities (*DS-CD*, January 13, 2000, 1557, 1566–1567).

Other agreements, more limited in scope, were reached to assure votes, such as the distribution of resources for infrastructure works in municipalities, previously included as amendments to the annual budget by deputies (this was one of the main demands PMDB representatives made) (*FSP*, December 16, 1999; January 12, 2000); the promise of granting R$30 million to sugar cane mill owners requested by deputies linked to the areas in which this lobby was strong (*FSP*, January 13, 2000); locating the

Agência Nacional de Saúde in the state of Rio de Janeiro, to get the favor of deputies from that district (*FSP*, January 13, 2000); and a specific deal with the "Igreja Universal" (an evangelical church), by which the government exchanged support for the authorization of media acquisitions by the church. To get the votes in the second round of voting, the federal government authorized the payment of R$694 million in parliamentary amendments to the budget (12 times the amount of 1999 and 65 percent of the total amount of amendments, that added up to R$1.1 billion) (*FSP*, "Governo atende deputados e aprova DRU," January 27, 2000). These concessions were critical for securing the votes of the deputies in the coalition. As the president approached the end of his second term in office, his partisan power and public support had eroded significantly (especially after the 1999 economic crisis). This had an effect on the concessions Cardoso had to make in order to pass reforms favorable for the central government. Nonetheless, these concessions were granted by the federal government after it had gained other sources of revenue which were not decentralized to the subnational governments. After one month, the bill passed in both rounds of voting, while the fiscal reform (under consideration at the same time) did not.

The approval and extension of the FEF was Cardoso's first important victory in relation to the balance of the federal equation during his presidency. The FSE/FEF/DRU severely altered the federal balance by increasing the central government's revenue and cutting that of subnational governments. It contributed to undermining the states' finances and to weakening their negotiating power with the federal government. As agreed during the negotiations for the FEF between the central government, governors, and mayors, although the federal government centralized 20 percent of subnational governments' revenue, absolute transfers to the states increased as a consequence of macroeconomic stability, growth, and higher tax collection. The cuts in transfers to states, although initially provisional, remained in place during most of Cardoso's term in office. Having weakened the governors by these reforms, the president went after other far-reaching changes that further contributed to debilitating state executives. In spite of the success in the extension of the reductions in federal transfers to the states, the president changed the approach for subsequent reforms. Apart from the FEF, Cardoso did not directly seek to centralize resources by taking revenues away from subnational governments. The large costs of this type of reform for the federal government probably influenced this decision.

Centralizing tax authority

Instead of continuing to centralize funds, the president sought to further alter the fiscal balance by curbing the tax revenues of subnational governments while he tried to expand those of the central government. In other words, Cardoso eliminated state taxes and reduced tax pressure at the sub-national level (exempting exports from states' sales taxes) at the same time that he created new federal taxes (called contributions), which were not part of the system of automatic transfers to subnational governments. In this manner, the president centralized tax collection and authority (the outcomes in terms of the federal balance were analogous to a straight-forward centralization of revenue), but not by directly taking it from the states and municipalities.

Cardoso sought to reduce state revenues and the funds the government allocated to municipalities by exempting several products for export from the states sales tax (ICMS). The main purpose of the bill, at least in the official discourse, was to reduce the trade and current account deficits by promoting exports (curbing the "Brazilian cost"; Interview with Antônio Kandir, September 11, 2006). In fact, however, the bill also stipulated serious cuts in the revenues collected by subnational governments and further increased their fiscal vulnerability. Antônio Kandir (PSDB-SP) introduced the Complementary Law bill 95/1996 (also known as the Kandir law) in the Chamber of Deputies on May 14, 1996. The bill was put to the vote in the Chamber of Deputies on August 27, 1996. Some members of the coalition voted against it (such as deputies of the PFL from Amazonas) because of the large costs it imposed on their states. Deputy Euler Ribeiro (PFL-AM) argued that the state of Amazonas would forfeit R$52 million due to the tax exemptions affecting export products manufactured in Manaus' Free Trade Zone (*DS-CD*, August 22, 1996, 23362). The PCdoB and the PT also opposed the reform (*DS-CD*, August 28, 1996, 24075). Despite some opposition, the bill and some amendments were passed by a large majority and then sent to the Senate. Seventeen days later, in an indication of the support the president had in Congress, the Upper Chamber approved the tax cut, turning it into Complementary Law 87 on September 13, 1996 (*DS-CD*, August 28, 1996, 24112).

The Kandir Law was not without costs for the central government. Governors exerted strong pressures on the central government to be reimbursed for the funds they would cease to collect. The total cost for the states due to the exemption of exports from their taxes was about R$1.6 billion a year (data for 1996; Rezende 1996, 12). The federal government conducted negotiations with governors, state secretaries of finance, and the legislative leaders in Congress through the now Minister of Planning, Antônio Kandir (*DS-CD*, August 28, 1996, 24113, 24115). As a result of those negotiations, the federal government finally agreed to create a reim-bursement fund to compensate the states for the lost revenue. This was a crucial concession from the president in the negotiations with state authorities (Interview with Antônio Kandir, September 11, 2006). But Cardoso also offered it with an expiration date: he insisted that the com-pensation should last for only one year. Federal authorities believed that this was sufficient time for subnational governments to adjust to the revenue cut. Governors strongly resisted those demands and the federal government finally agreed to exchange support for the bill for a five-year compensation (until 2002; Art.31, LCP 87/96; see also Annex to LCP 87/96; Melo, 2002, 92). It may seem that the federal government paid a large cost for this law, but this reform also represented a substantial loss for the states, as one of their most important sources of tax revenue was eliminated.

These five years were not an arbitrary figure. The period granted for the compensations expired the same year as the upcoming gubernatorial elections. That is, the president, through his delegation in Congress, guaranteed incumbent governors that they would not be affected by cuts in tax collection during their current terms in office. But that was not guaranteed after 2002, when the newly elected state executives were expected to take office. As in the case of the state bank privatizations (see below), the president made concessions to governors in the present in exchange for fiscal reforms that would strengthen fiscal stability and the power of the central government in the future, after governors have left office. Governors followed their minimax strategy: facing a strong president and having the fiscal incentives to negotiate, they sought to minimize losses and maximize compensation.

Compensation was not granted through cash transfers but rather through National Treasury bonds, which could be used by state authorities to pay their debts with the central government. Thus the president was able to exchange a crucial state tax for central government bonds, offered for a five-year period, which could be used to pay state debts with the central government. In the end, despite the compensations governors got for the revenue they ceased to receive, the Kandir Law represented an important loss in the states' tax base and a long-term reduction in tax revenue (Eaton, 2004, 162–163). It made states more vulnerable to the federal government, as transfers were guaranteed for a limited period and any increase or extensions had to be negotiated with the central administration.[48] As in the case of Argentina during the early 1990s, many governors opted for a short-term solution to their fiscal imbalances, replacing state taxing authority for federal compensation transfers that were expected to hold up during their administrations, even if the new law affected their districts' fiscal capacity in the longer run (something that would apply to future administrations). The president divided governors and played their interests against one another to the benefit of the central government.

Once the federal government had secured cuts in tax revenue and authority at the subnational level, it went after the creation of new federal taxes that were not meant to be shared with the states (the so-called contributions, or *contribuições*). Among the most important of these non-shared federal contributions was the CPMF (Provisional Contribution on the Movement or Transmission of Values, Credits, and Rights of Financial

Nature), a tax on financial transactions that was created in 1996, extended for two years in 1997, and remained effective until December 2007. The CPMF originally established a rate of 0.25 percent on all financial operations to finance public health care, social welfare, and a Fund to Eradicate Poverty (*Fundo de Combate e Erradicação da Pobreza*). Some analysts estimated that it collected about R$18 billion per year (out of a total R$280 billion of the government's total tax collection—tax revenue and pensions—in 2001) or R$284 billion in total during the period it remained effective (*FSP*, "FHC vai propor CPMF até 2004 sem isenção," June 29, 2001; "Governo anuncia emenda para manter CPMF até 2004," June 30, 2001). Other contributions were the CSLL (*Contribuição Social sobre o Lucro Líquido*), the PIS (*Programa de Integração Social*), and the COFINS (*Contribuição Social para o Financiamento da Seguridade Social*). Cardoso increased rates for the COFINS to collect more revenues for the central government. These contributions expanded the federal tax base and augmented the revenues the central government collected without decentralizing funds to the states (and municipalities).[49]

The IR and the IPI have historically been the main taxes for the federal government, collecting an average of about 5 and 2 percent of GDP, respectively. But the relevance of social contributions as a share of total tax collection increased substantially during Cardoso's term in office. Due to its capacity to generate revenue that is not shared with subnational governments, social contributions became one of the most important sources of revenue for the federal government (Giambiagi and Além, 1999, 196). For Giambiagi and Além (1999, 189) this was "the consequence of the attempts from the central government to augment its revenue as a reaction to the increase of decentralized tax revenue after the 1988 reforms." In a similar vein, Melo (2002, 48) argues that "as a result of [the] losses in the federal budget since 1988, the union began to make use of social contributions as a compensatory means to collect extra revenue."

Changes in the distribution of functions

The central government also increased states' (and municipalities') policy responsibilities. These new functions were not financed with extra fiscal transfers from the federal government but from federally imposed earmarking on state (and municipal) revenues. These reforms were another substantive change in the balance of the federal equation. The 1988 constitution decentralized new resources to subnational governments without stipulating new policy responsibilities for them. Cardoso sought to create the conditions so that sub-national governments could assume more responsibilities for delivering services, especially education and health care (Souza, 1997, 95).

With respect to education reforms, the president pressed Congress to pass Law 9,394 (LDB, or *Lei de Diretrizes e Bases da Educação Nacional*). The

LDB established that states had primary responsibility over secondary education and municipalities over primary education. The federal government was fundamentally (although not exclusively) in charge of higher education. It created a special fund (the *Fundo de Manutenção e Desenvolvimento do Ensino Fundamental e de Valorização do Magistério*, FUNDEF) that compelled states to assign 25 percent of their shares from tax revenues to basic education. The LDB set clearer divisions of responsibilities between the central government and sub-national governments; FUNDEF compelled states to finance their policy obligations in this area.

Reforms in health care followed a similar logic to those in education, redirecting policy responsibilities to subnational governments, especially municipalities, and centrally regulating the delivery of services through the so-called *Sistema Único de Saúde* (SUS).[50] The 1988 constitution established that the execution of primary health services was the responsibility of the municipalities, while complex health services and coordination activities were placed in the charge of the states. The federal government was in charge of regulating and planning them. But the constitution did not establish how each level of government was supposed to finance the delivery of health services. So health services basically depended on resources from the federal government, which financed almost 70 percent of the health care budget during the 1990s. This situation continued until the 29th constitutional amendment passed in 2000, which compelled the three levels of government to finance the system and gave more precision to the distribution of functions and responsibilities among them (regulated by the *Lei Orgânica da Assistência Social*, LOAS). The critical change was that the law demanded that states allocate 12 percent of their total budget revenue and 15 percent to municipalities to finance their health services (Mora and Varsano, 2001, 16; Ribeiro, 2005, 29–33).

These reforms altered the post-1988 federal balance established in the constitution, which had granted states more funds without any decentralization of administrative functions or policy responsibilities. During the Cardoso administration, states (and municipalities) were compelled to deliver health and education and to allocate a minimum share of their revenues to finance those social services. These reforms further contributed to strengthening the position of the central government in terms of the federal balance, as health care and education were now co-financed between the three levels of government and sub-national governments were under the control and supervision of the federal administration.

Central government controls on state spending

Once the aforementioned reforms were approved, Cardoso's challenge was to enforce these controls and restrictions on subnational governments. The president sought to secure the new balance of the federal equation in favorable terms for the central government by means of specific legislation that required three-fifth majorities to pass any changes to these agreements, reducing pressures from states on the federal budget. His political support in Congress, public opinion, and among allied governors, the distribution of compensation and dividing incentives to subnational governments, and the states' fiscal imbalances that put many governors on a defensive footing allowed him to consolidate the federal government's gains in the balance of power between the center and the states.

Early in 1995, Cardoso asked Congress to pass the so-called *Lei Camata* (*Lei Complementar* 82/1995, introduced by Deputy Rita Camata, PMDB-ES), which required the federal government, states, and municipalities to limit payroll expenditures to 60 percent of net revenues. The parties in the presidential coalition supported the bill because it imposed "discipline on the degree to which states could spend excessively on public employment" (Renato Vianna, PMDB-SC, *DS-CD*, December 4, 1991, 25405). The opposition criticized the bill because it violated subnational autonomy and threatened labor conditions of state and municipal public employees (a position sustained by the PT and PCdoB). The bill was passed, and the federal government brought its payroll spending to within the limits imposed by the law (58 percent) shortly after it was sanctioned, but not all state governments were able to do the same. Only six states were within this limit, while six others spent more than 80 percent of their revenues on payroll (Fleischer, 1998, 130).[51]

The fiscal situation of the federal government deteriorated sharply after the 1997 Asian financial crisis, worsening even further during 1998 in a prelude to the 1999 crisis. These crises, as argued in the theoretical section, reduced the costs of making changes in the status quo ante for the federal government and increased the costs of sustaining it for the states. In this context, a new project was introduced into the Chamber of Deputies during late 1998 to limit fiscal spending of the federal and subnational governments, modifying the *Lei Camata*. The *Lei Complementar* (96/1999), named *Lei Camata II*, which was approved on May 1999, reduced the limits on current spending to 50 percent for the federal government and maintained the 60 percent level for states and municipalities.

The *Lei Camata*, its amendments, and the increasing limits imposed on states from issuing debt was a gradual process that culminated in the sanction of the Fiscal Responsibility Law (*Lei de Responsabilidade Fiscal*, LRF), passed by Congress in May 2000. This law imposed personnel expenditure and public indebtedness limits for each level of government, compelled authorities to define annual fiscal targets, and created public finance control mechanisms for election years. It even imposed criminal sanctions on any office-holder who spent beyond her means (BNDES, 2000, 2). The LRF also prohibited states from issuing debts during the last year of a governor's mandate and on public works that could not be completed during the term of the incumbent administration (Melo, 2002, 167).

In general terms, governors did not coordinate actively against the LRF and the limits it imposed on them.[52] One of the main reasons was that they had fiscal incentives to do so. They were very much dependent on the central government to re-finance their debts, which once again increased dramatically during the 1999 currency crisis and subsequent devaluation of the real. State support for more spending restrictions, controls, and fiscal reforms were among the conditions agreed upon by the president and the governors to re-finance states' debt. Additionally, as a consequence of these reforms and restrictions, governors were severely weakened and faced strong collective action problems to coordinate against the central government. The president sent the LRF bill to Congress in the midst of the 1999 crisis. The financial turmoil generated strong pressures on the federal government to balance the fiscal deficit (Loureiro and Abrucio, 2003, 592) and harden fiscal controls on subnational governments. The costs of opposing the reforms for the governors were high, as the central government could refuse to re-finance their debts and limit access to bailouts and extra funds. The benefits were equally large. As states would very unlikely have access to loans without the guarantee of the central government, they also supported the law as a way of securing access to future credit. Moreover, the central government distributed discretionary transfers to secure support for the bill and guarantee that states would meet the terms of the law.[53]

Partisan differences among governors did not play a clear role. Governors from the PT cooperated and endorsed the reform because they needed to re-finance their debt with the central government and reduce spending. However, federal deputies and senators from this party rejected the bill, arguing that the revenue allocated to finance the debt swap should have been used on social spending. Other opposition parties shared this position, especially the PCdoB, which also rejected the bill. Federal legislators from the president's party and coalition had more (partisan and selective) incentives to support the president and stronger commitments to supporting the fiscal responsibility agenda (*DS-CD*, January 26, 2000, 3662–3665).[54]

The original bill was introduced in the Chamber of Deputies on April 15, 1999. The main opposition came from the PT and the PSB/PCdoB block. Opposition deputies claimed the bill sacrificed the autonomy of the states and municipalities and the capacity of subnational governments to implement social policies. Sérgio Miranda (PCdoB-MG) claimed that the LRF "is the end of the federal pact; [because] it imposes restrictions on governors and mayors in a rigid and authoritarian form" (*DS-CD*, January 26, 2000, 3662). Senator Heloísa Helena (PT-AL) strongly opposed it, claiming that "the Constitution determines the duties of the states: education, health, public security," and asking "why none of these issues can be protected [by law] and the only protected issue is debt and interest payments?" (*DSF*, April 11, 6954). Deputies supporting the government stressed the need to improve transparency and accountability in public administration and to institute a "new morality" in the administration of public resources. The LRF was passed in Congress after one year of deliberations, negotiations, and some modifications to the original bill. Despite the support the central government got in both chambers, it also had to make some concessions to key political actors, especially the governors (and mayors). One of the most significant of these concessions was an extension of the time by which expenditures on personnel had to be limited (the 1999 deadline had to be postponed to June 2000 due to the governors' and mayors' pressure).

In sum, Cardoso could rely on his power, public support, and legitimacy to continue with the structural reforms to stabilize the economy and weaken governors. Also, the 1999 crisis generated renewed incentives to continue the institutionalization of the reforms. Political actors, including governors, feared the previous equilibrium (the status quo ante before the Plano Real) and the costs it once imposed on them. This, in turn, contributed to diminishing the costs of reforms to consolidate the new status quo ante under Cardoso. Once sanctioned, the LRF imposed restrictions that have been difficult to alter. The LRF was a successful attempt of the central government to institutionalize the new balance of the federal distributive game, imposing restrictions and limits to the states, and reducing the probability of returning to the previous stage of the game.

The balance of the federal distributive game

The balance of the federal equation after the Cardoso reforms favored the president in relation to the governors: the federal executive got new funds and new taxes (increasing his resources, r_{jp}), and was able to delegate administrative responsibilities to subnational governments, thus diminishing the functions he had to deliver (P_{ip}). The central government kept some control and funding functions in the decentralization reform, and in this regard it was very different from that conducted by Menem during 1992–1993, who basically got rid of those functions by decentralizing them to the provinces. The new balance imposed costs on the governors: although they got more revenue (r_{jg}) in absolute terms, that revenue was reduced relative to that of the central government. Furthermore, the central government imposed more policy responsibilities on them and increased the functions they had to deliver (P_{ig}). In other words, the presidential net balance [$U = \Sigma(r_{jp} - P_{ip})$] improved significantly, while the gubernatorial net balance [$X = \Sigma(P_{ig} - r_{ig})$] worsened during the Cardoso administration.

In relative terms, the central government increased its share of revenue from 66.8 percent to 70.3 and its share of expenditures from 52.4 to almost 55 percent between 1994 and 1999. In contrast, the states' share of revenues decreased from 33.2 percent to 29.7 in the same period, while their share of expenditures diminished from 47.6 to 45 percent (IPEA Data; see Table 5.8). These changes were not radical if we consider that these shares increased dramatically after 1988. The main point here is that the decentralizing trend was reversed and that the central government, instead of being further weakened, began to alter the federal balance in its favor.

In absolute terms, the total tax revenue of the central government increased a total of 359 percent (from R$181.5 billion to R$651 billion) between 1994 and 2000. States' total revenue increased, in absolute terms, from R$41.7 billion in 1994 to R$152 million in 2000, a 365 percent increase for the period.

Despite the sharp increase in state revenue and federal transfers, the states' total spending rose from R$85.6 billion in 1995 to R$142.7 billion in 1998, a 167 percent increase in three years. Similarly, the total state debt (debt obligations plus interest rates) grew from R$3.1 billion in 1995 to R$5.7 billion in 1998, equivalent to a 184 percent increase. Ultimately, the states' primary fiscal deficit rose from R$4.4 billion in 1995 to R$21 billion in 1998, a 474 percent increase during the period (Data from *Secretaría do Tesouro Nacional*).

The main outcome of the reforms was that the president put an end to those institutional arrangements by which states were able to poach the central government's revenue (Loureiro and Abrucio, 2003, 590). The new rules fiscally constrained the states, imposing centrally determined fiscal goals upon them. These new regulations and their mandatory fiscally balanced budgets (possible in a context of a growing economy) reduced the states' fiscal incentives to alter the status quo and limited their capacity to predate the central government's revenue. The main cost of the reforms was a deep erosion in the states' fiscal autonomy and fiscal policy (see Table 5.9).

Table 5.8 Revenue and expenditure share of subnational units in Brazil (1994–2000)

Year	Revenue share	Expenditure share
1994	33.18	47.57
1995	31.04	46.09
1996	32.45	45.85
1997	31.50	44.77
1998	30.69	45.95
1999	29.69	–
2000	31.70	45.09

Sources: Data compiled and adapted from IPEA Data.

Table 5.9 Synthesis of the reforms and impacts on the federal balance (1995–1998)

Period of reforms	Subnational revenue (in relative terms)	Subnational functions	Subnational tax authority	Federal balance
Cardoso 1995–1998	Decreased (revenue share decreased from 33.2% in 1994 to 29.7% in 1999; the president retained 20% of state transfers) But increased in absolute terms	Relatively increased (imposed more policy responsibilities in health and education, together with municipalities and central control and planning)	Decreased (eliminated several state taxes, including export taxes, and replaced them with federal taxes—called social contributions; their revenue is not shared)	Favorable for the federal government $U = \Sigma(r_{jp} - P_{ip}) > X = \Sigma(P_{ig} - r_{ig})$

The federal distributive game during the latter part of the Cardoso government

After the LRF in 2000, Cardoso could not pass major changes in the distribution of federal funds, and he had to concentrate his efforts on maintaining the status quo ante. He was a relatively weaker president in Congress and in terms of public opinion, he did not have the political (and constitutional) opportunity to continue in office after the end of his second term, and the fiscal situation did not compel him to attack subnational governments as he once had.[55] Cardoso was able to keep support from a broad coalition of parties (PSDB, PFL, PMDB, PPB, and PTB) during most of his second term in office. But the erosion of the incumbent after the reelection bill and the waning support from public opinion had evident effects during his last year in office (between March and December 2002), when the PFL and the PTB abandoned the coalition. Cardoso maintained negative values during the final years of the administration (–22 percent in 2000, –13 percent in 2001, and –4 percent in 2002) (DataFolha, 1988–2001). The presidential coalition share of seats diminished substantially to 45 percent in the Chamber of Deputies and 25 percent in the Senate.

The drop in public opinion support and the reduction in the number of seats controlled by the federal executive's party and coalition notably reduced the partisan power of the president and his capacity to pass reforms, thereby altering the federal balance. The president still had fiscal incentives to stabilize federal accounts, but now he had fewer political resources to continue pressuring sub-national governments to centralize, reduce, and control the funds available to them. The erosion of presidential political power increased the expected costs and the probability of conflict over possible reforms endorsed by the federal executive against subnational governments. In an indication of this, close to the end of his second term in office, Cardoso proposed to pass a series of reforms, including a wide-ranging tax reform, but these proposals ended up deadlocked in Congress and were finally abandoned (as well as the judicial and a political reform).

The president announced he would propose that Congress federalize the ICMS and extend the CPMF (until 2004) in June 2001 (*FSP*, "Governo tenta de novo isentar Bolsa da CPMF," June 22, 2001; "FHC vai propor CPMF até 2004 sem isenção," June 29, 2001; "Governo anuncia emenda para manter CPMF até 2004," June 30, 2001). The creation of a federal VAT obviously threatened the continuation of the main state tax, the ICMS. So, if the tax reform bill endorsed by the president had passed in Congress, the states would have been the main losers. Opposition to the unification of the ICMS emerged immediately, including from members of the governing coalition, and the government expended little effort in pushing forward its proposal (*FSP*, "Aliados bombardeiam pacote tributário," June 29, 2001; "Estados rejeitam projeto do governo para unificar ICMS," July 7, 2001). Capitulating, Cardoso announced that, instead of pursuing a broad fiscal reform, he would focus his efforts only on extending the CPMF or what he called a "mini fiscal reform" (*FSP*, "Governo agora quer 'minirreforma'," June 22, 2000).[56] This is another indication that the president decided to (or could not do anything else but) concentrate efforts on maintaining the status quo ante achieved after the reforms rather than pushing forward more substantive changes.

Final comments: the tragedy for the pares

Benefits from changes to the status quo for the president after the Cardoso era reforms were substantial. These reforms had a huge fiscal impact on the states: governors saw their revenue cut (between R$9 and R$11 billion a year) and their functions augmented, all of which translated into a 180 percent increase in their debt and an over 470 percent increase in absolute terms in their fiscal deficit. The central government, on the contrary, improved its fiscal condition by reducing fiscal pressures from the states and above all by means of new tax revenue from social contributions, which are not shared with subnational governments.

The costs of the reforms during the Cardoso administration were not insignificant: just between 1997 and 2001, the federal government absorbed state debts for a total of R$205 billion and spent about R$45 billion on the privatization of state banks. To that we have to add compensations (for instance, the more than R$2 billion a year for the Kandir law) and costly concessions made to particular states and subnational leaders. Despite the costs, Cardoso did substantially alter the federal balance in favor of the central government in the most dramatic way since the transition to democracy.

How could Cardoso and Menem impose centralizing reforms on the strongest governors in the region? How can we explain centralizing reforms in a federation such as Brazil where, according to some scholars, institutions generate "centrifugal" forces that threaten the capacity of the president to achieve some of her agenda goals? Some authors claimed leadership was crucial; others that it was the distribution of costly selective incentives; others get into detailed historical accounts to explain this paradox; and still others claim that presidents, acting as strategic actors, distribute funds as a way to consolidate their power in key electoral districts.

The answer put forward in this chapter is in line with the argument presented by scholars who argue that the president's legislative powers are relevant variables that help explain reforms favoring the federal executive (Diniz, 1997; Figueiredo and Limongi, 1995, 1997, 2000; Santos, 1999a, 1999b). This claim can help us understand why presidents, in general, have had control over the legislative process and an important rate of legislative success. However, this claim faces some limitations to account for *when* reforms to the federal balance are more likely to occur. How can relatively stable institutional variables, such as the president's legislative powers (not to mention federal and electoral institutions, or party nomination procedures) account for these deep and recurrent changes in the federal balance?

The theoretical argument presented in Chapter 1 can help complement relatively static institutional arguments by providing a more dynamic account on these changes in the federal balance. It is out of the interaction between a sharp asymmetry of power in the setting of the federal distributive game and strong fiscal incentives that the actors can and would produce changes in the federal balance. It was not a matter of fiscal pressures alone. Both Cardoso and Menem faced strong fiscal incentives (i.e., the threshold for strong fiscal incentives was crossed) during most of their terms in office; however, they were capable of passing reforms to the federal balance during some relatively short and specific periods of time. When both presidents could concentrate partisan powers in Congress, maintain public support, and debilitate key political actors (among them, dividing the governors) (that is, when they crossed the threshold for partisan powers), they could give impulse to reforms (this happened, for instance, after the stabilization of the economy). This chapter has detailed how these factors interacted to account for the centralization processes in Argentina and Brazil. In the next chapter, I analyze some similarities, differences, and get into some of their implications for the functioning of these two federal democracies.

Notes

1 This helped him to tilt the balance to his favor, which gradually translated into an increasing support from a vast range of sectors and groups inside Peronism, including orthodox unionists (although he gradually diminished their influence in the party by dividing the CGT—General Labor Confederation—in a pro-Menem faction and another opposed to him), powerful party leaders, local bosses (especially those from the Buenos Aires' *Conourbano*), and naturally, legislators. Cafiero and his supporters ended up showing some signs of timid support to Menem.

2 For Calvo (2007, 270), almost 35 percent of all presidential initiatives were enacted by decree during Menem's presidency, most of them under the economic emergency and state reforms laws. Negretto (2002, 396) argues that during the first Menem presidency, DNUs represented 59.1 percent of all laws initiated by the federal executive and approved in Congress. This percentage diminished to 54.3 percent during his second term in office.

3 These averages, slightly smaller than those during Alfonsín's term (47.8 percent of the vote and 56.3 percent of the seats), reached 50.7 percent of the vote and 55 percent of the seats after 1991, and 54.7 and 57.1 percent respectively after 1997. Fifteen governors controlled more than 50 percent of their state legislative assemblies. Eight governors were elected with 50 percent of the vote or more. Nine governors were elected with similar percentages during

Alfonsín's presidency. The number of governors elected with these percentages reached 12 after the 1991 election and 13 after that of 1997.

4 Jones (2002, 159–167) claims that a provincial-level party, and to a lesser extent a national-level one, has a great deal of control over a legislator's access to the ballot and her position in the party lists for the federal legislative. However, in Jones's argument there is no variation according to the distribution of power between the federal and provincial levels. In this work, I claim that when governors are powerful in their provinces and the president is weak or federal party leaders are not influential, the lists are basically constructed in each district without much intervention from federal party members. However, when the president is strong and has control inside the party, she can have strong influence over the process of party list's formation in the provinces.

5 PJ legislators that opposed the president faced the costs of being expelled from the party or having to leave it, as occurred with the *Grupo de los Ocho* (Group of Eight) formed in January 1990, out of which the Frente Grande was created in 1993.

6 Some legislators from the incumbent party proposed a reform to the revenue-sharing regime, but the bill never reached the floor (Bill 5808-D-90, Trámite Parlamentario 230). The bill was signed by deputies from four provinces. Radical legislators presented several bills to include revenues from privatizations into the revenue-sharing regime, which were of course blocked in Congress (e.g., Bill 0751-S-90, Senator Solari Yrigoyen; Dirección de Información Parlamentaria).

7 Domingo Cavallo (who was appointed by the military junta as president of the Central Bank in 1982) had an antecedent and some indirect previous experience in this regard.

8 Despite this increase in provincial revenues, provincial governments faced large fiscal deficits during the entire period after the transition to democracy (the only exception was an overall surplus in 1983). The causes of these sustained deficits are several, and beyond the reach of this work. Some authors claim governors over-spent due to a series of perverse institutional incentives generated by the federal system (Jones *et al.*, 2000; Remmer and Wibbels, 2000; Rodden and Wibbels, 2002; Tommasi, 2002; Tommasi *et al.*, 2001) and to sustain clientelistic networks and their political machines (Domingo Cavallo endorsed this position). Others argue that they incurred permanent deficits because of the imbalances they face between the functions they have to deliver, the (few) funds they collect, and the insufficient funds they get from the central government (Nuñez Miñana and Porto, 1983; Pírez, 1986; Porto, 2003).

9 Between March 1991 and January 2002 the exchange rate was fixed in AR$1 = US$1 in Argentina.

10 Senator Malharo de Torres (UCR-Mendoza) asserted that she was shocked to see "we are considering practically the decentralization of the Argentine education system and we have to hurry and do it in fifteen minutes" (*DS-CSN*, November 13, 1991, 4042–4043).

11 This put the existence of previous agreements between the president and the governors into light. If there was not enough support for the bill, it would have been discussed in committees and then debated separately.

12 Deputy Cafiero (Buenos Aires) brought up divisions between PJ deputies: "our [legislative] delegation did not participate of this agreement and only today realizes that there is a bill to decentralize educational services [to the provinces]." He questioned the decentralization reform: "education is being analyzed through the prism and the microscope of the fiscal goals"; "the idea is to get rid of secondary, technical, and artistic schools." And finally claimed his province could not afford paying for those services (*DS-CDN*, December 5–6, 1991, 5326, 5327).

13 The last two governors to sign the bilateral agreements with the central government were Néstor Kirchner (Santa Cruz) and Eduardo Duhalde (Buenos Aires). Both were Peronists but from internal factions opposed to Menem, and the latter was, at that time, a serious partisan challenger to (and for) presidential power. Falleti (2003, 149) highlights that the financial impact of the decentralization reform was greater in the province of Buenos Aires than in the rest. Thirty percent of all the decentralized schools were in this province and the provincial government was compelled to equalize the salaries of former national and provincial teachers (provincial teachers' wages were lower than those of former national teachers, unlike the case of the rest of the provinces). The governor of this province was the last one to sign the agreements with the national government, in December of 1993.

14 Deputy Fontela (PJ-Buenos Aires) claimed that "this agreement ... decentralizes the cost of adjustment to the provinces." Deputy Baglini (UCR-Mendoza) argued that the "agreement simply covers ... the needs to finance national accounts." For him, "this cannot be a federal fiscal pact because ... it cannot have its origins in an act of force.... There is no federal fiscal pact when [the central government] takes advantage of the urgent necessities of the provinces." Deputy Molinas (AHTE-Santa Fe) accused this agreement as "an imposition based on the power [the central government] has to subjugate the provinces and make them accept all this."

15 Senator Aguirre Lanari (Liberal Party of Corrientes) argued the fiscal pact was a "adhesion contract" (*contrato de adhesión*) out of which "one of the parts—the strongest [i.e., the central government] imposes its conditions on the other [i.e., the provinces]—who theoretically may discuss and sign it or not, but who is [in reality] obliged to accept it even though it dislikes some of the clauses" (*DS-CSN*, September 2, 1992, 2311).

16 That was the case of the National Housing Fund (FONAVI), the Water and Sanitation Fund (COFAPyS), Fund for Electric Development of the Interior (FEDEI), and the Federal Highway Fund (*DS-CDN*, August 19–20, 2056). Other funds related to social assistance were also decentralized to the provinces, such as the Nutritional Social Program (PROSONU) and Communitarian Social Policies (POSOCO). These two funds represented more than AR$200 million annually.

17 It has been very difficult to get information of federal bailouts to the provinces. According to a crucial person interviewed during fieldwork in the Ministry of Economy, these data are processed but have not been made public "due to explicit requirement by federal authorities" (the identity of the person interviewed is kept anonymous for obvious reasons).

18 Menem tried to terminate these funds after five years. However, he and the incoming government of De la Rúa could not modify it as the Federal Tax Commission (CFI) determined that the fund had a "permanent and definitive character" (*Clarín*, "A diez años de un acuerdo secreto," January 11, 2004).

19 Before the decentralization reform, the central government was in charge of 831,132 secondary students (62.5 percent) and 98,334 professors (53.1 percent); in 1997, it had only 9,470 students (1.2 percent) and 3,021 professors (2.7 percent) (*Ministerio de Educación, Dirección General Red Federal de Información*, quoted in Repetto, 2001c, 29–30; Filmus, 1998, 4). According to Bisang and Cetrángolo (1997, 32), the decentralized hospitals employed about 9,200 agents and represented a cost of AR$110.7 million per year, or more than 22 percent of the total health care spending of the central government in 1991. In addition, the 1993 Federal Education Law increased mandatory primary school from seven to nine years, significantly increasing the costs for the provinces.

20 If we consider total federal transfers, this share dropped from 53 percent in 1992 to 45 percent in 1995.

21 Differences in the data from the Ministry of Economy, ECLAC, and the IMF are largely due to changes in the way in which municipal data are collected and classified into the aggregated categories and in the mechanisms for imputing data across the three levels of government.

22 In some provinces, such as Córdoba, the governor Ramón Mestre (1995–1999) initiated a similar decentralization process but in this case between the provincial administration and municipalities.

23 He and his closest supporters made that explicit as early as 1992. See for instance, the remarks made by Senator Sánchez (PJ-La Rioja) on September 2, 1992 (*DS-CSN*, September 2, 1992, 2319).

24 The PJ got almost 38 percent of the votes and 44 percent of the seats (136 seats in total), the UCR 20 percent of the vote and almost 25 percent of the seats (75 seats), and the Frente Grande 12.5 percent of the votes and 10 percent of the seats (minor parties controlled the rest of the seats).

25 To that we can add corruption scandals, feeble economic results (timid growth, large budget deficits), and a severe "social debt" (rising unemployment, poverty, and inequality) that diminished support for the president in public opinion, and encouraged social protests and the formation of a more coherent opposition front. The president's average positive image decreased from 36.6 percent during 1994–1995 to 12.8 percent by October 1996 (Nueva Mayoría).

26 Inflation had been under control since 1991, and GDP grew at a timid 2.25 percent, although it contracted 4.5 percent in 1995.

27 A transitory clause in the 1994 constitution stated that a new law should be approved by 1996. This constitutional clause has been systematically violated, as no new revenue-sharing regime has been sanctioned since 1988 (until today, 2015). Reforming revenue sharing is not a matter of constitutional enforcement but rather a consequence of the distribution of political power and fiscal incentives.

28 The president's positive image dropped below 20 percent during late 1996 and late 1999 (Data from Nueva Mayoría).

29 In exchange, provinces got more transfers (an extra AR$800 million) from an increase in the income tax (*La Nación*, "Senado: el PJ cumplió con el Gobierno"; "Fracasó el ajuste en Diputados," September 12; "Consiguió el PJ aprobar el paquete impositivo," September 19, 1996).

30 Menem also proposed to include the special compensation fund for the province of Buenos Aires that had been created in 1992 into the revenue-sharing scheme. He wanted to weaken Duhalde and his presidential aspirations (in an indication of tensions inside the PJ), but also to garner support from interior districts (*La Nación*, "Menem pediría que se elimine el fondo del conurbano bonaerense," January 29, 1998).

31 Porto (2003, 54) argues that, in fact, the central government appropriated a former provincial tax (on cars), further weakening subnational tax authority.

32 Even by mid-June (four months before the election), a DataFolha poll revealed that Lula enjoyed the support of 41 percent of the electorate, while Cardoso had the support of only 19 percent.

33 In exchange for their support, the PFL nominated the candidate for the vice-presidency, Marcos Maciel, and was granted three ministries in the first Cardoso cabinet (Energy and Mines, Social Security, and Environment).

34 The main partners, besides the PFL, were the PMBD, PTB, PL, PPR/PPB, and the PP. Cardoso gained the support of several PMDB members of parliament and governors by taking advantage of divisions inside this party and favoring the *governista* (pro-incumbent) faction. This latter group was composed mainly

of old state bosses, who were very much dependent on the federal government for running their states and maintaining their political clientele. Cardoso granted them positions in the federal administration, such as the Ministry of Transportation and areas linked to regional development. A similar strategy was replicated for the PPB. The president kept the most important ministries (Fazenda, Relações Exteriores, Saúde, and Educação) for key *tucanos* (Chagas, 2002, 342–343).

35 Between January 1995 and April 1996, the PSDB, PFL (which got two ministries in the cabinet), PMDB (with three ministries), and PTB formed the coalition. The president controlled 290 deputies or 56 percent of the seats in the Chamber of Deputies (almost the number required for a constitutional amendment, which was reached with the support from other minor parties); and 56 senators or 69 percent of the Senate. Between April 1996 and 1998, the PPB joined the coalition. With its support, Cardoso controlled a stunning 77 percent of the seats in the Chamber of Deputies and more than 90 percent of the Senate, the largest shares since 1985. Between March and December 2002, the PFL and the PTB left the coalition, substantially diminishing the presidential share of seats to 45 percent in the Chamber of Deputies and 25 percent in the Senate (Figueiredo, 2006, 13). For more details on how the distribution of ministerial posts between the parties in the coalition affected the legislative vote in Brazil, see Amorim Neto, 2000.

36 The PSDB controlled São Paulo (Mário Covas), Minas Gerais (Eduardo Azeredo), and Rio de Janeiro (Marcello Alencar); the PMDB won in Rio Grande do Sul (Antônio Britto), and the PFL in Bahia (Paulo Souto, supported by ACM).

37 During this entire year, despite the challenges his administration faced, his positive image averaged about 26 percent. Although it declined to an average of 17 percent in 1996, it partially recovered to 23 percent by 1997 (DataFolha, 1988–2001).

38 The PSDB won six governorships and the PFL, the other main party in the electoral alliance, won in two others. Nine states were in the hands of the PMDB, which had been part of the governing camp since 1995. The other parties in the governing coalition got four governorships: the PPR/PPB won three and the PTB one. The PL and the PP did not get any state government. Only five governors were from parties that were not formal members of the governing coalition.

39 After the 1994 election, 11 governors out of 27 (41 percent) were elected with 50 percent of the vote or more; a percentage that was lower than that during the 1986 and 1990 elections (74 and 48 percent respectively). Eleven governors had to deal with a state legislature in which an opposition party (or parties) controlled a larger share of the seats than the party of the governor (there were eight such cases during the Collor and none during the Sarney administration).

40 A major change in the institutional dimension of gubernatorial power was the possibility of reelection for governors and mayors, approved in June 4, 1997.

41 Annual inflation rates fell from 2,489 percent in 1994 to a 12.5 percent average annual rate between 1995 and 2002. GDP grew at an average 4.1 percent between 1994 and 1997.

42 Several scholars stressed the role of states' fiscal crisis in increasing the costs of the status quo ante for governors (Interviews with Antônio Kandir and Fernando Abrucio, September 11, 2006; Eduardo Kugelmas and Fernando Limongi, September 12, 2006).

43 Transfers to the states and municipalities were expected to grow by 25 percent in 1995 in relation to the previous year, controlling for inflation.

44 ACM also declared that "The federal government does not intend to call a vote on the tax reform because it is now comfortable lying on the FEF mattress" (*FSP*, "Congresso reage a críticas e ACM culpa o governo," July 2, 1997).

45 According to data from the Chamber of Deputies' Budget Advisory Board, states and municipalities lost R$1.73 billion in 1996 due to the cuts imposed by the FEF. In addition, subnational units were compelled to devolve the tax revenue the central government did not retain during January and February 1996 (about R$60 million from the IR) (*FSP*, February 14, 1996, 1–7).

46 The FEF, renamed DRU, was extended until December 2003 and later on until 2011. This last extension of the FSE-FEF-DRU was voted together with the extension of the CPMF, but the latter measure was rejected in the Senate (*Jornal do Senado*, December 20, 2007, 3).

47 Governor Dante de Oliveira (PSDB-MG) sent telegrams to deputies asking them to vote against the extension of FEF (*FSP*, "Presente de Grego," May 2, 1997), and some legislators reacted favorably, announcing they would act in accordance (*FSP*, "Amigo da Onça" May 3, 1997).

48 For states exporting few products, this tax was not a crucial source of revenue, so they did not actively oppose the bill. For some others, receiving transfers, although in the form of federal bonds from the central government, was seen as better than having this revenue cut by the central government (their worst case, but possible, scenario) or even having to collect it by themselves in a context of fiscal urgency (another sub-optimal option in relation to the federal transfers; see González, 2012).

49 The IOF (*Imposto sobre Operações Financeiras*) is another tax on financial transactions not shared with the states. Its rates were increased to 0.38 percent after the CPMF extension was not approved in Congress.

50 The central government increased federal transfers and spending only for subnational governments unable to meet a minimum level of health care (through the *Piso de Assistência Básica*, or PAB). A similar solution was agreed and implemented for education.

51 A series of corruption scandals contributed to creating a climate favorable for more restrictions in spending at the subnational level (one of the most far-reaching was the so-called *CPI dos Precatórios*).

52 The reactions from mayors were more significant, and they organized large demonstrations in Brasília against the LRF. One of the possible reasons for their militancy was that most governors had already re-financed their debt obligations with the central government but most municipalities had not (*FSP*, "Concessão aos Municipios," July 6, 1999).

53 Discretionary transfers increased 37 percent between 2000 and 2001. The amount of discretionary transfers distributed from the central government in 2001 was the largest in the decade between 1997 and 2007 (Data from *Secretaría do Tesouro Nacional*).

54 Governors were mainly worried about the tax reform, which was also being discussed at that time, rather than with the Fiscal Responsibility Law. This strategy of conducting several reforms at the same time and exchanging support for one of them in exchange of concessions in others was also characteristic of the negotiations to extend the FSE/FEF/DRU analyzed earlier.

55 For some political analysts, For Chagas (2002, 356–357), the weakening of the president began earlier. During the reelection negotiations, Cardoso's power was considerable but he had to exchange a substantive amount of selective incentives for winning support for the constitutional amendment. After his reelection, similar to what happened during Menem's second term, pressures from the opposition grew stronger and bargaining in Congress more

demanding. Additionally, the 1999 economic crisis affected the popularity of the president, which fell to its lowest level in July 1999.
56 Cardoso probably introduced this bill as a bargaining chip to trade, withdrawing it in exchange for the extension of the CPMF. According to Arno Augustin, Secretary of Finance of Rio Grande do Sul, through this way "the [federal] government gets the CPMF and later blames the states for the rejection of the tax reform" (*FSP*, "Estados rejeitam projeto do governo para unificar ICMS," July 7, 2001).

References

Abrucio, Fernando Luis, *Os Barões da Federação: Os Governadores e a Redemocratização Brasileira* (São Paulo: Coleção Comentário, USP, 1998).

Acuña, Carlos, "Politics and Economics in the Argentina of the Nineties (Or, Why the Future No Longer is What It Used to Be)"; in: Smith, William C., Carlos H. Acuña, and Eduardo A. Gamarra (eds.), *Democracy, Markets, and Structural Reform in Latin America* (Miami: North-South Center and Boulder, CO: Lynne Rienner, 1994).

Acuña, Carlos, "Algunas Notas sobre los Juegos, las Gallinas y la Lógica Política de los Pactos Constitucionales (Reflexiones a partir del Pacto Constitucional en la Argentina)"; in: Acuña, Carlos H. (ed.), *La Nueva Matriz Política Argentina* (Buenos Aires: Ed. Nueva Visión, 1995).

Alfonsín, Raúl, *Democracia y Consenso: A Propósito de la Reforma Constitucional* (Buenos Aires: Corregidor, 1996).

Amorim Neto, Octavio, "Gabinetes Presidenciais, Ciclos Eleitorais e Disciplina Legislativa no Brasil," *Dados*, Vol. 43, No. 3, 2000, pp. 479–519.

Baer, Werner, *The Brazilian Economy: Growth and Development* (London: Lynne Rienner, 2008).

Bisang, Roberto, and Oscar Cetrángolo, "Descentralización de los Servicios de Salud en la Argentina," *Serie de Reformas de Política Pública* No. 47, CEPAL, 1997.

BNDES (Banco Nacional do Desenvolvimento), "Fiscal Accountability Law: A Primer" (BNDES, 2000).

Calvo, Ernesto, "The Responsive Legislature: Public Opinion and Law Making in a Highly Disciplined Legislature," *British Journal of Political Science*, Vol. 37, No. 2, 2007, pp. 263–280.

Carrizo, Carla, "Entre el Consenso Coactivo y el Pluralismo Político: La Hora del Pueblo y el Pacto de Olivos (1973–1993)," *Desarrollo Económico*, Vol. 37, No. 147, 1997, pp. 389–418.

Cetrángolo, Oscar, and Juan Pedro Jiménez, "El Conflicto en Torno a las Relaciones Financieras entre la Nación y las Provincias. Primera Parte: Antecedentes de la Ley 23.548," *Serie de Estudios* No. 9, Centro de Estudios para el Cambio Estructural, 1995.

Cetrángolo, Oscar, and Juan Pedro Jiménez, "El Conflicto en Torno a las Relaciones Financieras entre la Nación y las Provincias. Segunda Parte: Desde la Ley 23.548 hasta la Actualidad," *Serie de Estudios* No. 10, Centro de Estudios para el Cambio Estructural, 1996.

Cetrángolo, Oscar, and Juan Pedro Jiménez, "Las Relaciones entre Niveles de Gobierno en Argentina. Raíces Históricas, Instituciones y Conflictos Persistentes," *Serie Gestión Pública* No. 47, CEPAL, 2004.

CECE (Centro de Estudios para el Cambio Estructural), *Federalismo Fiscal en Argentina* (CECE: Buenos Aires, 1997).

CGE (Confederación General Económica), *El Libro Azul de las Provincias: las Economías Regionales en la Transformación Económica de la República Argentina* (Buenos Aires: Instituto de Investigaciones Económicas y Financieras, 1993).

Chagas, Helena, "Relações Executivo-Legislativo"; in: Lamonier, Bolívar and Rubens Figueiredo (eds.), *A Era FHC: Um Balanço* (São Paulo: Cultura Editores Associados, 2002).

Couto, Cláudio Gonçalves, and Rogério Bastos Arantes, "¿Constitución o Políticas Públicas? Una Evaluación de los Años FHC"; in: Palermo, Vicente (ed.), *De Collor a Lula: Política Brasileña en Años de Transformación* (Buenos Aires: Siglo Veintiuno de Argentina Editores, 2004).

Diario de Sesiones de la Cámara de Diputados de la Nación (DS-CDN), December 5–6, 1991.

Diario de Sesiones de la Cámara de Diputados de la Nación (DS-CDN), August 19–20, 1992.

Diario de Sesiones de la Cámara de Senadores de la Nación (DS-CSN), November 13, 1991.

Diario de Sesiones de la Cámara de Senadores de la Nación (DS-CSN), August 19–20, 1992.

Diario de Sesiones de la Cámara de Senadores de la Nación (DS-CSN), September 2, 1992.

Diario de Sessões da Câmara dos Deputados (DS-CD), December 4, 1991.

Diario de Sessões da Câmara dos Deputados (DS-CD), November 2, 1995.

Diario de Sessões da Câmara dos Deputados (DS-CD), August 22, 1996.

Diario de Sessões da Câmara dos Deputados (DS-CD), August 28, 1996.

Diario de Sessões da Câmara dos Deputados (DS-CD), July 11, 1997.

Diario de Sessões da Câmara dos Deputados (DS-CD), December 8, 1999.

Diario de Sessões da Câmara dos Deputados (DS-CD), January 13, 2000.

Diario de Sessões da Câmara dos Deputados (DS-CD), January 26, 2000.

Dillinger, William, and Steven Webb, "Fiscal Management in Federal Democracies: Argentina and Brazil," Policy Research Working Paper 2121 (Washington, DC: World Bank, 1999).

Diniz, Eli, *Crise, Reforma do Estado e Goverabilidade, Brasil, 1985–95* (Rio de Janeiro: Editora Fundação Getúlio Vargas, 1997).

Eaton, Kent, "Decentralisation, Democratisation and Liberalisation: The History of Revenue Sharing in Argentina, 1934–1999," *Journal of Latin American Studies*, Vol. 33, No. 1, 2001a, pp. 1–28.

Eaton, Kent, "Political Obstacles to Decentralization: Evidence from Argentina and the Philippines," *Development and Change*, Vol. 32, No. 1, 2001b, pp. 101–127.

Eaton, Kent, "The Logic of Congressional Delegation: Explaining Argentine Economic Reform," *Latin American Research Review*, Vol. 36, No. 2, 2001c, pp. 97–117.

Eaton, Kent, *Politicians and Economic Reform in New Democracies: Argentina and the Philippines in the 1990s* (University Park, PA: Penn State University Press, 2002).

Eaton, Kent, "La Lógica de la Delegación de Poderes Legislativos: la Reforma de la Promoción Regional Argentina," *Desarrollo Económico*, Vol. 42, No. 168, 2003, pp. 499–518.

Eaton, Kent, *Politics Beyond the Capital: The Design of Subnational Institutions in South America* (Stanford: Stanford University Press, 2004).

ECLAC-CEPAL (Comisión Económica para América Latina y el Caribe), *Economic Survey of Latin America and the Caribbean, 1996–1997* (Santiago de Chile: CEPAL, 1997).

ECLAC-CEPAL (Comisión Económica para América Latina y el Caribe), *Economic Survey of Latin America and the Caribbean, 2004–2005* (Santiago de Chile: CEPAL, 2005).

Falleti, Tulia, "Federalismo y Descentralización Educativa en Argentina. Consecuencias (no queridas) de la Descentralización del Gasto en un País Federal"; in: Calvo, Ernesto and J. Abal Medina (eds.), *El Federalismo Electoral Argentino: Sobrerrepresentación, Reforma Política y Gobierno Dividido en Argentina* (Buenos Aires: EUDEBA, 2001).

Falleti, Tulia, "Governing Governors: Coalitions and Sequences of Decentralization in Argentina, Colombia, and Mexico," Ph.D. Dissertation, Northwestern University, 2003.

Ferreira Rubio, Delia, and Matteo Goretti, "Cuando el Presidente Gobierna Solo. Menem y los Decretos de Necesidad y Urgencia hasta la Reforma Constitucional (julio 1989—agosto 1994)," *Desarrollo Económico*, Vol. 36, No. 141, 1996, pp. 443–474.

Figueiredo, Argelina Cheibub, "Formação, Funcionamento e Desempenho das Coalizões de Governo no Brasil," paper prepared for delivery at the 5th Encontro da ABCP, July 26–29, FAFICH/UFMG, Belo Horizonte—MG, 2006.

Figueiredo, Argelina Cheibub, and Fernando Limongi, "Mudança Constitucional, Desempenho do Legislativo e Consolidação Institucional," *Revista Brasileira de Ciencias Sociais*, Vol. 10, No. 29, 1995, pp. 175–200.

Figueiredo, Argelina Cheibub, and Fernando Limongi, "O Congresso e as Medidas Provisórias: Abdicação ou Delegação?," *Novos Estudos*, CEBRAP 47, São Paulo, 1997.

Figueiredo, Argelina Cheibub, and Fernando Limongi, "Presidential Powers, Legislative Organization, and Party Behavior in Brazil," *Comparative Politics*, Vol. 32, No. 2, 2000, pp. 151–170.

Filmus, Daniel, "La Descentralización Educativa en Argentina: Elementos para el Análisis de un Proceso Abierto," *Reforma y Democracia*, No. 10, 1998.

Fleischer, David, "The Cardoso Government's Reform Agenda: A View from the National Congress, 1995–1998," *Journal of Interamerican Studies and World Affairs*, Vol. 40, No. 4, Special Issue: Brazil: The Challenge of Constitutional Reform, 1998, pp. 119–136.

Flynn, Peter, "Collor Corruption and Crisis: Time for Reflection," *Journal of Latin American Studies*, Vol. 25, No. 2, 1993, pp. 351–372.

Flynn, Peter, "The Politics of the 'Plano Real'," *Third World Quarterly*, Vol. 17, No. 3, 1996, pp. 401–426.

Gerchunoff, Pablo, and Lucas Llach, *El Ciclo de la Ilusión y el Desencanto. Un Siglo de Políticas Económicas Argentinas* (Buenos Aires: Ariel, 1998).

Giambiagi, Fábio, and Ana Claudia Duarte Além, *Finanças Públicas: Teoria e Prática no Brasil* (Rio de Janeiro: Campus, 1999).

González, Lucas, "The Distributive Effects of Centralization and Decentralization across Sub-National Units," *Latin American Research Review*, Vol. 47, No. 3, 2012, pp. 109–133.

Hagopian, Frances, Carlos Gervasoni, and Juan Andres Moraes, "From Patronage to Program: The Emergence of Party-Oriented Legislators in Brazil," *Comparative Political Studies*, Vol. 42, No. 3, 2009, pp. 360–391.

IADB (Inter-American Development Bank), *Latin America after a Decade of Reforms* (Washington, DC: IADB, 1997a).

IADB (Inter-American Development Bank) *Fiscal Stability with Democracy and Decentralization* (Washington, DC: IADB, 1997b).

Jones, Mark, "Explaining the High Level of Party Discipline in the Argentine Congress"; in: Morgenstern, Scott and Benito Nacif (eds.), *Legislative Politics in Latin America* (New York: Cambridge University Press, 2002).

Jones, Mark, Pablo Sanguinetti, and Mariano Tommasi, "Politics, Institutions, and Fiscal Performance in a Federal System: An Analysis of the Argentine Provinces," *Journal of Development Economics*, Vol. 61, No. 2, 2000, pp. 305–333.

Jones, Mark, Sebastián Saiegh, Pablo Spiller, and Mariano Tommasi, "Amateur Legislators—Professional Politicians: The Consequences of Party-Centered Electoral Rules in a Federal System," *American Journal of Political Science*, Vol. 46, No. 3, 2002, pp. 656–660.

Lardone, Martín, "Bancos Multilaterales de Desarrollo y Reforma del Estado: Un Análisis Comparado de Casos Provinciales en Argentina," paper presented at the Primer Encuentro de la Red de "Federalismo y Política Subnacional: Argentina en Perspectiva Comparada," Buenos Aires, Universidad Torcuato Di Tella, June 27–28, 2008.

Levitsky, Steven, *Transforming Labor-based Parties in Latin America* (Cambridge: Cambridge: Cambridge University Press, 2003).

Llanos, Mariana, "Understanding Presidential Power in Argentina: A Study of the Policy of Privatisation in the 1990s," *Journal of Latin American Studies*, Vol. 33, No. 1, 2001, pp. 67–99.

Lopreato, Francisco Luiz, *O Colapso das Finanças Estaduais e a Crise da Federação* (São Paulo: Editora UNESP-IE Unicamp, 2002).

Loureiro, Maria Rita, and Fernando Luis Abrucio, "Política y Reformas Fiscales en el Brasil Reciente"; in: Palermo, Vicente (ed.), *De Collor a Lula: Política Brasileña en Años de Transformación* (Buenos Aires: Siglo Veintiuno de Argentina Editores, 2003), pp. 573–610.

Melo, Marcus André, *As Reformas Constitucionais no Brasil: Instituições Políticas e Processo Decisório* (Rio de Janeiro: Editora Revan, 2002).

Mora, Mônica, and Ricardo Varsano, "Fiscal Decentralization and Subnational Fiscal Autonomy in Brazil: Some Facts of the Nineties," Texto para Discusão 854, Rio de Janeiro, 2001.

Mustapic, Ana María, "Oficialistas y Diputados: las Relaciones Ejecutivo-Legislativo en la Argentina," *Desarrollo Económico*, Vol. 39, No. 156, 2000, pp. 571–595.

Negretto, Gabriel, "¿Gobierna solo el Presidente? Poderes de Decreto y Diseño Institucional en Brasil y Argentina," *Desarrollo Económico*, Vol. 42, No. 167, 2002, pp. 377–404.

Novaro, Marcos, *Pilotos de Tormenta. Crisis de Representación y Personalización de la Política en Argentina (1989–1993)* (Buenos Aires: Letra Buena, 1994).

Nuñez Miñana, Horacio, and Alberto Porto, *Distribución de la Coparticipación Federal de Impuestos: Análisis y Alternativas* (Buenos Aires: Consejo Federal de Inversiones, 1983).

O'Donnell, Guillermo, "Delegative Democracy," *Journal of Democracy*, Vol. 5, No. 1, 1994, pp. 55–69.

Palanza, Valeria, "Espacios de Consenso Alternativos: Los Consejos Federales de la Política Social en Argentina," Working Paper 71, CEDI, 2002.

Panizza, Francisco, "Lula's Change: Redemption Songs or Dancing to the Music of Times?" unpublished paper, Department of Government, The London School of Economics, 2003.

Pereira, Carlos, and Bernardo Mueller, "The Cost of Governing: Strategic Behavior of the President and Legislators in Brazil's Budgetary Process," *Comparative Political Studies*, Vol. 37, No. 7, 2004, pp. 781–815.

Pírez, Pedro, *Coparticipación Federal y Descentralización del Estado* (Buenos Aires: Centro Editor de América Latina, 1986).

Porto, Alberto, "Etapas de la Coparticipación Federal de Impuestos," Documento de Federalismo Fiscal No. 2 (La Plata: Universidad Nacional de La Plata, 2003).

Power, Timothy, "Brazilian Politicians and Neoliberalism: Mapping Support for the Cardoso Reforms, 1995–1997," *Journal of Interamerican Studies and World Affairs*, Vol. 40, No. 4, Special Issue: Brazil: The Challenge of Constitutional Reform, 1998, pp. 51–72.

Power, Timothy, "Blairism Brazilian Style? Cardoso and the 'Third Way' in Brazil," *Political Science Quarterly*, Vol. 116, No. 4, 2002, pp. 611–636.

Remmer, Karen L., and Erik Wibbels, "The Subnational Politics of Economic Adjustment: Provincial Politics and Fiscal Performance in Argentina," *Comparative Political Studies*, Vol. 33, No. 4, 2000, pp. 419–451.

Repetto, Fabián, "Transferencia de Recursos para Programas Alimentarios en las Provincias: Un Analisis de lo Sucedido en los Años '90," Working Paper 54, CEDI, 2001a.

Repetto, Fabián, "Descentralización de la Salud Pública en los Noventa: Una Reforma a Mitad de Camino," Working Paper 55, CEDI, 2001b.

Repetto, Fabián, "Transferencia Educativa hacia las Provincias en los Años '90: Un Estudio Comparado," Working Paper 57, CEDI, 2001c.

Rezende, Fernando, "O Processo da Reforma Tributária," Texto para Discução 396, IPEA, Brasília, 1996.

Ribeiro, Leandro Molhano, "Partidos e Políticas Sociais nos Municípios Brasileiros (1996–2003)," unpublished Ph.D. Dissertation, Instituto Universitário de Pesquisas do Rio de Janeiro, Rio de Janeiro, 2005.

Rigolon, Francisco, and Fabio Giambiagi, "A Renegociação das Dívidas e o Regime Fiscal dos Estados," Textos para Discussão 69, Banco Nacional de Desenvolvimento Econômico e Social, 1999.

Rodden, Jonathan, *Hamilton's Paradox: The Promise and Peril of Fiscal Federalism* (Cambridge: Cambridge University Press, 2006).

Rodden, Jonathan, and Erik Wibbels, "Beyond the Fiction of Federalism: Macroeconomic Management in Multitiered Systems," *World Politics*, Vol. 54, No. 4, July 2002, pp. 494–531.

Samuels, David, "Fiscal Straitjacket: The Politics of Macroeconomic Reform in Brazil, 1995–2002," *Journal of Latin American Studies*, Vol. 35, No. 3, 2003, pp. 545–569.

Santos, Fabiano, "Democracia e Poder Legislativo no Brasil e na Argentina"; in: Lladós, José María and Samuel Pinheiro Guimaraes (eds.), *Perspectivas Brasil y Argentina* (Brasília: IPRI-CARI, 1999a).

Santos, Fabiano, "Instituicões Eleitorais e Desempenho do Presidencialismo no Brasil," *Dados*, Vol. 42, No. 1, 1999b.

Souza, Celina, *Constitutional Engineering in Brazil: The Politics of Federalism and Decentralisation* (London: Macmillan, 1997).

Tommasi, Mariano, "Federalism in Argentina and the Reforms of the 1990s," Working Paper 69, CEDI, 2002.

Tommasi, Mariano, Sebastián Saiegh, and Pablo Sanguinetti, "Fiscal Federalism in Argentina: Policies, Politics, and Institutional Reform," *Economia*, Spring 2001, pp. 157–211.

Wibbels, Erik, "Decentralization, Democracy, and Market-Reform. On the Difficulties of Killing of Two Birds with One Stone"; in: Montero, Alfred and David Samuels (eds.), *Decentralization and Democracy in Latin America* (Notre Dame, IN: University of Notre Dame Press, 2004).

World Bank, *Beyond the Washington Consensus: Institutions Matter* (Washington, DC: World Bank, 1998).

6 Conclusions

Some projections of the federal distributive game

The focus of this work has been in the post-transition presidencies until the late 1990s. These were periods of profound reforms, both decentralizing and centralizing, in which we can see variation in the distribution of funds and functions between levels of government. Despite limitations of time and space, I outline some brief comments on the subsequent presidencies in this section.

De la Rúa (1999–2001) and beyond

Fernando De la Rúa was a relatively weak president who faced strong but divided governors under a context of economic recession and severe fiscal pressures. He did not control Congress, was a weak leader in his party and coalition, and faced deep divisions inside his cabinet. Although he got elected with 48.5 percent of the vote (against Duhalde's 38.09), his coalition, the *Alianza*, had a plurality in the Chamber (49.4 percent) so it could not reach quorum by itself and was in a clear minority position in the Senate (35 percent of the seats; Peronism had 54.2 percent).

Governors, contrary to the president, were powerful actors in their provinces. Most of them had an important degree of control over their districts in partisan terms (the average gubernatorial partisan powers index was 1.76; a high value). However, the crucial difference between the Radical presidents (Alfonsín and De la Rúa) and Menem was that during the UCR presidencies, most governors opposed the president, while during Menem's time in office, most of them supported the federal executive. Additionally, the PJ president was powerful enough to prevent coordination against him. The Alianza won only in six out of 24 governorships. Peronism won in 14, including the three largest.

The critical difference between Alfonsín and De la Rúa was how much governors were able to coordinate against the president. Despite divisions, PJ governors coordinated against Alfonsín after 1987. During De la Rúa's term, Peronism was profoundly divided, not only after the serious conflict between Menem and Duhalde over the presidency of the party, but also over the presidential nomination after De la Rúa's term in office.

In economic terms, the Alianza government had to cope with difficult challenges: international volatility, decreasing investment, a long-lasting recession, large fiscal deficits, increasing debt and debt payments, and, consequently, strong tensions between the federal government and the provinces over the distribution of diminishing revenue-sharing funds. Governors also had large fiscal incentives to improve their federal balance. When De la Rúa got to power, several provinces were in deep fiscal crisis and at the brink of social turmoil. Corrientes, Tucumán, and Río Negro could not pay for either their public employees' salaries nor government's suppliers of goods or services (especially serious were the cases of hospitals and penitentiary services), leading to some violent demonstrations from public servants and teachers, during which some people died (*La Nación*, "Salarios impagos en varios distritos," November 11, 1999). As revenue-sharing transfers were used as guarantee for provincial debt obligations with public and private banks, some provinces suffered sharp reductions in these funds. The most dramatic case was Río Negro, a province that should have received AR$152 million in revenue-sharing funds between January and July 1999, but instead it received only AR$3 million; the rest went to lenders (*La Nación*, "En nueve años se sextuplicó el gasto público," December 18, 1999). Total provincial deficits doubled, increasing from AR$6.1 billion in 2000 to AR$12.3 billion in 2001.

Both the president and the governors had huge incentives to alter the federal balance's status quo ante, but neither of them concentrated enough political resources to do so. Federal legislators had increasingly weaker incentives to support the president as he gradually lost political support and popularity, did not have profound control of careers inside his party (Alfonsín was stronger than he was in the UCR), and had fewer resources to reward loyal legislators for their support. But at the same time, members of Congress feared that boycotting the central government and supporting governors in their attempts to extract more federal funds could lead to a fiscal debacle and affect their own career prospects.

De la Rúa made serious efforts to cut transfers from the central government to the provinces and control provincial spending, but they were strongly resisted by governors (especially those from the PJ, although Alianza's governors gradually increased their opposition to the president as their fiscal situation worsened). Despite facing a relatively weak president and being powerful in their provinces, factionalism inside Peronism was high, and it mounted as no leader emerged out of the struggles. Some strong governors were consolidating their power in their provinces and building alliances among other Peronist leaders to reach the PJ presidential nomination.

The political scenario was prone to gridlock in relation to the federal balance. Despite this, negotiations between the president and the governors led to the signature of a fiscal pact in 1999, out of which the central government increased taxes but the collected revenues would not be shared with the provinces. The federal government agreed, in exchange, to guarantee monthly transfers to the provinces in 2000 (AR$1.35 billion per month) and 2001 (AR$1.365 billion per month), regardless of tax collection levels, and to renegotiate provincial debts. Shortly after, governors demanded an increase in the revenue-sharing floor negotiated earlier because the fiscal situation in the provinces turned increasingly critical. The president, gradually weakened and without capacity to either alter the federal balance or resist gubernatorial pressures, feared PJ governors would coordinate against him (as during Alfonsín's times) and agreed to increase automatic transfers to the provinces, refinance their debts, and decentralize social programs to the provinces. In exchange, governors committed to freezing public spending until 2005.

To make things even more complicated for the president, De la Rúa was defeated in the midterm elections on October 14, 2001. The Alianza lost almost 20 percent of the votes it got in the 1999 legislative elections (from 40.5 percent in 1999 to 23.1 percent in 2001), giving up its plurality in the Chamber of Deputies and consolidating the strength of Peronism in the Senate. Following the elections, as we could expect, tensions between the president and the governors augmented. The situation seemed very similar to the one Alfonsín faced after the 1987 electoral defeat. However, it was different in some crucial aspects: Peronism was divided and struggles inside the party prevented them from coordinating and taking action against the federal government.

De la Rúa, in the context of a quickly deteriorating economy, demanded a reduction in transfers to the provinces of about AR$1.4 billion a month. He did not manage to convince the provincial leaders to accept this reduction, failing to reach a formal agreement with the governors during October 2001. Not only did governors oppose this reduction, but they also demanded the AR$250 million the central government owed in past transfers to the provinces. This refusal from the governors meant deadlock between the executive, provincial leaders, and Congress, which contributed to undermining the credibility of the government and raised speculations about its ability to control the fiscal deficit and avoid a default of its debt. Tensions finally erupted after a delay in the submission of revenue-sharing funds (for around AR$850 million) that the central government was compelled to allocate to the provinces. After negotiations between the president and governors failed, subnational executives, even those in the Alianza, took a more hostile stance toward the president (*La Nación*, "Mandatarios aliancistas dispuestos a dar pelea," November 2, 2001).

Governors began to issue local bonds as a way to pay for their debts and salaries (a form of issuing money). These decisions severely impacted the federal government, in fiscal and political terms. The crisis broke with a run on private sector deposits, which fell by more than AR$3.6 billion

(6 percent of the deposit base) during November 28–30 (IMF, 2003, 58–63). Demonstrators in Buenos Aires and major cities took to the streets demanding their savings, while poorer neighborhoods in the main urban areas across the country suffered looting and unrest a few days later. Violence caused the death of more than 30 people during revolts. After declaring the state of siege and the resignation of the whole cabinet on December 19, De la Rúa called for a government of national unity: a desperate call to put an end to deadlock and regain some political leverage to deal with the crisis. Peronism and even the UCR refused the offer. Absolutely isolated, he resigned on December 20. A Brazilian newspaper asked Cavallo what his biggest mistake was in commanding the economy during those years. He replied "I should have been more emphatic in denouncing the governors as responsible for the Argentine debacle" (*FSP*, "Cavallo elogia Brasil, mas vê 'debilidade'," August 31, 2005).

Beyond De la Rúa: the interim presidencies (2001–2003)

After De la Rúa resigned in December 2001, four presidents followed him in ten days. All of them were Peronists designated by a legislative assembly, but with the consensus of the governors. The interim president Adolfo Rodríguez Saá, former governor of San Luis, was nominated by a group of powerful governors, including Carlos Ruckauf, José Manuel de la Sota, and Néstor Kirchner (*La Nación*, "El día en que el peronismo regresó al poder," December 22, 2001). Rodríguez Saá promised to call for elections after two months of being in office, but in the end he sought to consolidate power for himself and terminate what was left of De la Rúa's term. That granted him strong opposition inside the Peronist party, especially from those governors expecting to run as candidates during the upcoming presidential elections. His support base eroded dramatically. After requesting the Peronist governors to buttress him, only six out of 14 answered his call from the city of Chapadmalal. Strong governors, especially those from Córdoba and Santa Fe, directly opposed him and rejected his call for party unity. In his resignation letter, Rodríguez Saá underscored the lack of support from Peronist governors.[1] After six days as the head of the federal executive, his resignation led to a crisis of succession that reflected the increasing fragmentation inside Peronism and the immense power governors can have when that of the president vanishes. After four presidents, although Peronist governors were divided over the designation, they finally agreed that Eduardo Duhalde, former governor of Buenos Aires, should be the president. Duhalde was designated president by the legislative assembly but negotiations were carried out by a federation of governors.[2]

The economic situation during the period was dramatic. Duhalde announced a devaluation of 70 percent of the peso after a decade of parity with the dollar. Real GDP fell by about 11 percent in 2002 while the unemployment rate rose above 20 percent and the poverty rate escalated to over 50 percent of the population. The public debt ratio more than doubled from 63 percent of GDP at the end of 2001 to about 135 percent of GDP at the end of 2002 (IMF, 2003, 44–45, 61–63). In this critical context, the president negotiated a reduction in the fiscal pressures on the federal budget with the governors. He proposed to retain 62 percent and allocate 38 percent to the provinces (that ratio was 56 to 44 percent). Governors drastically rejected the reform (*La Nación,* "No hubo acuerdo con los gobernadores," February 20, 2002). The federal government was able to eliminate guarantees on minimum revenue-sharing levels and to reduce them by about 20 percent. But governors' pressures on the central government resulted in significant concessions for subnational leaders, including 30 percent of the total amount collected by the tax on credits and debits of checking bank accounts (which was incorporated to the total revenue-sharing fund) and the rollover of provincial debts in favorable terms for the provinces (*La Nación,* "Las provincias y La Nación sellaron el pacto por la coparticipación," February 27, 2002).

There was not a clear winner in the federal distributive game during this period of profound political, social, financial, and fiscal turmoil. Neither the president nor the governors could impose profound changes to the federal balance. After a series of protests that produced the death of two demonstrators and having arranged who was going to be the man he and his Peronist machine in Buenos Aires province supported, Duhalde called for elections in April 2003.

Argentina began the twenty-first century with a profoundly weak president, very strong but uncoordinated governors, and the deepest economic crisis since the 1930s. The economic and fiscal crisis was partially reversed in 2003, and the president was able to concentrate power in relation to the governors, who remained deeply divided and fiscally dependent on the central government. That meant a new cycle of a relatively powerful president under a more benign fiscal context and no significant changes in the federal balance. Under these conditions, President Néstor Kirchner used the fiscal surplus to build up political support and consolidate power for himself, increasing federal spending in the provinces. The setting of the federal game changed again in 2009, under Cristina Fernández de Kirchner, a year in which the president lost enormous power (after a bitter conflict with the farmers), the fiscal context deteriorated dramatically (nationally and internationally) and, as we could expect, gubernatorial pressures on the federal government gained renewed strength. At the end of the Kirchner's decade, the president has concentrated power to limit demands from the governors and maintain the status quo, while governors began to exert renewed pressures on the federal government requesting the sharing of revenues from export taxes and the tax on checks and financial transactions. Due to the imbalances in the distribution of funds and functions between levels of government and the grievances they generated (particularly for governors), Argentina seems to be preparing for a new cycle of power struggles and institutional reforms to alter, once again, the balance of the federal distributive game.

The (first) Lula presidency (2003–2007)

Luiz Inácio Lula da Silva was a relatively powerful president who got increasingly more power and faced gradually weaker and divided governors under a growing economy and moderate fiscal pressures. He won the 2002 presidential election with the support of 46.4 percent of the votes (61.3 percent in the run-off). His party, the PT, got 17.74 percent of the total seats in the Lower Chamber and 18.5 percent in the Upper Chamber but Lula was able to construct working coalitions in Congress. The core parties in his coalition were the PT, PL, PCdoB, PSB, PTB, PV, PMDB, and the PSL (other parties joined and left the coalition at different times). His support in the Chamber oscillated between 43 percent of the seats at the very beginning and about 60 percent later during his term. In territorial terms, Lula could count on the support from nine governors elected from parties in his governing coalition. When the PMDB joined the coalition, after 2004, he could count on five more governors. The two main opposition parties (PSDB and PFL) controlled eleven governorships.

Some governors were still powerful in partisan terms in their states and all of them had considerable institutional resources. However, the average gubernatorial partisan power index was 1.16, lower than that during Cardoso's first period in office (1.23), Collor's (1.6), and Sarney's (2.2). The trend in which governors saw their power diminished began during Collor, deepened during Cardoso, and continued during Lula.

At the beginning of his term in office, Lula had limited political power and faced some fiscal urgency to consolidate the fiscal balance of the federal government (and consolidate domestic and international impressions on the health of the economy) as well as pressures from governors to increase transfers to the states. Gradually, the president increased his power at the same time that fiscal strain, and thus, the incentives to reform the federal balance, eased. Governors did not have the political power and faced moderate incentives to alter the status quo ante. The results were similar to those in Argentina between 2001 and 2003: minor changes in the federal balance, but for very different reasons.

Out of the theoretical expectations, a relatively powerful president in the context of relative fiscal stability, low fiscal pressures, and reasonably soft budget constraints is not going to be compelled to change the balance of the federal equation either by centralizing resources or decentralizing functions. These expected costs from these reforms would be larger than the expected benefits. Under those conditions, the president would try to keep the status quo ante and negotiate the distribution of funds obtained from the budget surplus (in the form of pork, social plans, infrastructure projects, or discretionary transfers) with the governors in exchange for their political support. Weak governors facing a powerful president in a context of fiscal surplus can either cooperate and offer support to the president, and in exchange get budget transfers and discretionary funds for their states, or they can conflict with the president and get limited or simply no extra funds. Since there were neither large fiscal incentives nor significant concentrations of political power at any level of government, we would expect that the status quo ante regulating the distribution of federal funds and functions would not suffer substantial changes during the period. Lula did not need to put governors under control in fiscal terms either (the LRF did that) or limit their political power to prevent coordination and predation of federal resources (Cardoso did that before him). Both options were still very much available in Argentina.

The key reforms, those that occupied most of the presidential agenda and legislative effort at the beginning of Lula's term in office, were the pension and the tax reform. One of the most important objectives behind them was the president's intention to consolidate the federal balance and the budget surplus. Without them, economic authorities feared they would not reach the fiscal goals agreed to with the IFIs, a situation that could undermine investors' confidence in the Brazilian economy. Of the two, the tax reform was oriented to change the federal balance to a more comfortable situation for the federal government.

The original bill, sent to Congress in April 2003, proposed to extend the DRU and the CPMF, to unify the ICMS (this was also a 2001 proposal Cardoso made), and eventually to replace it with a federal VAT. According to federal authorities, these reforms would help strengthen the federal budget surplus and terminate the "fiscal wars" among states. Negotiations were intense as several issues divided the central government and the governors. Due to the governors' resistance, tensions between them and the central government, and the increasing defections from the governing coalition, the president decided to concentrate efforts in gathering political support for the core of the reform (the "*miolo da picanha*," as Lula called it), which would help maintain the federal budget stabilized during 2003. The focus of negotiations became the extension of the CPMF and the DRU until the end of 2007. To ensure the vote in favor of this "minimum" version of the tax reform, the president made significant concessions to states (and municipalities), such as the decentralization of 25 percent of the revenue collected by the CIDE, a R$8.5 billion per year compensation that states and municipalities demanded due to the end of the ICMS on exports, and the creation of the Regional Development Fund (FDR) (*FSP*, "PSDB decide apoiar a emenda da Previdência," November 12, 2003).[3] As a result, the states were expected to get a total of at least R$4.5 billion in new transfers: R$2.5 billion from CIDE and R$2 billion from the FDR (*FSP*, "Concessões do governo aos Estados dividiram bloco dos governadores," September 5, 2003). The Chamber of Deputies eventually approved the tax reform, in the minimal version endorsed by the president, 346 votes to 92 on September 24, one month later than the pension reform and after nearly five months of negotiations and several concessions. The Lower Chamber approved changes to the ICMS but these reforms were later rejected in the Senate. Changes to the ICMS were also opposed by all governors (*FSP*, "Estados 'pobres' tentam desforra no Senado," September 24, 2003).

To make things worse for the president, a political crisis erupted due to corruption scandals involving the PT and some members of the government. A tax increase ended up deadlocked and other bills followed the same path in Congress (such as the broader tax reform, the labor and trade reforms, and other bills deepening the fiscal adjustment). The tax reform ended up deadlocked in the Chamber of Deputies at the end of 2003, waiting for an agreement with the governors (*FSP*, "Agenda econômica fracassa no Congresso," November 19, 2005). Despite eight long months of negotiations, the balance of the federal distributive game was not dramatically changed with the tax reform. Lula could only extend the DRU and the CPMF, and could neither reform the ICMS nor create a federal VAT. After substantial efforts, Lula could barely keep the status quo ante during the first years of his administration. It was not a minor achievement since the federal government continued to have a budget surplus.

In the end, there were no clear winners of the federal distributive game. As expected, the president concentrated his efforts in maintaining the status quo ante, and governors focused on exchanging support for some concessions and specific gains. This was their minimax strategy. The main institutional framework regulating the distribution of funds, tax powers, and functions remained basically unchanged during this period. During Lula's administration, the setting of the federal distributive game in Brazil is characterized by a relatively powerful president, weakened governors, and a more benign fiscal context. Under these conditions, and following our theoretical framework, we should expect no significant changes in the federal balance but rather a president who will use the fiscal surplus to build up political support and consolidate power. We would expect governors to keep their strategy of supporting presidential reforms in exchange for fiscal transfers to their states. Contrary to Argentina, which seems to be preparing for a new cycle of power struggles, Brazil has entered a sequence of more moderate federal tensions between president and governors and more stable federal institutions. How long will this setting last? It depends on the distribution of power in the federation and the fiscal incentives the actors face. These factors seems to be slowly changing at the beginning of Dilma Roussef's second mandate.

The federal distributive game and its implications for the performance of federal democracies

I have argued in this work that changes in fiscal relations between the central and subnational governments are expected to occur when there are important asymmetries in the distribution of political power among levels of government, when presidents and governors face hard budget constraints, and when they find themselves pressed by fiscal crises that encourage them to produce changes in the rules regulating the distribution of funds and functions. I found some statistical evidence supporting this argument for a group of countries in Latin America, both federal and unitary, and I analyzed two cases in depth. In line with the main argument, governors imposed decentralizing reforms when they were able to coordinate and concentrate political power against a weak president in an adverse fiscal context and under hard budget constraints. This is what happened in 1988 during the Alfonsín administration, when governors improved the provincial net balance between the functions that governors had to deliver and the funds they received and collected, increasing their net revenues and imposing considerable costs on the president. They substantially augmented legally mandated fiscal transfers from the central government to the provinces (from 48 percent to 57 percent of the total shared tax revenue), created and incorporated new taxes into the revenue-sharing scheme, and restricted the central government's capacity to use discretionary transfers and federal infrastructure programs, incorporating these sources of revenue into the common pool of funds to be distributed among provinces. The main result was that the revenue share of the subnational governments almost doubled (from 21 percent to 41 percent) between 1987 and 1988.

Also in 1988, President Sarney in Brazil was unable to counteract pressures from subnational governments and was forced to increase funds decentralized to the states and expand their tax base and authority (abolishing five former federal taxes). At the same time, he could not make governors responsible for the delivery of social services (mostly delivered by the federal administration). With all these changes, the revenue share of subnational governments increased around 130 percent in three years (from 18.1 percent of the total revenue in 1987 to 41.6 percent in 1989).

In both cases, the fiscal costs for the central government were profound, and many economists pointed out that this large increase in transfers to the states and provinces was one of the critical sources of hyperinflation during the late 1980s and early 1990s. In Argentina, economic and fiscal chaos also translated into political turmoil and the resignation of the federal executive. Drastic changes in federal relations and large costs for the federal government definitely had a political impact that contributed, together with other factors, to the aforementioned outcomes.

On the other hand, when presidents were able to concentrate political power and divide the governors under large fiscal pressures and hard budget constraints, they imposed centralizing reforms on states and provinces. This happened in Argentina during the Menem administration between 1992 and 1994, when the president centralized more than 15 percent of the total transfers to the provinces, eliminated provincial taxes, and decentralized education and health care services to subnational governments without the funding needed to deliver those services. These changes substantially altered the federal balance in favor of the central government. Provinces lost 49 percent of their revenue as a consequence of the centralizing reforms implemented during the Menem administration, while their share of expenditures increased by 23 percent (Cetrángolo and Jiménez, 2004). More functions and fewer funds produced not only such fiscal problems as more spending (a 70 percent increase between 1992 and 1995), larger deficits (a 200 percent rise), and increased debt (which grew more than 300 percent during the period), but also social turmoil, violent demonstrations, protests, and popular uprisings.

The flip side of the excruciating fiscal costs for the president imposed by gubernatorial pressures, macroeconomic chaos, and political turmoil was social mobilization and violence in the provinces caused by the inability of provincial governments to deliver basic social services. Although we lack clear indicators related to the social impact of the decentralization of health care and education services to provinces and municipalities, not a single provincial employee or expert interviewed claimed that these services' delivery improved after their "provincialization." Improving the provision of these services was clearly not the goal of federal authorities, so it is hardly surprising that this was not the outcome (see Table 6.1).

In a similar way, although with different results, the Cardoso administration passed a series of centralizing reforms that reduced the revenue decentralized to the states, eliminated state taxes (replacing them with federal ones whose tax collection was not shared with subnational governments), compelled states to co-finance education and health care, and imposed tight controls on state spending and their capacity to contract debt. As a result, between 1995 and 1998, the states augmented their total spending by more than 170 percent, their total debt by more than 180 percent, and their primary fiscal deficit by over 470 percent. On the other hand, the total tax revenue of the central government increased by more than 80 percent between 1994 and 1995 and almost 360 percent between 1994 and 2000, very different from Argentina where it rose by about 60 percent between 1991 and 2000 (or 48 percent between 1991 and the 2001 crisis). States in Brazil saw their share of expenditure decrease from 53 in 1992 to 44.7 percent in 1997 and their share of revenue from 37 in 1990 to 29.7 percent in 1999, the lowest level in the post-transition period. By contrast, the Argentine provinces increased their share of expenditures by 23 percent but reduced their share of revenue by 49 percent.

Table 6.1 Synthesis of the results by period of reform (1983/1985–2000)

Period of reforms	Subnational revenue (in relative terms)	Subnational functions	Subnational tax authority	Federal balance
Alfonsín 1987–1989	Increased (revenue share more than doubled; from 17% in 1985 to 42% in 1988; the Regional Development Fund was shared among provinces)	No substantial changes	Increased (new taxes included in the revenue-sharing scheme: VAT, on profits, excise, on fuels and lubricants, financial operations, lotteries and sporting events)	Favorable for provinces $X = \Sigma(P_{ig} - r_{ig}) > U = \Sigma(r_{jp} - P_{ip})$
Sarney 1987–1989	Increased (revenue share increased from 18.6% in 1987 to 30% in 1989).	No substantial changes	Increased (expanded the tax base of the ICM, five federal taxes, on transport, energy, fuels, minerals, and communications, were transferred to the states to create the ICMS)	Favorable for states $X = \Sigma(P_{ig} - r_{ig}) > U = \Sigma(r_{jp} - P_{ip})$

Menem 1991–1993	Decreased (revenue share fell from 38% in 1991 to 17% in 1996; the president retained 15% of provincial revenue-sharing funds). But increased in absolute terms	Increased (transferred health, education, housing; more than 1,500 schools, 800,000 students, and 95,000 teachers, total annual cost of $1.2 billion).	Decreased (eliminated provincial and local taxes: tax on the transport of fuels, natural gas, and electric energy, *impuesto a los sellos*, and on bank accounts, replacing them with federal taxes; their revenue is not shared).	Favorable for the federal government $U=\Sigma(r_{jp}-P_{ip}) > X=\Sigma(P_{ig}-r_{ig})$
Collor 1990–1992 and Itamar 1992–1994	Decreased (revenue share diminished from 37% in 1990 to 31% in 1995). But increased in absolute terms	No substantial changes	No substantial changes	Favorable for the federal government $U=\Sigma(r_{jp}-P_{ip}) > X=\Sigma(P_{ig}-r_{ig})$
Cardoso 1995–1998	Decreased (revenue share decreased from 33% in 1994 to 29.7% in 1999; the president retained 20% of state transfers). But increased in absolute terms	Relatively increased (imposed more policy responsibilities in health and education, together with municipalities)	Decreased (eliminated several state taxes, including export taxes, and replaced them with federal taxes—called social contributions; their revenue is not shared)	Favorable for the federal government $U=\Sigma(r_{jp}-P_{ip}) > X=\Sigma(P_{ig}-r_{ig})$

In exchange for these reforms, the Brazilian federal government had to pay the substantial costs of refinancing state debts (about R\$205 billion between 1997 and 2001), privatizing state banks (about R\$45 billion), and providing compensations for the Kandir Law (over R\$2 billion a year). These sums do not even take into account other costly concessions made to particular states and subnational leaders.

As expected by the theoretical model advanced in this work, the status quo prevailed when one of the crucial conditions was not met, that is, when neither the president nor the governors concentrated political power and/or when the key political actors did not have the fiscal incentives to alter the federal balance (that is, when they had fiscal alternatives for funding or when they faced soft budget constraints). Under those conditions, negotiations over the federal balance were deadlocked, and no reforms were passed in Congress.

When are the crucial conditions met?

The power of presidents depends on the electoral support given to them upon assuming office as well as on their Congressional and public support (understood in a broad sense to include that from interest and pressure groups). This study examined several cases of federal executives whose power weakened in their terms in office (Sarney, Alfonsín, and Collor de Mello, and even De la Rúa). In these cases, presidential powers seem to have receded gradually until a turning point was reached in which a relevant event or a series of events (such as the failure to control inflation by Alfonsín and Sarney or the corruption scandals that plagued Collor and De la Rúa) ignited a process by which presidential support in the governing coalition, inside the president's party, among powerful socio-political, economic, and financial actors, and in public opinion was drained. The loss of presidential power, in turn, triggered an "issue linkage process." At this point, previously uncoordinated actors were more likely to coordinate (in order to initiate other recipes to stabilize the economy or to remove "corrupt" political elites whose decisions and actions were costly for them), and opposition to the president grew stronger. Under such circumstances, as governors face larger fiscal incentives to alter the status quo ante and the budget constraints are harder, it will be more likely that they will try to coordinate to change the federal balance. These events or processes may be the prelude to major changes in the federal system, especially in terms of the distribution of functions and resources.

On the other hand, imposing centralizing reforms has depended on the capacity of the president to build up partisan power and weaken the governors' coordination efforts. The process of constructing presidential power in Argentina has been very much subject to the logic of what O'Donnell calls delegative democracy and its cycle of crisis (O'Donnell, 1994, 59, 64–65): in a context of crisis, the president wins the election and receives support from key socio-political and economic actors (as Menem did) or gathers this backing after the election (as Kirchner did). Under such circumstances, the federal executive has strong incentives, broad support, and substantial leverage to reform and alter the status quo without being subject to checks from the legislature and other institutions of "horizontal" control. As long as the president demonstrates the ability to control inflation (during the first administration after the democratic transition) or to generate economic growth and employment, the executive can count on the support of political elites and public opinion. Without these "policies [being] recognized as successful by electorally weighty segments of the population" (O'Donnell, 1994, 67), there is a new cycle of crisis, a profound erosion of presidential power, a new electoral contest (sometimes anticipated), a new winner, and a new cycle of delegation and crisis.

This same logic applies to Brazil during the presidencies of José Sarney and Fernando Collor (O'Donnell, 1994, 64). However, beginning with the administration of Fernando Henrique Cardoso, the basis of partisan competition and coalition formation has been more programmatic, coalitions have been more stable, and as a result policy outcomes have also been more stable. Next, I offer some possible reasons why this might have been the case in relation to the federal distributive game.

One of the critical conditions for explaining reforms to the federal balance is the political capacity of political actors to conduct reforms. But as we have seen throughout this study, fiscal incentives are another. These incentives are associated with the overall fiscal conditions presidents and governors face and how strong the pressures on their budgets are. New democratic administrations had to deal with the results of catastrophic economic performances during military rule (especially in Argentina), including a series of structural (international and domestic) imbalances and such conjunctural factors as fluctuations in international prices and budget cycles, in turn linked to their own economic mismanagement and the outcomes of previous stages of the game.

Some key questions linked to this are how weak must the president be, how strong must the governors be, and how severe must the economic crisis be before the actors lead to reforms to the federal balance. To begin with, there are cut points: for political power, when presidents have a simple majority in Congress and their legislators are disciplined; for fiscal crisis, the cut point is when presidents and governors face an imbalanced budget, that is a deficit. For gubernatorial power, the cut point is when a majority of the governors are powerful in their provinces, and they can coordinate against a weak president. These cut points put presidents and governors in different games. Magnitudes become relevant after these cut points have been crossed; changes *will be more likely* to occur when the values the key variables take after the cut points are larger. In other words, centralizing changes to the federal balance will be more likely when presidents are more powerful (that is, when they concentrate more seats after they reach a majority) and the deficit they face is larger (and budget constraints are harder). The same can be said about governors and their decentralizing reforms.

Some similarities in the reform process

The reform process in both countries shared some common characteristics in addition to being implemented under the conditions specified by the main hypothesis. First, one of the major objectives behind the reforms, although clearly not the only one, was to stabilize federal accounts, reduce fiscal deficits, and diminish inflationary pressures on the federal budget. In other words, the main actors' fiscal incentives were the most important driving force behind the reforms in Argentina and Brazil. In terms of the discourse legitimizing the reforms, presidents and legislators of the main coalition parties raised the specter of a return to instability and hyperinflation if reforms did not pass the Congress. Through such threats, they gave a common discourse to their core supporters and appealed to voters, a majority of which favored stability.

Second, presidents used their political power to push for reforms, dividing governors and fostering majorities in Congress. Federal executives did that through different means: on the one hand, they used debt rollovers and renegotiations to foster support for core presidential reforms, divide governors' coordination efforts, and reduce subnational fiscal pressures on the federal budget. As presidents had to rescue states from their increasingly unbearable debt, they demanded that governors implement reforms in line with goals of fiscal prudence and control. On the other, presidents made concessions to governors in order to reduce the probability of conflict during the negotiations.[4] These concessions were also combined with specific (or particularistic) agreements with some political forces or Congressional delegations in exchange for legislative support.[5] The opposition in both countries strongly criticized these "obscure pacts" between the president, governors, and some legislators in order to pass reforms. Presidents in both federations also distributed discretionary transfers to foster parliamentary support.

Third, many reforms were implemented with sunset provisions, which set an extinction date and delayed negotiations over the maintenance of these rules. Furthermore, many crucial reforms were also conducted with an initiation date generally set after the end of the incumbent governor's term in office.[6] Using such means, presidents imposed costs on subnational governments that were not borne by the governors in office (unless they were reelected but, even then, the costs were set for the period after the election).

Fourth, and related to the previous arrangements, the president granted several concessions to incumbent governors until the end of their terms in office. Both in Argentina and Brazil, many governors opted for a short-term solution to their fiscal imbalances, which affected provincial/state fiscal autonomy in the longer run. For instance, several governors supported relinquishing state tax authority in exchange for federal compensatory transfers that were expected to last until the end of their administrations (sometimes these concessions ended up extending beyond the original deadline). Hence, they had fiscal relief during their terms in office but they ended up reducing their states' fiscal capacity in the longer run (especially affecting incoming administrations). These rules attempted to reduce the costs of passing the reforms and the probability of conflict between president and governors in the short term.

Fifth, in both cases there is much more movement vis-à-vis subnational revenue and subnational tax authority (columns 2 and 4 in Table 6.1) than vis-à-vis subnational functions (column 3). The distribution of administrative functions as opposed to fiscal authority seems to be "stickier" in both cases.

Sixth, even powerful presidents after the transition to democracy in Argentina and Brazil could not reform the main institutional frameworks regulating the distribution of funds and functions. The main reason was that neither Menem nor Cardoso could gather enough support in Congress to amend those rules, and they faced strong resistance from governors.[7] In Argentina and Brazil, modifying those rules was very costly and the probability of conflict was high, even for Menem and Cardoso. Despite the costs, both of these presidents could change the legal frameworks linked to these rules (trimming the share of funds before they were distributed among states).[8]

The most substantive reforms to the abovementioned institutional frameworks occurred in a period of acute fiscal crises in which governors were relatively powerful and presidents comparatively weak. The erosion of presidential power in both federations had large implications for the functioning of these federal democracies. Brazil could sustain the reforms passed during the 1990s because presidents were relatively popular, they had legislative support in Congress (not enough to pass reforms, but clearly enough to prevent others endorsed by the governors), and governors were deeply weakened during the period. The political scenario in Argentina immediately after Menem was quite different.

Some substantive differences in the reform process

Despite the aforementioned similarities, other characteristics sharply differentiate the aggregated outcomes of these two cases in terms of the distribution of resources, functions, and the institutions created, as well as the consequences for political stability in these two democracies. To begin with, there was always greater fiscal urgency in Argentina than in Brazil. This generated stronger incentives for political actors to produce (profound) reforms in the federal balance. Urgency was used (and abused) by successive presidents to pass rushed reforms (in a manner that resonated with O'Donnell's delegative democracy argument). The decentralization of education and health care services was passed in Congress in only ten days, and the First Fiscal Pact was approved in 22 days. Of course the crucial negotiations, carried out by the president and members of the cabinet and the governors, were conducted before the bill was taken into Congress. Nevertheless, there were no substantive debates on the fiscal pacts in Congress (legislators simply rubberstamped the decisions made between the federal and provincial executives), and as a result the "quality" of these bills suffered, and they lacked a genuine consensus. In O'Donnell's (1994, 62) words, a delegative democracy has the "apparent advantage of allowing swift policy making, but at the expense of a higher likelihood of gross mistakes, of hazardous implementation, and of concentrating responsibility for the outcomes on the president."

By contrast, fiscal crises, the sense of urgency, and the fiscal incentives to reform facing presidents and governors were systematically more moderate in Brazil. Hence, reforms in Brazil were, in general, more gradual and protracted. Most negotiations in Congress took months and some even years. In many cases, the president could not get his preferred reforms passed in the expected time, and approval was delayed for months; this was the case for the extension of the FSE and FEF. This does not mean that Argentine presidents could always pass the reforms they wanted in the time frame they desired. In fact, in many cases (such as the revenue-sharing bill itself) Menem had to give up on reforms. But nonetheless, several crucial reforms in Argentina were negotiated in a critical fiscal context under which the president pressed Congress to expedite reforms.

Second, following from the two prior characteristics, reforms in Argentina tended to be more unilateral, as the actor who led negotiations and prevailed in terms of power relations could impose key conditions on the weaker most of the time. Brazilian presidents were at no time able to concentrate as much political power as their Argentine counterparts did. Although presidents had to make concessions in both cases, these were more extensive in the Brazilian case. Cardoso led several parallel reforms and exchanged support for some key bills for concessions in some others. In order to secure the passage and subsequent extensions of the FSE, for example, the president made concessions in the pension, tax, and administrative reforms. Thus, the most important bills related to the federal balance (such as the FEF/DRU) were approved, but other reforms were not. Lula followed some of these negotiation strategies.

Third, as a consequence of deep fiscal crises and the periods of profound concentration of power in one level of government, changes in the distribution of funds and functions (decentralization versus centralization) were always sharper and deeper in Argentina. The 1988 decentralization process imposed large costs on the federal government, and four years later, the president not only reversed these reforms but also imposed huge costs on the provinces. In Brazil, the process of reversing the profound changes governors imposed on the central government in 1988 took more than a decade of long negotiations and concessions to accomplish. In the end, changes were substantial, but so were the compensations.

Fourth, although the main objective of the reforms in Argentina was to stabilize the federal government's fiscal deficit, the reforms were also part of Menem's strategy for political survival: making governors more fiscally dependent on the central government was also a way to debilitate them. Provincial fiscal dependency and vulnerability may be a permanent source of fiscal, economic, and social instability and turmoil at the subnational level, but it is also a political asset for the president. Fiscal goals were present in Brazil too, but programmatic targets also accompanied the reforms of federal institutions regulating the distribution of funds and functions. The main reforms in Brazil were debated and discussed extensively in Congress under broad labels, such as "tax reform." Discussions had a programmatic component linked to the main parties' ideological positions (PSDB, PFL versus PT, PCdoB; less clear for the PMDB) in Congress, the key arena for negotiations (this goes in line with the argument of Hagopian *et al.*, 2009). In Argentina, the main changes were debated between the president and the governors through "fiscal pacts." During these negotiations, few if any programmatic issues were discussed; the key was the federal distribution of revenue. Once agreement was reached on the main reforms, the bill was sent to Congress for approval, where it was usually sanctioned in expeditiously and without substantial changes. Fiscal restrictions on current spending and debt, as well as the need to have balanced budgets, were considered general goals for the Center-Right coalition led by Cardoso, crystallizing in the 1995 Camata Law and the 2000 LRF. In Argentina, limits to subnational current spending and indebtedness were more difficult to enforce, in part because the central government imposed a costly decentralization of social services and could not oblige provinces to accept additional conditions during these negotiations. Also, these decentralizing reforms were so costly that it was difficult for most provinces to balance their budgets without issuing debt. Brazilian governors were never compelled to accept such stringent limitations.

As a consequence, and in the fifth place, the institutional setting regulating the distribution of funds and functions was changed in a more gradual way and by building a broader consensus in Brazil than in Argentina, especially after Cardoso. As O'Donnell (1994, 62) claims, "decision making in representative democracies tends to be slow and incremental and sometimes prone to gridlock." Many reforms in Brazil demanded constitutional amendments and three-fifths majorities, which made changes, especially drastic changes, more costly. Congress was the crucial arena for negotiations, despite the fact that parallel negotiations took place with governors (and mayors)[9] over most of the reforms oriented toward changing the federal balance. In Argentina, agreements with the governors have been the keystone for reforms that seek to alter the federal balance, although these agreements must be ratified by the legislature and enacted into law.

Sixth, in Brazil the central government played a stronger and clearer role in planning, controlling, and financing decentralized functions (compensating subnational governments which could not meet basic fiscal requirements through the FUNDEF-LDB and the SUS-PAB). In Argentina, the federal administration basically offloaded key functions entirely to the provinces, resulting in a much weaker role (de jure but also de facto) for the federal government in planning, controlling, and financing. The Menem government guaranteed an absolute floor in the decentralized funds to the provinces. But inflation (which grew gradually despite being low after 1991) and increasing salaries and infrastructure costs rendered these guarantees irrelevant and useless.

In exchange, the central government in Argentina could not impose conditions on the governors, and provincial governments were not compelled to spend minimum percentages of their revenue on such areas as health care and education (most funds were not earmarked), as Brazilian states (and municipalities) had to do. This was a critical element during the negotiations for decentralization reforms in Argentina, as governors could freely use revenue-sharing funds for the decentralized social services in other areas. The federal government did not allocate extra funds to finance the decentralized functions; hence, it could not compel provinces to allocate budget revenue to social services. Menem also decentralized specific funds (such as housing and road funds) to facilitate negotiations with the governors and win their support for the bill that decentralized services. The decentralization of these funds was achieved through ad hoc political negotiations with each governor, without any programmatic criteria or transparent requirements for the allocation and distribution.

As a result, the overall federal balance today is very different in the two cases. Argentina is a deeply *imbalanced federal system*: the federal government has decentralized several policy responsibilities to the provincial level at the same time that it has centralized fiscal revenue and the mechanisms to distribute it, making Argentine governors gradually more dependent on the central government in fiscal terms. Brazil, by contrast, is a more *balanced federation*: fewer policy obligations are in the hands of the states (and they share them with municipalities but with significant central government regulations), states have more fiscal autonomy than in Argentina, and the central government has a clearer compensatory role and more control over subnational governments. A crucial difference between the two federations is that Brazilian states received more absolute transfers over the course of the entire period, and they were compensated for the new functions they assumed by the central government. They also shared policy responsibilities with municipalities. Argentine provinces also received more transfers in absolute terms during some years but these were not as substantial as in Brazil. Moreover, as the economy went through periods of expansion and sharp contraction, the fiscal situation of the provinces became more volatile, erratic, and, in the end, more precarious.

Why the differences between cases?

What explains the differences in the reform process between the two cases? The literature has highlighted several factors, among them, the role of leadership. Several scholars claimed, for instance, that Brazil's status quo is characterized by centrifugal pressures from subnational governments and aggregated problems of governability (Ames, 2001; Mainwaring, 1997, 1999; Samuels, 2003). However, Cardoso reversed this situation based on his exceptional leadership skills, coalition building and maintenance, presidential performance, and ability to realize reform objectives, but without altering the main features of Brazilian federalism (Samuels and Mainwaring, 2004, 122, 124–125). Some of these scholars further claim that reforms were passed because of the large costs the federal government assumed during negotiations (Samuels, 2003).

Others have stressed the role of the institutional resources in the hands of presidents, more precisely a set of legislative powers that allowed them to enforce discipline in Congress and pass most of their reform agenda (Figueiredo and Limongi, 1995, 1997, 2000; Limongi and Figueiredo, 1995, 1998). These scholars, as stressed before, argue that there is a substantial difference in the aggregated consequences for the democratic regime. Brazil's presidents are politically powerful, and they have been capable of passing most of their reform agenda in Congress.[10]

A third group of scholars have underscored the relevance of parties and the party system. Some of these authors claimed that Brazilian parties have shown substantial discipline in Congress (Nicolau, 1999). Others have stressed the relevance of the ideological dimension and programmatic commitments. For Hagopian *et al.* (2009, 362), market reforms created a programmatic cleavage and diminished the resource base for state patronage, making Brazilian deputies increasingly party oriented because of the greater utilization of party-programmatic strategies as opposed to those based on patronage. In a similar vein, other scholars claimed that while the PSDB and PT are more programmatic parties that carried out reforms based on policy goals, the PJ (similar in some regards to the PMDB in Brazil) has weaker programmatic commitments, more clientelistic networks, and based most of its reforms on a strategy oriented toward building up and concentrating political power (Santos, 1999a). As a consequence, reforms in Brazil were more programmatic and negotiated, while in Argentina they tended to be more unilateral and asymmetrical (led by the more powerful actor), and mainly sought to balance the fiscal deficit of the central government as a strategy to consolidate the president's power.

This work agrees with the former two arguments, which claim that Brazilian presidents have had institutional and partisan resources to pass reforms and that they have been effective in doing so, but I also emphasize the key variables in this study's main theoretical argument in order to explain the changes in the distribution of funds and functions in both federal systems. First, we need to compare the distribution of political power in both cases. The degree of concentration in either the central or provincial level of government, and the asymmetries in the distribution of political power between them, have always been larger in Argentina. Brazilian presidents traditionally were forced to negotiate because the support of their own parties was never sufficient for passing reforms. Although both Cardoso and Menem could reach majorities to pass crucial bills, Menem's party controlled almost four times the share of seats in the Chamber of Deputies that Cardoso's party controlled.[11] Menem concentrated more partisan powers, which allowed him to impose more conditions on the governors than his counterpart in Brazil. Cardoso faced weak governors, who were further weakened during his administration. Argentine governors were stronger during Menem's term in office than during Alfonsín's; their power in partisan terms increased systematically after 1983.[12] Menem confronted strong potential opponents who could draw upon substantial political resources in their provinces. He needed to keep them under control and prevent them from coordinating against the central government. He accomplished this goal in two ways: first, through partisan powers and partisan linkages (here the Peronist territorial structure was a critical resource); and second, through the distribution of selective incentives and compensation. Once governors supported the president, they conferred significant political resources upon the federal executive and his political agenda.

Second, we have to take into account the fiscal incentives and budget constraints the actors faced. Fiscal crises were significant in both countries, but they were regularly larger and more recurrent in Argentina.[13] These fiscal results have had important implications for the federal game. Brazilian presidents have always faced softer budget constraints than presidents in Argentina, even during critical periods, and neither they nor Brazilian governors have ever had to confront the same fiscal urgency their counterparts faced in Argentina.

Federal fiscal relations in the period after the transition to democracy in Argentina have tended to be fairly conflictive and highly unstable. One of the main reasons is that presidents and governors have faced strong fiscal incentives to alter the status quo ante. Under weak presidents who could not deliver fiscal relief to them or who were unpopular or weak in partisan terms, governors have had strong fiscal incentives to alter the status quo ante in their favor. Governors in Argentina are currently unco-ordinated but they remain potentially powerful; the stability of the status quo ante depends on the capacity of the president to divide them and resist their pressures. Since the reforms, the federal balance in Brazil has been more favorable for the president, who has been able to contain the governors and induce them to adhere to strict fiscal rules. Under those rules, and considering that subnational leaders have faced milder fiscal pressures than in Argentina, they have had weaker incentives to alter the status quo ante and would face larger costs to do so (since these regula-tions require qualified majorities in both chambers).

Contra *and* inter pares *federalisms?*

Argentina's federal system has been prone to a *contra pares* type, in which winners are more likely to impose costly reforms on their opponents. Gov-ernors were likely to engage in praetorian coordination when the pres-ident was weak, while presidents, when they could, imposed costly reforms on subnational governments. Borrowing an expression taken from a very different context, "looting" seems to be a rational (and the expected) behavior for all actors (O'Donnell, 2010, 43). This was a strategy of polit-ical survival rather than a way to make the federal balance more stable, efficient, or redistributive.

Brazilian federalism has been more inclined to be an *inter pares* type, in which reforms have been more difficult to impose unilaterally. One of the reasons for this difference is that neither presidents nor governors have historically concentrated enough power to impose reforms on each other. Presidents have needed to engage in long and protracted negotiations to pass reforms altering the federal balance, and governors have been more likely to be divided and uncoordinated. Differences between Argentina and Brazil have not depended so much on leaders' personality or negoti-ating skills as they have on the restrictions imposed by their capacity to concentrate power and the fiscal incentives they faced.

The aggregated results on the political system and the democratic regime have been substantial: Argentina has faced recurrent conflicts and instab-ility, while federal institutions regulating relations among levels of govern-ment have not been able to protect presidents and governors from each other's potential assaults. Moreover, in the absence of policy goals and pro-grammatic objectives during the implementation of the reforms studied here, there were also devastating consequences in terms of policy outcomes. The decentralization of education and health care services, the provincial incapacity to deliver them (both in fiscal and administrative terms), and con-texts of economic decline followed by the 2001–2002 collapse translated into violent protests, demonstrations, and social turmoil, all of which contributed to increasing tensions between governors and the president.

In Brazil, a less concentrated (or more fragmented) distribution of power and less pressing fiscal incentives have been associated with more costly changes of the rules of the federal game, more institutional stability, and a less chaotic delivery of services. The results, in turn, were fewer tensions and less conflictive fiscal and political relations between president and governors. Federal institutions in Brazil have been more likely to protect presidents and governors from each other's potential assaults.

Some comparative notes for federal democracies

In more developed federal nations, the rules that distribute tax authority, administrative functions, and revenue have certainly been modified at times, but overall they have tended to be relatively stable over time.[14] These institutions not only endow stability to federal relations; they also contribute to relieving tensions between levels of government, protecting each of them from potential assaults from the other.

In the United States, stability in the federal institutional structure regulating the distribution of funds and functions has been the consequence of two main factors. On the one hand, the president has been able to concentrate political power in such a manner that the federal executive has become the most prominent political actor in the federation. Presidential power has grown to a degree that has not been paralleled by that of the governors, and this has been clear at least since the reforms implemented during the presidency of Franklin Delano Roosevelt.

Roosevelt essentially moved the center of partisan power from the party organization, at that time dominated by state (and local) structures, to the White House (Milkis, 1993, 86). He initiated the process of dramatic expansion in presidential power that led to the decline of governors' and traditional parties' political relevance (the latter were very much linked to regional and local leaders). Roosevelt contributed to the creation of a thickened presidential administration by centralizing administrative powers and constructing a political constituency directly linked to the president. These processes essentially represented a move of political power away from state and local partisan structures, very much dominated by governors, to the presidency (and the bureaucracy).

The 1930s economic crisis provided the autonomy and gave the president the necessary room of maneuver for a radical change in the party system and in the relation between the executive and regional parties (Skowronek, 1993, 296). Truman, Eisenhower, Kennedy, and Johnson continued the expansion of presidential capacities, weakening state and local partisan structures, and building direct appeals to the electorate (Milkis, 1993, 151). These processes, which were continued by different post-modern presidents, further contributed to the decline of the traditional state party apparatus.[15]

As a consequence of this dramatic increase in presidential power, gubernatorial pressures and predation have been limited and controlled by a strong federal executive. During the twentieth century, the US has never experienced anything similar to the gubernatorial coordination we have seen in Argentina and Brazil during the late 1980s mainly because governors were never that powerful and presidents never that weak.

On the other hand, governors never faced the fiscal pressures their Argentine and Brazilian counterparts had systematically faced after their last transition to democracy. This is the consequence of two key factors: first, the revenue share of the South American states and provinces is much lower than in the US.[16] So, the fiscal imbalances between administrative functions and sub-national resources to finance them (the vertical imbalance) are greater in the former two cases than in the latter one. Second, the fiscal pressures due to fiscal crises have never been as acute in the US as they have been in Argentina, and to a lesser extent in Brazil.[17] US governors never had the fiscal incentives to alter the status quo ante that their counterparts in Argentina and Brazil had. Their revenue share has been quite stable over time (IMF, 2001) and never subject to the enormous fluctuations experienced in the two developing federations. Economic turmoil and fiscal crises gave both Argentine and Brazilian presidents and governors strong incentives to alter the regulations governing the distribution of funds, tax authority, and government functions. Federal fiscal imbalances were the consequence of huge fiscal deficits and hyperinflationary processes that the US never faced. Subnational fiscal crises produced shortfalls in the provision of basic social services and the payment of salaries, which translated into provincial protests, mobilization, and violence. In extreme circumstances, particularly in the case of Argentina, the mere capacity of the provincial state to deliver basic functions, including not only health services and education but even security (achieved by paying salaries to provincial police forces) was jeopardized. Fiscal crisis never threatened the capacity of the states to deliver basic functions in developed federations, such as the US (and Canada, for instance). US governors have mostly claimed more federal funds for certain policies or reforms, such as during the recent health care bill endorsed by President Barack Obama (*New York Times*, "Governors Balk over Emerging Health Bill Because of Cost," July 20, 2009). Fiscal pressures and deficits have been more or less large, but they never threatened the capacity of the states to function as such or to contain protest and social turmoil. Having fewer fiscal incentives to alter the status quo and less power to face a strong president has meant more institutional stability in the frameworks regulating the federal balance in the US and other developed countries with federal systems than in Argentina and Brazil.

In developing federations, institutions regulating the distribution of funds and functions (the dependent variables) tend to be very much contested. In these federations, political actors tend to see changes in the frameworks that regulate the distribution of resources as an option for reversing unfavorable fiscal situations and improving their federal balance in the struggle for power. The actors aggrieved by the status quo ante see institutional change as a possible means of reversing the costs they faced and imposing them on other actors. In such a context, the dynamics of the federal game affect not only the distribution of funds and functions but also the institutional frameworks regulating them. That is, changes in the federal balance not only have fiscal implications for macroeconomic stability (because they affect the fiscal deficit and the amount of debt of the central and subnational governments) and for shortcomings in the delivery of basic social services. They also exercise an important impact on the degree of conflict and tensions among levels of government in the federation, which in extreme cases can lead to problems of territorial integrity; this is the problem of *weakly checked federal pressures*. Changes in the federal balance also influence the strength of institutional checks on presidential power, which in extreme cases can lead to presidential assaults on state autonomy; this is the problem of *weakly checked centralized power*.

Post-transition Argentina and Brazil are cases in which the outcomes of the federal game have resulted in periods of deep macroeconomic instability and serious problems in the delivery of social services. Subnational politicians have traditionally been regarded as over-spenders, especially as the transfers they get from the federal government have grown (and the vertical imbalance between the functions they deliver and the resources they collect in their states has become larger; see Rodden, 2006). This work provides some historical analysis that questions this assumption and generates some debate, rather than takes it as a "given" datum of reality. Under some conditions, subnational governments *had* to spend more because they became responsible for more functions. They incurred large deficits and debt because they did not have legitimate sources of revenue to pay for these services. It is difficult to know whether governors, in general, prefer spending more (the debate is open and we need more studies on this topic); but from this work it seems clear that sometimes they could not do anything else. More comparative work is needed to inform this discussion.

Beyond the fiscal implications of the federal distributive game, the tensions and conflicts between levels of government, macroeconomic instability, and social turmoil may *also* affect the political stability of a federal democracy, particularly under conditions of a large concentration of power at the gubernatorial or presidential level. Argentina during the administrations of Alfonsín and De la Rúa and perhaps also Brazil under Collor are examples of political instability that resulted from several causes, but one of them was the tensions between governors and the president over the distribution of revenue.[18] During critical periods, governors may have contributed to economic and fiscal instability due to their pressures for more fiscal transfers (this was one of the consequences of their attempts to remain in power and improve their fiscal balance), but in other circumstances they also represented checks on presidential power. This was probably the case during the Rodríguez Saá and the Duhalde administrations in Argentina (and even later, during those of the Kirchners). In these cases, not only Congress and the Judiciary—which were very much weakened during the period of crisis in the delegative democracy—but also governors were the actors in charge of setting limits to presidential attempts to concentrate excessive power.

Governors have also contributed to checking presidential power in other federations. In Mexico, for example, the gradual weakening of the federal executive and the increasing power of governors translated into subnational pressures to decentralize revenue and functions. Eventually, the gains governors achieved in fiscal, administrative, and electoral power challenged the 71-year PRI executive monopoly. In the elections of June 1997, the PRI lost its legislative majority as well as its control of several state governorships, which were critical springboards for federal politics.[19] Opposition governors (and even some PRI governors) actively coordinated in the National Conference of Governors (CoNaGo) and pressured the central government to increase the shares of federally generated revenues allocated to the states. The governors demanded more transfers in order to increase the amount of revenue available to autonomously administer from the central government (in order to deliver more services and increase their political relevance in the federation). Governors achieved some of their demands, but "decentralization was gradual, limited in degree, and based on the transfer of expenditures and grants with high levels of federal discretion." The federal government maintained control over the tax system, including the collection of the main tax, the value-added tax (Montero, 2001, 47). As claimed by Willis *et al.* (1999, 47),

> Revenue-sharing and transfers to lower levels of government have increased, government agencies have become more decentralized, and state and particularly local governments have gained new fiscal powers. Yet the striking feature of Mexico, when viewed in comparative perspective, is the continuing weight of presidential authority in this process.

Despite the limited results achieved by governors in fiscal and administrative terms, the pressures they brought to bear on the central government represented a fundamental change in Mexican politics. Struggles and conflicts between PRI presidents and governors as well as increasing electoral competition from the PAN and PRD in both national and subnational elections, have meant unprecedented threats to the historical pattern of sustained centralization (Montero, 2001, 49). Although Mexico remains relatively centralized in political, fiscal, and administrative terms, governors have been crucial political actors in limiting presidential power and the PRI monopoly, operating as an institutional check (together with the legislative and judicial branches of government) to restrain executive dominance over national politics.

Governors were also crucial in setting limits on presidential power in the case of Venezuela. The difference in this case is that the monopoly of power was not in hands of a single party but in two. Governors were historically weak in Venezuela, but during the late 1980s a process of erosion of presidential power and a legitimacy crisis in the partyarchy of AD and COPEI (Coppedge, 1994) was accompanied by profound economic and fiscal turmoil. Once regional leaders were granted political and administrative autonomy (direct election and faculties to administer portions of their own budget), they bullied the federal executive for fiscal and administrative autonomy. Between 1990 and 1992, elected governors demanded that the central government should decentralize more funds and responsibility for the administration of public services to sub-national governments. The president (and allied party elites) successfully resisted.

The two failed coup attempts in 1992 and the profound political crisis that ensued resulted in the removal of President Carlos Andrés Pérez from office by a decision of the Attorney General and the Supreme Court due to corruption scandals. He was replaced by Ramón Velázquez. The interim federal executive assumed power in a very weak position and subnational leaders took advantage of this situation to demand more transfers. The new president could not resist the renewed pressures from governors, who actively coordinated within the Association of Venezuelan Governors (AGV), and finally had to increase fiscal transfers to the states from 15 to 20 percent and raise the Intergovernmental Decentralization Fund (FIDES) for a total of $4.5 billion between 1993 and 1994 (Penfold-Becerra, 2004, 166, 171). Several authors have claimed that the 1989 reforms turned the centralized political system not only into a more federal democracy but also into one in which new partisan elites could compete for power and the influence of the traditional parties was limited.

Powerful governors can pressure the president for more fiscal and administrative powers. But, if governors are weakly checked, their demands can go even further. When the president is too weak, governors are powerful, and the institutional rules protecting the autonomy of each level of government are unstable and very much contested (or even seen by political actors as illegitimate), the territorial integrity of the federation can be challenged. This is the problem of *weakly checked federal pressures.*

After the collapse of the Soviet Union, the Russian federation was on the brink of disintegration. Regional pressures dominated Russian politics from the early to the mid 1990s (Alexander, 2004, 235). President Boris Yeltsin had neither the political power nor the fiscal resources to gain control of regional pressures, and he was unable to resist the demands emanating from very strong subnational politicians. As a consequence, the republics and regions were notably strengthened, resulting in a federal balance that was more favorable to them during the period. In 1994, the president granted regional and local governments substantial revenue-raising powers by decree. Subnational governments were also allowed to introduce new regional and local taxes and to change the tax rate on profits in their jurisdictions (De Silva *et al.*, 2009, 34). Some analysts estimated that during the Yeltsin administration approximately 60 percent of the taxes collected in the regions was not retained at the central level but distributed back to regional budgets (Lavrov 1998, 34; quoted in Konitzer and Wegren, 2006, 511).

The 1998 economic crisis generated incentives for strong regional politicians to step up their demands on a weakened central government. But fiscal demands were only the beginning. Some regions pressed for more institutional autonomy, and some even threatened to secede.[20] These regions were precisely those that contributed a large share of revenue to the central government and received few fiscal benefits in return.[21] As claimed by Alexander (2004, 234), after the 1998 economic crash, Russia "de facto moved dramatically in the direction of a confederation, with a number of strong regions and a weak center." The territorial integrity of the federation was at stake not only because of fiscal or administrative demands from subnational governments, but also because of profound cleavages between levels of government, which translated into strong centrifugal forces.

The opposite problem is a *weakly checked centralized power*, where neither governors nor other institutional checks can resist the assaults of presidents that are able to concentrate power. In some extreme cases, federal struggles can result in challenges to state autonomy and even undermine democracy in federal systems. Venezuela under Hugo Chávez is one example. Russia under Vladimir Putin is another.

Despite being historically weak, governors got stronger during the late 1980s and early 1990s in Venezuela. After gaining some power during a period of a weakened president and strong fiscal incentives, they had to face a powerful federal executive who sought to centralize revenue and consolidate power. In December 1998, Chávez assumed office with the largest margin of votes in Venezuelan history.[22] With a significant political power in his hands and strong fiscal incentives to centralize, he carried out comprehensive reforms. The president wanted not only to improve the federal balance and centralize fiscal revenue but also to debilitate subnational officials (especially those in the opposition who had their strongholds in state governorships) and consolidate his power. The asymmetry in the federal distribution of political power exercised an impact on governors, who could resist only some attacks from the president.

Fiscal centralization came first. The federal government centralized the distribution of funds and retained other fiscal transfers instead of distributing them among the states.[23] As a result, the share of revenue of subnational governments decreased from 29 percent of the total in 1998 to 21 percent in 2004, 19 percent in 2005, and 17 percent in 2006 (Mascareño, 2007, 19).

This was not the end of the centralization process. Subsequently, Chávez reformed the constitution, increasing his institutional powers by extending his mandate from five to six years and allowing for reelection. He also reduced the autonomy of subnational governments and regional legislatures, and trimmed the power of governors by eliminating the Senate, which had the effect of increasing his control over Congress and reducing the influence of opposition governors over the legislature. He also significantly reduced the fiscal transfers and administrative functions of the Metropolitan Mayor's office (Alcalde Metropolitano), which was a key district in the hands of the opposition. To replace it, he named a metropolitan authority and allocated to it about 90 percent of the revenue and several of the functions that previously belonged to the Mayor. A series of elections and referenda between 1999 and 2000 allowed Chávez to increase his control over the legislature, the judiciary, and, naturally, over subnational governments (Penfold-Becerra, 2004, 175).

The boundaries between fiscal centralization and political domination (or hegemony in extreme cases) have been easily crossed by the most powerful presidents who wished to concentrate political resources and remain in power. Governors can impose limits on presidential power, but only when they have political resources and institutional protections to resist the president's attacks. Notwithstanding the assaults from the president and his partisans, some Venezuelan federal institutions (for instance, the direct election of governors and mayors) could not be reformed due to demands from subnational politicians and opposition forces. Despite being debilitated and challenged by presidential assaults, opposition subnational leaders were one of the few and among the most important checks to president Chávez in Venezuela. Many of these opposition leaders were arrested or barred from running for office (these arrests continued and even increased during Maduro's term in office). Many of them were the politicians in the opposition who had the largest share of support among public opinion and still have some (clearly weakened) institutional protections to voice their disagreement with the president.

As presidents and governors concentrate more power and their fiscal incentives to alter the status quo ante are larger, changes to the federal institutional frameworks will be more likely. When cycles between concentration of power in one level of government are more recurrent under strong fiscal imbalances, these federal rules will be more volatile. In cases of high concentration of political power, fiscal institutions can end up being extremely vulnerable and unstable. Sometimes these rules are not the only ones subject to profound changes. Under some conditions, assaults from the powerful actor can mean the institutional destruction or disappearance of the other.

With the Russian Federation challenged by centrifugal pressures during the Yeltsin administration, the decentralizing trend was drastically reversed after the election of Vladimir Putin in March 2000. He was a powerful president[24] who had strong incentives to concentrate fiscal resources due to the deep economic crisis the country had been facing since 1998. Under those conditions, as we could expect given the setting of the federal distributive game, Putin augmented the central government's control of regionally collected revenue and centralized fiscal resources.[25]

Putin improved the fiscal balance for the federal government as a means of strengthening his control over subnational politicians. As Vishnevskii (2002) argues, "the 'budgetary rope' is being pulled [toward the center] ... because the center wants to strengthen its own power" (quoted in Konitzer and Wegren, 2006, 512). Having secured a more favorable federal balance, Putin began a profound centralization process to contain centrifugal pressures from the regions and put regional elites under centralized control. He created seven federal districts under the command of presidential representatives, reconfigured the selection processes for deputies to the Upper House of Parliament (the Federation Council), and brought regional legislation and constitutions in line with the Russian Constitution and federal laws (Alexander, 2004, 234). In December 2004, he decreed the elimination of regional elections and replaced elected governors with executives selected "by recommendation of the president" (this was, in fact, a system of quasi-appointment whereby the president presents his candidates to regional legislatures for approval). These reforms represented, according to some analysts, "the greatest threat to Russian federalism in the federation's entire post-communist history" (Konitzer and Wegren, 2006, 503, 510–511).[26]

The resulting centralization process, the most extensive of all in the post-Soviet era, has raised concerns about the democratic status of the union. The legislature and judiciary, as well as some other public organizations (such as the press and the mass media) suffered similar assaults by the federal executive. Governors, strengthened during the Yeltsin years, could not resist the attacks of a powerful president who had strong fiscal incentives to centralize and claimed the need to avoid territorial disintegration as one of the justifications for the centralization process. The outcomes of the federal game had significant implications for the territorial integrity of the union and the democratic condition of the Russian Federation.

Despite the imprecision of these comparative notes, I would claim that sharp changes in the federal balance can have profound implications, not only for the macroeconomic stability of the entire federation and the states' capacity to deliver essential social services (as was evident in

Argentina and Brazil), but also for the dynamics of electoral competition (as in Mexico and Venezuela), the territorial integrity of the union (Russia), and even the checks on presidential power (Venezuela and Russia).

What is clearer, though, is that institutions in developing federations, particularly the rules regulating the distribution of funds and functions, are not a stable feature of the setting in which political actors interact. They are recurrently subject to major changes according to the distribution of political power and the fiscal incentives the actors face. What this study makes clear is that some federations may move toward becoming more institutionalized. Such a change can take place either because presidents and governors agree upon some basic rules or because one of them imposes these rules on the other actor without generating profound grievances. The framework of this study suggests that the latter path is the more likely. In any case, and in both scenarios, political actors are more likely to play the game without having the incentives to alter its fundamental rules every time it is their turn to reshuffle the deck. In other developing federations, these rules are still subject to the praetorian dynamics by which the winner of the game imposes costly reforms on the other actor, and both of them see this as a way (and perhaps the only way) to survive politically. In the end, "looting" is the rational behavior for all actors. Large concentrations of political power and strong fiscal incentives are variables that play a key role in these cases. In the most extreme situations, the winner can even try to make the other actor (institutionally) disappear. There is still much we have to understand about political struggles in developing federal democracies. This study is an attempt to show their relevance. In the end, it is not only the distribution of power and resources that is at stake in the federal game in these federations. It is also the actual functioning of democracy itself.

Notes

1 He declared that "[s]ome governors who do not understand the severity of this moment, have decided not to support me anymore" (quoted in Mustapic, 2005, 273). The newspaper *Clarín* stated that he left office because he could not get PJ governors to support his program for government (*Clarín*, "Renunció Rodríguez Saá y volvió a abrirse otra pelea en el PJ por la presidencia," December 30, 2001).

2 He was the candidate who generated less conflict with the governors from the Liga Federal and the big provinces, especially Córdoba and Santa Fe (*La Nación*, "Duhalde, el candidato de mayor consenso," December 31, 2001).

3 The federal government also made some specific concessions to certain states to secure the vote from some of their representatives, especially from the Northern states (which got the extension of the special regime in the Manaus Free Trade Zone from 2013 to 2023).

4 Some examples were the possibility of reelection for governors and the short-term compensations for the Kandir Law in Brazil, as well as the "floors" in fiscal transfers to the provinces or the increase in the percentages of some shared taxes in Argentina.

5 Such as the industrial promotion schemes in both countries, the negotiation for the Zona Franca de Manaus, some infrastructural works, the installation of federal offices in certain states, and the decentralization of specific funds—such as the R$2 billion Regional Development Fund in Brazil, the annual AR$650 million for the Buenos Aires Province Fund, or the annual AR$18 million for Santa Cruz.

6 State debts in Brazil were refinanced along a period of 30 years without any payments during the immediate 2 years, in order to prevent incumbent governors from having to pay for the adjustment process during their last years in office and before the elections. Governors also extended the time limits to begin adjustments in personnel expenditure as demanded by the LRF.

7 In some cases, presidents could pass those reforms and even further tilt the federal balance in their favor; see notes on Russia and Venezuela below.

8 The FEF cut 20 percent of the funds allocated to states, and Fiscal Pact I reduced these transfers by 15 percent.

9 As indicated earlier, the relevance of mayors in Brazil is a crucial difference in relation to the Argentine case, in which local officials hardly ever participate in negotiations in the federal Congress. Their capacity to negotiate depends, first of all, on their relations with the governor.

10 Some of them claim that relations between the legislature and the president could be defined as "forced cooperation" (Santos, 1999b).

11 Menem's party could almost reach a majority in the Chamber of Deputies with his own legislators between 1991 and 1995, and had a comfortable majority after 1995 (46.3 percent in 1991; 48.2 percent in 1993; and 51.4 percent in 1995). Between 1989 and 1995 he counted on the support of other minor parties allied to him. These deputies in his coalition showed high discipline rates. He also controlled a large majority of the Senate during his entire term in office (average of 56.5 percent of the seats). With this support, Congress approved over 60 percent of the executive bills between 1993 and 1994, the core period of the reforms. Cardoso's PSDB controlled only 12.3 percent of the total seats in the Lower Chamber and 11 percent of those in the Upper Chamber after the 1994 election. His governing coalition (mainly PFL, PMDB, PTB, and PPB) was crucial to constructing majorities in both chambers.

12 The average gubernatorial power index for Cardoso's first term was 1.23 and 1.37 for his second period in office, lower than Collor's (1.6) and Sarney's (2.2). The average value during the Menem administration was 1.86 (higher than the 1.71 after 1983 and 1.56 after 1987, during Alfonsín's term).

13 Brazil's GDP grew at an average of 2.6 percent between 1985 and 2002. Its GDP decreased only in three years, at an average of –1.7 percent. Argentina's GDP grew to half of Brazil's during the period (at an average 1.4 percent between 1983 and 2002), decreasing in nine years out of 20. The largest falls were a –7.6 in 1985, a –7.5 in 1989, and a –11 percent collapse in 2002. Brazil never experienced anything similar. The Argentine fiscal deficit was –2.2 percent of GDP average between 1987 and 2004; in Brazil the operational deficit was –1.5 percent of GDP between 1985 and 2001, 32 percent smaller than the Argentine.

14 In these cases, as indicated in Chapter 1, federal frameworks can be considered, for analytical reasons, as "given."

15 On average, US presidents controlled 51.35 percent of the votes in national elections since 1824 (the first year for which the popular vote has been recorded), and almost 53 percent of the votes since the first FDR presidency.

16 Argentine provinces controlled 27.6 percent of the total revenues in 1984; in 2000, this share decreased to 18.5 percent. In Brazil, the states' revenue share has been historically higher: 37 percent in 1990 and 29.7 percent in 1999, but

considerably lower than the share of the US subnational governments, whose share was 42 percent in 1998.

17 The average real GDP growth rate for the US between 1935 and 2015 (March) (chained 2009 dollars, inflation-adjusted) was 4.4 percent (according to data from the US Bureau of Economic Analysis).

18 A positive aspect to consider is that post-1983 the stability of government has been at stake several times, but not the stability of the regime (Pérez Liñán, 2007). Federal conflicts have not challenged democratic stability (although sometimes they affected governments' survival).

19 The most notable case was Vicente Fox, opposition (PAN) governor of Guanajuato, who became president in 2000.

20 The central government granted regions more institutional autonomy, including the "ownership of natural resources and land, wider budgetary and tax powers, and the right to engage directly in foreign economic relations" (Alexander, 2004, 237).

21 Other regions demanded autonomy or wanted to secede based on ethnic or religious conflicts with central authorities (e.g., the Chechen Republic). In fact, 15 republics separated from the Russian Federation after the collapse of the Soviet Union in December 1991.

22 He won the election by more than a million votes over his nearest rival, carrying 20 of 23 states, and winning 56.2 percent of the vote. In 2000 he was reelected with 59 percent of the vote. In the 2004 election, the Chavismo got another state (21 of the 23). In 2005 it got total control of the National Assembly, as the opposition withdrew from the election (Mascareño, 2007, 20; McCoy, 1999, 72).

23 Such as the Macroeconomic Stabilization Fund. The federal government delayed transfers to subnational governments for over $12 billion during 2006 (Mascareño, 2007, 19).

24 After the December 2003 election, his party, United Russia, dominated the State Duma with 68 percent of the seats. The party was the only one that had deep territorial penetration in a continental state, with branches in each of Russia's 89 regions. Furthermore, Putin consistently enjoyed a popularity rating of 60–80 percent from the time he was elected until 2005 (Konitzer and Wegren, 2006, 504, 509–510).

25 The federal government increased its share of regional tax revenues from approximately 50 percent of the total to 62 percent in 2002, with the regions having to pay for these changes (Alexander, 2004, 252). In 2003, a new revenue-share scheme was established, out of which approximately 70 percent of the collected revenue was allocated to the central government (Konitzer and Wegren, 2006, 511).

26 The president has taken advantage of regional fiscal dependency on the central government to restrain subnational pressures. Regional executives "see membership in the pro-Putin United Russia as a means to increase their access to financial resources and gain the necessary finances to meet their regional obligations." Also, "[u]nder new laws that allow the president to remove governors of 'bankrupt' regions from their posts, access to financial resources are a critical factor in maintaining office" (Konitzer and Wegren, 2006, 512).

References

Alexander, James, "Federal Reforms in Russia: Putin's Challenge to the Republics," *Demokratizatsiya*, Vol. 12, No. 2, 2004, pp. 233–264.

Ames, Barry, *The Deadlock of Democracy in Brazil. Interests, Identities, and Institutions in Comparative Politics* (Ann Arbor: University of Michigan Press, 2001).

Cetrángolo, Oscar, and Juan Pedro Jiménez, "Las Relaciones entre Niveles de Gobierno en Argentina. Raíces Históricas, Instituciones y Conflictos Persistentes," Serie Gestión Pública No. 47, CEPAL, 2004.

Coppedge, Michael, *Strong Parties and Lame Ducks: Presidential Partyarchy and Factionalism in Venezuela* (Stanford: Stanford University Press, 1994).

De Silva, Migara, Galina Kurlyandskaya, Elena Andreeva, and Natalia Golovanova, *Intergovernmental Reforms in the Russian Federation: One Step Forward, Two Steps Back* (Washington, DC: The World Bank, 2009).

Figueiredo, Argelina Cheibub, and Fernando Limongi, "Mudança Constitucional, Desempenho do Legislativo e Consolidação Institucional," *Revista Brasileira de Ciencias Sociais*, Vol. 10, No. 29, 1995, pp. 175–200.

Figueiredo, Argelina Cheibub, and Fernando Limongi, "O Congresso e as Medidas Provisórias: Abdicação ou Delegação?," *Novos Estudos*, CEBRAP 47, São Paulo, 1997.

Figueiredo, Argelina Cheibub, and Fernando Limongi, "Presidential Powers, Legislative Organization, and Party Behavior in Brazil," *Comparative Politics*, Vol. 32, No. 2, 2000, pp. 151–170.

Hagopian, Frances, Carlos Gervasoni, and Juan Andres Moraes, "From Patronage to Program: The Emergence of Party-Oriented Legislators in Brazil," *Comparative Political Studies*, Vol. 42, No. 3, 2009, pp. 360–391.

IMF (International Monetary Fund), *Government Finance Statistics* (GFS), 2001.

IMF (International Monetary Fund), "Lessons from the Crisis in Argentina," paper prepared by the Policy Development and Review Department, October 8, 2003.

Konitzer, Andrew, and Stephen Wegren, "Federalism and Political Recentralization in the Russian Federation: United Russia as the Party of Power," *Publius: The Journal of Federalism*, Vol. 36, No. 4, 2006, pp. 503–522.

Lavrov, Aleksei, "Budgetary Federalism"; in: Azrael, Jeremy and Emil Payin (eds.), *Conflict and Consensus in Ethno-Political and Center-Periphery Relations in Russia* (Washington, DC: Rand, 1998).

Limongi, Fernando, and Argelina Figueiredo, "Partidos Políticos na Câmara dos Deputados: 1989–1994," *Dados*, Vol. 38, No. 3, 1995, pp. 497–524.

Limongi, Fernando, and Argelina Figueiredo, "Bases Institucionáis do Presidencialismo de Coalizão," *Lua Nova*, No. 44, pp. 81–106.

Mainwaring, Scott, "Multipartism, Robust Federalism, and Presidentialism in Brazil"; in: Mainwaring, Scott and Matthew Shugart (eds.), *Presidentialism and Democracy in Latin America* (Cambridge: Cambridge University Press, 1997).

Mainwaring, Scott, *Rethinking Party Systems in the Third Wave of Democratization: The Case of Brazil* (Stanford: Stanford University Press, 1999).

Mascareño Quintana, Carlos, "El Federalismo Venezolano Re-Centralizado," *Provincia*, No. 17, January–June, 2007, pp. 11–22.

McCoy, Jennifer, "Chávez and the End of Partyarchy in Venezuela," *Journal of Democracy*, Vol. 10, No. 3, 1999, pp. 64–77.

Milkis, Sidney, *The President and the Parties: Transformation of the American Party System since the New Deal* (Oxford and New York: Oxford University Press, 1993).

Montero, Alfred P., "After Decentralization: Patterns of Intergovernmental Conflict in Argentina, Brazil, Mexico, and Spain," *Publius: The Journal of Federalism*, Vol. 31, No. 4, Fall 2001, pp. 43–64.

Mustapic, Ana María, "Inestabilidad sin Colapso. La Renuncia de los Presidentes: Argentina en el Año 2001," *Desarrollo Económico*, Vol. 45, No. 178, 2005, pp. 263–280.

Nicolau, Jairo Marconi, "Disciplina Partidaria e Base Parlamentar na Camara dos Deputados no Primeiro Governo Fernando Henrique Cardoso (1995–1998)," mimeo, IUPERJ, Rio de Janeiro, 1999.

O'Donnell, Guillermo, "Delegative Democracy," *Journal of Democracy*, Vol. 5, No. 1, 1994, pp. 55–69.

O'Donnell, Guillermo, *El Estado Burocrático Autoritario* (Buenos Aires: Prometeo, 2010).

Penfold-Becerra, Michael, "Electoral Dynamics and Decentralization in Venezuela"; in: Montero, Alfred P. and David J. Samuels (eds.), *Decentralization and Democracy in Latin America* (Notre Dame, IN: University of Notre Dame Press, 2004).

Pérez Liñán, Aníbal, *Presidential Impeachment and the New Political Instability in Latin America* (Cambridge: Cambridge University Press, 2007).

Rodden, Jonathan, *Hamilton's Paradox: The Promise and Peril of Fiscal Federalism* (Cambridge: Cambridge University Press, 2006).

Samuels, David, *Ambition, Federalism, and Legislative Politics in Brazil* (Cambridge: Cambridge University Press, 2003).

Samuels, David, and Scott Mainwaring, "Strong Federalism, Constraints on the Central Government, and Economic Reform in Brazil"; in: Gibson, Edward L. (ed.), *Federalism and Democracy in Latin America* (Baltimore: Johns Hopkins University Press, 2004).

Santos, Fabiano, "Democracia e Poder Legislativo no Brasil e na Argentina"; in: Llados, José María and Samuel Pinheiro Guimaraes (eds.), *Perspectivas Brasil y Argentina* (Brasília: IPRI-CARI, 1999a).

Santos, Fabiano, "Instituicões Eleitorais e Desempenho do Presidencialismo no Brasil," *Dados*, Vol. 42, No. 1, 1999b, pp. 111–138.

Skowronek, Stephen, *The Politics Presidents Make* (Cambridge: Belknap Press, 1993).

Vishnevskii, Boris, "Vsia Vlast'—Mne! Kak Federal'nyi Tsentr Zanimaetsia Peretiagivaniem Biudzhetnogo Kanata," *Nezavisimaia Gazeta*, September 3, 2002.

Willis, Eliza, Christopher da C.B. Garman, and Stephan Haggard, "The Politics of Decentralization in Latin America," *Latin American Research Review*, Vol. 34, No. 1, 1999, pp. 7–56.

Index

Page numbers in *italics* denote tables, those in **bold** denote figures.

Abrucio (1998) 11, 19, 96, 129, 134, 146, 149, 164, 176, 188, 231
Abrucio and Samuels (1997) 97, 164
Abrucio, Fernando 268n42
accountability, local 224
Acuña (1994) 103, 109–10, 203
AD *68–9*, 84n41, 302
adjustment 15, 17, 33, 64, *69*, 72–3, *78*, 82n22, 109, 145, 176, 189–90, 209, 230, 266n14, 283, 307n6
administration, means of 92
administrative functions 4–6, 25–6, 31, 33, 44n29, 56–7, 85n42, 146, 149, 151, 256, 298, 304
Agência Nacional de Saúde 252
Alencar, Marcello 268n36
Alexander (2004) 302–3, 305, 308n25
Alfonsín, Raúl 6, 30, 33, 42n10, 90, 100–1, **101–2**, 103–10, **110**, *111*, **113**, 113–14, 116–17, 118–19, **121**, 121–3, 125, *126*, 127, 147, 150–1, 153n20, 154n27, 155n42, 155n43, 197, 199–204, 210, 212, 227, 264n3, 265n3, 276–8, 284, *286*, 288, 296
Alianza 227, 276–8
Amapá 132, 152n7, 157n58
Ames (2001) 11–12, 27, 164, 295
Angell, Lowden and Thorp (2001) 4, 16, 41n7, 42n8
Angeloz, Eduardo César 156n47, 199
antiparty and antipolitician 166
approval rating *111*, *138*, *172*, 179, *180*, 200, *238*
Argentina 1–2, 4–7, 8n4, 8n7, 10–14, 16, 23, 33, 41n4, 42n10, 54–5, 57, 60–1, 65, *66–9*, 74–5, *76*, *79*, 80n3, 83n33, 89, 91–4, 96–9, 100–1, 104–7,

116, 119, *125*, 128–9, 132–3, 135, 140, 147, 150–1, 155n46, 164, 186, 197, 200, 203, *203*, 209, *225*, 231, 235, 254, 264, 265n9, 280–5, 288–94, 296–7, 299–301, 306n4, 307n13
Arnaudo, Bernabé 216
arrears 230
Artana and López Murphy (1994) 41n7, 41n8
Asian financial crisis 257
Association of Venezuelan Governors (AGV) 302
autonomy 2–3, 14, 61, 96, 157n66, 197, 258, 298, 300, 302–4, 308n21; fiscal 1, 11, 26, 260, 291, 294; institutional 3, 303, 308n20; political 8n6, 64; provincial 95, 217, 223–4; subnational 1–2, 10, 257
Azeredo, Eduardo 268n36

Bacha (2001) 197, 204, 206, 208
Bacha, Edmar 179, 186, 188, 190
bailouts 37, 184, 189, 211, 218, 236, 240–1, 248, 258, 266n17
balance: operational 136, 170, 179, *179*, *237*; of power 4, 20–1, 23, 30, 122, 257; primary 170, 179, 182
bargaining chips 249
barões da federação 231
Barry, Luis 212
Basic Education Maintenance and Development Fund (FUNDEB) 152n9
basic services 2, 40, 231
Belgium 1
Benton (2008) 48, 102n33
Bevilaqua (2002) 153n15

bicameral legislature 154n25
bilateral agreements 219, 266n13
bill, draft of the 230
Bisang and Centrángolo (1997) 266n19
bonds 189, 203, 254, 269n48, 278;
    National Treasury 254
Brazil 1–2, 4, 6–8, 10–12, 14, 16, 23, 33,
    41n1, 41n4, 42n10, 54–5, 57, 60–1,
    65, *66–9*, 74–5, *77*, *79*, 80n3, 83n33,
    89, 91, 95–104, 108, 122, 128–37, *145*,
    146–51, 152n9, 153n16, 155n46,
    158n69, 164, *170*, 179, *190*, 191–2,
    197–8, 203, 211, 218, 231–3, *234*,
    235–6, *237*, 240, 242, 253, *260*, 263–4,
    268n35, 279, 282–5, 288–300, 306,
    306n4, 307n5, 307n6, 307n9, 307n13,
    307n15
Brazilian Democratic Movement Party
    (PMDB) 129–32, 134, *138*, 140–1,
    157n59, 157n64, 166–8, 172, 176,
    178, 186–7, 192n1, 193n11, 233–5,
    251, 257, 262, 267n34, 268n35,
    268n35, 268n36, 268n38, 281, 293,
    295, 307n11
Bresser Pereira, Luis Carlos 147
Britto, Antônio 268n36
Brizola, Leonel 166
budget: allocations 4, 247; constraints
    5, 32–4, 37–8, 44n30, 110, *112*, 114,
    119, 120–2, 136, *139*, 142, 170, *173*,
    174–5, *181*, 183–4, 191, 205, *207*,
    208–10, 223, 236–7, *239*, 240–7, 281,
    284–5, 288, 290, 296; deficit 2, 40,
    115, 119, 169, 175, 215, 267n25;
    federal 6, 113, 164, 188, 220, 243,
    247, 255, 257, 280, 282; law 98, 117,
    221; surplus 261, 282
Burgin (1975) 93

Cafiero, Antonio 199, 264n1, 265n12
Calvo (2007) 27, 153n20, 264n2
Calvo and Abal Medina (2001) 18, 150
Camata, Rita 257
campaign 21, 165–6, 188, 193n11, 227,
    232
Campos Sales, Manuel 95
Canada 1, 299
Cardoso, Fernando Henrique 30, 41n4,
    42n10, 100, *101*, **102**, 146, 157n57,
    175, 178–9, 185–92, 193n13, 197–8,
    211, 216, 231–4, *234*, 235–7, *238*,
    240–1, **241–2**, 243–53, 255–7, 259,
    261, 262–4, 267n32, 267n33, 267n34,
    268n34, 268n35, 269n55, 270n56,

281–2, 285, *287*, 289, 291–3, 295–6,
    307n11
career prospects 12, 39, 210, 243, 248,
    277
Carmagnani (1993) 19, 41
cases, distribution of 100, *101*, **102**
causal mechanism 90
Cavallo, Domingo 204, 210, 213, 220,
    248, 265n7, 265n8, 279
CECE (1997) 222
Center Democratic Union (UceDe)
    199, *206*, 217
centralization: of administrative powers
    55; degrees of 1; fiscal 3, 15, 62, 70,
    72, 95, 170, 304; of power 92; process
    3, 10, 55, 151n5, 231, 264, 304–5;
    re-centralization 2, 17, 165
centralizing reforms 37–8, 63, 73, 94–6,
    175, 178, 184, 197, 210, 224, 232,
    246, 263, 285, 288
Centrão 142–3
centrifugal: institutional configurations
    164; pressures 150, 295, 305
Cetrángolo and Jiménez: (1995) 221;
    (1996) 204; (1997) 152n10; (2004)
    213, 215, 218, 224
Chávez, Hugo 1, 3, 303–4
checks and balances 108, 134
Cheibub and Limongi (2002) 11–12,
    165
Chiaramonte (1993) 41n5
Chiebub, Figueiredo, and Limongi
    (2002) 11
Chile 7, 33, 54–5, 57, 65, *66–9*, 80n3,
    80n6, 81n14
clash 6, 38–9, 57, 114, 120, 140, 149,
    184, 208, 242, 246
cleavages 32, 144, 303
clientelistic networks 295
coalition: electoral 233; governing 61,
    186, 188, 199, 233, 235, 262, 268n38,
    281–2, 307n11; working 233
coercion, means of 3, 92
collective action, problems 24, 32, 94,
    113, 119, 142, 144, 150, 246, 258
Collor de Mello, Fernando 100,
    157n59, 164–5, **171**, 171, **176**, 288
commodity prices 109
Communitarian Social Policies
    (POSOCO) 266n16
comparative analysis 5, 18, 81n11, 90
compensation 39, 202, 208–9, 211, 213,
    216, 219–21, 223–4, 254, 257,
    267n30, 282, 296

Compensation Fund for the Export of Industrialized Products (FPEX) 152
concessions 187–8, 199, 217, 227, 231, 247–52, 254, 259, 263, 269n54, 280, 282–3, 288, 290–3, 306n3
confederation 303
conflict, probability of 29, 36, **38**, 38–40, 117, 120, 140–2, 178, 184, 186, 188, 208–9, 212, 216, 218, 221, 242, 246, 262, 291
confrontational 184, 209
Constitution (1853) 98–9, 106
Constitution (1988) 1, 99, 137, **138**, 143, 145–7, 149, 169–70, 177, 184–6, 244, 246, 255–6
Constitution (1994) 153n19, 153n22, 267n27
constitutional: amendment 188, 256, 269n55; assembly 137, 140–3, 145–6, 149, 164, 170, 227–8; convention 143, 150, 227; reform 136–7, 142, 147, 149, 153n19, 164–5, 225, 229, 234, 246
context: fiscal 5, 20, 29–30, 33, 38–9, 43n28, 54, 57, 71–2, 75, 80, 94, 100, *101*, 104, 108, 110, 113, 119–20, 130, 135–6, 140, 164, 166, 168, 175, 177–9, 203, 208–9, 212, 224, 227, 229, 232, 236, 241, 245, 280, 283–4, 292; historical 90, 103, 129, 165, 232; international 109
contribuções 254
Contribuição de Intervenção no Domínio Econômico (CIDE) 152n9
Contribuição Social para o Financiamento da Seguridade Social (COFINS) 255
Contribuição Social sobre o Lucro Líquido (CSLL) 255
Contributions from the National Treasury (*Aportes del Tesoro Nacional*, ATN) 98, 124, 152n10, 152n11, 220
control mechanisms 59, 257
Convertibility: Law 204, 210; Plan 200, 204, 224
coordination: mechanisms 60, 107, 135; partisan 23, 42n17, 114, 157n64, 201; regional 24, 168
COPEI 302
Coppedge (2012) 19, 90–1
Coppedge and Mejía (2001) 21, 59, 62, 78–9, 82n17
Corbacho (1998) 107
corruption scandal 177
coup attempts 302

Covas, Mário 268n36
CPI dos Precatórios 269n51
credit claiming 219
Crimea 1
criminal sanctions 257
Cruzado plan 132, 185
cut points 289

Da Nóbrega, Maílson 147
Dahl (1986) 41n7, 92
De la Rúa, Fernando *101*, 132, 227, 231, 266n18, 276–9, 288, 300
De la Sota, José Manuel 227, 279
De Luca, Jones and Tula (2002) 108, 154n30
De Silva, Kurlyandskaya, Andreeva, and Golovanova (2009) 303
De Souza (1999) 136
deadlock 103, 117, 164–5, 175, 192, 278–9
debt: burden 108–9, *112*, 114; default 2; domestic 136, 169, 187; foreign 108–9, 135, 154, 204; issuing 10, 32–4, 37, 188, 210, 257, 293; moratorium 119; obligations 135–6, 189, *239*, 240, 244, 260, 269n52, 277; provincial 110, 112, 119, 139, 173, 181, 204; public sector 135, 203; re-negotiation 244–5; rollover 176, 236; swap 258
decentralization: administrative 8n6, 11, 31–2, *78*, 80n1, 80n4, 91, 221; bill 215; degree of 8n1; fiscal 6, 26, 31, *31*, 32, 42n10, 43n28, 56, 58, *78–9*, 80n8, 100, 147, 228; policies 4, 11, 16–17, 55, 75; political 8n6, 80n5; reform 213, 222, 259, 265n12, 266n19; of secondary education 213
decentralizing trend 2–3, 94, 212, 260, 305
decree 11, 21, 41n1, 59–60, 111, 132–3, *138*, 153n22, 165, 167, 172, 174, *180*, 193n5, 200–1, 205, *206*, 217, 220, 235, *238*, 264n2, 303; authority 81n10, 105–6, 133; power 11, 21, 59, *111*, 133, *138*, 165, *172*, *180*, 200, *206*, *238*; provisional 234–5
defection, cost of 211
defensive coordination 210
deficit: operational fiscal 136; provincial *207*; trade 204
delegative democracy 288, 292
Democratic Alliance 130

Democratic Labor Party (PDT) 129, 166, 168, 186, 249
Democratic Social Party (PDS) 129–31, *138*, 157n62, 168
demonstration effect 247
Desposato (2002) 13
devaluation 258, 279
Deviated Union's Revenue (*Desvinculação de Receitas da União*, DRU) 251–2, 269n46, 269n54, 282–3, 292
Di Gropello and Cominetti (1998) 54
Díaz Cayeros (2006) 4, 17, 19–20
Dillinger and Webb (1999) 10, 41, 215
Diniz (1997) 12, 263
Dirección Nacional de Coordinación Fiscal con las Provincias *79*, 110
direct election of senators 229
discipline: absolute 199, 206; party 12, 41n2, 59, 104; rate 167, 234; relative 199
discretion 6, 25–6, 43n22, 98, 108, 114, 117, 147, 219, 301
distribution: of functions 4, 8n7, 20, 98, 190, 255–6; primary 74, 97, 124, 215; of resources 2, 4, 7, 10, 13, 17–18, 23–4, 28, 30, 32–3, 40, 72, 81n15, 93, 97–8, 117, 119, 122, 134, 137, 142, 166, 193n5, 198, 220, 229, 236, 251, 291, 300; secondary 97
divided government 23, 106, 123, 168, 202, 236
do Couto e Silva, Golbery 95
Duhalde, Eduardo 227, 266n13, 267n30, 276–7, 279–80, 301, 306n2
Dutra, Eurico Gaspar 233
Dutra, Olívio 245

Eaton and Dickovick (2004) 4, 19
Eaton: (2001a) 16, 19, 56, 85, 218; (2002a) 19, 121, 230; (2004) 4, 14, 16, 19, 42n9, 56, 94–7, 115, 129, 137, 144, 203, 213, 218, 220, 230, 254
ECLAC-CEPAL: (1997) 64, *78–9*, 109, *203*, *203*, 205; (2005) 64, *78–9*, 203, *203*, 205
Economic Emergency Law (23, 697) 204
economic growth 55, 64, 109, *112*, 135, *139*, *173*, *181*, 204, *207*, *239*, 289
Ecuador 7, 55, 57, 65, *66–9*
education 2, 6, 10, 22, 43n24, 54, 57–8, 94, 99, 152n9, 158n68, 186–7, 211–12, 213–15, 221–3, *226*, 231, 248,

255–6, *261*, 265n12, 266n19, 269n50, 285, *287*, 292, 294, 297, 299
effective budget revenue 136
effective number of parties (enp) 18, 42n17, 63, *67*, *70*, 71, *78*, 192n3
Elazar (1991) 41
electoral: competition 103, 236, 306; democracies 200
Electoral College 130
elites, political 93, 166, 188, 288–9
Emenda Airton Sandoval 96
Emenda Passos Porto 96
Emendão 176
emergency powers 60, 133
Escobar-Lemmon (2001) 17–18, 22, 58, 64, 71, 73, 80n8, 81n10, 82n24, 150
Estado Novo 95, 110n5
exclusive initiative 60, 133, 234
Executive Comittee on Fiscal Reform (or *Comissão Ary Oswaldo Matos Filho*, CERF) 176
expected: benefits 37–9, 113, 117, 120, 122, 141, 143, 174, 178, 183–4, 186, 209, 242–4, 246, 281; costs 30, 33, 37, **38**, 39, 114, 117, 120, 140, 143, 155n37, 171, 175, 178, 183–4, 188, 208, 210, 212, 242–3, 246, 262, 281
expenditure share 8n1, 58, 70, 74, *78–9*, 81n9, 83n33, 85n43, 124, *125*, 145, *190*, 225, *260*
external shocks 236
extraordinary powers 107

factionalism 227, 277
Falleti: (2003) 11, 43n21, 44n31, 80n5, 213–14, 223, 266n13; (2005) 4, 8n6, 19, 80n3, 80n5; (2010) 11, 19, 22, 43n21
Faoro (1979) 41n5
Fausto (2006) 41n5
federal: balance 2, 5, 8n2, 30, 33, 39–40, 44n28, 75, 89–90, 94, 97, 99, 101, 104, 108, 110, 113, 118, 122, 125, *126*, 128–9, 131, 135, *148*, 149–51, 157n60, 164–6, 170, 184, 189–91, *191*, 197–8, 210–11, 221, *226*, 228, 231–2, 242, 245–7, 252–3, 256, 260, *261*, 262–4, 277–8, 280–3, 285, *286*, 288–9, 292, 294, 297, 299–300, 303, 305, 307n7; councils 60, 223; countries 1, 6, 8n3, 13, 17, 20, 29, 33, 55–7, 63, 71, 75, 82n20, 92; democracies 2, 4–8, 10, 14–15, 24, 34, 40, 42n11, 55, 89, 198, 232, 264, 284,

291, 298, 306; distributive game,
setting of the 100, 131–3, 164–5, 171,
178, 198, 243, 264, 283; districts 305;
institutions 5–6, 10–11, 14, 30, 34,
197, 283, 293, 297–8, 304; public
works 124; system 15, 18, 56, 63, *78*,
186, 265n8, 288, 294, 297
Federal Council on Culture and
Education (CFCE) 223
Federal Council on Health and
Sanitation (COFESA) 223
Federal Council on Investment (CFI)
223, 266n18
Federal Education Law 266n19
Federal Highway Fund 266n16
Federation Council 305
Feris, Romero 123, 154n31, 156n50
Fernández de Kirchner, Cristina 7, 280
Ferreira Rubio and Goretti (1996)
153n24, 200–1
FIEL (1993) 94
Figueiredo and Limongi: (1997) 11–12,
27, 165, 263, 295; (2000) 11–12, 27,
41n3, 165, 235, 263, 295
Filmus (1998) 266
financial guarantee clause 218
Finot (2001) 41n7, 41n8
First Republic 95–6
fiscal: adjustment 33, 109, 189, 190,
283; context 5, 20, 29–30, 33, 38–9,
43n28, 54, 57, 71–2, 75, 80, 94, 100,
101, 104, 108, 110, 113, 119–20, 130,
135–6, 140, 164, 166, 168, 175, 177–9,
203, 208–9, 212, 224, 227, 229, 232,
236, 241, 245, 280, 283–4, 292; crises
1, 5, 16–17, 25–6, 30n3, 31, 40, 57–8,
74–5, 100–1, 129, 150, 198, 241, 284,
291–2, 296, 299; deficit 31, 37, 72,
78–9, 96, **102**, 108–9, *110*, *112*, 114,
119, 136, **137**, *139*, 150, 154n33,
169–70, **171**, *173*, 174–5, *181*, **182**,
182–3, 185, 187, *203*, 203–4, **205**, *207*,
209, 214, 217, 221, 228, **228**, 232,
236–7, *239*, **241**, 248, 258, 260, 263,
278, 285, 293, 296, 300, 307n13;
exemptions 202; imbalance 2, 40,
109, 113, 142, 149, 151, 154n27,
155n37, 165, 164–5, 204–5, 214–15,
228, 230–1, 248, 254, 257, 291, 299,
304; incentives 5, 34–6, 40, 89, 95,
102, 104, 108, 113–14, 116–18, 128,
130, 140, 150, 165, 177, 184, 188–9,
191, 197–8, 232, 236, 245–7, 254, 258,
260, 262, 264, 267n27, 277, 282–3,

288–90, 292, 296–9, 303–4, 306;
pressures 5, 83n33, 110, *112*, 128,
135–6, 139, 149, 155n36, 169–70,
173, 174, 179, *181*, 183–4, *207*, 209,
211, 223, 228, 236–7, *239*, 240, 244,
263–4, 276, 280–1, 285, 290, 297, 299;
targets 257; wars 282
Fiscal Pact: I 216, 307n8; II 217
Fiscal Responsibility Law (*Lei de
Responsabilidade Fiscal,* LRF) 257–8,
259, 262, 269n52, 269n54, 282, 293,
307n6
Fiscal Stability Fund (*Fundo de
Estabilização Fiscal,* FEF) 249–52,
269n44, 269n45, 269n46, 269n47,
269n54, 292, 307n8
Fleischer (1998) 257
Flynn (1993) 178, 182, 234
*Fondo de Compensación de Desequilibrios
Regionales* 219
Fondo Nacional de Incentivo Docente 230
fragmentation 12, 18, 63, 71, *78*, 100,
164, 166, 168, 171, *173*, *181*, 243, 279
free trade 93, 253, 306n3
Frente Grande 199, 227, 265n5, 267n24
Frepaso 199
Frondizi, Arturo 94
functions, provincial 98
Fund for Electric Development of the
Interior (FEDEI) 266n16
Fund for Financing Social Programs in
Buenos Aires Metropolitan Area
(*Fondo de Reparación Histórica del
Conourbano Bonaerense*) 220
Fund to Eradicate Poverty (*Fundo de
Combate e Erradicação da Pobreza*) 255
*Fundo de Manutenção e Desenvolvimento do
Ensino Fundamental e de Valorização do
Magistério* (FUNDEF) 158, 256, 294

game-theoretical analysis 34, 90
García Delgado (1997) 15
García, Hélio 188
Garman, Haggard, and Willis (2001b)
4, 86, 150, 164
Garman, Leite, and da Silva Marques
(2001a) 41n7
General Labor Confederation (CGT)
264n1
Generality 91
Gerchunoff and Llach (1998) 109–10,
154–5, 204
Giambiagi and Além (1999) 97, 135–6,
147, *170*, 182, 255

Gibson (2004) 22, 41, 42n11
Gibson and Calvo (2000) 41, 42n11
Gibson and Calvo and Falleti (2004)
    42n11
Gibson and Falleti (2004) 4, 19–20, 56,
    92
González: (2008) 22, 74; (2012) 32,
    43n20, 43n23, 211, 220, 225, 269
governability 187, 225, 232, 295
government spending 190, 204, 209
governors' politics (*políticas dos
    governadores*) 95
governorships 118, 129–32, *138*, 140,
    153n19, 166, 168, *173*, 178, *181*, 235,
    239, 268n38, 281, 301, 303
gradualism 130
Great Depression 95, 154n33
gridlock 117, 277, 293
grievances 280
Grindle (2000) 4, 19
Group of Eight (*Grupo de los Ocho*)
    265n5
guarantees on minimum revenue-
    sharing levels 280
gubernatorial: elections 96, 117, 129,
    166–8, 200, 254; partisan powers
    index *138*, *173*, 202, *239*, 276;
    predation 197

Haggard and Webb (2004) 18, 19, 150
Hagopian (1996) 129, 151
Hagopian, Gervasoni, and Moraes
    (2009) 243, 293, 295
Hardin (1968) 128
health care 2, 6, 10, 43n24, 54, 57–8,
    94–5, 211–13, 221–3, 231, 255–6,
    266n19, 269n50, 285, 292, 294, 297
hegemony 3, 304
historical: background 89, 91, 99;
    context 90, 103, 129, 165, 232;
    struggles 90–1, 99

IADB (1997) 11, 72, *78*, 80n2, 80n8,
    82n22, 224
ICM-ICMS 136, 146, *148*, 152n7,
    153n16, 158n69, 177, 189, 253,
    262–3, 270n56, 282–3
Igreja Universal 252
Illia, Arturo Umberto 94
imbalances 2, 4, 6, 37, 40, 109, 113, 142,
    149, 151, 154n27, 155n37, 165,
    174–5, 204–5, 211, 214–15, 228,
    230–1, 236, 248, 254, 257, 265, 280,
    289, 291, 299, 304

IMF (2001) 1, 10–11, *78–9*, 80n7, 81n9,
    124, *125*, 145, *145*, 299
Immediate Action Plan (*Plano Real*)
    189–90, 192, 203, 233, 235–7, 240,
    243–4, 250, 259
impeachment 177, 179
*Imposto Provisório sobre Movimentações
    Financeiras* (IPMF) 177, 185
independence 83, 92, 95
indexing system 190
India 1
industrial promotion schemes 307n5
inflation 89, 96, 108–9, *112*, 113–14,
    117–19, 120–1, 123, 127, 135–7, *139*,
    154n33, 166, 168–70, *173*, 174–6,
    179, *181*, 183–4, 187, 189–90, 200,
    203–4, *207*, 209, 212, 218, 232–3, *239*,
    240, 243–4, 250, 267n26, 268n41,
    268n43, 288–9, 294, 308n17;
    hyperinflation 2, 33, 40, 127, 187,
    198, 201, 210, 244, 246, 284
infrastructure: plans 98; works 251
institutional: configurations 11–12, 20,
    134, 232; power of governors 134;
    protections 304; resources 61, 81n15,
    105–6, 108, 134–5, 165, 179, 192, 200,
    234–5, 281, 295; stability 298
interest: groups 25, 198; payments 109,
    135, 179, 187
Intergovernmental Decentralization
    Fund (FIDES) 302
international credit 136, 142
International Financial Institutions
    (IFIs) 16–17, 73, 183, 209, 212, 282
interventor 220
IOF (*Imposto sobre Operações Financeiras*)
    153, 269n49
issue linkage process 288
Italy 1
Itamar, Franco 100, 164, 166, 178–9,
    182, 183–6, 188, **191**, 191–2

Jobim, Nelson 193n11
Joga, Vicente 220
Jones (2002) 12, 26–7, 104, 199–200,
    265n4, 265n8
Jones and Mainwaring (2003) 18, 63, *78*
Juárez, Carlos 108, 154n31
Justo, Agustín Pedro 93

Kandir, Antônio 185–6, 243, 253,
    268n42
Kingstone (2000) 190

Kirchner, Néstor 7, 30, *101*, 154n31, 220, 226n13, 279–80, 289
Konitzer and Wegren (2006) 305, 308n24, 308n25, 308n26
Kraemer (1997) 41n7, 41n8
Kugelmas (2001) 144
Kugelmas and Salum (1989) 129–30, 140
Kugelmas, Eduardo 129, 268n42

Laakso and Taagepera (1979) 18, 63, 78, 192n3
Lamounier (1990) 132
Lanusse, Alejandro Agustín 42n10, 94
Lardone (2008) 17, 212
Latin America 4, 6, 11, 13, 15, 20, 22, 54, 65, 234, 284
Law 20.221 115, 124, 155n38
Law 23.548 123–4, 152n10
Law 24.049 215, 218
Law 8.727 (*Lei do Acordo de Renegociação das Dívidas*) 189
Law 9.394 (*Lei de Diretrizes e Bases da Educação Nacional*, LDB) 255–6, 294
leadership 30, 103, 167, 192n4, 263, 295
legislative: elections 109, 199, 227, 278; powers 12, 62, 70, 132–3, 153n22, 263–4, 295
legitimacy 30, 96, 104, 129, 131, 140–2
Lei Complementar: 77 185; 82/1995 (*Lei Camata I*) 257; 96/1999 (*Lei Camata II*) 257
Lei delegada (LDs) 133
Lei Orgânica da Assistência Social (LOAS) 256
Leite (2005) 189
Levitsky (2003) 199
Liberal Front Party (*Partido da Frente Liberal*, PFL) 130–2, *138*, 140, 157n59, 157n64, 166–8, 176, 178, 187–8, 192n1, 192n4, 193n10, 232–3, 235, 248, 253, 262, 267n33, 267n34, 268n35, 268n36, 268n38, 281, 293, 307n11
Liga Federal 306n2
Lijphart (1999) 10, 56, 71, 107
Limongi and Figueiredo (1998) 295
Limongi, Fernando 174, 244, 268n42
Litvack, Ahmad and Bird (1998) 41n7, 41n8
Llanos (2001) 12–13, 105, 201
local bonds 278
looting 127, 279, 297, 306
López Murphy (1995) 41n7, 80n8

Lopreato (2002) 15–16, 136, 141, 149, 170, 245
Love (1993) 41n5
Luder, Italo Argentino 104
Lula da Silva, Luis Inácio 7, 30, 100, 232, 281

McCoy (1999) 308n22
Maciel, Marcos 267n33
Macroeconomic Stabilization Fund 308n23
Maduro, Nicolás 3, 304
Maestro, Carlos 220
Magalhães, Antônio Carlos 177, 188, 192n4
Mainwaring and Pérez Liñan (1998) 27, 157n62
Mainwaring and Shugart (1997) 21, 58, *78–9*, 132–3
Mainwaring: (1995) 11, 27, 164; (1997) 11, 27, 129, 164; (1999) 11–12, 21, 27, 29, 137, 164, 166
majority, three-fifths 233
Maluf, Paulo 130
Manaus Free Trade Zone 306n3
Manor (1999) 16–17
Maranhão 131
Marques Moreira, Marcilio 176
Mascareño (2007) 304, 308n22, 308n23
mass media 166, 240, 305
Massaccesi, Horacio 156n47
medidas provisórias (MPs) 133, *138*, 157n57, 167, *172*, 179, *180*, 193n8, 234–5, *238*
Melo (2002) 147, 177, 240, 254–5, 257
Menem, Carlos Saúl 30, 41n4, 42n10, 100, *101*, **102**, 103, 151n4, 153n24, 155n39, 197–205, **205**, *206*, **208**, 209–13, 216, 218–21, 223–4
Mestre, Ramón 267n22
Metropolitan Mayor (*Alcalde Metropolitano*) 304
Mexico 6–7, 54–5, 57, 65, *66–9*, 80n3
midterm elections 278
military: coup 94, 96; government 42n10, 94, 210, 212; junta 94, 265n7; power 89; regime 96, 103, 129–31, 135
Milkis (1993) 298
Minas Gerais 130, 152n7, 176, 178, 188, 245, 268n36
minimum revenue guarantee 230
Minister: of Economy 116, 209, 212–13; of Foreign Affairs 234
minmax 39; strategy 120, 127

minority coalition (*coalizão minoritária*)
    167
miolo da picanha 282
Moine, Mario 220
Monarchy 95
monetary emission 109, 119, 204
money, printing 32–4, 37, 136, 142,
    183, 205, 243
Montero: (2001a) 18, 150, 301–2;
    (2001b) 18, 150, 301–2
Mora and Varsano (2001) 99, 256
Morgenstern and Nacif (2002) 13, 27
Musgrave (1959) 41n7, 42n8
Mustapic: (2000) 12, 41n2, 105–6;
    (2002) 12
Mustapic and Goretti (1992) 12, 103,
    105, 153n18

Nash equilibrium 113, 120, 208, 216, 242
National Conference of Governors
    (CoNaGo) 301
National Constitutional Assembly
    (*Assembleia Nacional Constituinte*,
    ANC) 140, 142–3, 150, 157n65
National Council for Economic Policy
    (*Conselho Nacional de Política
    Fazendária*, Confaz) 152n7
National Housing Fund (FONAVI) 266
National Pedagogic Congress (*Congreso
    Pedagógico Nacional*, NPC) 212
National Treasury 146, 254; Grants
    (*Aportes del Tesoro Nacional*, ATNs) 98,
    124, 152n10, 152n11, 220
natural resources 127, 308n20
Negretto: (2002) 133, 157n57, 167,
    264n2; (2004) 27; (2009) 21, 58, 62
net balance 34–6, 147, 191, 193n14,
    208, 224, 242, 259, 284
Neustadt (1989) 21, 42n13
Neves, Tancredo 130–1, *138*
Nicolau, Jairo 79, 192n1, 233
Nigeria 1
nominal vote 215
normal form game 36, **36**, **113**, 120,
    121, 141, **141**, **176**, 208, **208**, 242, **242**
Novaro (1994) 200
Nunes Leal (1997) 95
Nuñez Miñana and Porto (1983) 265n8
Nutritional Social Program
    (PROSONU) 266n16

Oates: (1977) 41n7; (1998) 42n8
Obama, Barack 299
O'Donnell: (1994) 200, 288–9, 292–3;
    (2010) 92, 297

O'Donnell and Schmitter (1986) 103
Old Republic (*República Velha*) 95
Olivera-Tanzi effect 109
O'Neil: (2003) 151; (2005) 151
Onganía, Juan Carlos 94
Operação Desmonte 149
Ostrom (1999) 128
Oszlak (1997) 41n5
outsider 165
over-spending 127, 245
overgrazing 193n6

PAC 123, 156n50, 217
Palanza (2002) 223
Palermo (2000) 41n3
PAN 301, 308n19
Panizza: (1999) 80n9; (2000) 165, 169
pares 89, 101, 103, 117, 128, 130, 149,
    151, 151n1, 164, 192, 197, 225, 263,
    297
Partido Justicialista (PJ) 103–6, 114, 116,
    118, 121–5, 127, 153n18, 153n19,
    153n21, 155n44, 156n49, 156n50,
    198–9, 201, 205, 210–11, 215, 217,
    220, 227, 229–30, 265n5, 265n12,
    266n14, 267n23, 267n24, 267n29,
    267n30, 276–8, 295, 306n1
party: discipline 12, 41n2, 59, 104;
    lists 82n18, 202, 265n4; system 12,
    18, 42n8, 42n17, 62–3, *67*, *70*, 71,
    78, 83n29, 134, 164–5, 167–8, 295,
    298
Party of National Reconstruction
    (PRN) 166–7, *172*
patronage 164, 213, 243, 295
payoff 35–6, 38–9, 91, 113, 120, 140–1,
    175, 208, 242
payroll 153n15, 182, 189, 213, 257
Pedro: I 95; II 95
Penfold-Becerra (2004) 18, 150, 302,
    304
pension system 2, 216–17, 222, 230, 248
Pereira and Mueller (2004) 27, 43n25,
    243
Pérez, Carlos Andrés 302
Pérez Liñan (2007) 308n18
Perón, Juan Domingo 42n10, 94
Piauí 131, 157n59
Pírez: (1986a) 94, 115, 117, 154n27,
    155n39, 265n8; (1986b) 93, 265n8
Piso de Assistência Básica (PAB) 269n50,
    294
Plan Austral 106, 109, 113, 118
Plan Primavera 109

Plano Brasil Novo 169
Plano Collor 169
Plano Real 189–90, 192, 203, 233, 235–7,
    240, 243–4, 250, 259
plebiscite 199, 227
plurality *78*, 198, 227, 276, 278
policy: goals 213, 231, 295, 297; making
    292; responsibilities 4, 8n2, 10,
    43n24, 255–6, 259, *261, 287*, 294–5
political: allies 200, 233–4; instability
    151, 300; stability 291, 300; support 14,
    25–6, 29, 31, 33, 44n28, 98, 104, 116,
    119, 121, 129, 131–2, 142, 149–50,
    157n61, 177–8, 186, 188, 190, 192,
    198, 209, 213–14, 219, 235, 280, 282–3
port 92–3, 146
Porto: (2003) 41n7, 93, 215, 217,
    221–2, 265n8, 267n31; (2004) 41n7
positive: image 27, 84n33, *138, 172,
    180, 206*, 234, *238*, 267n25, 267n28,
    268n37; sum game 144
post-transition federal balance 89
power: institutional 59, 70, 105–8, 132,
    134, 168; of governors 8, 22–3, 59,
    61, *68*, 71, 82n27, 83n32, 106, 118,
    132–4, 146, 149, 167, 201, 231, 235,
    301, 304; partisan 21–2, 30, 39, 58,
    61–2, 65, *66, 68, 70*, 70–1, 74, 82n17,
    82n27, 83n33, 84n33, 84n35, 85n43,
    102, 104, 106, *112*, 131, 134, 142,
    167, 179, 225, 236, **241**, 252, 262,
    281, 288, 298; of the president 13, 21,
    57–8, *68*, 70–2, 74, *78–9*, 81n10,
    82n27, **102**, 106, 117, 124, 131–2,
    166, 198, 227, 231, 233, 235, 262;
    sharing 56, 92
Power: (1998a) 133, 167, 179, 234;
    (1998b) 133, 137, 167, 179
power relations 3, 19–20, 34, 36, 118,
    292
Prado (2003) 146
praetorian: dynamics 3, 306; struggles 5
PRD 301
pre-coparticipation 216
predatory coordination 60
presidential: assaults 300, 304;
    capacities 298; institutional powers
    105, 132; partisan power 83n33,
    84n33, 104, 131; systems 6, 20; veto
    111, 120, 122–3, 140, 156n48
PRI 301–2
price controls 119
primus 101, 103, 117, 128, 130, 151,
    151n1, 192, 197, 225, 232

Proceso de Reorganización Nacional 94
Programa de Integração Social (PIS) 255
programmatic: ideas 231; parties 295
protectionist 93
protests 2, 6, 40, 225, 231, 267n25, 280,
    285, 298–9
provincial: banks 218; legislatures 106–7,
    153n19, 229; parties 109, 115–18,
    122–5, 153n19, 156n50, 199, *206*, 217;
    police forces 299; spending 222, 277
provincialization 285
Provisional Contribution on the
    Movement or Transmission of
    Values, Credits, and Rights of
    Financial Nature (CPMF) 177, 254–5,
    262–3, 269n46, 269n49, 270n56,
    282–3
Prud'homme (1995) 41n7
Przeworski (1991) 29, 34, 118
Przeworski, Alvarez, Cheibub, and
    Limongi (2000) 65, 78, 82n23
public opinion, support from 27, 104,
    132, 200, 262
Putin, Vladimir 1, 3, 303, 305, 308n24,
    308n26

Radical Party (*Unión Cívica Radical*,
    UCR) 93, 103–4, 107, 109, 113,
    115–16, 118, 122, 123, 127, 153n17,
    153n18, 153n19, 155n41, 155n44,
    156n47, 156n50, 199, *206*, 214–15,
    217, 227, 265n10, 266n14, 267n24,
    276–7, 279
recession 108–9, 120, 135, 168, 170,
    174, 189, 276–7
reelection 107, 154n29, 188, 193n12,
    221, 227–9, 231, 249, 262, 268n40,
    269n55, 304, 306n4
reform: administrative 249; pension
    283
Regency 95
regional: caudillos 92; interests 142,
    144
Regional Development Fund (FDR)
    124, 282, 307n15
Remmer and Wibbles (2000) 265
Repetto: (2001b) 219; (2001c) 212–15,
    266n19
representative democracies 200, 293
Resende, Andre Lara 183
revenue: fiscal 5, 24, 107, 128, 145, 151,
    184, 294, 303; provincial 2, *79*, 125,
    156n54, 212, 224, *226, 287*; share of
    1–2, 259, 285, 303–4

Revenue-Sharing Law (*Régimen de Coparticipación Federal de Impuestos*) 115, 123, 127, 152n11, 154n27, 203, 209, 211, 216, 221
Rezende (1990) 144
Rezk: (1997) 41; (1998) 41
Ribeiro (2005) 256
Rigolon and Giambiagi (1999) 189, 245
Riker (1964) 20, 41n7, 56
Roarelli (1994) 192n4, 193n7
Rodden (2006) 41n7, 42n8, 54, 58, 80, 189, 240, 265n8, 300
Rodríguez Saá, Adolfo 154, 227, 279, 301, 306n1
roll-call: data 199; votes 104, 234
Roosevelt, Franklin Delano 298
Roussef, Dilma 283
Ruckauf, Carlos 279
Russia 1, 3, 6, 48, 303, 307n7, 308n24, 308n26
Rodden: (2002) 41n7, 42n8; (2004) 41n7, 42n8, 80; (2006) 41n7, 42n8, 54, 58, 80, 189, 240, 300
Rodden and Wibbels (2002) 265n8
Rondinelli, Nellis and Cheema (1983) 15, 41n7

Saadi, Ramón 108, 154n31
Samuels: (2003a) 11, 18, 150, 164, 240, 295; (2003b) 11, 18, 147, 150, 164, 240, 295
Samuels and Mainwaring (2004) 11, 41n7, 164, 295
Samuels and Snyder: (2001a) 42n11; (2001b) 42n11
Santos: (1999a) 12, 263, 295; (2001) 59, 134
Sarney, José 30, 33, 42n10, 90, 100–1, *101*, **102**, 104, 122, 129–35, 137, **137**, *138*, **141**, 141–3, 147, *148*, 149–51, 153n22, 156n56, 157n65, 165–8, 177, 179, 197, 232, *234*, 235–6, 240, 244, 268n39, 281, 284, *286*, 288–9, 307n12
Sawers (1996) 41n5
Schlesinger (1965) 59
Second Republic 95
selective incentives 13, 25, 27–8, 35, 37, 106, 119–21, 150, 198, 202–3, 211, 214, 218–19, 224, 233, 240, 243, 248, 269, 296
sense of urgency 183, 186, 292
Sergipe 132
Serra and Afonso (1999) 145–6

Serra, José 157n66
service delivery, shortages in 224
sesión sobre tablas 217
settings 44n28, 100, 113, 119, 140, 205, 240, 242
shared authority 99
shock measures 169
Shugart and Carey (1992) 21, 27, 58, 62, *78–9*, 105, 132
Silva (1981) 95
Skowronek (1993) 34, 43n27, 293
Smoke (2003) 41n7, 42n8
Snyder and Samuels (2004) 42n11
Sobisch 154n31, 227
social: contributions 80n9, 153n15, 255, *261*, 263, *287*; mobilization 15–16, 64, 73, *78*, 151, 285; programs 10, 43n24, 98, 132, 150, 220, 278; services 6, 99, 146, 213, 215, 218, 228, 231, 256, 284–5, 293–4, 300, 305; spending 37, 147, 258
Social Emergency Fund (*Fundo Social de Emergência*, FSE) 185–9, 191–2, 193n11, 193n12, 216, 247–9, 252, 269n46, 269n54, 292
Sola, Lourdes 149
Souto, Paulo 268n36
Souza (1997) 1, 4, 16, 19, 41n7, 42n8, 42n11, 129, 131, 137, 140, 142–6, 149, 157, 158n68, 255
Soviet Union 302, 308n21
Spain 1, 103
stabilization plan 169, 179, 189, 200, 211–12, 237, 248
stalemate 186, 229
Stallings (1992) 17
state: assemblies 106, 134, 154n25, 202; autonomy 300, 303; banks 146, 175, 183–5, 188, 237, 245, 248, 263, 288; legislature 6–1, 134, 154n25, 268n39; of siege 127, 279
States' and Federal District's Participation Fund (*Fundo de Participação dos Estados e do Distrito Federal*, FPE) 98–9, 145, 152n7, 152n12, 153n15
States' and Municipalities' Participation Fund (*Fundo de Participação: dos Estados* e *Municípios*; FPEM) 96; *dos Estados e do Distrito Federal* (FPE) 98–9, 145, 152n7, 152n12, 153n15; *dos Municípios* (FPM) 98, 145, 153n15
statistical section 90
Stein (1998) 41n7, 42n8

Stepan: (1999) 11–12, 20, 41n7, 56;
    (2001) 11–12, 20, 56
strategic motivations and interactions 90
subnational autonomy 2, 257
subsidies 81n9, 109, 169, 220
substantive shifts 1, 5
sunset provision 188
Supreme Court 200, 302
surplus 31, 37, 72, 83n33, 100, **102**, **110**,
    119, **137**, 154n34, 169, **171**, *173*, 179,
    182, **205**, 222, **228**, 237, **241**, 265n8,
    280–3

tacit approval 200
Tauguinas, Rolando 220
tax: authority 2–3, 11, 43n20, 93–4,
    96–9, *126*, *148*, 157n63, *191*, 218, *226*,
    232, 246, 252, *261*, 267n31, *286*, 291,
    298–9; base 145–6, *148*, 254–5, 284,
    286; centralizing 252; collection 25,
    93, 119, 125, 152n13, 153n13,
    153n16, 157n66, 182–3, 190, 204, 210,
    214, 218, 248, 252–5, 278, 285; on
    credits and debits 280; exemptions
    218–19, 253; export (IE) 153n15;
    federal 176, 204, 219, 230, 255,
    266n18; financial transactions
    (*Imposto sobre Operações Financeiras*,
    IOF)153n15, 269n49; import (II)
    153n15; income (*Imposto de Renda*,
    IR) 95, 143, 145, 152n7, 152n8,
    152n10, 152n13, 153n14, 153n15,
    156n55, 158n68, 220–1, 255, 267n29,
    269n45; industrialized products (IPI)
    143, 145, 152n7, 153n5, 177, 255;
    inflationary 175, 243, 245; inheritance
    and gifts tax (ITCMD and ITBI)
    153n16; on large fortunes (IGF)
    153n15; motor vehicles registration
    (IPVA) 153n16; provincial *79*, 156n6,
    217–18, 231, 267n31; reform 176,
    262, 296n44, 269n54, 270n56, 282–3,
    293; revenue *79*, 93, 147, 152n6,
    152n7, 158n67, 170, 176, 183, 186,
    190, 240, 249, 254–5, 260, 263,
    269n45, 284–5; Rural Propriety (ITR)
    152n9, 153n15; value-added (VAT)
    126, 152n8, 152n13, 156n52, 177,
    204, 221, 262, 282–3, *286*
tax-free zone 220
taxing powers 3, 93, 151
Teichman (2001) 17
Tendler (1997) 16, 41n7, 42n8
tequila crisis 224

theoretical expectations 43n28, 70,
    85n43, 90, 103–4, 113, 119, 131, 140,
    166, 175, 184, 209, 221, 232, 241, 281
theory building 5–6
thickness 91
Tiebout (1956) 41n7, 42n8
Tommasi (2002) 265n8
Tommasi, Saiegh and Sanguinetti
    (2001) 265n8
Torres (1961) 41n5, 95
tragedy of the commons 128, 151,
    193n6
transfers: automatic 44n31, 97, 124,
    153n14, 204, 209, 253, 278;
    discretionary 4, 37, 98, 132, 149–50,
    156n54, 192n4, 193n7, 216, 269n53,
    282, 284; legally mandated 74, 97–8,
    132, 157n67, 222; other legally
    mandated 98, 152n8, 152n9; revenue-
    sharing 152n11, 204, 222, 224;
    voluntary (*transferências voluntárias*)
    98, 152n12
transition to democracy 2, 15, 89, 94,
    97, 100–1, 103–4, 107–8, 128–9,
    132–5, 140, 147, 149, 164, 168,
    192n3, 197, 231–2, 240, 265n8, 291,
    296, 299
Treisman (2007) 41n7, 42n8, 80n8
Tribunal de Contas da União (TCU)
    152n7
tucanos 268n34
turmoil 2, 6, 89, 109, 127, 151, 164, 183,
    204, 258, 277, 280, 284–5, 293,
    298–300, 302
turning point 288
TV Globo network 166

Ukraine 1
unemployment 108, 267n25, 280
Unified Health System (*Sistema Único de
    Saúde*, SUS) 152n9, 256, 294
unions 25, 29, 103, 127, 198, 225
unitary countries 6–7, 55–7, 61, 63, 65,
    71, 80n6, 81n14, 82n19
United Kingdom 1
United States 1, 6, 59–60, 234, 298
uprisings 225, 285
urgency clauses 154n28
Uruguay 7, 55, 57, 65, *66–9*

Vargas, Gétulio 95–6
Vasconcelos, Jarbas 234
Velázquez, Ramón 302
Venezuela 1, 3, 6, 42n9, 55, 57, 65, *66–9*

vertical imbalance 299–300
veto 11–12, 21, 59–60, 105–6, *111*, 114, 120, 122
Viola, Roberto 108
votación sobre tablas 123

Wallis and Oates (1988) 80n8
Water and Sanitation Fund (COFAPyS) 284
Weingast (1995) 42n8, 44n30
Weyland: (1993) 165, 167; (1998) 169
Wibbels: (2000) 41n7; (2004) 210, 223; (2005a) 41n7, 56

Willis, Garman and Haggard (1999) 6, 17, 43n21, 301
Worker's Party (PT) 166, *172*, *180*, 186–7, 193n12, 232, *238*, 248, 250–1, 253, 257–8, 281, 283, 293, 295
World Bank: (1997) 11; (1998a) 54, 224; (1998b) 54, 224; (2001) 54, *78–9*

Yeltsin, Boris 3, 303, 305
Yugoslavia 1

zero-sum game 32–3, 144
Zorraquín Becú (1953) 41n5

For Product Safety Concerns and Information please contact our EU
representative GPSR@taylorandfrancis.com
Taylor & Francis Verlag GmbH, Kaufingerstraße 24, 80331 München, Germany